Karl Wohlmuth, Achim Gutowski, Magda Kandil,
Tobias Knedlik, Osmund O. Uzor (Eds.)

Macroeconomic Policy Formation in Africa –
Country Cases

D1785724

African Development Perspectives Yearbook

Edited by the

Research Group on African Development Perspectives Bremen:
Karl Wohlmuth, Achim Gutowski, Magda Kandil,
Tobias Knedlik, Osmund O. Uzor

Vol. XVII

LIT

Karl Wohlmuth, Achim Gutowski, Magda Kandil,
Tobias Knedlik, Osmund O. Uzor (Eds.)

Macroeconomic Policy Formation
in Africa – Country Cases

LIT

Bibliographic information published by the Deutsche Nationalbibliothek
The Deutsche Nationalbibliothek lists this publication in the Deutsche
Nationalbibliografie; detailed bibliographic data are available in the Internet at
http://dnb.d-nb.de.

ISBN 978-3-643-90522-2

A catalogue record for this book is available from the British Library

©LIT VERLAG GmbH & Co. KG Wien,
Zweigniederlassung Zürich 2014
Klosbachstr. 107
CH-8032 Zürich
Tel. +41 (0) 44-251 75 05
Fax +41 (0) 44-251 75 06
E-Mail: zuerich@lit-verlag.ch
http://www.lit-verlag.ch

LIT VERLAG Dr. W. Hopf
Berlin 2014
Fresnostr. 2
D-48159 Münster
Tel. +49 (0) 2 51-62 03 20
Fax +49 (0) 2 51-23 19 72
E-Mail: lit@lit-verlag.de
http://www.lit-verlag.de

Distribution:
In the UK: Global Book Marketing, e-mail: mo@centralbooks.com
In North America: International Specialized Book Services, e-mail: orders@isbs.com
In Germany: LIT Verlag Fresnostr. 2, D-48159 Münster
Tel. +49 (0) 2 51-620 32 22, Fax +49 (0) 2 51-922 60 99, E-mail: vertrieb@lit-verlag.de

In Austria: Medienlogistik Pichler-ÖBZ, e-mail: mlo@medien-logistik.at
e-books are available at www.litwebshop.de

Contents Volume 17
African Development Perspectives Yearbook, 2014
MACROECONOMIC POLICY FORMATION IN AFRICA - COUNTRY CASES

The Research Group on African Development Perspectives Bremen

The aggravating social, political and economic crisis of the African continent forces institutions, organisations, researchers, development practitioners, ad hoc working groups and networks on Africa, and all others involved in African development affairs to intensify the analytical and conceptional work on alternative development visions and designs for Africa. There exist a growing number of plans and programmes, strategy conceptions, researches, and ideas for policy action and projects being published worldwide and focussing on the peculiarity of the African crisis, Africa's recent growth dynamics, the chances for structural adjustment and transformation, the issue of planning development beyond mere adjustment, and on the necessary responses to the globalisation trend. The discussion referring to Africa's development problems and perspectives is widening. However, it is difficult to get an overall view of the different approaches and proposals and, subsequently, to make the discussion useful for the programming and co-ordinating of development policies. So there is a need for a comprehensive publication that compiles, evaluates, and analyzes the scattered material and the often not easily available sources.

To fill this gap, the *Research Group on African Development Perspectives Bremen*, established at the University of Bremen, is presenting the African Development Perspectives Yearbook, being published since Volume 1 in 1989. Research activities of the group members comprised over the years country case studies and comparative country analyses; studies on macroeconomic policies and strategies, aspects of labour market policies and informal sector activities, human development policies and strategies, agriculture and food security policies; studies on natural resources development and environmental policies, but also researches on the promotion of small-scale industries, private sector development policies, entrepreneurship development, and assessments of sector and structural adjustment policies, trade and regional integration policies, as well as reviews of economic diversification options.

The *African Development Perspectives Yearbook* is the first English-speaking periodical published in Germany relating to development problems and perspectives in Africa. African, European and North-American experts from universities, international and regional organisations, and from non-governmental and donor organisations are reporting on problems and on possible solutions, on new political and economic approaches, on specific economic programmes, and on visions for alternative African development paths.

Africa's future will depend on both, on its economic and political connections with the international community at the Pan-African, sub-regional, national, provincial and sectoral levels, and on local projects and development efforts at the micro level. Most important are own African development visions, programmes, strategies and policies. The *African Development Perspectives Yearbook* contains information and analyses with regard to these various dimensions. Global analyses, regional and country studies, sectoral studies and individual project evaluations are published in the *African Development Perspectives Yearbook*, as well as statements and declarations on Africa submitted as the result of international conferences, important documents of African regional organisations and of individual African states, and important programmes of African civil society organisations and African self-help groups.

Beside the analytical, comparative and documentary character of the *African Development Perspectives Yearbook*, the editors successfully established an extensive network for the exchange of news and information and are so relating and connecting development organisations and research institutions that are working in and for Africa. The members of the *Research Group on African Development Perspectives* are interested to deepen the contacts with partners in and outside of Africa who are sharing similar objectives.

The *African Development Perspectives Yearbook* is targeted to decision-makers and research personnel in development policy institutions and to experts and staff in project consultancies, media, research and development, donor and aid institutions, and to all others that are interested in Africa's development. It offers comprehensive analyses and information about recent developments with regard to the African continent. Main focus is on development perspectives. Thus, the African Development Perspectives Yearbook is reporting on

- visions and conceptions with regard to long-term development strategies for Africa;
- strategies that emphasise a longer-run planning process that goes beyond conventional structural adjustment policies;
- successful projects and programmes concerning countries, regions, institutions, or specific sectors of African economies, by analysing the conditions of their success;
- resourceful and creative activities of socio-economic interest groups, local development initiatives and NGOs, which could serve as models for other regions;

- innovative strategies for and prospects of regional integration in Africa; and on
- economic, social, and political trends in Africa's sub-regions, nation-states, provinces, towns and local communities.

The *African Development Perspectives Yearbook* takes into account sources and information from all relevant levels of action, planning, discussion, and research, i.e. from international, regional, and national organisations and institutions, committees, working groups, and NGOs, but with particular emphasis given to those ideas and approaches originating from Africa.

Address:
Research Group on African Development Perspectives Bremen
c/o

Professor Karl Wohlmuth, Volume Editor,
University of Bremen
Department of Economics and Business Studies
P.O. Box 330 440
28334 Bremen, Germany
Phone: +49 421 218-66517
Fax: +49 421 218-4550
Email: wohlmuth@uni-bremen.de

Professor Tobias Knedlik, Managing Editor
Fulda University of Applied Sciences
Marquardstr. 35
D-36039 Fulda
Germany
E-mail: Tobias.Knedlik@w.hs-fulda.de

Internet: http://www.iwim.uni-bremen.de/africa/africanyearbook.htm

Foreword and Acknowledgements

This Volume 17 of the *African Development Perspectives Yearbook* with the title „Macroeconomic Policy Formation in Africa – Country Cases" has benefited from many contributions, from various inputs and from important support. The great number of contributions to this volume was made possible because of the continuing support from African and international organisations, from numerous research and development institutions, and from many individual experts working continuously on Africa. International and regional organisations, such as UNDP (United Nations Development Programme), ILO (International Labour Office), UNESCWA (United Nations Economic and Social Commission for Western Asia), UNECA (United Nations Economic Commission for Africa), WAMA (West African Monetary Agency), WAMI (West African Monetary Institute), and the Arab Planning Institute (API) in Kuwait City have directly supported the Yearbook project on "Macroeconomic Policy Formation" with contributions, expertise and suggestions. Many organisations, like the African Development Bank (AfDB), the United Nations Economic Commission for Africa (UNECA), the OECD (Organization for Economic Cooperation and Development) Development Centre, the African Union (AU) and the NEPAD (New Partnership for Africa's Development) Secretariat, have contributed with information and encouragement. We, as the Editors of the Yearbook, are always interested in their advice and guidance so as to structure the future work on the *African Development Perspectives Yearbook*.

For Volume 17 of the *African Development Perspectives Yearbook* the Editors took up the event of the Independence of the Republic of South Sudan on July 9, 2011 to publish a special *Unit 1* on *New Economic Policies for Sudan and South Sudan - The Need for a Strategic Economic Cooperation* in order to highlight the need for new macroeconomic strategies and policies and to focus on the many interdependencies between these two countries. The Editors were enthusiastically supported in this endeavour by groups of authors from the two countries. While the authors of this *Unit 1* are convinced that new macroeconomic policies and a strategic economic and political cooperation between the two countries are necessary, the politics in these two countries has not yet learned the lessons from the many decades of conflict between and within these two countries. Even new wars inside the South Sudan since December 2013 and continuing wars in Sudan make millions of people in both countries suffering.

Various groups of researchers in Nigeria from academic institutions and from governmental and non-governmental offices in Nigeria have contributed to Volume 17 of the *African Development Perspectives Yearbook* by making possible the *Unit 2* on *Macroeconomic Policies in West Africa*. Researchers from academic institutions in Nigeria and from WAMA (West African Monetary Agency) and WAMI (West African Monetary Institute) have contributed with their expertise - by writing various essays on the case of Nigeria's macroeconomic policy formation process (including impacts of macroeconomic policies on productive economic sectors) and an essay on the future role of the West African regional economic and monetary integration process (by analysing the new structure of the West African Monetary Zone around countries like Nigeria and Ghana). In order to compare and contrast the established CFA-based West African Economic and Monetary Integration process with the new WAMZ (West African Monetary Zone) integration process in *Unit 2*, Senegal was included as a country case for the CFA Zone.

Unit 3 of Volume 17 contains a great number of book reviews and book notes and so is a valuable source of new books, journal issues, documents and research papers with a focus on macroeconomic policy formation in Africa. All the entries to this *Unit 3* are highly relevant for the main theme Macroeconomic Policy Formation in Africa. The many reviews are grouped according to the headings: Macroeconomic Policy formation in Africa; Macroeconomic Policies in Africa; Global Economic Reports; Regional African Economic Reports; Arab Spring Economies in North Africa; Post-Conflict Countries in Africa; Development Policies and Development Aid.

Volume 17 is complementary to Volume 16 on „Macroeconomic Policy Formation in Africa – General Issues". For Volume 16 senior researchers gave inputs to the *Unit 1* on General Issues with regard of Macroeconomic Policy Formation. The essays in *Unit 1* of Volume 16 have set the theme for the Volumes 16 and 17 with contributions on employment-targeting, on new macroeconomic policy regimes by considering vulnerability and resilience to shocks, and on ways to react in macroeconomic policies to demands for inclusive growth and to adapt in macroeconomic policies to economic globalization pressures and economic governance pressures. These introductory essays are so important for the theoretical focus of Volumes 16 and 17. Many researchers and international organisations have also supported strongly the idea to publish a *Unit 2* in Volume 16 on the Economics of the "Arab Spring" Countries. It was possible to work on such a *Unit 2* because of the early involvement of researchers from Egypt, Tunisia and from international organisations being active in the North Africa/Western Asia Region, like UNESCWA Beirut, UNDP Cairo and API, Kuwait City.

Many other institutions have contributed with news, information, publications, and various forms of encouragement. Many regional and international organisations, like the African Development Bank (AfDB), the African Union (AU), the UNECA (United Nations Economic Commission for Africa), the World Bank, UNCTAD (United Nations Conference on Trade and Development), UNDP (United Nations Development Programme), IMF (International Monetary Fund), UNIDO (United Nations Industrial Development Organization), and ILO (International Labour Organization), continue to support our scientific effort by sending us - always timely - new strategy documents and drafts of their researches for publication and review. Also UNU-WIDER (United Nations University - World Institute for Development Economics Research) as an institution of global importance has continuously supported our work with most recent research papers, publications and information about important scientific events. Furthermore, we would like to thank all these institutions by informing so many others about our work for Africa.

We would also like to express our gratitude to Dr. Magda Kandil, Executive Director and Director of Research at the Egyptian Center for Economic Studies (ECES), Cairo and now acting as a senior expert at IMF, Washington. She was the first expert to submit a paper for the *Unit 2* of Volume 16 on the Economics of the "Arab Spring" Countries in North Africa, and she accepted the invitation to join the team of volume editors for both editions – Volume 16 and Volume 17. Dr. Tobias Knedlik, the Managing Editor of the *African Development Perspectives Yearbook,* and Professor Karl Wohlmuth, the Volume Editor, are also thankful to Dr. Osmund O. Uzor for bringing in his expertise on Nigeria as the main Unit Editor for *Unit 2* of Volume 17 and to Professor Dr. Achim Gutowski for his continuous work as Book Review/Book Notes Editor of the *African Development Perspectives Yearbook*; his *Unit 3* is in this Volume 17.

We have to thank all contributors and supporters of the *African Development Perspectives Yearbook* for their hard work, their steady encouragement and their continuous assistance. The valuable input from leading African research institutions and experts has contributed over the years to the success of the *African Development Perspectives Yearbook* as an outstanding publication on and for Africa. The readers of the various Yearbook volumes have contributed with critical comments and encouragement so that over time a valuable network between readers, contributors and editors was created.

Various institutions have made donations over the years and have funded allocations to the *African Development Perspectives Yearbook* project, but the support of the University of Bremen, Bremen, Germany is of invaluable importance. The University of Bremen was awarded by the German scientific research community in June 2012 the title "Excellence University", and the

Research Group on African Development Perspectives Bremen is very proud about this distinction.

These donations, supports and research grants to the project have helped us to research on African development issues, to distribute the various volumes of the Yearbook to African partner universities and to major African research institutions, and to invite research scholars from leading African research institutions to work with us in Bremen. Institutions like the Volkswagen Foundation and the Humboldt Foundation have generously financed the stay of senior researchers at IWIM (Institute for World Economics and International Management) in Bremen. The Africa Research Workshops are regularly held in Bremen at the University to discuss the draft papers which are intended for publication. These Africa Research workshops serve as forums for the intensive discussion of the draft papers and related research topics. The Editors also have to thank the many reviewers of draft contributions for their committed work. By this input the *African Development Perspectives Yearbook* has become over the years a fully refereed publication.

Many persons have given support, advice, and encouragement; others have helped with frank and critical assessments. However, the responsibility for the final product remains with the editorial team of the *Research Group on African Development Perspectives* in Bremen. While Volume 17 and the companion Volume 16 both are released in 2014, the Research Group now works on Volume 18 for 2015 with the title *"Africa's Progress in Regional and Global Economic Integration"*.

In the name of the Editorial Team:

Karl Wohlmuth, Bremen University, Volume Editor, and
Tobias Knedlik, Fulda University and IWH Halle, Managing Editor

List of Abbreviations and Acronyms

AAA	Addis Ababa Agreement
AC	Arab Countries
ACBF	African Capacity Building Foundation
ACR	African Competitiveness Report
ADB	Asian Development Bank
ADCR	Arab Development Challenges Report (of UNDP)
ADF	Augmented Dickey Fuller Unit Root Test
ADL	Autoregressive Distributive Lag Model
ADPY	African Development Perspectives Yearbook (Research Group in Bremen)
AEC	African Economic Community
AEO	African Economic Outlook
AERC	African Economic Research Consortium
AfDB	African Development Bank
AFEM	Autonomous Foreign Exchange market
AFRISTAT	Observatoire Economique et Statistique d'Afrique Subsaharienne, Bamako
AFT	Agence France Trésor/AFT
AGRIC	Agricultural Sector
AGRSH	agriculture (sector)
AGS	Accelerated Growth Strategy (in Senegal)
AIAE	African Institute for Applied Economics (in Enugu, Nigeria)
AIMS	Aid Information Management System
AMP	Aid Management Platform
AMU	Arab Maghreb Union
APF	African Partnership Forum
API	Arab Planning Institute (in Kuwait)
APRM	African Peer Review Mechanism
APTBEF	Association Professionnelle Tunisienne des Banques et des Établissements Financiers
ARA	Autonomous Revenue Agency
ARDL	autoregressive distributed lag (model)
ARP	Agriculture Revival Programme (of Sudan)
ASEAN	Association of South East Asian Nations
ASF	Agriculture Support Fund
AT	Aide Transparency
AU	African Union
AU	African Union

AUC	African Union Commission (of African Union)
BAD	Banque Africaine de Developpement (AfDB)
BCEAO	Banque Centrale des États de l'Afrique de l'Ouest
BCV	Banco de Cabo Verde
BD/GDP	Budget Deficit/GDP
BDD	Budget Deficit (Dummy)
BDF/TR	Budget Deficit Financing by the Central Bank/Tax Revenue
BEAC	Banque des Etats de l'Afrique Centrale
BFPME	Banque de Financement des Petites et Moyennes Entreprises
BIS	Bank for International Settlements
BM	Base Money
BOF	Budget Office of the Federation (of Nigeria)
BoG	Bank of Ghana
BOP	Balance of Payments
BPD	Barrel Per Day
BRIC	Brazil, Russia, India, and China
BRICS	Brazil, Russia, India, China and South Africa
BSD	Budget Surplus (Dummy)
BSDP	Border-States Development Programme
BSP	Budget Sector Plans
BSSCDC	Border States Security, Cooperation and Development Commission
BSWG	Budget Sector Working Group
BTS	Banque Tunisienne de Solidarité
BVMT	Bourse des Valeurs Mobilières de Tunis
CAEMC	Central African Economic and Monetary Community
CAI	Consultancy Africa Intelligence
CAP	Comprehensive Adjustment Program
CAPMSE	Central Agency for Public Mobilization and Statistics of Egypt
CAREPP	Commission d'Assainissement et de Restructuration des Entreprises à Participations Publiques
CARICOM	Caribbean Community
CB	Central Bank
CBAF	Cross-Border Assistance Framework (CBAF
CBE	Central Bank of Egypt
CBK	Central Bank of Kenya
CBN	Central Bank of Nigeria
CBOS	Central Bank of Sudan
CBSS	Central Bank of South Sudan

CBSS	Central Bureau of Statistics of Sudan
CBSSu	Central Bureau of Statistics Sudan
CBSSy	Central Bureau of Statistics Syria
CBT	Central Bank of Tunisia
CBWAS	Central Bank of West African States (BCEAO)
CCC	Community Customs Code (of ECOWAS)
CDP	Community Development Program
CE	Capital Expenditure
CEM	Country Economic Memorandum of World Bank
CEMAC	Communauté Économique et Monétaire de l'Afrique Centrale (Economic Community of Central African States)
CET	Common External Tariff
CFA	Communaute Financiere Africaine (Francs)
CFA Francs	Communaute Financiere Africaine (Francs)
CGD	Commission on Growth and Development
CIA	Central Intelligence Agency (of USA)
CIC	Currency in Circulation
CIS	Community of Independent States
CM	Common Market
CNS	Comprehensive National Strategy of Sudan
CO	Crude oil prices
CODESRIA	Council for the Development of Social Sciences Research in Africa
COM	Council of Ministers of Sudan
COMESA	Common Market for Eastern and Southern Africa
Congo, DR	Congo, Democratic Republic
Congo, Rep.	Congo, Republic
CoV	Coefficient of Variation
CPA	Comprehensive Peace Agreement for Sudan
CPI	Consumer Price Index
CPIA	Country Policy and Institutional Assessment
CPRC	Chronic Poverty Research Centre (University of Manchester)
CRDC	Chaire de recherche du Canada en développement des
CRES	Consortium pour la Recherche Economique et Sociale
CSAE	Centre for the Study of African Economies
CSO	Civil Society Organization
CSPLP	Cellule de Suivi du Programme de Lutte contre Pauvreté
CTA	Comprehensive Transformation Agenda
CTS	Community Tax for Solidarity
CU	Customs Union

DAS	Dutch Auction System
DC	Development Centre (of OECD)
DCBS	Development Commission for the Border States
DDR	Disarmament, Rehabilitation and Reconstruction
DESA	Department of Economic and Social Affairs (of the UN)
DESP	Document of Economic and Social Policy (Senegal)
Dev.	Development
DFES	Direction of Forecast and Economic Studies (Senegal)
DFID	Department For International Development (UK)
DGID	Direction Générale des Impôts et Domaines (Senegal)
DMBs	Deposit Money Banks
DMO	Debt Management Office (of Nigeria)
DPEM	Dummy variable for PEM
DPLs	development policy loans
DR	Developing Region
DR of Congo	Democratic Republic of Congo
DRP	Debt Restructuring Programme (for Nigeria)
DSRI	Development Studies Research Institute (in Khartoum)
EAC	East African Community
EAP	East Asia and Pacific
EBRD	European Bank for Reconstruction and Development
ECA	Economic Commission for Africa
ECA	Excess Crude Account
ECA	Europe and Central Asia
ECB	European Central Bank
ECDPM	European Centre for Development Policy Management
ECES	Egyptian Center for Economic Studies
ECM	error correction mechanism
ECO	ECO (Proposed Currency for WAMZ)
ECO	European Consultants Organisation
ECOWAS	Economic Community of West African States
EFR	Economic & Financial Review (of CBN)
EGP	Egyptian Pound
EGPC	Egypt's General Petroleum Company
EGX100	Egypt's Stock Exchange Index 100
EGX30	Egypt's Stock Exchange Index 30
EIB	European Investment Bank
EITI	Extractive Industries Transparency Initiative
EIU	Economist Intelligence Unit
EMU	European Monetary Union
EOP	Economic Orientation Plan (Senegal)

EPCMU	Economic Policy Coordination and Monitoring Unit (Senegal)
EPSI	Economic Policy Support Instrument (Senegal)
ER	Exchange Rate
ERD	Economics and Research Department (Asian Development Bank)
ETLS	ECOWAS Trade Liberalisation Scheme
EU	European Union
EXRT	(Nominal) exchange rate
F. CFA (XAF)	Franc de la Coopération Financière en Afrique Centrale
F.CFA (XOF)	Franc de la Communauté Financière d'Afrique
FDI	Foreign Direct Investment
FG	Federal Government
FGN	Federal Government of Nigeria
FGT	Foster–Greer-Thorbecke (poverty index)
FLAC	Fiscal Liquidity Assessment Committee
FMF	Federal Ministry of Finance (of Nigeria)
FMIS	Financial Management Information System
FONDAD	Forum on Debt and Development, The Hague
FR	Fiscal Revenue
FRBSL	Federal Reserve Bank of St Louis
FSP	Fiscal Strategy Plan
FTA	Free Trade Area
FY	Fiscal Year
GADET	Pentagon Generation Agency for Development and Transformation
GAFTA	Greater Arab Free Trade Area
GCC	Gulf Cooperation Countries
GCF	Gross Capital Formation
GCI	Global Competitiveness Index
GDP	Gross Domestic Product
GEAC	German Economic Advisory Committee (to the government)
GER	Gross Foreign Exchange Reserves
GFC	Global Financial Crisis
GFCF	Gross Fixed Capital Formation
GFPI	Guarantee Fund for Priority Investment
GFS	Government Finance Statistics
GGFCE	General Government Final Consumption Expenditure
GIGA	German Institute for Global and Area Studies (in Hamburg, Germany)

GMT	Grilli, Masciandaro, and Tabellini (methodology)
GNI	Gross National Income
GNP	Gross National Product
GNSs	Gross National Savings
GoNU	Government of National Unity
GOSS	Government Of Southern Sudan
GOVEXP	Government expenditure
GRSS	Government of the Republic of South Sudan
GVC	Global Value Chains
H1	First Half of the Year
HCE	Household Consumption Expenditure
HDI	Human Development Index
HDR	Human Development Report
HIES	Household Income and Expenditure Surveys
HIPC	Highly Indebted Poor Country (programme)
HIV	Human immunodeficiency virus
HRV	Hausmann/Rodrik/Velasco (growth diagnostics approach)
I(0)	Variable Stationary at Levels (Stationarity test)
I(1)	Variable Stationary at first difference (Stationarity test)
IAA	Non-accumulation of Internal Arrears
IBRD	International Bank for Reconstruction and Development (World Bank Group)
ICRG	International Country Risk Guide
ICT	Information and Telecommunication Technology
IDA	International Development Association (World Bank Group)
IDB	Islamic Development Bank
IDEA	The International Institute for Democracy and Electoral Assistance
IDP	internally displaced people
IDR	World Development Indicators
IDRC	International Development and Research Council
IDS	Institute for Development Studies (in Sussex, UK)
IFC	International Finance Corporation (World Bank Group)
IFEM	Interbank Foreign Exchange Market
IFI	International Financial Institutions
IFMIS	Integrated Finance Management Information System
IFMS	Integrated financial Management System
IFPRI	International Food Policy Research Institute
IFRS	International Financial Reporting Standard
IGAD	Intergovernmental Authority on Development

IGC	International growth Centre/Ideas For Growth
IIAEG	Ibrahim Index of African Economic Governance
IIDS	Indian Institute of Dalit Studies
IILS	International Institute For Labour Studies (of ILO)
ILO	International Labor Organization
IMF	International Monetary Fund
INDSH	industry (sector)
INF	Inflation Rate
INV	Aggregate Investment/Real Gross Domestic Capital Formation
IOM	International Organization for Migration
IPC-IG	International Policy Centre for Inclusive Growth
IPD	Initiative for Policy Dialogue (at Columbia University, New York, USA)
IPPDR	Interim Public Procurement and Disposal Regulation
IPRSP	Interim Poverty Reduction Strategy Paper for Sudan
ISF	Industry Support Fund for Sudan
ISIC	International Standard Industrial Classification
IT	Inflation Targeting
IWIM	Institut für Weltwirtschaft und Internationales Management (der Universität Bremen)
IWVWW	Internationale Wissenschaftlichen Vereinigung Weltwirtschaft und Weltpolitik e.V., Berlin
JAM	Joint Assessment Mission
JEMSAP	Journal of Economic Management Studies and Policy
JLP-PPG	Joint Learning Programmes on Pro-Poor Growth
JO	Journal Officiel
JORT	Journal Officiel de la Republique Tunesienne
KCL	Karumasi Consultancy Limited
KILM	Key Indicators of Labour Market (of ILO)
KOF	Konjunkturforschungsstelle ETH Zürich (KOF Index)
KOFIG	KOF Index of Globalization
KSA	Kingdom of Saudi Arabia
LAC	Latin America and Caribbean
LAG	Liquidity Assessment Group
LAS	League of Arab States
LDC	Least Developed Countries
LE	Egyptian Pound
LGA	Local Government Act
LICs	Low-Income Countries
M1	Narrow Money Supply

M2	Broad Money Supply
MANSH	manufacturing sub-sector (part of industry sector)
mbd	million barrels per day
MDA	Ministries Departments and Agencies
MDG	Millennium Development Goals
MDTF	Multi-Donor Trust Fund (for Sudan and South Sudan)
MEF	Ministry of Economy and Finance (Senegal)
MEFMI	Macroeconomic and Financial Management
MEI	Middle East Insights
MENA	Middle East and North African (countries)
MFA	Macro Financial Assistance (loan)
MGI	McKinsey Global Institute
MI	Ministry of Interior (Senegal)
MIT	Massachusetts Institute of Technology
MLACD	Ministry of Legal Affairs and Constitutional Development
MMR	Money Market Rate
MoFEP	Ministry of Finance and Economic Planning
MOFNE	Ministry of Finance & National Economy Sudan
MOU	Memorandum of Understanding
MP	Member of Parliament
MPC	Monetary Policy Committee
MPI	Migration Policy Institute
MPI	Ministry of Planning and Industry
MPIA	Modeling and Policy Impact Analysis
MPIC	Monetary Policy Implementation Committee
MPR	Monetary Policy Rate
MPRA	Munich Paper Repec Archive
MPTC	Monetary Policy Technical Committee
MRR	minimum rediscount rate
MTEF	medium-term expenditure framework
MTEF	Medium Term Expenditure Framework
MTEF	Medium-Term Expenditure Framework
MTFASRP	Medium-Term Financial Adjustment and Structural Reform Program
MTFF	Medium Term Fiscal Framework
MTRF	medium-term revenue framework
MU	Monetary Union
MU	manufacturing capacity utilization
N	Naira (Nigerian currency)
NA	National Assembly of Sudan
NAC	National Action Council (of Malaysia)

NAC	National Audit Chamber
NASD	National Agency for Statistics and Demography (Senegal)
NBER	National Bureau of Economic Research
NBS	National Bureau of Statistics
NCB	National Central Bank
NCEPC	National Committee of Economic Policy Coordination (Senegal)
NCP	National Congress Party of Sudan
NDA	National Development Agenda
NDA	Net Domestic Assets
NEEDS	National Economic Empowerment Development Strategy
NEPAD	New Partnership for Africa's Development
NEPRU	Namibian Economic Policy Research Unit
NES	Nigerian Economic Society
NFE	Non-Formal Education
NGO	Non-Governmental Organization
NHDI	Non-Income Human Development Index
NHIS	National Health Insurance Scheme
NILS	National Institute for Legislative Studies
NIR	Net International Reserves
NIS	National Institute of Statistics (of Tunisia)
NISER	Nigerian Institute of Social and Economic
NIST	National Institute of Statistics of Tunisia
NLA	National Legislative Assembly
NPAID	Norwegian People's Aid
NPC	National Planning Commission
NPGG	National Program for Good Governance (Senegal)
NPM	New Public Management
NPS	New Planning System (Senegal)
NSAs	Non State Actors
NSESD	National Strategy for Economic and Social Development (Senegal)
NSPC	National Strategic Planning Council of Sudan
OANDA	Corporation for foreign exchange trading
OAPEC	Organization of Arab Petroleum Exporting Countries
OCA	Optimum Currency Area
OCDE	Organisation de Coopération et de Développement Economiques
ODA	Official Development Assistance
ODI	Overseas Development Institute (in London, UK)
OEA	Office of the Economic Advisor to the President

OECD	Organization for Economic Cooperation and Development
OLS	Ordinary Least Square
OPEC	Organization of Petroleum Exporting Countries
OPM	Oxford Policy Management
ORSA	Oil Revenue Stabilization Account (of Sudan)
ORSEF	Oil Revenue Stabilization and Equity Fund
PACT	International NGO (also working in Sudan)
PDG	Partnership for Democratic Governance
PE	Public Expenditure
PEFA	Public Expenditure and Financial Accountability
PEM	Public Expenditure Management
PEP	Partnership for Economic Policy
PERI	Political Economy Research Institute, Amherst, USA
PFM	Public Finance Management
PFMA	Public Financial Management Act
PI/TR	Public Investment/Tax Revenue Ratio
PMS	Premium Motor Spirit
POVCAL	Poverty Calculation
PP	Phillips Perron (test)
PPP	Purchasing Power Parity (exchange rates)
PPP	Public Private Partnership
PPU	Procurement Policy Unit
PREM	Poverty Reduction and Economic Management Network of the World Bank
PRGF	Poverty Reduction and Growth Facility
PRINV	Private Investment
PRS	Political Risk Services
PRSP	Poverty Reduction Strategy Papers
PSD	Private Sector Development
PUINV	Public Investment
PWPs	Public Works Programmes
R&D	Research and Development
RBNZ	Reserve Bank of New Zealand
RCC	Regional Center in Cairo (of the United Nations Development Programme)
RDA	Regional Development Agency (Senegal)
RDP	Research Discussion Paper
RE	Recurrent Expenditure
RECs	Regional Economic Communities
REER	Real Effective Exchange Rate
RER	Real Exchange Rate Stability Research

RIR	Real Interest Rate
RoS	Republic of Sudan
RPSAOC	Réseau de Recherche sur les Politiques Sociales en Afrique de l'Ouest et du Centre.
RWP	Research Working Papers
S&P	Standard and Poor's Credit Rating Agency
SADC	Southern African Development Community
SANE	South Africa, Algeria, Nigeria and Egypt (group of countries)
SANRB	South African National Reserve Bank
SAP	Structural adjustment policies
SAP	Structural Adjustment Program
SARB	South African Reserve Bank
SAS	South Asia
SBA	Stand-By Agreement (of IMF)
SC	State Council
SCAPE	Singapore Centre for Applied and Policy Economics
SCF	Stabilisation and Cooperation Fund (of WAMZ)
SDG	Sudanese Guinea
SERG	Sudan Economy Research Group (at University of Bremen)
SERVSH	services (sector)
SFEC	Strategic Framework for Economic Cooperation
SFSI	Sovereign Fund for Strategic Investments
SITC	Standard International Trade Classification
SLF	Statistical License Fee
SME	Small and Medium Enterprises
SMP	Staff Monitored Program (of IMF)
SPLA	Sudan People Liberation Army
SPLM	Sudan People Liberation Movement
SPN	Staff Position Note (of IMF)
SPPS	Survey on the Perception of Poverty in Senegal
SSA	Sub-Saharan Africa
SSAC	South Sudan Audit Chamber
SSACA	South Sudan Anti-Corruption Authority
SSACC	South Sudan Anti-Corruption Commission
SSBF	South Sudan Business Forum
SSCCSE	Southern Sudan Centre for Census, Statistics and Evaluation
SSCSA	South Sudan Civil Society Alliance
SSDP	South Sudan Development Plan
SSID	Senegalese Social Indicators Database
SSNAC	South Sudan National Audit Chamber (of South Sudan)

SSNBS	South Sudan National Bureau of Statistics
SSP	South Sudanese Pound
SSRN	Social Science Research Network
STI	Science, Technology and Innovation
SVR	Sachverständigenrat zur Begutachtung der gesamtwirtschaftlichen Entwicklung (der Bundesrepublik Deutschland)
SWF	Sovereign Wealth Fund
TD	Treasury Department (of South Africa)
TFP	Total Factor Productivity
TICQS	Tunisian Institute of Competitiveness and the Quantitative Studies
TJA	Transitional Justice Act
TM	thousand millions
TND	Tunisian Dinar
TPIP	Triennial Public Investment Program
TR	Total Public Revenue
TR/GDP	Tax Revenue/GDP
TRA	Temporary Relocation Agency (African Development Bank in Tunis)
TYEEP	Three-year Emergency Economic Program
TYESP	Three-Year Economic Salvation Program for Sudan
TYP	Ten-Year Plan of Economic and Social Development for Sudan
TYP-ESD	Ten-Year Plan of Economic and Social Development for Sudan
UAE	United Arab Emirates
UCAD	University Cheikh Anta Diop of Dakar
UCMEP	Unit for Coordination and Monitoring of Economic Policy
UEMOA	Union Economique et Monétaire Ouest Africaine (West African Economic and Monetary Union)
UGTT	Union Générale Tunisienne du Travail
UHC	Universal Health Coverage (for Senegal)
UK	United Kingdom
UN	United Nations
UN NGLS	United Nations Non-Governmental Liaison Service (in Geneva and New York)
UNCTAD	United Nations Conference on Trade and Development
UNDESA	United Nations Department for Economic and Social Affairs
UNDP	United Nations Development Programme

UNECA	United Nations Economic Commission for Africa
UNEMRT	Unemployment rate
UNESCWA	United Nations Economic and Social Commission for Western Asia
UNIDO	United Nations Industrial Development Organization
UNSD	United Nations Statistical Division
UNU-WIDER	United Nations university - World Institute for Development Economics Research
UNWTO	United Nations World Tourism Organisation
US	United States
US$	United States $
USA	United States of America
USAID	United States Agency for International Development
USD	United States Dollar
USPF	Universal Social Protection Fund (Senegal)
Ut	Error term or Residual term
UTICA	Union Tunisienne de l'Industrie, du Commerce et de l'Artisanat
VAR	Vector Autoregression Model
VAT	Value Added Tax
VECM	Vector Error-Correction Model
VP	Vice President
WACB	West African Central Bank
WAEMU	West African Economic and Monetary Union
WAMA	West African Monetary Agency
WAMI	West African Monetary Institute
WAMZ	West African Monetary Zone
WB	World Bank
WB/TR	Wage Bill/Tax Revenue Ratio
WBIFC	World Bank and International Finance Corporation
WDAS	Wholesale Dutch Auction System
WDB	World Bank, World Databank
WDI	World Development Indicators (of World Bank)
WEF	World Economic Forum
WRTSH	wholesale and retail trade (sector)
WTO	World Trade Organization

Unit 1: Macroeconomic Policy Formation in Sudan and South Sudan – The Need for a Strategic Economic Cooperation

New Economic Policies for Sudan and South Sudan and the Need for a Strategic Economic Cooperation

Karl Wohlmuth[1]

1   The Issues

The Constraints of the Sudanese Growth Model since Independence in the year 1956

Sudan has - after its independence in 1956 - seen only two periods of peace – the period 1972 - 1983 (Addis Ababa Agreement/AAA) and the transition period of 2005 - 2011 after the Comprehensive Peace Agreement/CPA of January 9, 2005. Millions of people died, millions were displaced and the economy was devastated along with the infrastructure and the institutions. At the end of the transition period South Sudan became on July 9, 2011 an independent republic. However, since independence of South Sudan new conflicts have emerged between the two states, at the international border and in the border regions on both sides. Also in other regions of the two countries conflicts with varying intensity occurred and one side accuses the other to be involved in accidents. Natural resources, like oil, land, livestock, minerals, water, etc., play a great role in these conflicts. A new approach is needed to address all these issues in an integrated way and to come to a sustainable development, growth and cooperation model.

The growth model in Sudan is itself an issue. The growth model in Sudan became – after independence in 1956 and the more so after 1999 on the basis of the oil export industry - more and more capital- and import-intensive, while the irrigated and semi-mechanized farming systems brought with it more and more land- and nature capital-intensive production systems. Traditional agriculture was consistently neglected in Sudan since independence. Economic shocks, social exclusion, political instability and civil war, neglect

---

of peripheral areas, and ecological shocks characterized the growth model since independence. Recent developments reinforce this pattern of growth. The hydropower installations associated with a number of newly constructed and projected dams (with high public investment, like the Merowe dam), the continuation of oil exploration (in ecologically sensitive areas), the gold mining activity (with around five hundred thousand workers mining under extremely dangerous production conditions and large-scale environmental destruction), other mining ventures (with negative ecological impacts), and the large-scale land lease deals (with domestic and foreign investors in areas with fertile land used by local producers) add to these problems, and lead to new conflicts.

The growth period since 1999 - when oil exports started - was also a period without recording any successes in broad-based agricultural development. Traditional rain-fed agriculture was not supported; irrigated agriculture and semi-mechanized farming were not properly maintained and regulated. The regional imbalances ("horizontal inequality") and the income disparities along the income ladder ("vertical inequality") may even have widened (The Republic of Sudan et al. 2010; Ahmed 2010). The oil industry sector became the main source of financing the continuation of the (civil) war(s) in Sudan, and it was also becoming the main source of conflicts in the ten border-states between North and South Sudan (as large-scale ecological destruction, displacement of the local population, and disputes over the distribution of oil revenues were escalating). The growth model of Sudan became increasingly one led by vertical and horizontal inequalities. While "vertical inequality" means a shift of incomes from lower income strata to higher income strata, "horizontal inequality" means a shift of opportunities from lower income regions/ethnic groups/social identity groups to higher income regions/ethnic groups/social identity groups. The successful negotiation of the CPA of 2005 is probably also the result of the collapse of this particular growth model as escalating costs of war have eroded the legitimacy and the top-down income transfer potential of the power elites.

However, no change of the growth model was effected in the transition period of 2005 to 2011 towards the Referendum. Reliance on the oil industry and the oil revenues, increasing income inequality and regional economic imbalances, neglect of broad-based economic development and the use of the state resources for consumption purposes (wages and salaries, subsidies, personnel, security) were the characteristics of development processes in the North and in the South Sudan. Many factors contributed to the lack of cooperation: mistrust about the distribution of oil revenues, unclear competencies between the central government in Khartoum and the autonomous government of the South in Juba, different interpretations of the wording of the CPA, border issues, and unsolved problems with regard of the Three Areas

(South Kordofan State, Blue Nile State, and Abyei). Conflicts between North and South Sudan and within the two states escalated after the independence of the South Sudan in July 9, 2011 – because of increasing horizontal inequalities, because of the lack of institutions for a broad participation of people in governance, and because of strongly prevailing economic incentives for starting rebellions (Wohlmuth 2012).

Part of the inherited growth model is also the "top-down" approach in planning and policymaking rather than combining this approach with a "bottom-up" approach by planning growth and making economic policy working also from the level of counties and states upward to the central government level. The "growth diagnostics" approach (developed by Hausmann/Rodrik/Velasco, 2005, abbreviated HRV 2005) is an instrument to look at the investor's choices, potentials and constraints at local levels. Such a growth strategy analysis – based on HRV 2005 – was already applied to the conditions of some states in the North Sudan and the South Sudan (South Kordofan State and Blue Nile State in the North, and Western Bahr el Ghazal State and Upper Nile State in the South). Such a growth strategy would – if implemented - give the basis for a more effective fiscal decentralization and for improved local economic governance (see for South Kordofan state: Klugman/Wee 2008, and for Upper Nile State and Eastern Equatoria State: World Bank 2009, chapter 6; for Western Bahr el Ghazal State and for Blue Nile State DSRI/Development Studies Research Institute staff in Khartoum has made a study for World Bank which was reported in Bonn at the International Sudan and South Sudan Studies Conference 2012: see Wohlmuth 2012). Such an approach requests however another model of development administration which is committed to inclusive development and a model of economic governance which is local-based, participatory and more transparent.

All the periods of economic policy formation in Sudan since 1956 (and even before since 1947 when the Juba Conference was held) saw the neglect of South Sudan in development plans and development strategies, but more important also the neglect in real resource allocation and fiscal funding for the South. In the context of Sudan's growth and development model, South Sudan is however not a special case. Increasing regional imbalances in the North Sudan fuel more and more conflicts: in the five states of Darfur, in North Kordofan and South Kordofan states, in Blue Nile State, in the three Eastern States, etc. Also in South Sudan increasing regional imbalances lead to escalating conflicts. Such conflicts also spill over the borders between the North and the South. Unsolved border conflicts between the North and the South associated with resource conflicts contribute to this pattern of conflicts. Lack of trust in the state agencies and lack of commitment in the negotiations for a new social contract are fuelled by this particular mode of production, distribution and growth in the two Sudans. "Horizontal inequality" (in its economic, political, social and cultural forms) is a major explanation of conflicts and war(s) in Sudan as this source of conflict is added to the numerous other factors like slow growth over the long run, volatile growth in the short run, bad economic governance and increasing "vertical inequality" (Gini income inequality coefficients increased especially in the 1990s to be considered as "extremely unequal"; UNDP 2006, p. 26).

Consistently the Sudan has grown far below its potential, with an annual growth rate per capita of not more than 1.3% over nearly 40 years (1965 - 2004), and poverty rates ranging in the regions between 50% and 90% of the population (Hansohm 2007, p. 185). If the period of 1960 - 1999 is considered (1999 is a turning point as oil exports started), a very low annual growth rate of only 0.39% per capita was recorded and this "near stagnation situation" was associated with a high volatility of growth (Ali/Elbadawi 2003, p. 9). This means that the pre-oil economy of Sudan was virtually stagnant. The oil export economy since 1999 brought some gains in recorded growth (annual real growth not lower than 5-6 per cent and up to 7-8 per cent; see World Bank 2009, p. 15; AfDB et al. 2012); this high growth was associated with very high volatility of growth. High volatility of growth has implications for fiscal policy and fiscal planning, and if medium-term fiscal planning is not properly done – as it is the case in Sudan – severe macroeconomic imbalances and deeper vertical and horizontal inequalities are resulting. Growth in Sudan since 2000 has rather fuelled centrifugal tendencies – because of increasing inequalities on the income ladder and in the geographic space, because of the concentration of economic and political power in and around Khartoum, and because of the erosion of political, economic and corporate governance. The expansion of the oil industry contributed to the severe loss of transparency in economy and society.

The stop of the oil production in the South Sudan early 2012 and the deadlock in the post-independence negotiations between Sudan and South Sudan had severe consequences for both states. This state of affairs led in both states to extreme forms of austerity policy, to a further strengthening of military and security sectors, to a halt of structural transformation and of an improvement of the social situation and the physical infrastructure, and to declining growth rates. The growth and development perspectives are increasingly uncertain for both states (see AfDB et al. 2012, 2013). The danger is great that the human development progress in some areas of the two states is not only coming to a halt but that it is heading for a reversal.

The Limits of the Sudanese Model of Development Administration and Governance

Beside of the peculiarities of the growth model in Sudan the mechanism of development administration is problematic. Various factors have to be mentioned to underline the continuity in Sudan's failed economic policies and its unsatisfactory economic progress (see Hansohm 2007, pp. 187-190): Development strategies lack information and a sound analytical basis for the strategies; there is a lack of realism, prioritization and sequence; the view is held that finance is the key factor to development so that the entry of Sudan into the global oil economy in 1999/2000 was seen as a new chance for development (thereby ignoring what broad-based development means and what the sources and modalities of such an oil-based growth are). Too little attention is devoted to implementation, management and coordination. Institutions and institution-building consistently were neglected as it was assumed that skills provision is the key factor. Private sector development was not given real priority despite of the rhetoric of liberalization and privatization since 1989 (ignoring the fact that private sector development requests the existence of market-supporting institutions and legal frameworks as well as of a sustained dialogue between the public and the private sector). Public regulation (over-regulation) and public intervention (of an ad hoc type) went parallel to the rather biased privatization and liberalization programmes. Local contexts and local knowledge were largely ignored in development strategy and so the development blueprints could not be implemented. External actors/partners were consistently overestimated in their role, and their economic and political interests were not properly evaluated (so the Sudan switched from Western to Socialist partners and then to Arab partners and again to Western partners and then to Asian and Arab partners). In this process Sudan has imported a lot of foreign development models but has not transformed (absorbed) them into a genuine and holistic development strategy (see Hansohm 2007 on more details about these continuities of Sudan's economic policy).

Most important in the context of development administration and governance is the concentration of political and economic power in Khartoum and some few other country states in Sudan. The small power group (of military, big business and some Islamic religious leaders) is moderated by President Bashir and favours huge dam projects for irrigation and electricity production, labour-intensive gold mining, further oil, gas and minerals exploration, and large-scale land leases to domestic and foreign investors, but all this consistently works at the expense of broad-based agricultural development and related agro-industrialization. Development planning and development administration are constrained by these power configurations of exclusion. The development model is excluding most of the regions and the majority of the people, and the institutions in the country are extractive (in the sense of Acemoglu 2012). The Agriculture Revival Programme (ARP) of the Sudan is an example; the programme is full of good ideas and intentions, but allocation of funds favours irrigated agriculture and big projects, not projects for broad-based development of agriculture and poverty alleviation (RoS/Republic of Sudan, 2008). However, the situation in South Sudan has developed since the CPA of 2005 (and similarly so since the 2011 independence) along similar lines. The Agriculture Sector is consistently neglected, as less than 2% of government expenditures were allocated from 2008 - 2011 (see Okwaroh 2012, p. 22). This is so, although international donors, like USAID, started with an Agricultural Revitalization Programme for Southern Sudan already in 2002, but it did not work as projected. Oil exploration, other mining activities and large-scale land leases in fertile land areas play an ever increasing role. Illegal timber logging is widespread. Communal land is appropriated by government for the benefit of private and public investors, domestic and foreign ones. The environmental and social consequences of this model are reported as severe. Broad-based agriculture is neglected to the extent that food insecurity is pervasive. The particular growth model and the particular type of development administration explain the poor economic results in Sudan and South Sudan; all this helps to explain the prevalence of past and current conflicts.

There is also an economic governance dilemma as the oil economy added to the major governance problems in Sudan by making a whole industry sector working without transparency and accountability (World Bank 2009, pp. 47-60; Hansohm 2009). The lack of economic governance in the oil sector spread to overall economic policy and to other sector policies, to regional and environment policies, and also to politics and economics in border regions between North Sudan and South Sudan (as oil production is mainly located in the border areas). All the major negotiations between the South and the North after the CPA were handicapped by lack of transparency about oil revenues, production volumes and shares, oil reserves, cost and profit, processing and transport costs, etc. Trust could not be restored at the level of the Government of National Unity (GoNU) and between the North and the South in the Interim Period of 2005-1011. Therefore, cooperation and coordination vanished between the two partners.

Foundations of Economic Policies in the new State of South Sudan

Economic policies in South Sudan are in a manifold dilemma situation. First, the new state has inherited a devastated country with so many displaced people and returning refugees, without adequate infrastructure and without an effective bureaucracy. Second, the continuing conflicts are binding resources for a vast security sector (army, militias, police, border troops, secret service, etc.) to the extent that funding for development is very small. Third, institutions were destroyed during civil wars and are still weak and not participatory; in the context of large-scale destruction by war and on-going conflicts the institutions for government effectiveness, rule of law, and private sector development cannot be built up. Fourth, geography plays also a role. South Sudan is a land-locked country and needs access to the coast. Transit of oil to Port Sudan is an issue because of the political conflicts in the border regions with Sudan; transit via Ethiopia to Djibouti and to Kenyan and Tanzanian ports is another issue because of infrastructure and cost problems and insecurity associated with these alternative trading routes. Fifth, South Sudan's neighbours also have political problems and conflicts which spill over to South Sudan (from Uganda, DR of Congo, and the Central African Republic, but to a lesser degree also from Kenya and Ethiopia), thereby affecting agricultural production and trade. Sixth, international agreements are of great importance for South Sudan but are not yet concluded (for a fair Nile waters distribution, and for a fair and effective cooperation in regional economic communities, like the East African Community /EAC).

The burden of history explains a lot of mistakes and disappointments, but the new state has to move to a sustainable development path. For South Sudan all this history means that the Sudanese growth model, the Sudanese characteristics of development administration and the Sudanese model of economic governance have to be overcome as they have led to and have perpetuated the known social, political and economic exclusion effects. Only marginal references can be found in the Sudanese development strategies and in the Sudanese development plans to the issues of the South while the major Regional Development Plan of 1979 for the South (handled at that time by the autonomous government for the South) never took off. Lack of transparency on government policies being relevant for the South, neglect of human resource and infrastructure development in the South, a trend of ad hoc decision making from the side of the central government towards the South, and lack of control about financial resources and entitlements of the South (mostly allocated as grants from the central government and only partly generated from within the autonomous region) were major problems in the South. As there was no chance to impact on central government decisions in Khartoum, the autonomous region was like a last resort of hope at participation. The subdivision of the autonomous region by President Numeiri had therefore serious consequences, and together with other factors (discovery of oil in the South, building of the Jonglei Canal, "divide and rule" policies affecting the coexistence of ethnic groups in the South) led in 1983 to the Second Sudanese Civil War. Implementation of development programmes in the South could never be evaluated and adjusted in the short periods of peace. The South had only two peace periods: 1972 - 1983 and 2005 - 2011. Both periods saw an initial phase with optimism and constructive policies and a second one characterised by lack of trust and increasing pessimism). In both periods an own growth model, based on its huge agricultural resources, could not be developed in the South, although in the first peace period the Regional Development Plan of 1979 and in the second peace period, the transition period to the referendum, a Growth Strategy (see GOSS 2010) and the foundations for a First Development Plan (GRSS 2011) were laid out.

However, the situation in South Sudan with regard of economic governance (and also political governance in more general terms) is more difficult as governance in the South Sudan region was contested already since the 1970s by the international aid business which was setting their own priorities and implementation modalities. The situation has not improved in this respect and the weak South Sudan state is operating more or less exclusively in the oversized security sector (see Grawert 2007 on the history of contested governance in South Sudan), while social services delivery is largely in the hands of the international aid business. Another severe limitation in South Sudan is the heritage of post-colonial state-building in terms of traditional (ethnic-based) rule: in the ten states of South Sudan counties after counties are created and based on tribal and ethnic criteria, thereby preventing a more open state formation at local levels (CODESRIA 2010) with economic interactions, immigration from other regions in South Sudan and exchanges of goods, services and factors. This has implications also for the widely practised land deals as the local governments make their own land lease businesses (largely without any control from higher state levels). The extent of such deals is huge, but the conditions of leases are not transparent, and such transactions are concentrated in the most fertile areas (NPAID/Norwegian People's Aid, 2011; The Oakland Institute 2011), cultivable land which would be needed for providing food security in South Sudan. Food insecurity has increased since 2006 despite of proclaimed action from the side of the government – which is presenting ambitious agriculture and infrastructure development plans. The reason for this regression is obvious: increasing conflicts (conflicts at the international border and in border-states and natural resources- and ethnic-based conflicts) lead to food insecurity, while lack of progress in agriculture production and distribution leads to conflicts.

Some positive steps of state building were taken in the first few years of the first peace period after 1972 but since 1977/78 the situation changed, and the Regional Development Plan of 1979 never got a chance for implementation. Various crises (Jonglei Canal dam, Chevron oil discovery, VP General Joseph Lago and political division in the South, macroeconomic imbalances spilling over from the North, lack of regular finance for the South, discussion and introduction of Sharia law, etc.) signalled the upcoming end of peace.

Also in the first few years of the second peace period - from 2005 to 2011 – some developments went in the right direction. South Sudan was starting to move from humanitarian assistance and a war economy to disarmament, rehabilitation and reconstruction (DRR), but soon the steps towards a deeper development of agriculture and infrastructure stalled. The utilization of the huge agriculture potentials was blocked by security considerations (an increasing number of conflicts on natural resources, like land and livestock, and because of unsolved political issues in border regions, and many rebellions against the central government and the supposed "Dinka predominance" in the army and the central government), and even the disarmament process was stopped. This pattern of conflict has even gained momentum after independence of South Sudan in July 9, 2011 (see Jok 2013).

On paper a Growth Strategy (GOSS 2010) and a Development Plan (GRSS 2011) were presented, probably with the good intention to implement these proposals and recommendations in South Sudan. But mistrust about the way of calculating the South's share of oil revenues by the central government in the North, power struggles among the South Sudanese political and military elites, lack of political and economic governance, financing needs for an oversized security sector, rumours about the intentions of the North with regard of the handling of the Population Census and the conduct of the Referendum, and conflicting economic and commercial interests among the power elites of the South with regard of a rapid oil and minerals exploitation and large-scale land leases changed the situation to the negative side. The Tamazuj ("intermingling") states along the border in the North and in the South continued their cooperation to some extent (the governors of the border-states in the South and in the North met regularly and made recommendations to the central governments in Khartoum and Juba, and even started on a modest scale Unity Fund Projects). This cooperation ended with independence.

The year from the independence of July 9, 2011 to July 9, 2012 has brought for both Sudans further tensions and an aggravation of the conflicts, caused by the deadlock in negotiations on the open CPA and separation issues, the stop of the oil production in the South, the destruction of the oil production facilities in Heglig (north of the border) by the South, and the bombing of facilities in Unity State by the North. Increasing conflicts in the three regions (Abyei, Blue Nile State and South Kordofan State) spilled over to the South and to other states in the North. Observers of the situation in Sudan and South Sudan (see Lesley on Africa, 2012) argue that politicians in both states of the Sudan have completely abandoned the idea of a development policy in the interest of the people as they behave consistently at the expense of the survival interest of their populations. The political calculus within narrow circles of the political and military elites is only related to the way of how to destabilize the other regime. Even military attacks are part of the game and obviously a political calculus is practised by the elites on both sides to preserve power in the home country, to avoid the merger of opposition forces against the regime, and to continue with a war economy as it allows it to keep intact the oversized security sector in both countries and the related distribution of resource rents. The stop of oil production in January 2012 in South Sudan led to a sharp reduction of foreign exchange reserves and savings, to large-scale leases of fertile land and the sale of licences for oil and minerals exploration, but also to new forms of external indebtedness in relation to new international actors (like China and Qatar) by mortgaging untapped oil resources for current government finance. The political situation also lead to the proliferation of highly unrealistic plans, such as building as quickly as possible alternative pipeline routes to Lamu, Kenya or via Ethiopia to Djibouti, and new railway lines to Mombasa and other places (in Uganda and Tanzania).

The fate of Sudan and South Sudan cannot forever be locked into a system of conflicts and wars, unsustainable growth, a climate of mistrust, weak governance institutions, non-inclusive development strategies, lack of economic incentives to develop productive sectors, further degradation of the environment, and the prevalence of strong incentives among power elites to go for war, rebellions and conflict. The danger is great that the tensions between Sudan and South Sudan lead to a new and probably a very long period of conflict and economic decline, if it is not possible to move quickly towards a Strategic Framework for Economic Cooperation (SFEC) between the two states, a framework that is beneficial to both states and that is also changing the inherited growth model in the North and in the South, the traditional characteristics of development administration and the inadequate structures of economic and political governance. Sudan has never come up to implement its proclaimed visions, strategies and plans, and the risk is great that South Sudan will follow this path. Against this background of failed development initiatives, and because of increasing disappointment and disillusionment on the side of the people in both Sudans a Strategic Framework for Economic Cooperation (SFEC) between Sudan and South Sudan was presented Wohlmuth 2012), based on new economic policies in the two countries. It is assumed that new macroeconomic policies and drastic structural changes in both Sudans and mutual political and economic commitments from both sides are in the interest of both countries and especially for the people. A win-win situation will be created.

2 The Contributions

The two contributions in this Unit highlight the complexities of macroeconomic policy formation in Sudan and in South Sudan. Both groups of authors analyse the development of economic strategies and of macroeconomic policies in these two countries as only analysis of the historical context of economic policies reveals the constraints in macroeconomic policy formation, such as the interest groups at work and the socioeconomic background of policies.

The three authors **Mosllem Ahmed Alamir, Ebaidalla Mahjoub Ebaidalla** and **Saef Alnasr Ibrahim Mustafa** present a paper on the **Macroeconomic Policy Formation in Sudan after the Secession of the South**. While it is a main purpose of the study to identify the consequences of the secession of South Sudan for Sudan's macroeconomic management, the study also highlights two important periods of macroeconomic policies, especially the 1970s with the oil price shocks and the period since 1999 up to 2010 when Sudan started its oil exports. There is also an analysis how Sudan used the oil revenues and how the country has managed its oil wealth. Then an analysis of the macroeconomic management after the secession of the South Sudan is presented. The study has an interesting methodological approach as the authors discuss the reaction of macroeconomic management to economic shocks. How was the reaction to the oil price shocks in the 1970s (*first shock*)? How was the reaction to the starting and on-going oil boom, a shock for the macro-management because the institutions in Sudan were not prepared for managing the oil revenues properly (*second shock*)? And, how was the reaction to the secession of the South Sudan, a shock to Sudan because of the loss of 75 per cent of its oil revenues (*third shock*)?

There are many studies available to give evidence on the reactions of Sudan to the *first shock*. The country reacted to the oil price shock by designing a new development strategy which was very ambitious – the Sudan should become a large-scale supplier of food and agricultural products to the oil exporters in the Near East (the label "Breadbasket Strategy" is also used in more recent times by politicians in Sudan and in South Sudan to advertise to foreign investors on their huge agricultural resources). The three authors highlight the main developments in macroeconomic management during these years. The increasing macroeconomic instability is analysed in detail.

The reaction to the *second shock*, the steep increase of oil revenues in 1999 in a context of fiscal and monetary institutions not being prepared for it, was also highly inappropriate. The policymakers were soon confronted with a serious dilemma situation. The on-going civil war requested enormous funding for the military, while a future-oriented and macro-economically sound use of the oil revenues would have demanded a specific development policy for the non-oil economy so as to protect agriculture and traditional export sectors. The start of the conflicts in Darfur (2003) was a new factor which led to a diversion of the oil revenues from development to war. While political and macroeconomic instability prevailed before the oil boom started in 1999, the escalating oil revenues brought new problems. The authors show that substantial economic policy changes were envisaged (from fiscal federalism to increasing development expenditures), the difficult political situation in the country prevented a success of the Medium-Term Financial Adjustment and Structural Reform Program/MTFASRP covering the years of 1997-2011, which was negotiated with and monitored by the IMF. The main objectives could not be realised (macroeconomic stability, private sector development, confronting post-conflict challenges, and poverty reduction measures). While the fiscal situation prior to the CPA was relatively stable, the CPA requested additional funds in accordance with the treaty provisions. Any fiscal space was lost quite soon after the CPA. The Oil Revenue Stabilization Account (ORSA) was used up fully for consumptive purposes. ORSA could have played a strong role to facilitate macroeconomic management after the secession, but no funds were left to manage the loss of public revenues and foreign exchange after 2011.

The reaction of the policymakers to the *third shock* was inadequate. Although strong austerity measures were undertaken, credibility in such measures from the side of the population was not there. This led to demonstrations, to further political instability, and to repression from the side of the regime in Khartoum. The political situation sharply deteriorated. The conflicts in the Three Areas intensified after the independence of South Sudan (in Blue Nile State, in South Kordofan State, but also in Abyei, where a consensus on the status could not be found yet). Other conflicts at the international border and in border-states north and south of the border also contributed to the climate of near war and conflict of varying intensity. The authors make it quite clear that all these shocks have can tell a similar story. Macroeconomic stability is possible only if a political consensus is found towards peace and development, if economic interest groups are part of a dialogue forum between the government and the business sector, and if the institutions for macroeconomic policy formation are continuously adjusted to the global and regional environment.

The analysis by the authors shows that Sudan has immense potentials to become an emerging economy, by reaching sustainably high growth rates through using agricultural resources and exploration of minerals, but good governance of the revenues from agriculture, agro-industries and from minerals is also a necessary precondition for this to happen. A medium-term planning and fiscal policy framework has to be used and implemented. However, inefficient macroeconomic management, lack of inclusive economic policies, lack of implementation of development plans, and long internal conflicts hinder the country to effectively utilize its resources. Therefore, the authors recommend policies to lay the economic foundation for a diversified, inclusive and sustainable development path. Successful policies require that political and technical issues are addressed competently and that resources are managed well by a committed bureaucracy and political class. However, it is necessary to invest into the "owners" of the resources, what requires that measures are undertaken for employment creation, the establishment of social safety nets, and programmes for poverty reduction. The paper suggests that Sudan's new strategy should focus on overcoming the legacies of long internal conflicts (and prolonged now by conflicts with South Sudan) and on building the economic foundation for a diversified economic structure and an inclusive growth process. To address these long-standing structural rigidities, Sudan needs policy measures that emphasize fiscal discipline and stable monetary policy along with underlying structural, social and political reforms.

In the second paper with the title **Macroeconomic Policy Formation in South Sudan: Building Fiscal Management** the authors **Asha Abdel Rahim and Dirk Hansohm** study the role of fiscal planning for the reconstruction and development of South Sudan. South Sudan has got its independence on July 9, 2011. It is a least developed country, a post-conflict country, a country without access to the sea, a country which is dependent on the oil exports (with up to 98 % of the foreign exchange earnings. Tax revenues are still very small, as resource revenues dominate the budget. It is a country with a huge security sector (army, militias, intelligence service, and various police troops) which claims the greatest share of the country's financial resources. It is a country in which international donors play a fundamental role in supplying humanitarian assistance (because of food insecurity and because of many refugee camps) and in providing social services to the rural population (because of the neglect of such services by the own government). It is a country with vast agricultural resources although these are not exploited yet. It is a country in which minerals exploration, oil and gas exploration and land leases play a dominant role. Therefore, Resource Curse and Dutch Disease effects are dangerous consequences of the growth model, threatening the development of agriculture and manufacturing sub-sectors. South Sudan is because of its geography dependent on (and even vulnerable with regard of) neighbouring countries as oil transit to Port Sudan harbour in Sudan and the transit of import and export goods are done via Kenya and Uganda. It is also a country with weak institutions and a still unfavourable investment climate. It is a country with widespread prevalence of corruption and bad governance. All the social, political, economic and structural indicators and as well the governance indicators are unfavourable. Because of the long civil wars form 1955 to 1972 and from 1983 to 2005 the structural transformation in the country was blocked. The country has a subsistence agriculture sector with very low productivity and a negligible manufacturing and crafts sector. Imports of food, and of industrial goods and services prevail. Details are presented by the two authors in the paper on South Sudan.

In this country context the authors study in great detail the role of fiscal planning and of fiscal policy. Medium-term fiscal planning is of great relevance for a country which aims at setting priorities for public expenditures and public revenues. Especially because of the dependence on oil revenues South Sudan has to consider the benefits of medium-term fiscal planning. Medium-term fiscal frameworks can help towards restructuring budgets and allocating public revenues towards non-oil production activities and non-oil incomes in the form of taxes and duties. Medium-term fiscal policies will enable the country to plan for public expenditure restructuring away from consumption to investment, from salaries and wages to productive inputs and infrastructure, and from defence/security to peace and development-related expenditures.

The authors have developed a specific methodological approach in order to study the issues of fiscal planning. First, the initial conditions of the country are identified, as the preconditions for development determine the framework for fiscal planning. The many constraints on development have to be analysed first so as to be able to use planning instruments fully, like the Growth Strategy and the new Development Plan and then the Medium-Term Fiscal Framework. Although macroeconomic policy formation is covering monetary, fiscal and exchange rate policies as well as other policies, the paper focusses largely on the processes and the quality of fiscal management in the country. Therefore, the state-building process in South Sudan, the fiscal planning process, and the fiscal management of the oil revenues matter most. The new fiscal planning instruments and their relevance for a country like South Sudan are discussed and evaluated. State-building, medium-term fiscal planning and fiscal management of the oil revenues are interconnected issues.

South Sudan has to learn the lessons from other countries, as the Sudan did not manage wisely, consistent and future-oriented the oil revenues so that nothing can be copied from these experiences. The problems for South Sudan may be even more severe than for Sudan because of the lack of experiences in negotiating contracts, the weakness of government institutions and agencies, the lack of infrastructure development, and the extent of security-related expenditures. All these factors may limit a control of the oil revenues and their use for development (see also Hickel, Jason, 2012). Progress in disarmament, demobilisation and reintegration (DDR) was very limited in south

Sudan so that the risks for the budget and for reconstruction and development are exorbitant. In order to sustain the huge army, militia, intelligence and police forces a dominant share of the public revenue is used. The DDR process is getting even more complicated because of the on-going conflicts with Sudan and the many internal conflicts. Growth has slowed down through the years 2009-2011, and the stop of the oil production meant a further reduction of growth. This is completely in contrast to developments to be expected for a post-conflict country after a peace agreement and being supported so much by international aid. As oil reserves may be used up by 2035 the time available for structural transformation and for restructuring the economic institutions through finance from oil revenues may be indeed limited.

The authors point out that institutions and measures at institution-building play a great role. Although some agencies function well, like the South Sudan National Audit Chamber (SSNAC) or the National Bureau of Statistics (NBS), many other institutions do not work well. While SSNAC makes a good job in presenting evidence and recommendations, the response to critical evaluations of government financial affairs from the side of those concerned is highly unsatisfactory, as nothing is done to improve on the mentioned issues. The great number of offices, agencies, commissions, ministries, administrations, and departments - at all government levels - contribute to the lack of transparency. It is more for employment creation purposes and as tool to prevent inter-ethnic conflicts in government. However, these measures have neither raised effectiveness of government nor have they reduced conflicts (see Jok 2013). Some offices are imaging concern about important issues, like the South Sudan Anti-Corruption Authority (SSACA), but the output is insignificant. The authors give also other interesting examples about a huge, but inefficient bureaucracy.

Even in the context of fiscal planning various institutions overlap – these are ministries, departments, commissions, and evaluation and monitoring agencies. Another major problem identified by the authors is the concept used for medium-term fiscal planning in a country like South Sudan. Most of the planning methods are relevant for Western countries and these are not so easily to be transferred to a least developed country – because of gaps in human resources, organisational differences, different reward and incentive systems, and communication problems. The new public management (NPM) approach as pushed by international donors has not been relevant as there have been high demands for complementary reforms in many areas at the same time. This was not realistic and still is not. It is argued that these instruments can only be applied in a post-conflict economy like South Sudan with considerable adaptations and on the basis of incremental improvements. The authors request an incremental strategy based on own resources and the development of feasible policies and strategies. For all this to work, the constitution, the fiscal federalism, the structure of the fiscal administration, and the whole budget cycle matter. A main outcome of the study is that the "downstream" budget functions (budget execution) are not working well while "upstream" budget functions (budget preparation) have improved considerably. Upstream functions are done by a small number of experts, while downstream functions require skills and capabilities at multiple levels, also in the states and counties.

While Public Finance Management (PFM) is built up, the basis for proper working is a functioning coordination of all government levels and an adequate financing of their respective tasks. Neither coordination nor finance issues have been improved in recent times. The states in South Sudan are not equipped with the funds they need to fulfil the tasks allocated to them according to the wording of the constitution (health and education services, etc.). Transfers to the states are not regularly made and they are even reduced in times of crisis (as it was after the stop of oil production and the loss of oil revenues since January 2012). Oil revenues and aid funds have to be managed properly by instruments of PFM. This is not only a management task, but also request political will and leadership. The paper brings out that both sources of revenue (oil and aid) are not well managed. A medium-term outlook is not included, coordination between providers and users of funds is not guaranteed, budget discipline is not strong enough, and boom-bust cycles in revenues are not considered. Aid funds and mineral rents are not yet adequately covered in PFM, and synchronisation with macroeconomic policy is not functioning. A medium-term planning approach for fiscal policy has to be used and implemented for oil and aid flows, and this is necessary in the context of development planning for all the productive sectors of the economy.

The authors present in great detail the history of public finance reform, the fiscal policy strategies, the fiscal policy designs and the process of policy formation. Also the institutions and actors are analysed in their functions and attitudes. A key finding of the study is that for South Sudan the establishment of organisations, laws and regulations is not sufficient to change macroeconomic policy-making and fiscal policy-making if the institutions are not embedded into the society, politics and economy. Furthermore, the existing institutions and human capabilities are not compatible with the practice of implementing sophisticated and demanding reforms in a short period of time. Instead, these reforms create a wide imbalance between the formation of organisations and their institutional grounding. Instead of international 'best practice' models, a gradual process of learning, prioritization, and sequencing is called for in the study.

The Strategy

Towards a New Economic and Social Policy for Sudan and South Sudan

Five elements matter in order to support development in Sudan and south Sudan. Policy recommendations are quite similar, although development level and resources endowment are different.

First, macroeconomic stability has to be provided. Fiscal deficits and current account deficits, high and accelerating inflation rates (especially food price inflation), weakening local currencies, increasing unemployment rates (and the more so youth unemployment rates), and increasing income inequality measures have to be mentioned for Sudan, and to some extent also for South Sudan (AEO/African Economic Outlook 2013, Internet Version: http://www.africaneconomicoutlook.org/en/). Macroeconomic instability has become a problem for Sudan after the independence of South Sudan on July 9, 2011 because of the 75% loss of oil revenues and the need for harsh austerity policies but it was already an aggravating problem after signing the CPA as demands for financial transfers to the South increased sharply and because of the escalating Darfur civil war. Macroeconomic instability is also a problem for South Sudan, despite of the high oil revenues potential. Structural problems (weak macroeconomic policy institutions, a weak finance and banking system, insufficient agricultural production, import dependency for food and industrial goods, and widespread food insecurity because of internal conflicts) lead to food price inflation, to pressures on the local currency and to fiscal and monetary control problems. Because of the stop of oil production in January 2012 by the government of South Sudan the macroeconomic instability problems were even aggravated in both countries and they are still severe. Most of the problems are structural so that macroeconomic institutions have to be rebuilt and strengthened. Both countries need to manage better their mineral rents (especially oil revenues) and have to protect and develop the non-oil economic sectors as a base for tax revenues. Cooperation between the two countries will definitely help in achieving macroeconomic stability in both countries (Wohlmuth 2012).

Second, a medium term public finance framework **is needed for both countries,** especially so because of the high volatility of oil revenues and the low importance of non-oil exports and non-oil revenues. Such medium-term public finance frameworks are not in place, and there is no Permanent Fund/Permanent Income approach at work to smooth the expenditures from the volatile oil revenues towards stabilization and long-term development objectives. The problem is more severe now for South Sudan as the country has to manage wisely the oil revenues up to 2035 – for generating savings for future incomes, for allocating priority expenditures to key sectors (like education and health) and for establishing elementary social safety nets on the basis of direct cash payments (to be taxed) to the people of South Sudan (see on such a distribution of oil revenues Hickel, Jason, 2012). Also Sudan has to move in this direction; gold mining, oil and gas exploration and production and exploration and production of other minerals request as well a similar future-oriented policy on mineral rents. Also for macroeconomic stability such "funds for the future" based on minerals rents are important to smooth expenditures. All this can only work if - by establishing a medium-term fiscal framework and adhering to it politically – the major expenditure items (security and defense, subsidies, and wages and salaries) can be brought under control while improving the tax structure and the tax administration (by emphasizing tax revenues over revenues from resource rents). The extremely high cost of "security" in both countries (claiming up to 70 per cent of the expenditure) can only be reduced by ending conflicts on the borders and internally and by preventing new conflicts. The high subsidies for food and fuel and the high payments for wages and salaries have also to be brought under control. Cooperation between Sudan and South Sudan will be helpful in laying the foundations for a strengthening of medium-term fiscal planning (Wohlmuth 2012).

Third, a _redirection of exports towards non-oil products_ is needed in both countries. However, the time since January 9, 2005 (Comprehensive Peace Agreement) was not used in the two countries for generating non-oil exports. Despite of the huge agricultural resources and agro-industrial opportunities, both countries are still large-scale food importers (and need as well humanitarian food assistance for millions of people in both countries). Both countries are considered as potential breadbaskets because of the rich endowment with agricultural resources, like cultivable land, livestock, forest cover and fishing grounds. However, a redirection of exports towards non-oil products requests a new course of action based on integrated policy frameworks. Three issues are important in this context. First, it is necessary to support linkages between agriculture and agro-industries (input industries and processing industries). Second, it is necessary to support specific agricultural and agro-industrial value chains with high potential for import substitution and export development. Third, it is necessary to support specific export products by strategies to convert comparative advantages into competitive advantages (with long-term strategic measures). While Sudan can support import substitution (with regard of sugar, wheat, and oilseeds) and the development of new export products (like processing Gum Arabicum to products for various industrial uses), South Sudan can benefit from exploiting in a sustainable way livestock resources, forest cover, and fishing grounds. Both countries need to work on a smooth process of finalizing World Trade Organization/WTO membership negotiations and on steps towards further (effective and non-overlapping) regional integration steps. Trade and industrial policies have to be streamlined towards a continuous support of these new (non-oil) export branches. Cooperation between the two countries in trade policies is important as the border-regions are very rich in these resources. Most important is however the promotion of non-oil exports by smoothing public expenditures which are based on volatile oil revenues. While the South Sudan has to do this for oil revenues, Sudan will also have to consider the revenues form gold mining and refined gold exports. Requested is nothing less than a permanent income approach so that also future generations can benefit from these non-renewable resources. Science, Technology and Innovation (STI) policies are important for linking agriculture and agro-industries, for strengthening agro-industrial value chains and for converting the comparative advantages into competitive advantages (Wohlmuth 2013). It is also necessary to support local manufacturing of agro-industrial products in the states what requires that strong federalism is built up by adequate financing of such a production base and by infrastructure development programmes to link the production centers of the states. Blueprints for such a strategy are available but it is important that determined action takes place in this direction.

Fourth, effective social safety nets **are needed to protect the poor and the poorest,** but also the middle class which became impoverished in recent years, as the available rudimentary social security and social safety systems have rather deteriorated. Public interventions in health and education sectors as well as towards the functioning of the labour market were highly inefficient and ineffective, and macroeconomic policies were not pro-poor. In the 1990s also the middle class of Sudan suffered from cost recovery measures in health and education. Also food price increases and fuel price increases in the 2000s eroded the income potential of the middle class. Poverty rates escalated in the North and in the South. The uneven distribution of incomes between states (horizontal inequality) and between income classes (vertical inequality) was becoming another issue. Youth unemployment and overall unemployment rates have increased rapidly. Most important, the social security system is only covering few percent of the working force and of the population, while direct poverty alleviation programmes only reach few percent of the poor and the poorest. Health and education institutions are often out of reach of the poor and of the poorest. This is also the case with the Islamic anti-poverty programmes (as these are programmes with high administrative cost). Allocation of public funds for health and education has further declined in recent decades (as a share of the GDP and of overall public expenditures). Because of the importance of such expenditures for productivity increases, labour market mobility was affected negatively also from this side. Macroeconomic policies were not pro-poor because of the inappropriate allocation and the unplanned use of oil revenues (mostly spent on security and defense, administration, wages and salaries, irrigation projects and dam-building).

New policy directions are therefore needed for South Sudan, using oil revenues for cash transfers to support the children and the women, for public works programmes, and for allocations to the poor and the poorest, but also for key projects in education and health sectors. Sudan has to redirect funds from untargeted food and fuel subsidies and from defense and security expenditures towards establishing social safety nets, public works programmes and broad-based labour market intervention programmes, but also revenues from oil production and from gold exports can be used for this purpose. Social safety nets will also help to make macroeconomic policies more effective as income stability over time is promoted by such measures. Public works programmes may help in both countries to address the growing problems of unemployment of the youth; food assistance programmes can be combined with them for improving the preconditions of agricultural production. Sudan has gained a successful history of such works programmes in the 1970s and 1980s.

***Fifth, effective reductions of horizontal and vertical inequalities* are requested** but the reality in both countries is that the regional imbalances and the income inequalities have rather increased since the CPA of 2005 and since the Independence of South Sudan. This has repercussions on political and economic stability in both countries and on the perspectives of cooperation between the two countries and in the border-belt states north and south of the new international border. An important policy to address the horizontal inequalities is the strengthening of the system of fiscal federalism (the way of financing the federal state, the states and the counties as well as the social security systems) so as to create viable local economic units which are financed regularly by central transfers. Combined with a bottom-up growth strategy, which is based on the mobilization of the local resources, the endogenous growth potential can be developed. Examples of "growth diagnostics" studies for some states in the north and in the south show that it is feasible to develop adapted local growth strategies by identifying the binding constraints to growth (either lack of readiness to invest in a particular area or a lack of finance sources and credit, or problems with availability of human capital and infrastructure needed for productive activities, or lack of institutions or lack of security). Many reasons can impede local growth so that a realistic and adapted package of support is needed. Central transfers have in the past played a role to punish and to reward local politicians and local ethnic groups, but were not used as an instrument of development. The central transfers were not based on the level of poverty and the potential for economic development but were allocated on the basis of a fixed sum and a share proportional to the number of people in the state. Regrettably the payments often were done irregularly. The same formulae for allocating central transfers is applied now in South Sudan, and the same type of reward/punishment system is in place as in the North.

Vertical inequalities as well can be addressed by determined policy action – the taxation system and the subsidy system play a crucial role as various income sources are not properly taxed, mainly real estate and direct incomes, while non-targeted food and fuel subsidies favour the well-off people. Some small producers and traders are overtaxed as a myriad of taxes and duties affects their production and trading activities. Social safety nets and cost recovery policies have to be revised in order to change the (vertical) income distribution. In Sudan and in South Sudan the strong presence of privileged military and security officers and a well-paid class of political actors protect their incomes at the expense of other income earners. Cash income transfer payments and public works programmes are helpful to change the income distribution patterns towards the poorer segments. However, most important is the context of food insecurity and violent conflict in the two countries. In Sudan and in South Sudan violent conflicts generate widespread food insecurity while food insecurity leads to new waves of conflict. Demand for international human assistance has increased in both countries since 2006 (immediately after the CPA). Therefore, the major forces at work in generating conflicts have to be eliminated (such as horizontal inequalities, economic incentives to rebellions, and the lack of institutions for a broad participation of the people in governance mechanisms). A combination of policies to redress horizontal and vertical inequalities is feasible for both countries, but this requests a holistic and a long-term approach.

A Strategic Economic Cooperation between Sudan and South Sudan is needed

Successful negotiations on the Post-CPA and Separation Agendas are only the first important step towards a Strategic Framework. Ten cross-border policy areas are of importance and have to be addressed as components for a Strategic Framework (see Wohlmuth 2012). Five programmes are Core Programmes as they will change the growth model of the two Sudans, while five other programmes are Supplementary Programmes as they will support the implementation of the Core Programmes (Wohlmuth 2012). The five Core

Programmes and the five Supplementary Programmes have to be looked at as integrated and interlinked programmes.

Of first priority is core programme one - *a Border-States Development Programmes for Sudan and South Sudan.* An integrated development programme is needed for the five (now six) border-states in the North (Southern Darfur, now southern Darfur and Eastern Darfur, Southern Kordofan, White Nile, Sennar, and Blue Nile) and the five border-states in the South (Western Bahr El Ghazal, Northern Bahr El Ghazal, Warrap, Unity, and Upper Nile), plus the contested area of Abyei. Such a programme is needed because of the economic and political interdependencies, the cross-border effects of horizontal inequalities, and the development opportunities associated with an integrated use of resources in the area. The huge potential of natural resources in the area (see Saeed 2010) can be ideally combined with the human resources potential to the benefit of both countries, for peace and development. Such a border-states development programme will contribute considerably to the generation of tax and non-tax revenues and foreign exchange earnings, so that the harsh austerity policy could be modified and softened. Although in the transition period (2005 – 2011) some few attempts in this direction were made (Tamazuj States Initaitve/TSI), with coordination meetings of the governors of the Tamazuj states and some development projects launched with funds out of the Unity Fund, nothing sustainable came out of this in terms of economic cooperation after the separation of the South. The meetings of the governors highlighted the issues and they reported their recommendations on security, economic, social and political issues to the central government in Khartoum and to the autonomous government of South Sudan. There was also an attempt to develop common programmes and projects by using finance from the Unity Fund. Most of these attempts have however failed, and a new approach in this direction is therefore needed. The African Union (AU) pressured in their mediation efforts since 2012 to make the Abyei area a centre for cooperation between the two countries, with parts of oil revenues of the Abyei area to be used for development projects in the surrounding areas in the North and in the South. The problem of the Abyei elections and the final status of the area are still unresolved issues.

A Development Commission for the Border States (DCBS), including public sector, private sector and civil society representatives from the ten (eleven) states and from Abyei area, should be formed to develop common platforms for the development of the regional economy on the basis of a "soft" border regime. Earlier, a Border States Security, Cooperation and Development Commission (BSSCDC) had been proposed to work on visions, development plans and action plans, but also on operational programs and concrete projects for the area (Saeed 2010, Wohlmuth 2012). There should be functional committees (looking at security, trade, investment, taxation and customs, agriculture and agro-industries, crafts, pastoral management, infrastructure, water, energy, environmental issues and climate change adaptation, etc.), and there should be also committees looking at particular products (like oil and gas, other mineral resources, particular agricultural and livestock products, such as cereals, tree crops, oilseeds, meat, etc.). The assembly and the committees of the DCBS should be supported by sufficient staff and by highly qualified technical experts (to be funded by the oil revenues generated in the border region). Such an organization (headed mainly by regional politicians, businessmen and civil society representatives from the North and the South) should have a clear mandate for specific policy areas, and so could contribute to the development of both countries – Sudan and South Sudan.

A "soft" border regime, to allow for an easy transit of people, livestock, goods, services, and labour, would be a great chance for the area to reach peace and development. Most of the problems that generate now the conflicts in the area (conflicts because of lack of participation in governance, conflicts because of horizontal inequalities, conflicts because of economic incentives for rebellions, and conflicts because of intensified competition for natural resources) can be eased by cooperation and by allowing such movements of people, livestock, services, goods, and labour. Taxation, customs and administrative issues and any upcoming conflicts can also be solved by such a Development Commission for the Border States (DCBS) – by exchanging information, by discussing issues with conflict parties, by preventive action, and by coordinating the identification, funding and execution of related projects and programmes. Some pooling of resources from the two central governments and from international donors would be possible and would be helpful, as well as mobilizing additional sources of finance emanating from a new oil revenues sharing agreement between the two Sudans to the benefit of the border region. Development assistance and humanitarian assistance could be initiated, targeted and executed for the whole border region in the context of a Cross-Border Assistance Framework (CBAF). Cross-border public works programmes could become a useful instrument for peace and development.

Strategy formation is needed alongside the earlier mentioned and discussed tasks and issues (prior to independence of South Sudan): Security and Disarmament, Demobilization and Reintegration/DDR; Food Security and Agricultural, Forestry, Fisheries, and Livestock Development; Employment Creation and Improvement of Labour Conditions; Human Development; Water, Hydropower and Energy Development; Environmental and Climate Change Adaptation Policies; as well as Policies on Oil Concessions, Oil Industry Development, and on Oil Transport. A major task of the DCBS would be to work out studies for "growth and employment diagnostics" and "poverty alleviation and nutrition status diagnostics" for the states, localities and counties in the area (along the lines of the already available studies for Upper Nile State, Western Bahr el Ghazal State, Blue Nile State and South Kordofan State). These studies for the eleven states and Abyei area should become the basis for cross-sector and cross-border support programmes. Bottom-up and top-down development programmes could be merged and implemented effectively.

Implementation of the new development strategies for the border-region – the Border-States Development Programme (BSDP) - should be monitored closely by the governments of the ten (eleven) states and by the Abyei administration but also by the civil society and by private business sector in the form of dialogue forums to be initiated at various levels. Such development strategies and programmes can be financed by regular own revenues of the ten (eleven) states and Abyei area and by Common Funds (to be financed by central governments after a new oil revenues sharing agreement has been concluded between the two Sudans and by the oil funds of the oil-producing states at both sides of the border after negotiating with their central governments a fair share of the locally generated oil revenues), to which also international donor funds could contribute. DDR programmes when financed by such Common Funds can help to integrate the former officers and fighters of militias, rebel groups and official and unofficial armies into training and employment programmes, especially so in the form of new type Public Works Programmes (PWPs) which may have lasting impact on infrastructure development. Economic incentives for rebellions could be removed thereby. Horizontal inequalities can also be reduced by such steps. Local governance and governance in the whole border-region will be improved and so the broader participation of the people will further peace and development. Training, vocational education, information, extension and research centres have to be located in the area of the border-states in order to be near the huge resource base. Mediation of conflicts in the area will be very important, and so innovative modern and traditional forms of conflict prevention and resolution will be needed at various levels; mediation teams appointed by the DCBS can function on a low-cost basis. An interaction of the Border-States Development Programme with an Infrastructure Cross-Border Development Programme (to be planned by the two countries) is urgently requested, so as to use in the future fully the traffic infrastructure (of railways, rivers, airports and roads) and as well the energy and water supply and information and telecommunication infrastructure in the region.

Fiscal decentralization and fiscal federalism will work better than in the past on the basis of this Border-States Development Programme (BSDP) as it is to be based on growth, employment and poverty alleviation and nutrition status diagnostics and on related demands for development action and funds. This development programme would also help to decentralize political power, financial resources, responsibility, and overall development efforts. The Growth Diagnostics studies for Upper Nile State in the South and South Kordofan State in the North show that any lasting development progress will be dependent on an assessment of the "binding constraints" for growth at state and county level (like low investment returns or inadequate finance, land rights, poor geography, low human capital, bad infrastructure, government and market failures, low domestic saving and poor finance intermediation, etc.).

Problems in South Kordofan State are the thin own public revenue basis and the inadequate federal transfers (see Klugman/Wee 2008), but a structural transformation of these revenue systems depends on identifying, first of all, a strategy towards coping with the "binding constraints" for growth. Better projects can attract more funds and better revenue and expenditure management can contribute to relaxing the "binding constraints" to growth. Most important, public investment is highly inadequate and basic social and economic services are minimal. A Border-States Development Programme (BSDP) can contribute to a better financed public investment programme. External development assistance for the South Kordofan State was always limited. Donors' contribution to the extended public investment programme will be highly relevant. Private business activity is affected by inadequate infrastructure and the lack of market access; the BSDP will contribute to alleviate such shortcomings. The growth diagnostics studies (also the one for the better-off Upper Nile State: see World Bank 2009, chapter 6) reveal that local growth can be enhanced by governance reforms, by local finance reform, by local investment programmes, and by local agro-industrial development action, directed to small farmers and to micro-, small- and medium-sized agro-industrial enterprises.

Local-level solutions are advantageous as social, environmental, cultural and ethnic aspects of development (projects) in the state and in the county can be better considered. Based on this "growth diagnostics" approach, support strategies can be proposed for county and state levels; also at higher government levels - for the region of the border-states and at the federation level – strategies can be developed and implemented. On the basis of the "growth diagnostics" framework a sound basis for cross-border economic cooperation can be created. Government failures, such as with the lease practices regarding land rights, can be better assessed on the basis of the "growth diagnostics" framework (as the small farmers are still the backbone of the rural economy, and not some few large-scale investors from outside). Land tenure issues are prominent factors in explaining South Kordofan's severe development problems got worse since the 1970s when large-scale agricultural development investments, Gum Arabic production, and oil exploration and production got momentum (see Klugman/Wee 2008). In the context of a "growth diagnostics" framework, such investments could have been better planned and executed (with much less negative social impact and environmental damage). Also in Upper Nile State - with large-scale agricultural schemes aside of medium-scale and small-scale agriculture ventures - the "binding constraints" to growth can be better assessed on the basis of a growth diagnostics approach, such as the volatility of own public revenues, the land rights issues and related resource conflicts (World Bank 2009, Chapter 6).

Border-states wide development planning will be facilitated on the basis of these "growth diagnostics" instruments as they allow it to work out programmes in a more participatory manner and in a bottom-up process in conjunction with the traditional top down-planning style. However, the governance of such planning processes matters; governance improvements are important for the success of local growth initiatives.

References

Acemoglu, Daron, 2012, The world our grandchildren will inherit: the rights revolution and beyond, Essay prepared for: Economic Possibilities for Our Grandchildren, edited by Ignacio Palacios-Huerta, MIT Press, forthcoming, 30 pages

AEO/African Economic Outlook 2013, Internet Version Web Access: http://www.africaneconomicoutlook.org/en/

Ahmed, Medani M., 2010, Global Financial Crisis Discussion Series Paper 19: Sudan Phase 2, London: ODI/Overseas Development Institute, February 2010

AfDB/African Development Bank/DC of OECD/Development Centre of The Organisation for Economic Co-operation and Development/UNDP/United Nations Development Programme/ UNECA/United Nations Economic Commission for Africa, 2012, African Economic Outlook 2012, Special Theme: Promoting Youth Employment, with full-length country notes at: http://www.africaneconomicoutlook.org/en/countries/

AfDB/African Development Bank/DC of OECD/Development Centre of The Organisation for Economic Co-operation and Development/UNDP/United Nations Development Programme/ UNECA/United Nations Economic Commission for Africa, 2013, African Economic Outlook 2013, Special Theme: Structural Transformation and Natural Resources, with full-length country notes at: http://www.africaneconomicoutlook.org/en/countries/

Ali, Ali Abdel Gadir/Elbadawi, Ibrahim A., 2003, Explaining Sudan's Economic Growth Performance, November 2003, Draft for: Cambridge General Economic Surveys of Africa: Eastern and Southern Africa, 32 pages

GRSS/Government of the Republic of South Sudan (GRSS; 2011): South Sudan Development Plan 2011-2013, Juba, in August 2011

CODESRIA/Council for the Development of Social Sciences Research in Africa, 2010, The Post-Referendum Sudan, National and Regional Questions, a Conference held in Nairobi on 28 February-1 March 2011 under the theme "Post-Referendum Sudan Conference 2011"

GOSS/Government Of Southern Sudan, 2010, GOSS Growth Strategy 2010 – 2012, January 2010

Grawert, Elke, 2007, The Aid Business in South Sudan after the Comprehensive Peace Agreement, pp. 387-401, in: Hans-Heinrich Bass/ Tobias Knedlik/Mareike Meyn/Maren Wiegand-Kottisch (Hrsg./Eds.), Ökonomische Systeme im Wandel der Weltwirtschaft/Economic Systems in a Changing World Economy, Band 16 der Schriftenreihe des Instituts für Weltwirtschaft und Internationales Management (IWIM), Berlin: LIT Verlag Dr. W. Hopf 2007

GRSS/Government of the Republic of South Sudan, 2011, South Sudan Development Plan 2011-2013, Realising freedom, equality, justice, peace and prosperity for all, Juba, August 2011

Hansohm, Dirk, 2007, Sudan's Economic Strategies 1956 – 2007, Constances dominate Changes, pp. 173- 192, in: Hans-Heinrich Bass/ Tobias Knedlik/Mareike Meyn/Maren Wiegand-Kottisch (Hrsg./Eds.), Ökonomische Systeme im Wandel der Weltwirtschaft/Economic Systems in a Changing World Economy, Band 16 der Schriftenreihe des Instituts für Weltwirtschaft und Internationales Management/IWIM, Berlin: LIT Verlag Dr. W. Hopf 2007

Hansohm, Dirk, 2009, Oil and Foreign Aid: Chances for Pro-Poor Development in Sudan?, pp. 105-145, in: Wohlmuth, Karl, Reuben Adeolu Alabi, Philippe Burger, Achim Gutowski, Afeikhena Jerome, Tobias Knedlik, Mareike Meyn, Tino Urban (Eds.) (2009), African Development Perspectives Yearbook (ADPY), Volume 14: New Growth and Poverty Alleviation Strategies for Africa – Institutional and Local Perspectives, Berlin : LIT Verlag 2009

Hausmann, Ricardo/Dani Rodrik/Andres Velasco, 2005, Growth Diagnostics, Harvard Kennedy School, Center for International Development, Harvard University, Cambridge, Mass., USA, 35 pages

Hickel, Jason, 2012, Can South Sudan learn from the Alaska model?, The Africa Report, accessed via: http://theafricareport.com/index.php/20120629501814512/news-analysis/can-south-sudan-learn-from-the-alaska-model-501814512.html

Jok, Madut Jok, 2013, Mapping the Sources of Conflict and Insecurity in South Sudan, Special Report No. 1, The Sudd Institute, Juba, January 12, 2013, 21 pages

Klugman, Jeni/Asbjorn Wee, 2008, South Kordofan: A Growth Diagnostic, Sudan Multi-Donor Trust Funds, MDTF-National, Sector Policy Note, March 31, 2008, Khartoum: Multi Donor Trust Fund – National, Technical Secretariat, The World Bank, ix plus 50 plus xxxvii pages

Lesley on Africa, 2012, Does War Serve Political Interests in Sudan and South Sudan?, Comment 28 April 2012, accessed: lesleyannewarner.worldpress.com

NPAID/Norwegian People's Aid, 2011, The New Frontier, A baseline survey of large-scale land-based investment in Southern Sudan, by David K. Deng, Researched by GADET-Pentagon and the South Sudan Law Society Report 1/11 (March), 48 pages, Information and Access: http://www.npaid.org/filestore/NPA_New_Frontier.pdf

Okwaroh, Kenneth, 2012, South Sudan, Resources for poverty eradication: A background paper, Nairobi, Kenya: Development Initiatives: Africa Hub

RoS/Republic of Sudan, 2008, Executive Programme for Agricultural Revival, Agriculture and Articulate a Future Vision and Action Plan for Agricultural Revival, Khartoum: Republic of Sudan, Council of Ministers, General Secretariat, April 2008

Saeed, Abdalbasit, 2010, Challenges Facing Sudan after Referendum Day 2011, Persistent and emerging Conflict in the North-South Borderline States, Sudan Report 2010:1, CMI/Chr. Michelsen Institute, Bergen, Norway

World Bank, 2009, Sudan – Toward Sustainable and Broad-Based Growth, Country Economic Memorandum, in consultation with ministries of the Government of National Unity (GoNU) and the Government of Southern Sudan (GoSS), December 2009, by Poverty Reduction and Economic Management Unit, Africa Region, Report no. 52514-SD, Washington D. C.: 2009

Wohlmuth, Karl, 2012, Towards A Strategic Framework for Economic Cooperation between Sudan and South Sudan, Sudan Economy Research Group (SERG) Discussion Papers Number 40, IWIM/SERG, University of Bremen, Bremen, September 2012, 61 pages

Wohlmuth Karl, 2013, The Role of Science, Technology and Innovation (STI) in Promoting Agriculture, Agro-Industry and Agribusiness in Africa, pp. 21-36, in: Berichte, April-Juni 2013, Schwerpunktthema: Afrika - Entwicklungspotential und Risiko, hrsg. vom Forschungsinstitut der Internationalen Wissenschaftlichen Vereinigung Weltwirtschaft und Weltpolitik (IWVWW) e. V. in Berlin

Macroeconomic Policy Formation in Sudan after the Secession of the South

Mosllem Ahmed Alamir[1], Ebaidalla Mahjoub Ebaidalla[2]and Saef Alnasr Ibrahim Mustafa[3]

1 Introduction

The secession of South Sudan in July 2011 represented a significant transition point in the recent history of Sudan[4]. Following the secession, Sudan faces a significant oil shock similar to the two historical oil shocks of 1973 and 1999 but with very different outcomes for Sudan. The global oil prices hike in 1973 – as a negative oil shock - has resulted in a severe decline in growth and productivity of Sudan as an oil-importing country. This was largely accounted for by chronic economic problems such as increased foreign debts, shortage of foreign exchange, national currency depreciation, high inflation rates, and internal and external disequilibria. Accordingly, the agricultural export proceeds declined, specially of the main cash crops like Cotton and Gum Arabic, owing largely to the lack of imported capital and intermediate goods.

The advent of oil in 1999 – as a positive oil shock - has fundamentally changed the position of Sudan's economy as it became an oil-exporting country. A substantial increase in global oil prices beside the huge amount of FDI

---

[1] Assistant Professor at Department of Economics, University of Khartoum; E-mail: mosllem@hotmail.com
[2] Lecturer at Department of Economics, University of Kassala; Email: ebaidallamahjoub@yahoo.com
[3] Lecturer at Department of Economics, University of Khartoum; E-mail: safeibrahim@hotmail.com
[4] The results of the South Sudan's self-determination referendum were finalized on February 7th, 2011, with over 98 percent of the votes for secession. Sudan has accepted the secession outcome, and the formal international recognition of an independent South Sudan was conducted on July 9th, 2011 when the Comprehensive Peace Agreement (CPA) Interim Period was ended.

inflow in the last decade had contributed to this robust performance. Sudan's economic growth has been strong by regional standards since 2000. Over this period, oil accounted for about 90 percent of the total exports and contributed about 15 percent and 60 percent to GDP and government revenues, respectively[5]. Overall, real GDP growth averaged about 9 percent, placing Sudan among the top performers in the region. The size of the Sudan's economy has grown fivefold—from $10 billion in 1999 to $53 billion in 2008[6].

The secession of South Sudan – as a negative oil shock – has translated the position of Sudan – by provoking the loss of three-quarters of Sudan's oil production and by enforcing from Sudan daunting adjustment challenges to a permanent external and fiscal shock[7]. Since July 9, 2011 Sudan is no longer receiving any revenue share from Southern oil fields, which previously accounted for three-quarters of Sudan's total oil production, about half of its fiscal revenues, and around two-thirds of its international payment capacity. The immense and complex adverse impact of the secession is largely transmitted through the fiscal and external accounts.

Sudan has experimented with a diversity of macroeconomic management and policy formation approaches with a view to maintain economic stability and to remove structural rigidities and negative economic conditions that were associated with the three oil shocks (1973, 1999, and 2011). During the 1970s' oil shock, Sudan has pursued economic policies that were motivated by governmental market interventions through import-substitution policies which were associated with restrictive international trade measures. These measures were also associated with nationalization and interventionist policies, including heavy restrictions on markets, prices and wages, using mechanisms of control. Private enterprises were nationalized, and the whole system of financial intermediation was controlled by the state. Directed credit and foreign exchange restrictions were also imposed.

Associated with the onset of the oil boom (1999-2010), Sudan has taken various macroeconomic policies motivated by transforming the economy from state control policies to free-market economy principles, including international and domestic trade liberalization. Rising oil production together with sustained stability-oriented policies have created a low risk economic environment, with real growth rates increasing to historic highs.

The main objective of the paper is to identify the consequences of secession on macroeconomic management in Sudan. The paper raises several questions, including the following: How have the fiscal and monetary poli-

---

[5] See CBOS/Central Bank of Sudan Annual Report – different issues
[6] World Bank: Sudan Country Economic Memorandum (CEM), September 2009
[7] IMF 2012a, "Article IV Consultation for Sudan", September 7, 2012

cies worked in recent years/decades in Sudan? What were the impacts of the oil shocks on macroeconomic stability, and on exchange rate and trade policies? Why has the Oil Stabilization Fund not worked in recent years? How is the process of macroeconomic policy formation in Sudan, and what are the main institutions being responsible for the process of macroeconomic policy formation in Sudan, and how effective are they? How does the macroeconomic management work after the secession of the South Sudan? What are the new economic policy priorities? What are the short-term and medium-term adjustment measures to cope with the loss of the largest share of oil revenues? How important is economic cooperation with South Sudan for macroeconomic management?

The remainder of this paper is organized as follows. Section two reviews Sudan's macroeconomic management in response to the 1970s oil price hike. Section three highlights Sudan's macroeconomic management over the advent of the oil boom (1999-2010). Section four discusses how Sudan has managed its oil resources, focusing on government failure. Section five addresses the consequences of South Sudan's secession on Sudan's macroeconomic management, while section six reviews Sudan's macroeconomic management institutions to assess their efficacy. Section seven highlights the medium-term reform agendas for Sudan, while section eight presents conclusions and policy recommendations.

2 Sudan's Macroeconomic Management in Response to the 1970s' Oil Price Hike

Oil price hike shocks in the 1970s have had significant effects on Sudan's macroeconomic variables (economic growth, employment, balance of payments and government accounts), given its dependence on oil imports[8]. In response to these global oil shocks, Sudan has adopted restricted demand-side macroeconomic management policies, accompanied with extensive government market intervention and regulation of the economy. During this episode, trade and foreign exchange rate policy had greatly depended on fixed currency arrangements, direct controls and regulations on the foreign exchange market, and tightened international trade policy measures that contained the imposition of duties and customs on both exports and imports

---

[8] The 1973 oil crisis started in October 1973, when the members of Organization of Arab Petroleum Exporting Countries (OAPEC) imposed an embargo that led the price of crude to rise from $3 per barrel to $12 by 1974.

sides[9]. As a result, private enterprises were nationalized, and the whole financial intermediation system was controlled by the state.

The main macroeconomic management feature of this period was the direct government involvement in economic activities, accompanied with increased public investments in state-owned enterprises, including the following measures:

- Introducing regulated and controlled pricing systems on goods and services, and imposing high tax rates on domestically produced goods and commercial activities.

- Adopting monetary policy measures that were characterized by a heavy reliance on monetization in the financing of budget deficits, financial repression, and direct credit controls and ceilings. These credit ceilings and controls included ceilings on sectoral credit allocation, floors on sectoral allocation, regional credit allocation, Central Bank prior approvals for large loans, Central Bank cost-charged lending facilities; and individual bank credit ceilings. As a result, the financial system consisted of few rather small banking sector and insurance companies, which were poorly performing and repressed in their activities; there was no stock market, and there was only a weak regulatory framework associated with the dominating fiscal policy (Abdalla Elhassan/Kamal Yousif and Badreldin Hassien, 2004).

- Applying fixed exchange rate arrangements and imposing direct controls on the foreign exchange markets and restricting the dealing in the hard currencies (Haidar Abbas/Mustaf I. Abdelnabi, and Selma Salih, 2006).

- Pursuing tightened international trade policy measures based on the imposition of duties and customs on both exports and imports sides. These measures included restricting the country's payments for luxury imports and encouraging exports through preferential exchange rates and incentives.

Despite all these policy measures, Sudan's economy remained very weak - with a persistent macroeconomic instability. The breakdown of peace negotiations in 1984 led to regime transitions and intensified the civil war in

---

[9] Historically, Sudan did not attempt to prepare a medium-term economic program or a national development plan until the 1960s. Then after, the Ten-Year Plan of Economic and Social Development (TYP-ESD) of 1961-1970 was formulated. The TYP-ESD's ambitious goals were frustrated by the civil war in the South and by lack of funds, depleted foreign exchange reserves and a shortfall in foreign investment capital; all these factors had threatened the continuation of implementing the plan.

South Sudan. During the period, Sudan has experienced two regime transitions, extreme political repression and predatory economic measures in favor of the ruling party and against traditional entrepreneurs. As a result, the economy faced persistent and negative growth rates, a heavy monetization of financing the budget deficit, an acute shortage of foreign exchange reserves, and declining export competitiveness in the global market (see figure 1, upper panel). Arrears accumulated and relations to creditors worsened.

Figure 1: Sudan's Economic Growth and Overall Inflation Rate, 1960-1989

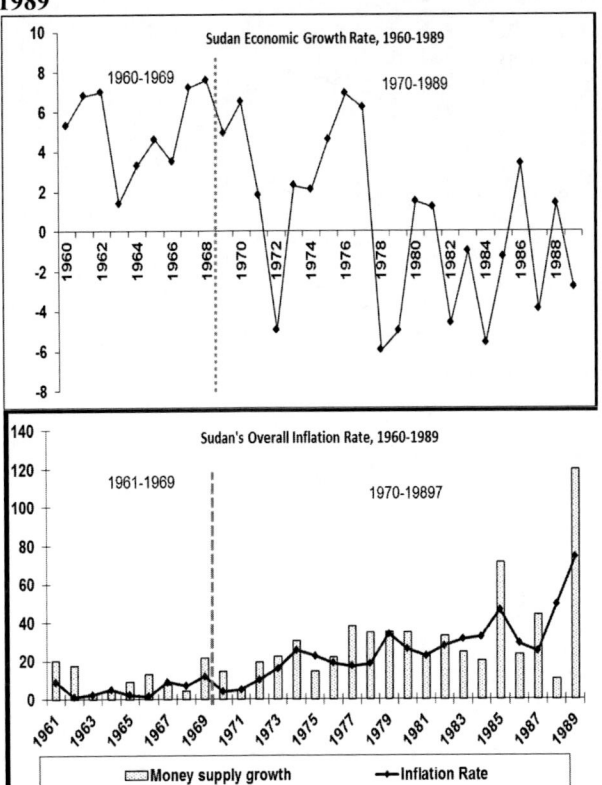

Source: Central Bureau of Statistics of Sudan (CBSS 2012) and World Bank's World Development Indicators 2011 (World Bank 2011b).

The country suffered double-digit inflation rates for the first time; they stood at 25.4 percent in 1974 compared to 6.1 percent during the 1960s (see figure 1, lower panel). This trend was attributed to increased import costs, a surge of energy prices, and a money supply expansion reflecting accelerated deficit financing. The failure in maintaining price stability has fuelled uncertainty, slowed private investment and distorted resource allocation.

Figure 2: Sudan's Budget and External Sector Performance, % of GDP, 1960-1989

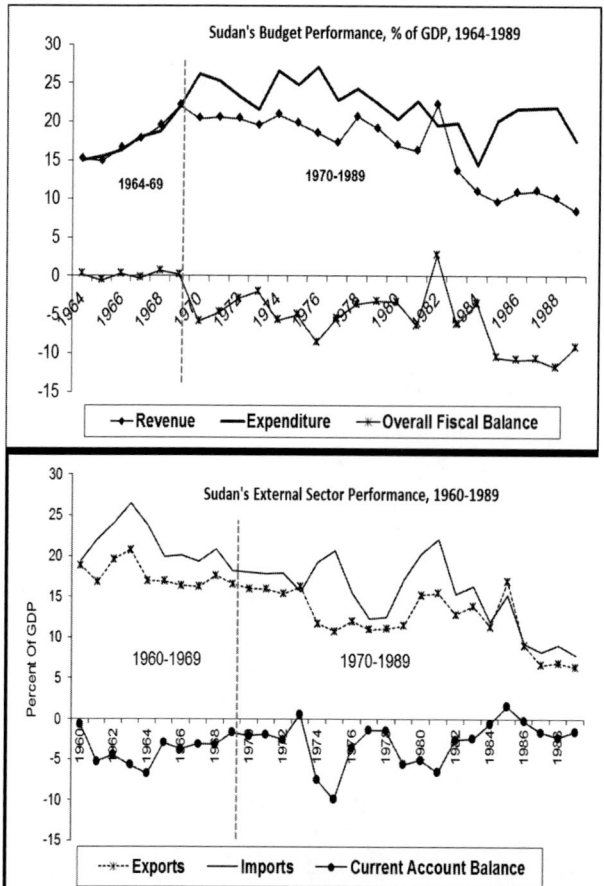

Source: Ministry of Finance & National Economy/MOFNE and Central Bank of Sudan/CBOS - Annual Reports – different issues.

The economy has experienced a significant persistent deterioration in the overall budget position (see figure 2, upper panel). The overall budget balance deteriorated from a surplus in the 1960s to a deficit of 5 percent of the GDP in 1970s. The increased fiscal imbalance was a result of large increases in expenditure while total revenue remained low and even declined, while coinciding with a steep decline in net capital inflows.

Sudan's total revenue has experienced a steady decline, mostly as a result of a decline in non-tax revenue and a low customs duty tax base (see table 1). The drop in non-tax revenue was attributed to the sharp drop in profit transfers from public enterprises and a weak collection of fees and charges. Total expenditure was high relative to revenue collections over 1978-1989. Several factors have accelerated the expenditure over 1978-1989, including (i) the break out of the Civil war in the South in 1983 and (ii) natural disasters that had hit the country, mainly drought and desertification that started in 1984 and rainfalls and floods that affected large areas in August/September 1988; all that had caused widespread devastation throughout the country.

Table 1: Trends and Composition of Public Budget, (% of GDP) 1965-1989

Items	1965-1969	1970-1977	1978-1989
Total revenue	18.4	19.2	10.6
Tax revenue	13.8	13.5	8.2
Direct tax	1.2	2.2	1.9
Indirect tax	12.6	11.3	6.2
Non-tax revenue	4.6	5.8	2.5
Total expenditure	17.5	26.3	19.7
Current expenditure	16.7	18.9	15.5
Development expenditure	0.8	7.3	4.3

Source: Ministry of Finance & National Economy/MOFNE, Annual Economic Report – different issues

The burden of financing the growing fiscal deficit has increasingly been borne by government borrowing from the central bank (money creation). The striking feature of the fiscal stance was the heavy reliance on domestic banking borrowing to finance the overall budget deficit; all this had even more expansionary effects on the money supply than was ever the case in the previous periods.

The overall balance of payments has experienced pertinent deteriorations. Export has slowed down from 17.7 percent of GDP during the 1960s to 11.4 percent over the 1970s (see figure 2, right panel). The overvalued, multiple exchange rates - together with import and export controls - had distorted the incentive system, especially for exports, and resulted in the emergence of some shortages of imported production inputs, a low capacity utilization in industry, and the emergence of a wide spread between the official and the parallel exchange rates. Several factors had accounted for the deteriorated balance of payments position, including:

Export side	*Import side*
➢ the deterioration of export competitiveness, due to both supply and demand bottlenecks, and high production costs due to domestic inflationary pressures and exchange rate devaluation; ➢ relatively low prices and weak demand for Sudan's exports; ➢ low profitability of exports as a result of the explicit and implicit exchange rate devaluation which has induced increases in the cost of imported and domestic raw materials and capital goods, factors which coincided with low productivity; ➢ lack of production inputs and spare parts; and ➢ the severe drought, desertification and famine events that occurred.	➢ marked rise in imported machinery and spare parts required for the economic development projects; ➢ increase in imported crude petroleum and petroleum products due to increased domestic consumption and higher international oil prices; ➢ increased private imports as a result of expanded economic activity, especially in the industrial sector; especially private imports of transport equipment due to the declared policy to mitigate transportation bottlenecks and to allow for an expansion of economic business activities; and ➢ the continued depreciation (devaluation) of the Sudanese pound which has substantially affected imports' prices.

3   Sudan's Macroeconomic Management over the Advent of the Oil Boom (1999 - 2010)

Sudan's macroeconomic stance had been volatile until the advent of oil[10]. Despite the substantial policy measures and structural reforms that were adopted over the period 1989 - 1997, the economy has remained subject to significant structural rigidities that hampered seriously the role of the private

---

[10] Sudan exported its first oil in August 1999, and its revenues have increasingly become important in the budget resource envelope, especially during the recent surge in oil prices.

sector in the economy[11]. These rigidities include an inefficient public sector, heavy price distortions, cumbersome regulations, an inward-looking development approach and an anti-export bias, a restrictive tariff and trade regime, a repressed financial sector, and overall inadequate policy instruments (IMF, Staff Report 1998).

The basic features of Sudan's economy before the advent of oil boom were four-folds:

- Sudan predominantly was an agricultural economy with the export of agricultural raw materials - mainly cash crops and livestock - for earning the foreign exchange being necessary for imports required as well as being the basis for the generation of government revenue. There has not been much structural transformation of Sudan's economy in the relative contribution of economic sectors to the GDP or to its growth over the last four decades (see table 2).

- Sudan's agriculture sector performance has been disappointing from the point of view of its huge potential; while there was rapid growth in other sectors, there were difficulties in reforming the agriculture sector and improving its performance. The political instability in the 1980s and the drought in 1983 have substantially lowered the contribution of agriculture to GDP and livelihoods provision.

- Sudan suffered from triple digits inflation associated with a double digits premium on the dollar over the official foreign exchange rate; and

- Sudan had an extensive public sector involvement and regulation of the economy, an economy which was dominated by public enterprises, including much of agriculture and most of large-scale industry, transport, electric power, banking, and insurance. This was due

---

[11] Over 1989 - 1997, Sudan has initiated several programmes to resolve the country's economic problems, including the Three-Year Economic Salvation Program/TYESP (1990-1993) and the Comprehensive National Strategy/CNS (1992-2002). These programmes aimed at addressing the structural rigidities and stimulating the economy's potential through liberalizing the economy – moving toward an environment which relies more on the private sector. The main focus of the these plans was on liberalization of international and domestic trade, including liberalization of agricultural prices and marketing, removal of agricultural subsidies, reduction in trade tariffs and removal of non-tariff barriers to trade, liberalization of the foreign exchange rate system, liberalization of the financial sector and of interest rates, and provision of various forms of investment incentives.

to the nationalization of the financial and the real sectors as well as the private sector's inability to finance major development projects. The advent of oil resources exploitation in 1999 has provided immense opportunity to Sudan and has led to a shift in its macroeconomic management that helped to restore macroeconomic stability and to create a low risk economic environment. Oil production has increased from 63,000 barrels per day in 1999 to about 480,000 bpd in 2010; inducing a remarkable growth in construction, trade, hotels and restaurants businesses. The contribution of the oil sector to GDP has increased from 2 percent in 1999 to 15.1 percent and to 20.1 percent in 2005 and 2007, respectively (World Bank, Sudan CEM, 2009).

Table 2: Sectoral Contribution to Real GDP, 1960-2006 (% of GDP)

Episodes	1960-69	1970-77	1978-89	1990-97	1998-2006
Agriculture	**41.9**	**36.2**	**34.0**	**40.8**	**35.9**
Industry	**14.3**	**15.4**	**14.0**	**12.1**	**19.6**
Mining & Quarrying	0.2	0.3	0.1	0.2	6.1
Manufacturing	5.9	9.1	7.8	6.2	7.9
Electricity & Water	3.3	1.9	1.3	1.0	0.8
Building & Construction	5.0	4.1	4.8	4.7	4.8
Services	**43.7**	**48.4**	**52.0**	**47.1**	**44.6**
Commerce & Hotels	13.3	16.9	18.5	21.5	15.8
Transport & Communic.	6.2	7.8	10.1	8.4	12.0
Finance & Insurance	3.3	6.0	9.6	8.0	8.0
Government services	8.9	12.5	7.7	3.6	4.7
Others	12.0	5.2	6.0	5.6	4.1

Source: Ministry of Finance & National Economy/MOFNE and Central Bank of Sudan/CBOS- Annual Reports – different issues.

The government had designed a Medium-Term Financial Adjustment and Structural Reform Program/MTFASRP covering the years 1997-2011, which was running with the supervision/consultation of the International Monetary Fund (IMF) under the so-called IMF Staff-Monitored Program

(SMP). The intentions of this macroeconomic management approach were restoring macroeconomic stability, creating a better environment for the private sector, addressing the post-conflict challenges (reconstruction and rehabilitation of the war-affected areas and solving the issues of displaced population settlements), and implementing poverty reduction actions. Substantial fiscal policy measures, combined with monetary and exchange rate reforms as well as trade liberalization reforms, were undertaken over the period 1999-2011. The subsequent discussion gives more information about the highlights.

Fiscal Policy: Several policy measures were taken to contain domestic imbalances and to maintain fiscal sustainability — notably through:

Revenue measures	*Expenditure measures*
➤ Rising receipts from oil exports through several attempts to encourage investment in oil exploration and production;	➤ Rationalizing public expenditure and improving public resource management, fiscal controls and fiscal reporting;
➤ Strengthening non-oil revenue, notably by vertically and horizontally broadening the tax base;	➤ Ensuring efficient inter-sectoral and intra-sectoral allocation of expenditures;
➤ Strengthening the structure and administration of the tax system and initiating tax reform;	➤ Increasing development and maintenance expenditures with a view to increase public investment in infrastructure and human development;
➤ Eliminating tax and customs exemptions;	➤ Improving public investment planning, and improving fiscal transparency;
➤ Improving equity and enhancing tax collection efficiency;	➤ Implementing Government Finance Statistics (GFS) classifications; and
➤ Adjusting customs duty rates on domestic industry products, with an aim to improve its competitiveness;	➤ Reforming the federal-states fiscal relations; and initiating a civil service reform program.
➤ Reducing tax rates on profit gains, with a view to encourage private investment and production; and	
➤ Eliminating subsidies and adjusting user's fees and charges to reflect the real production costs, taking into account the social and economic circumstances of the beneficiaries.	

A series of revenue and expenditure measures and key fiscal adjustments were implemented since 1999 (MOFNE, Annual Economic Review, different issues). The number of import tariff bands was gradually reduced from 7 in 1997 to 4 since 1999; the maximum tariff rate was limited from 125 percent to 40 percent, while the minimum tariff rate was reduced from five percent to zero percent. Export duties rates were reduced from 10% (cotton & gum Arabic), 3% (livestock, fruit and vegetables) and 5% (other exports) to zero percent (full exemption) since 2000, except hides & skins. The consumption tax was eliminated as a result of the VAT introduction in 2000. Substantial discretionary direct tax measures were implemented in the context of the business profit tax rates, which were reduced from 40-45 percent to 10% for individual entrepreneurs, 0% for agriculture companies and associations, 15% for limited public and private partnerships, and 35% for bank and insurance companies (MOFNE/Ministry of Finance and National Economy, different issues).

The structure of composition of total revenue has significantly changed over the four decades. The highlights are as follows:

❖ The oil revenue share rapidly increased from zero percent up to the year 1999 to constitute more than half of total revenue since the year 2003. However, this has a serious implication as it exposed the budget to instability in the event of adverse trends associated with world market prices of crude oil.

❖ The bulk of tax revenue has come from indirect tax collections, which constituted more than half of the total revenue generated up to 1998. However, the historical "lion share" of indirect taxes rapidly decreased to about one-third of total revenue since 2000, mostly due to the adopted supply-side fiscal measures that aimed at further liberalizing foreign trade and improving competitiveness.

❖ The direct tax share substantially increased from 18 percent during the years 1978-1989 to about one-quarter of total revenue, reflecting the implemented demand-side fiscal measures that aimed at curtailing the ability of individuals and institutions to purchase and spend on goods and services (so as to reduce the level of aggregate demand in the economy).

❖ The share of non-tax revenue has demonstrated a sharp decline, as non-tax revenue decreased from around one-quarter of total revenue to less than ten percent. This was mostly the result of a sharp reduction in profit transfers from public enterprises due to the rapid privatization process that had been adopted (MOFNE, Annual Economic Review, different issues).

Several expenditure measures were implemented to improve budgetary controls and the enforcement of expenditure management and monitoring, including financing the budget from real resources and limiting the government borrowing from the central bank. Several effective expenditure controls were also imposed on all government ministries, including the establishment of accounts' monitoring units at ministries and major government departments. Internal controls were also strengthened, which were aimed at restricting the ability of line ministries to grant exemptions and to retain internally generated revenues from fees and charges; strict controls were imposed with respect to the issuance of government guarantees. A budget monitoring system was developed, including the preparation of daily reports on the government's cash position, weekly estimates of the budget position, monthly budget reports to the Council of Ministers (COM) which included forecasts for the remainder of the year, and quarterly reports to the National Assembly (NA) on fiscal developments. Additional measures were also implemented with a view to eliminate off-budget expenditures and to maintain relatively transparent and consolidated public budget.

During the oil-boom, the composition of total expenditure has shifted further in favour of federal transfers to sub-national government and development expenditure; the transfers to states increased from about 5 percent of total expenditure during the years 1990-1997 to about 12 percent over the more recent years since 1999. This shift accounted for the government's commitment to fiscal decentralization through grants. Development expenditure has increased from 14 percent of total expenditure to 20 percent, reflecting the continued intensive needs for social and infrastructure expenditures. The share of current expenditure was reduced from 81 percent of total expenditure during the early 1990s to about two-thirds over the more recent years, mostly on account of the adoption of fiscal decentralization which laid the responsibility of social services delivery on the states. However, a great share of public investment went to dam-building, and the supply of social services from the side of the states remained weak in terms of quantity and quality (MOFNE, Annual Economic Review, different issues).

Significant progress was made in maintaining fiscal sustainability, and the volatility of the fiscal deficit was contained to the minimum levels, reflecting an increased resource envelope (see figure 3). The budget deficit was reduced substantially from an average of 3 percent of GDP during 1990-1997 to about 1 percent of GDP during 1998-2004, reflecting significant increases in revenue collection. Revenue collections increased significantly – from a low base of 6 percent of GDP in 1997 to 20 percent in 2006. The sizable increase in revenue was accounted for by higher revenues from oil, which had provided a desired acceleration to the budgetary resources, due to a surge in international oil prices in late 1999 (MOFNE, Annual Economic Review, different issues).

Figure 3: Sudan's fiscal stance (% of GDP), 1985-2010

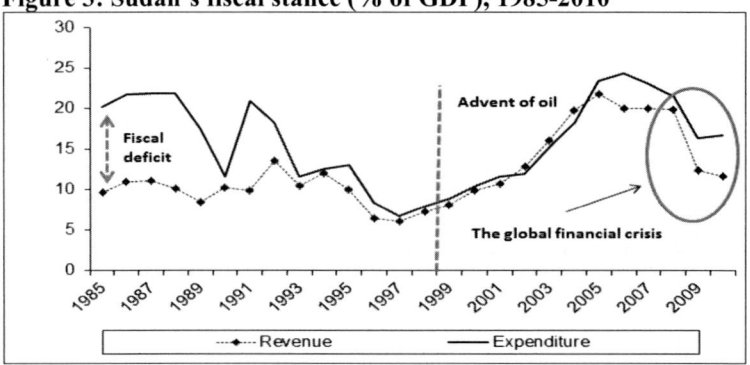

Source: Ministry of Finance & National Economy/MOFNE, Annual Economic Report – different issues.

However, the fiscal stance has turned to deteriorate and growing deficits emerged since 2005 following three years of surplus; new obligations were associated with the signed Peace Agreement (CPA)[12]. The average fiscal deficit remained slightly above 3 percent of GDP during this period relative to a surplus of 1 percent of GDP in the years 2002–2004. Public expenditures have grown sharply — from a low base of 7 percent of GDP in 1997 to 24 percent in 2006 (nearly four times) — using fully the fiscal space from oil revenues (MOFNE, Annual Economic Review, different issues).

The budget deficit was mainly domestically financed, especially by bond sales in the domestic non-bank sector. Domestic deficit financing was two-thirds of total deficit financing during 1998-2006. The bulk of domestic financing was non-bank sector borrowing (e.g. Government *Musharka* Certificates and Government Investment Certificates), which accounted for 71 percent, 69 percent and 54 percent of total deficit financing in 2001, 2005 and 2006 respectively. Domestic bank borrowing was reduced from 75 percent of total deficit financing in 1998 to 1.7 percent in 2005, reflecting tightened and reoriented monetary policy measures (MOFNE, Annual Economic Review, different issues). The predominance of borrowing from the non-bank sector has had likely very serious implications on investment and resource allocation through its impact on the cost of finance and the amount of credit available to the private sector. Severe crowding-out effects emerged.

Monetary policy: A comprehensive adjustment program (CAP) was introduced for further liberalizing the financial system (UNDP, 2006), mostly by:

---

[12] The CPA has brought new obligations in favor of state governments, including revenue sharing with the South Sudan to enhance fiscal federalism.

- using effective indirect monetary policy instruments (to mop up and manage banks' excess liquidity) and changing rules of lending;
- narrowing the gap between reserve requirements on domestic and foreign currency deposits, which were eventually unified since 2001;
- lowering the required reserve ratio on both domestic and foreign currency to 14 percent;
- eliminating the central bank role in determining the internal liquidity ratio that banks should hold to meet their liability; and
- eliminating direct monetary controls and easing the credit ceiling on trade.

Some progress was made in the implementation process of these financial reforms. The number of banks and branches was increased, and banking infrastructure and technology was strengthened. Also, the Central Bank of Sudan (CBOS) moved toward market-based monetary policy instruments. Despite this progress, shortcomings of the Islamic mode of finance and strong seasonality trends remained key factors that constrained financial intermediation (Kireyev, 2001). A banking sector restructuring strategy was initiated in the year 2000 with the aim of strengthening the capital base of the banks. The strategy included privatizing public banks, merging, liquidizing or recapitalizing small banks, reducing non-performing loans, and improving loan evaluation (Sabir M. Hassan, 2004). In reward, a significant improvement in the financial development indicators was achieved; the credit to private sector to GDP ratio increased from 3.9 percent in 2001 to 12.9 percent in 2010; the financial deepening (M2/GDP) ratio has increased from 12.8 percent in 2001 to 22.8 percent in 2010; and the market capitalization to GDP ratio increased from 4 percent in 2001 to 18 percent in 2010 (CBOS, Annual Report, different issues).

Substantial progress was made in maintaining price stabilization since 2000 (figure 4, lower panel). Inflation rate was contained at single-digit levels, reflecting the tight stance of fiscal and monetary and credit policies pursued in recent years that were associated with a sharp reduction in money aggregate growth. The expansion of money supply was reduced from an average of 72 percent during the years 1990-1996 to less than 30 percent during the years 1998-2010 (figure 4, lower panel). This was largely attributed to a notable government borrowing reduction from the central bank on account of curtailing the budget deficit to around less than 1 percent of GDP (CBOS, Annual Report, different issues.

However, inflation rate has jumped significantly in 2008 to 14.3 percent, breaching the double-digit mark for the first time since mid-1999. Rising food prices (cereals, rice, food oils, meat, vegetables and fruits) had driven inflation. Recent developments in food price increases in Sudan were driven by the global oil price increases during the first-half of 2008 and by domestic supply-side uncertainties, including weather-related production shortfalls. The pass-through exchange rate effect had a significant impact on imported consumer goods and also moderately affected the cost of locally produced ones - through higher cost of imported raw materials (CBSS 2012, Monthly Bulletin of Consumer Price Index, various issues).

Figure 4: Oil fundamentally changed the Sudan economy performance, 1985-2010

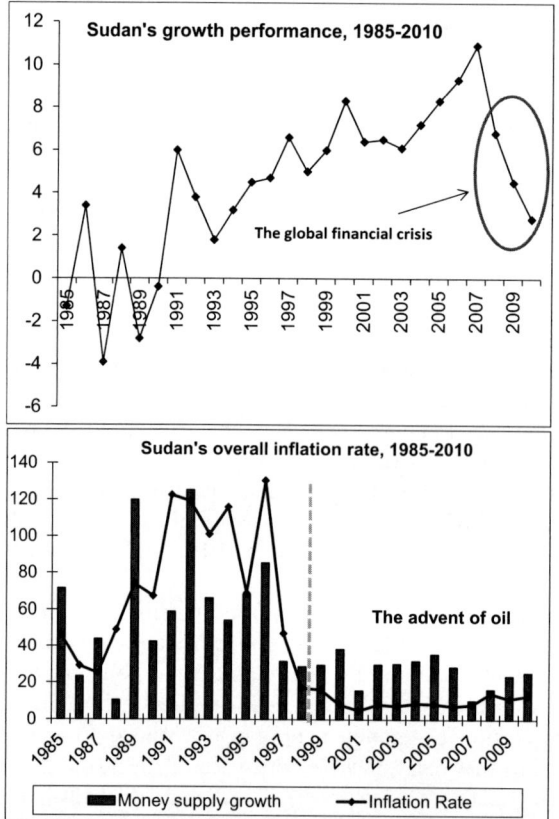

Source: Central Bank of Sudan Annual Report – different issues and World Bank's World Development Indicators 2011

A number of short-term policy measures was implemented to contain inflationary pressures and to mitigate their impact on the vulnerable poor. These measures included economy-wide policy measures (e.g. reducing administrative user-fees and import tariffs, releasing grain stocks, introducing export restrictions and price controls). The authorities had also used tightened monetary measures, through raising the required reserve ratio on deposits and by strengthening open-market operations. A number of safety net and social protection programs was introduced (e.g. cash transfer, school feeding, free health support, and agriculture and industry support funds). However, not too many persons could benefit from these measures.

Exchange rate policy: Substantial exchange rate system reforms were introduced, aimed at gradually liberalizing the de facto fixed exchange rate to a unified market-determined exchange rate regime so as to narrow the spread between the parallel market rates and the official exchange rates (Haidar Abbas et. al., 2006). These reforms include:

- increasing foreign exchange market transparency and removing all restrictions on the foreign exchange market;
- elimination of surrender requirements to the Bank of Sudan on foreign exchange receipts from exports;
- development of indirect monetary instruments for managing excess liquidity and for intervening in the unified foreign exchange rate market;
- unifying the various exchange rates (e.g. customs exchange rate, commercial exchange rate) with the official rate; and
- ensuing tightened monetary and fiscal policies.

In practice, the managed-float exchange rate regime was formally introduced and the remaining restrictions on current account transactions were lifted in 2002. Since then, the official exchange rate was determined on a market forces basis, and the current account was freed from any restrictions. The exchange rate has positively responded to these policy measures. A relative stabilization of nominal and real effective exchange rates was achieved and the spread between the official and the parallel exchange rates was also reduced (see figure 5 on the effective real exchange rate). The advent of oil brought a remarkable growth in foreign exchange inflows and a reduction in balance of payment pressures. The stabilization of the exchange rate was accounted for by four factors: (i) the sustained reforms of gradually liberalizing the exchange rate system which have reduced pressures on the foreign exchange situation and also have reduced the spread between the official and free market exchange rates; (ii) the oil-related inflows of foreign currency; (iii) the level of foreign exchange reserves, and (iv) the increasing inflow of international capital, such as foreign direct investment and migrants' remittances.

Figure 5: Effective real exchange rate, 1981-2006

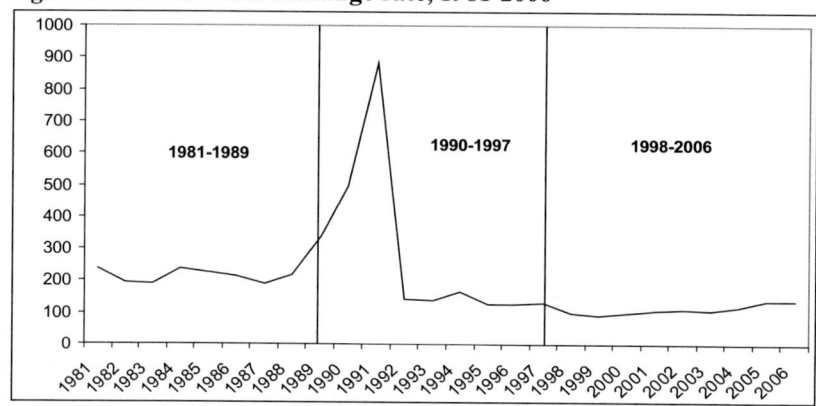

Source: Sudan: IMF Staff Monitoring and Consultation Reports – different issues

Trade Policy: The pace of trade liberalization, launched in 1992, has speeded up since 1998 as emphasis has been shifted in favour of an outward-oriented trade development strategy. The reforms undertaken were focused on removing restrictions on imports and exports and on removing retentions of export earnings; measures taken are as follows:

- eliminating and reducing customs duties and taxes on exports;
- reorienting credit and financial policies in favour of exports;
- encouraging exports-oriented industrialization;
- simplifying administrative and institutional arrangements for exports;
- strengthening export's infrastructure and ensuring better quality control;
- removing the remaining foreign exchange surrender requirements;
- eliminating all limits on exporters' holdings of foreign exchange; and
- maintaining a trade regime relatively free of quantitative import restrictions.

In practice, tariff bands were reduced from many as 13 in 1996 to 4 since 1999, comprising a zero rate, 10 percent, 25 percent, and 40 percent in 2000. The tariff maximum rate was reduced from 125 percent in 1997 to 45 percent in 2001, while the minimum rate was reduced from 5 percent to zero percent. All exports were exempted from customs duties since 2000, except hides and skins, while export revenue surrender requirements to the central bank were totally removed (CBOS, Annual Report, different issues). However, the extent of export diversification reached in Sudan remained minimal despite of all these measures.

The external current account deficit was contained at about 5 percent of GDP during the years 1999-2004, reflecting mainly the increase in oil-related export volumes and revenues (see figure 6). Overall exports have increased significantly from 12.5 percent of GDP in 1998 to more than 20 percent of GDP since 2000 as a result of the oil export boom and the higher export prices. Oil-related export has increased significantly from zero to about 15 percent of GDP since 2003. Non-oil related exports were however depressed by the recent exchange rate appreciation, the sharp decline in international commodity prices, especially for cotton, the Gulf countries' ban on Sudanese livestock for health reasons, the high domestic demand for potential export goods, and the severe transportation bottlenecks and the associated high transport costs (CBOS, Annual Report, different issues).

Figure 6: Sudan's external current account position (% of GDP), 1985-2010

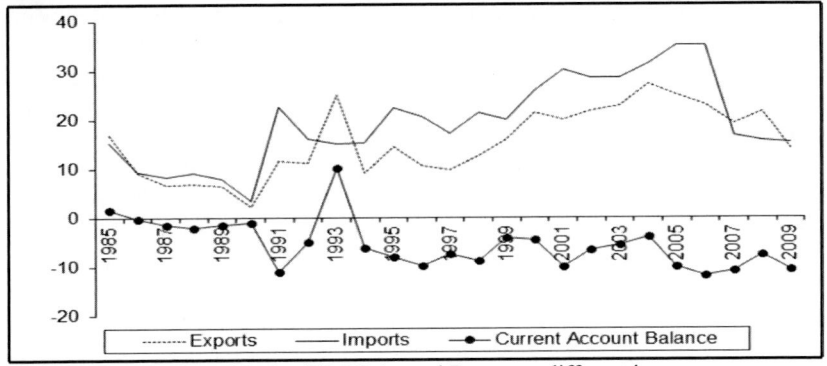

Source: Central Bank of Sudan/CBOS Annual Reports – different issues.

The historical composition of Sudan's exports has changed markedly in favour of oil-related exports since oil products exportation started in mid-1999. Oil-related exports accounted for a great share of Sudan's exports of goods and services. The share of non-oil goods exports has sharply dropped from an average of 86 percent in the later 1970s to less than 20 percent since the early 2000s. The stagnation of the non-oil export share was accounted for by supply factors related generally to the difficulties facing the agriculture sector, the low productivity due to the deteriorated infrastructure, and the heavy state taxation. Sudan has still to wait for a real and effective export diversification strategy.

Imports have also increased significantly, mainly as a result of foreign direct investment-related imports, and because of higher petroleum product imports so as to meet the demand of the rapid accelerated transportation sector in the country. Also policy factors (trade policy and exchange rate policy) played a role in this regard.

4   How Sudan has managed its oil resources? Is it a case of government failure?

Oil has provided a great opportunity for Sudan to become an emerging economy. Nonetheless, Sudan has failed to effectively manage and spend oil resources to build an economic foundation for a diversified, inclusive and sustainable growth path and to invest in its citizens as "the owners of the resources". The exploitation of oil in Sudan has generally been associated with a shrinking of the non-oil tradable goods sector (real sectors). All of Sudan's fast growing sectors were either related to oil or are non-tradable services, while the growth of agriculture and manufacturing sectors has been slower than the growth rate of the overall economy. The share of agriculture declined from about 42 percent in 1990–98 to about 35 percent for the period 1999–2010, and export competitiveness of agro-sector products has declined even more (CBSS, Sudan Annual Statistical Book, various issues).

The historical composition of Sudan's exports was dominated by oil-related exports since oil exportation started in 1999. More than 95 percent of Sudan's exports were coming from the oil sector, while the share of non-oil exports has fallen from nearly 100 percent of GDP in the eve of oil to less than 2 percent in 2008 (CBOS Annual Report – different issues). The shift in the composition of exports can be attributed to the exchange rate appreciation, supply factors related generally to the difficulties facing the agriculture sector, low productivity due to deteriorated infrastructure, and heavy state taxation.

Similar evidence of structural change has come from the shift in the composition of imports. The share of consumption goods in total imports has increased in recent times from an already high base. The flip side of increased imports of consumption goods is a decline in the manufacturing sector's share in total output. The appreciation of the real exchange rate (during the years 2006-2008) was likely to have played a role in making imports more attractive than domestic manufacturing.

The Oil Revenue Stabilization Account (ORSA) was not able to provide relief to Sudan from oil revenue shortfalls. Savings into the ORSA led to accumulations of $1.4 billion by the end of 2008. However, almost all the savings were subsequently depleted through continuous withdrawals, although oil revenues were 42 percent above budget figures (MOFNE, Annual Economic Review – different issues). An opportunity for saving was missed, and all this was completely against the objective of the ORSA, to save for future fiscal periods, for human capital investments and for future generations. If properly managed, the ORSA would have dramatically lowered the negative fiscal impact and the foreign exchange shortage associated with the secession of South Sudan.

The incidence of poverty is high in Sudan (46.6 percent) and varies significantly between urban and rural areas, with 57.6 percent of households being below the poverty line compared to 26.5 percent of the urban population[13]. Poverty in Sudan varies significantly by states, ranging from almost 70 percent in Northern Darfur to 50 percent in Gadarif and 26 percent in Khartoum (see figure 7).

The oil boom has also failed to provide enough jobs for a rapidly growing labor force, especially for the youth and the women. The unemployment rate remains very high in Sudan, with 13 per cent in 2009 compared to 15.9 per cent in 2008 and 11.2 per cent in 1993 (see Table 3); some estimates are still higher. The unemployment rate varies significantly between urban and rural areas as well as between the states, with around 10 per cent in urban areas compared to around 13 per cent in rural areas (CBSS, Sudan National Households Budget Survey 2009; Central Bureau of Statistics, Khartoum, Sudan).

The failure to manage the oil wealth coincided with the destruction of the economy caused by the escalating costs of civil war. The macroeconomic reforms undertaken in Sudan could not have a lasting impact on efficiency and sustainability. While the ongoing civil war prevented a better management of the oil wealth, the oil wealth gave the basis for financing the continuation of the civil war. The Comprehensive Peace Agreement (CPA) of January 9, 2005 provided a window of opportunity to push socio-economic reforms on a broader scale, but the lack of trust between the North and the South eroded quickly the potentials for peace and development.

---

[13] Government of Sudan, Sudan's Interim Poverty Reduction Strategy Paper (IPRSP) 2012

Figure 7: Poverty incidence in Sudan, 2009

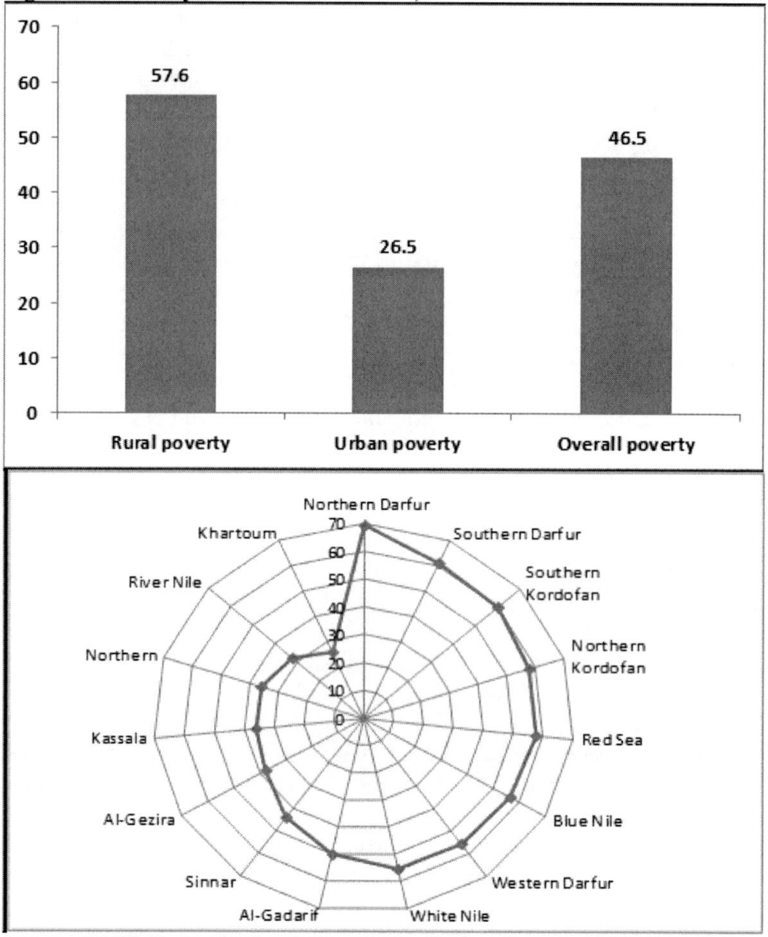

Source: CBSS, Sudan National Households Budget Survey 2009, Central Bureau of Statistics, Khartoum.

Table 3: Sudan's Unemployment Rate, 1993-2009

	Overall	Male	Female	Urban	Rural
1993	11.2	11.2	11.1	13.7	10.1
1996	15.1	12	23.4	13.9	19
2008	15.9	13.7	24.7	12.3	17.5
2009	13	9	23	10	13

Source: CBSS, Sudan National Households Budget Survey 2009, Central Bureau of Statistics, Khartoum.

5   South Sudan Secession's Consequences on Sudan's Macro-economic Management

The secession of South Sudan in July 2011 brought an immense permanent resource/revenue shock to Sudan, leading to severe pressures on the fiscal position and on the exchange rate similar to that of the oil shock in the early 1970s. The difference is the permanency of the oil shock. The loss of about three quarters of the country's oil production left Sudan with roughly half of its previous fiscal revenues and only a third of its export proceeds (IMF 2012 a). The oil sector's contribution to GDP dropped to 5 percent in 2012 compared with around 15 percent in 2007 (see figure 8). Real GDP growth is projected at -3.3 percent and -11.1 percent in 2011 and 2012 respectively, compared to 5 percent in 2010 (International Monetary Fund 2012a, "Sudan—Staff Report for the 2012 Article IV Consultation").

The secession of South Sudan has hit Sudan's fiscal position significantly, reflecting the adverse fiscal costs of the secession on the economy. Oil revenues declined sharply, accounting - for the first time since 2000 - for less than 30 percent of total public revenue. Previously oil revenue used to account for more than half of total public revenue. The extent of the resources shock is causing a major fiscal adjustment, and is forcing the government to amend both the 2011 and 2012 budgets in the second half of the year just after their approval by the National Assembly (MOFNE, 2012 Amended Budget). The oil revenue fall is more likely to threaten the sustainability of fiscal finances, given the insufficient fiscal space to implement increased spending pressures due to the development agenda and the significant domestic and foreign debt arrears. Unfortunately – as mentioned - Sudan missed the vast opportunities created by the oil boom to make significant progress to diversify its economy, including using in an active way the Oil Revenue Stabilization Account (ORSA).

Figure 8: Sudan's Oil sector contribution to GDP

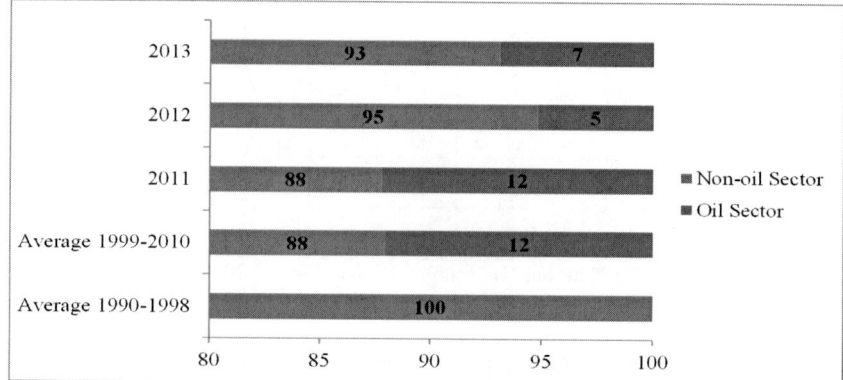

Source: IMF: Sudan SMP report, 2012 a. **Note**: The 2011 figure is an estimate, while 2012 and 2013 figures are projections.

The loss of the main source of foreign exchange flows and the increasing uncertainty over the economic prospects put significant depreciation pressure on the local currency, with international foreign exchange reserves running down to critical levels in (failed) attempts to defend the exchange rate. Inflation rates substantially accelerated, reaching 45 percent in October 2012 as a result of the rising import cost of basic goods; this again being a result of the weakening local currency value (CBSS/Central Bureau of Statistics Sudan 2012, "Monthly Bulletin of Consumer Price Index", various issues).

In response to the secession of South Sudan shock, Sudan has formulated the "Three-year Emergency Economic Program/TYEEP 2011-2013" which includes a number of comprehensive reforms to address the severe deterioration of the country's economic and financial situation. The program aimed to reverse the external imbalance - notably through promoting import substitution for foodstuffs and by stimulating production and exports of gold and of various agricultural commodities. It set ambitious goals of self-sufficiency by the year 2013 for a number of agricultural products, such as wheat, sugar, and cooking oil. It also aimed to increase exports of cotton, processed meat, gum Arabic, and of gold. The program embodies a number of macroeconomic policy measures to contain the deterioration of economic conditions. However, the assumptions are over-optimistic.

Fiscal policy: The government has announced major fiscal measures in early January 2011 aimed to adjust the fiscal position to the reality of Secession. These measures include reducing public expenditures (notably on goods and services), increasing public revenues (by reducing subsidies on petroleum products and on sugar) and establishing several safety-net measures (MOF-NE, Minister of Finance & National Economy to the National Assembly, January 2011). The measures are as follows:

Expenditure measures	Revenue measures
• 25% reduction in salaries of senior ministerial positions.	• Increasing the price of diesel to 6.5 SDG (per gallon)
• 30% reduction of the budgets for travelling abroad.	• Increasing the price of benzene to 8.5 SDG per gallon.
• 10% reduction of the diplomatic missions' budgets.	• Increasing the price of cooking gas to 13 SDG (per container).
• Halt on purchases of new government cars.	• Increasing the price of fuel jet to 6.5 SDG per gallon.
• Stop on approval of new constructions and purchases of new furniture for government units.	• Levying a 20 SDG excise tax on each sack of sugar (i.e. 50 kg).
• 30% reduction of purchases of goods and services during the first quarter of 2011.	**Strengthening safety nets measures**
• Downsizing central and state governments.	• Increasing the monthly salary of civil service employees by 100 SDG; this applies also to pensions.
• 20% reduction in development budgets of all public corporations.	• Providing a free meal to poor students and a subsidized meal to all students.
• Freezing on new staff recruitment except for newly established ministries.	• Providing tuition fees for poor students.
• Freeze on the creation of new government units.	• Providing bursaries to 200,000 students.
• All public units are required to deposit foreign exchange proceeds in their accounts with CBoS.	• Giving support to 500,000 families.
• Transfer of all royalties collected by public corporations to the national budget.	• Increasing free health support through the health insurance program.
• Privatizing all public companies by end of 2011.	• Establishing an Agriculture Support Fund (ASF) with an amount of US$ 150mn.
• Sale of all government shares in joint investments to the private sector.	• Establishing an Industry Support Fund (ISF) with an amount of US$150mn.
• Eliminating VAT exemptions granted on commodities.	• Granting special incentives to investors from the Arab region (Presidential Decree).

Source: World Bank/WB, Sudan Economic Brief, World Bank, February 2011.

However, it is not at all clear which of these measures were really implemented and to which budgetary effect. Concerning the social safety net measures, it is not at all clear what the impact on poverty alleviation will be.

Monetary policy: The Sudan has undertaken several monetary policy measures to contain inflationary pressures and to mitigate their adverse impact on the vulnerable poor. The Central Bank had used tightened monetary measures through raising the reserve requirement ratio on deposits and the strengthening of open-market operations. The reserve requirement ratio was increased from 15 percent to 18 percent and the Central Bank deposits of commercial banks were rolled back (CBOS Annual Report, 2011).

Exchange rate policy: Similar to the early 1970s, the policies place a significant emphasis on the demand-side as tools for macroeconomic management through exchange rate measures and monetary policy measures to reverse the fiscal and trade deficits. The Central Bank of Sudan has imposed a series of intervention policies to reduce the pressure in the foreign exchange market and to broadly close the gap between the official and the parallel market rates. These measures included the reduction of the allowances for amounts of hard currency being available to individuals travelling abroad. Individuals travelling abroad were only permitted to take a maximum of the equivalent of 2,000 Euros of any foreign currency after providing the supporting documentation. The importation of selected goods was restricted, a 100% cash margin was imposed on most imports, and use of foreign exchange was limited primarily to serve genuine market needs. Customs duties on all the imported goods were increased with the exception of food items, wheat, sugar and capital goods as used by local manufacturers, measures which were projected to result in a 15% - 20% drop in imports (CBOS Annual Report, 2011).

A "premium concept" was also introduced on top of the official exchange rate to encourage holders of foreign exchange to sell their positions at a rate close to the street market rate. The premium rate is waved up-and-down following developments in the parallel market exchange rates, which would send a signal to the market about the temporary nature of the exchange rate level. The premium rate was initially set at 16.29 percent above the official price in December 2010, but it was reduced to 4.77 percent end of April 2011. The Central Bank of Sudan (CBOS) has also imposed regulations on export traders. Previously export traders were allowed to access dollars through a letter of credit under the condition that they return the hard currency within a period of six months; this condition was now cut to three months under the new directives (CBOS Annual Report, 2011).

Despite the various implemented demand-side policy measures, the adverse impact of the Secession continues to affect heavily vital economy activities, causing serious economic imbalances and increasing the hardship for the poor. These measures provided a temporary breathing space only, but did not address the source of the deterioration in economic conditions, which are likely to be structural in nature.

Progress in restoring macroeconomic stability has remained weak and the financial situation continued to be very difficult; external and domestic imbalances were even further deteriorated. The overall budget deficit has continued to expand and the burden of financing has increasingly relied on government borrowing from the Central Bank of Sudan (CBOS) which resulted in reserve money growing. Inflation has accelerated sharply to remain double-digits compared to around one-digit since 2003, reflecting rising import cost of basic goods and weather-related production shortfalls what adds to the economic duress for the poor and vulnerable.

Despite the interventions by the Central Bank, Sudan continues to face considerable foreign exchange market instability driven by supply-related shortages in foreign exchange. The exchange rate continued to depreciate sharply and remained unpredictable. Despite of the premium that existed over the official exchange rate, the gap between the official and the black market rates widened, partly due to the growing economic uncertainties. The overall balance of current account drastically turned into a large deficit position, reflecting the lower oil export that was only partially offset by the increase in gold exports.

Sudan has introduced a new comprehensive austerity package in June 2012, which combines fiscal adjustment, increased exchange rate flexibility and a tightening of the monetary stance to restore macroeconomic stability and to avoid a further deterioration of the economic conditions. As a result, Sudan's budget for 2012 was amended on June 18, 2012 to reflect the new reality resulting from the delayed post-CPA arrangement on oil revenue division/oil transfer fees; the revised budget proposed fiscal austerity measures to absorb the revenue shortfalls. The amended budget has however embarked on a fiscal reform path, aiming at addressing the budget imbalances resulting from the secession of South Sudan. The key fiscal measures adopted are:

Expenditure measures	*Revenue measures*
• Phasing out fuel subsidies. The diesel price was increased to SDG 8 per Gallon from SDG 6.5, while the prize of benzene was increased to SDG 12.5 per Gallon from SDG 8.5. • Liberalizing the price of sugar. • Consolidating ministries at all levels of government.	• Increasing the VAT from 15 to 17 percent; • increasing the development tax from 10 to 13 percent; • Increasing the Business profit tax on the banking sector from 15 to 30 percent; • Increase the stamp duties on financial transactions and international flights; • Repealing the negative list used to limit imports and imposing instead import tariffs; • Enhancing revenue collection and lifting discretional tax exemptions; and • Eliminating the rights of foreign exchange revenues retention of some ministries and public corporations.
Social safety nets spending • Raising the salary of civil servants and pensioners by 100 SDG per month. • Establishing tax and duty exemptions for wheat, flour, sugar and basic food items, and reducing customs duties on powder milk and food oil. • Widening the social insurance networks from 500,000 poor families to 750,000. • Lowering customs duties on main staples and exempting medicine. • Strengthening micro-finance measures.	

Source: IMF, Sudan SMP Report, IMF, 2012 a.

The austerity package also includes measures that aim to lessen the pressure on the exchange rate and to safeguard external reserves. The Central Bank adopted new exchange rate measures in June 2012 centered on a devaluation of the Sudanese pound and a reform forward to a more flexible exchange rate regime. The Sudanese pound was devaluated to 4.42 per US dollar. The Central Bank also allowed licensed foreign exchange dealers and commercial banks to set the value of the local currency closer to the parallel market rate (CBOS, Amended Monetary and Financial Policies for 2012).

Despite these measures, the macroeconomic stability conditions continued to deteriorate, partially reflecting the delayed agreement with South Sudan on oil transit fees that represented almost 30 percent of the total revenues in the original budget (IMF 2012 a). Inflation continued to accelerate hitting the rate of 45 percent in October 2012, twice the rate of inflation early this year (see figure 9). The rising inflation rate is being fuelled by increased fuel prices, by supply bottlenecks, and by rising pressures on the local currency. Unless there are considerable improvements in regard of the extreme foreign exchange shortage and the associated supply-side bottlenecks, it is more likely that inflation will stay at very high levels (based on assessments by the authors).

The gap between the official and the parallel market exchange rate is still significant (see figure 9), due to the increasing shortage of foreign exchange and the negative expectations on the agreement about oil transit fees with South Sudan. As well, the commercial bank exchange rates still fall short of the prevailing parallel market rate, meaning that the premium concept does not really work.

New conflicts between Sudan and South Sudan in the border regions of the two countries prevent any consolidation of economic reform policies and the strengthening of macroeconomic institutions and policies.

6   Sudan's Macroeconomic Management Institutions

Four major institutions are effectively participating in macroeconomic policy formulation and implementation, namely: National Assembly, National Strategic Planning Council, Ministry of Finance & National Economy, and the Central Bank of Sudan. In addition to these four institutions other institutions also play a role, like the President's Office, the ruling National Congress Party/NCP, the Council of Ministers, the States Council, Big Business, and other organizations like the Sudanese Businessmen and Employers Federation, the Sudanese Workers and Trade Unions Federation, and the Sudan Banks Union. However, there is a hierarchical and top down approach, and the known weaknesses of the governance system (as measured by various governance indicators) affect the policy formulation as well as the policy outcomes. A major weakness is the lack of an institutionalized policy dialogue between business, labour and government. Nonetheless the four major institutions referred to above play a role in macroeconomic policy-making.

Figure 9: Sudan's inflation rate and exchange rate, January 2009-October 2012

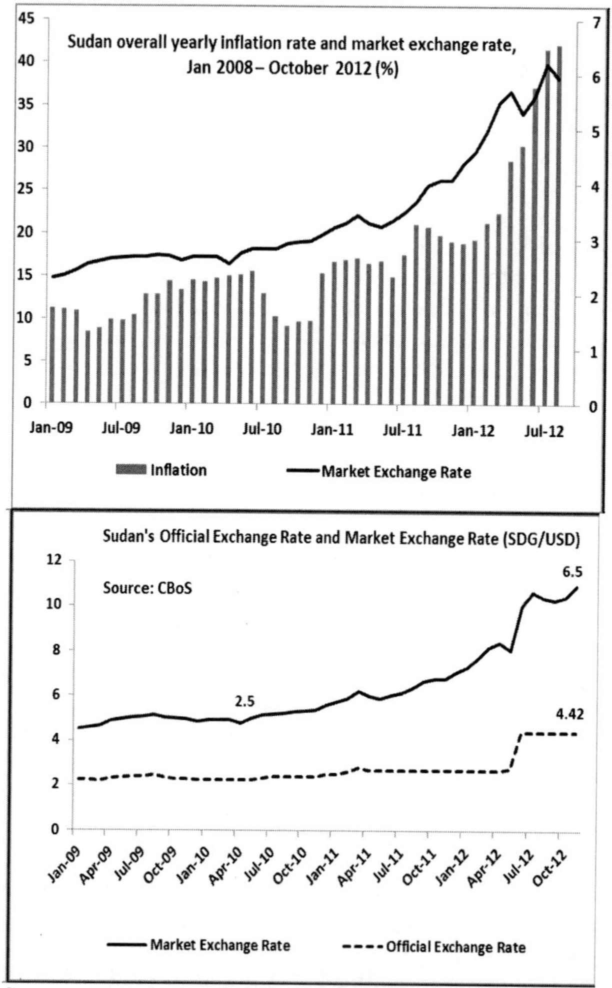

Source: Central Bank of Sudan, Monthly Economic Review (Monthly Inflation Report – different issues) and Central Bureau of Statistics (Monthly Inflation Report – different issues).

Ministry of Finance & National Economy (MOFNE): The Ministry is responsible for fiscal policy formulation and implementation. The preparation of the national government budget is the key task of the Ministry of Finance, and it involves the participation a number specialized committees formed of officials from different national and sub-national bodies such as state level authorities, public entities, and independent councilors. The national budget is then submitted to the National Parliament for approval. The process of the national budget preparation starts with formulations by a Macroeconomic Committee which is responsible for developing the macroeconomic framework. Then the budget circular is initiated and distributed. After that the MOFNE Undersecretary meets with line ministries and General Directors of public corporations on the budget circular. The MOFNE Minister then meets with state governments' representatives. The budget proposals of the line ministries and of government units are then reviewed and discussed by the Sectoral Committee. A first draft of the budget is also shared with different social actors (trade unions, civil society) for consultation. A second draft is then prepared and approved by the Higher Committee and signed by the MOFNE Minister; it is then submitted to the Council of Ministers, approved and then submitted to the National Parliament for endorsement[14]. It is not clear who really decides on the objectives and modalities of fiscal policy and what the formal and informal role of other actors is.

The Central Bank of Sudan (CBOS): The CBOS is responsible for monetary policy formulation and governing the banking sector to insure financial stability and safety. It determines the money supply growth, selects the monetary policy instruments, and is responsible for the process of implementation and the monitoring of the performance. The CBOS establishes a number of committees to formulate its monetary policy, a policy draft which is then shared with commercial banks managers and the academia for broad consultation. Although the CBOS is the responsible body for monetary policy management, coordination with the Ministry of Finance is taken into consideration. During policy formulation, both the CBOS and the Ministry of Finance determine - through a joint committee - the main targeted macroeconomic indicators (e.g. economic growth, inflation, exchange rate, and banking credit to different economic sectors). While the banking sector is supervised by the CBOS, the stock market (Khartoum Stock Exchange) and the insurance sector are governed by independent supervisory bodies. The Khartoum Stock Exchange Board of Directors and the Insurance Supervisory Authority are responsible for the management of the stock market and the insurance companies, but they work in collaboration with the CBOS. It is not clear to what extent the autonomy of the CBOS is really preserved and what autonomy means for the functions of the main officials. However, some changes have taken place towards more institutional autonomy based on recommendations of IMF Staff Monitoring Reports. For some time, fiscal policy used to domi-

---

[14] World Bank (2007), "Sudan: Public Expenditure Review".

nate monetary policy and the CBOS used to change the monetary aggregates and the financial resource direction in favor of the government budget requirements. However, CBOS gained some independence and legislation was issued so as to limit the government borrowing from the CBOS. The CBOS now determines the level of government borrowing from the banking system independently (Tajeldin I. Hamed and Mohamed O. Ahmed, 2009).

National Strategic Planning Council (NSPC): The NSPC is the think-tank of the country, and it is the key body that develops the national plans both short-term and long-term. It determines the national vision, mission, and objectives. It also determines the challenges and opportunities, strengths and weaknesses in all national issues, and then sets the strategic goals. The Council works in collaboration with all segments of the society, governmental and non-governmental and civil society organizations, universities and research institutions as well as political parties and international organizations. The Council is required to submit the plans that it formulates to the National Parliament for approval, before they become mandatory for other institutions to follow in their plans. It is not clear how independent the NSPC really is, and how much influence is exerted from main parties and organizations, from big business and from high level government bodies. The National Strategic Planning Council (NSPC) is leading the chain of the policy formulation in the country, and it collaborates with all key institutions through joint committees during the formulation of the national strategic plans. Then each institution develops its sub-national plan in which intermediate goals, instruments and related stages are determined. In doing so also joint committees are formed as in the case of the coordination between Ministry of Finance and the Central Bank of Sudan. It is not clear who takes the lead in developing strategic goals and objectives, but the NSPC plays definitely some role.

The National Assembly (NA): The National Assembly represents the interests of the whole Nation, and it is the responsible body for issuing legislations and rules, for monitoring the executive government management, and for maintaining the Government system. Its responsibilities include: amendment of the constitution; declaration of war; discussing the presidential speeches; approval of the government budget; resignation of the president and the vice-president; and any other responsibilities stated in the constitution. Following the referendum on the right of self-determination for South Sudan, which opted for the establishment of an independent state "South Sudan", the Parliament Constituencies and the relative representation lists which are connected to the population distribution have changed. Accordingly, the Parliament is composed of 354 elected members representing ten different political parties with the majority coming from the ruling National

Congress Party (NCP). The National Assembly is participating effectively in the macroeconomic policy formulation through its right to discuss and to approve the national plans submitted by the National Strategic Planning Council (NSPC) and the Government Budget submitted by the Ministry of Finance and National Economy (MOFNE), and any other economic and financial matters and legislations submitted for approval by any relevant government body. The National Assembly does this through its two special-ized committees: The Economic Affairs Committee and the Industry, Invest-ment and Foreign Trade Committee. The National Assembly also has the authority to question any government body working closely with the General Auditor to ensure transparency and to fight corruption. It is not really clear to what extent the National Assembly (NA) has impacted on macroeconomic policies in the decisive periods of Sudan's development.

It is not clear how these four institutions interact among each other and how they coordinate with other actors who show interest in and are part of economic policy. As the civil war has dominated the politics in Sudan for decades, it might be expected that all fiscal and economic policies were sub-jugated to these basically political and military decisions.

7   Medium-term Reform Agendas for Sudan: The Way Forward

The Sudan development path implies that resources endowment is not enough. Success requires addressing technical issues and managing resources endowment well so as to encourage economic diversification and to invest in the "owners" of the resources (the people). Sudan has immense potentials to become an emerging economy, including fertile land and water resources (farming, livestock production and related agro-processing industries) and minerals (oil, gold, etc.) which are in high demand globally. Sudan is also rich in human resources and capabilities. It is in the neighborhood of wealthy countries (Europe and Arab oil-exporting countries), which provides poten-tially a strong market for the products of Sudan.

However, inefficient macroeconomic management and internal conflict hinder Sudan to effectively utilize its natural resources so as to build an eco-nomic foundation for a diversified, inclusive and sustainable development process. Despite the substantial policy measures and structural reforms that were adopted since the 1960s, Sudan's economy has remained subject to significant structural rigidities that need to be addressed in order to achieve any sustainable economic development path.

Since its independence in 1956, Sudan has been hindered by several armed conflicts, including South Sudan, the East Front, Darfur, Blue Nile State, South Kordofan State and Abyei. These past and various ongoing conflicts pose challenges for governance, human development, and for growth and poverty reduction in Sudan. Key among these challenges is the huge loss of lives by armed conflicts and the destruction of infrastructure. These factors have severely debilitated the country's capacity for development as well as undermined the development projects in areas affected by armed conflict.

Sudan's new strategy should focus on overcoming the legacies of long internal conflicts and building the economic foundation for a diversified and inclusive growth. To address these long-standing structural rigidities, Sudan needs a mix of policy measures that emphasis fiscal discipline and a strict monetary policy along with underlying structural reforms, including:

➤ bringing durable peace throughout the country and addressing the post-conflict challenges (reconstruction and rehabilitation of the war-affected areas and of the displaced population settlements);

➤ providing broad opportunities for socio-economic recovery in all parts of the country;

➤ creating an enabling environment for the private sector, increasing competitiveness and speeding up the further diversification of the economy;

➤ strengthening public finance management (taxation, expenditure management, controls, auditing and monitoring);

➤ increasing the effectiveness of monetary policy and deepening and restructuring the financial sector (by new accounting and monitoring systems, by enforcing prudential regulations, and by introducing new monetary instruments); and

➤ introducing a more flexible exchange rate regime and an open trade system (by unification of exchange rate systems and by tariff and trade reforms).

8   Conclusion

The oil exploration since 1999 has provided an immense opportunity for Sudan to become an emerging economy, but the country failed to effectively use the oil resources to build an economic foundation for a diversified, inclusive and sustainable development path.

The Secession of South Sudan in July 2011 represented a significant transition point in the recent history of Sudan, causing serious economic imbalances and increasing hardship for the population. The country was left with immensely fragile economic conditions that were transmitted largely through the fiscal and external accounts. The loss of about three quarters of the oil production left Sudan with only half of its previous fiscal revenues and only a third of its export proceeds. These challenges created negative fiscal and balance of payments implications that strained the economic, social and political stability.

Macroeconomic stability has sharply deteriorated following the Secession of South Sudan. The budget deficit has increased dramatically, reflecting pressures emerging from the significant loss in oil revenues and exports. Inflation rates continued to be volatile and increased, reaching double digit rates as a result of rising import cost of basic goods (as a result of the weakening local currency value). The exchange rate has sharply depreciated and the overall balance of external accounts has experienced persistent deteriorations.

Similar to the policy responses during the oil shock in the early 1970s, Sudan has adopted restrictive demand-side macroeconomic management policies in response to the macroeconomic shock of the Secession of South Sudan. The policy measures in the 1970s have centered on extensive government market interventions and on regulations of the economy. However, the economy has not responded positively to these measures and the economic fundamentals continued to deteriorate. To avoid a further deterioration of the country's economic and financial situation after the Secession shock, Sudan has introduced a new comprehensive austerity package in June 2012, including harsh fiscal adjustment measures and allowing for more exchange rate flexibility. The fiscal stance has responded positively to these measures and some progress has been made in maintaining fiscal sustainability. However, the continuing conflicts in Sudan and the tensions with South Sudan lead to a massive use of scarce resources for defense and security at the expense of development.

Although the June 2012 policy measures are an important step towards restoring macroeconomic stability, Sudan's policymakers need to use a two-tier macroeconomic management process. Policy measures need to focus on short-term adjustment measures to avoid a further deterioration of the economic and social conditions, and on a medium-term and long-term structural reform to build the economic foundation for a diversified and inclusive growth process. This underscores the need to expand its agriculture and domestic manufacturing sectors through structural reforms, more exchange rate flexibility and specific production incentives to the primary sectors.

References

Abdalla Elhassan, Kamal Yousif, and Badreldin Hassien, (2004), "The Evaluation of Monetary and Financial Policy Instruments during 1980 – 2002", CBOS Studies Series, CBOS

AfDB, OECD, UNDP and UNECA (2012), "African Economic Outlook - Sudan", available via the internet at http://www.afdb.org/fileadmin/uploads/afdb/Documents/ Publications/Sudan%20Full%20PDF%20Country%20Note.pdf

Bird, G. (2001), "Conducting macroeconomic policy in developing countries: piece of cake or mission impossible?", Third World Quarterly, Vol. 22, No 1, pp. 37-49

Brinkerhoff, D. and Goldsmith, A. (2003), "How Citizens Participate in Macroeconomic Policy: International Experience and Implications for Poverty Reduction", in: World Development, Vol. 31, No. 4, pp. 685–701

Cantore, N., Alessandro A. and Paulo, A. (2012), "Energy price shocks - Sweet and Sour consequences for developing countries", Working Paper 355, Overseas Development Institute/ODI, UK; available via the internet at: www.odi.org.uk/resources/docs/7794.pdf

CBOS/Central Bank of Sudan, annual reports (various issues); available via the internet at: http://www.cbos.gov.sd/

CBOS/Central Bank of Sudan, Monthly Economic Review (various issues), available via the internet at: http://www.cbos.gov.sd/

_____, Amended Monetary and Financial Policies for 2012

CBSS/Central Bureau of Statistics Sudan (2012), "Monthly Bulletin of Consumer Price Index", Khartoum

_____ (2009), "Sudan National Budget Households Survey", Sudan

_____ "Sudan Annual Statistical Book", various issues, Sudan

Haidar Abbas, Mustaf I Abdelnabi, and Selma Salih, (2006), "The Documentation of Exchange Rate Policy in Sudan during 1956- 2006", CBOS Studies Series (in Arabic), No. 7

IMF/International Monetary Fund (2012a), "Sudan—Staff Report for the 2012 Article IV Consultation", September 7, 2012

_____ (2012b), "Macroeconomic Policy Frameworks for Resource-rich Developing Countries", http://www.imf.org/external/np/pp/eng/2012/082412a.pdf

_____(2012c), "Macroeconomic Policy Frameworks for Resource-rich Developing Countries—Analytic Frameworks and Applications—supplement 2, http://www.imf.org/external/np/pp/eng/2012/082412b.pdf

_____(2012d), "Fiscal Regimes for Extractive Industries: Design and Implementation", http://www.imf.org/external/np/pp/eng/2012/081512.pdf

_____ (2011a), "Sudan: Second Review Under the 2009–10 Staff-Monitored Program -Staff Report"; Staff Supplement; and Statement by the Executive Director for Sudan, http://www.imf.org/external/pubs/ft/scr/2011/cr1186.pdf

_____ (2011b), "Policy Formulation, Analytical Frameworks, and Program Design", Prepared by the Policy Development and Review Department, http://www.imf.org/external/np/pdr/2004/eng/policy.pdf

_____(1998), "Sudan—Staff Report for the 1998 Article IV Consultation", Washington D.C.

Kireyev, (2001), "Financial Reforms in Sudan: Streamlining Bank Intermediation", IMF Working Paper, WP/01/53

MEFMI (2001) "Institutional Aspects of Macroeconomic Policy Co-ordination in MEFMI Member Countries", by Macroeconomic and Financial Management Institute of Eastern and Southern Africa, Vol. 1: Main Report, Available via the internet at: http://www.mefmi.org/admin/cms/publication/pub-2001-study-institutional-aspects-of-macroeconomic-policy-coordination-volume1.pdf

MOFNE, Annual Economic Review, different issues

_____, 2012 Amended Budget Book

_____, Minister of Finance & National Economy to the National Assembly, January 2011

Montiel, P. and Serven, L. (2006), "Macroeconomic Stability in Developing Countries: How Much Is Enough?", in: The World Bank Research Observer, vol. 21, no. 2, pp:151-178

Sabir Mohamed Hassan (2004), "Issues in the Regulation of Islamic Banking (The Case of Sudan)", CBOS/Central Bank of Sudan, Khartoum

Government of Sudan, Sudan's Interim Poverty Reduction Strategy Paper (IPRSP) 2012

Tajeldin I. Hamed and Mohamed O. Ahmed (2009), "The Islamic Central Bank between Dependency and Independence, With reference to CBOS experience", CBOS, Research Series (in Arabic, No. 21

Tanaka, O. (2010), "China's Macroeconomic Policy Shift in 2008 - Political Process from Tightening to Easing", in: Public Policy Review, Vol. 6, No. 3. pp., Policy Research Institute, Ministry of Finance, Japan

UNDP (2006), "Macroeconomic Policies for Poverty Reduction: The Case of Sudan", Khartoum, Sudan.

Weisbrot, M., Ray, R., Johnston, J., Cordero, J. and Montecino, J. (2009), "IMF-Supported Macroeconomic Policies and the World Recession: A Look at Fourty One Borrowing Countries", Center for Economic and Policy Research, Washington, D.C.

World Bank (2011a), "Sudan Country Economic Brief", The World Bank – Africa Region – PREM Unit, Available via the internet at: http://siteresources.worldbank.org/ INTSU-DAN/Resources/Sudan_Economic_Brief-July_2011.pdf

_____(2011b), " World Bank's World Development Indicators" (accessed on 30\11\2012)

_____ (2009), "Sudan Country Economic Memorandum (CEM)", World Bank, Washington DC

_____(2008), "Revitalizing Sudan's Non-Oil Exports: A Diagnostic Trade Integration Study (DTIS)", Prepared for the Integrated Framework Program (December 2008), World Bank, Washington D.C.

_____(2007), "Sudan: Public Expenditure Review", World Bank, Washington D.C.

_____ (2003), "Sudan Stabilization and Reconstruction, Country Economic Memorandum", Volume 1: Main Text, World Bank, Washington D.C.

Yagci, F. (2001), "Choice of Exchange Rate Regimes For Developing Countries", The World Bank, Africa Region Working Paper Series No.16, Available via the internet at: http://www.worldbank.org/afr/wps/index.htm

Macroeconomic Policy Formation in South Sudan: Building Fiscal Management[1]

Asha Abdel Rahim[2] and Dirk Hansohm[3]

1 Introduction

South Sudan became independent on July 9, 2011 and is the newest state on the globe; in the same month it became the 193th member state of the United Nations. However, the independent state was preceded by six year interim period as an autonomous region, as stipulated in the Comprehensive Peace Agreement (CPA) of 2005. The Southern Sudan region enjoyed in these years already a high degree of political autonomy. In this interim period the reconstruction after a long civil war started and also the building up of a public administration began.

South Sudan is unique by combining challenges of different country groups:

- It is a least developed country where modern development has really only begun very recently;
- It is a post-conflict economy with its particular challenges of state-building and reconstruction;
- It depends highly on oil exports as a basis of the economy and of the state budget and so is subject to 'resource curse' effects;
- It is land-locked and can only reach the world market principally either through Sudan or Kenya.

Each of these characteristics is a heavy burden on its own. But the country holds also promise with its wealth of natural resources, a young population (51% under 18 years), and support granted by numerous donor countries.

[1] The authors thank Lwiza Mawage Kee, Evarist Twimukye and Steven Wondu for useful information and discussions. However, the authors take alone all the responsibility for the content of this document.
[2] Assistant Prof., Head of Economics Department, University of Juba, Email: asha.farag@gmail.com
[3] Technical Advisor, Policy and Research Unit, Ministry of Eastern African Community, Nairobi, Email: dirk@hansohm.com

It is in many respects a virgin country as it was neglected for most of its co-lonial and post-colonial history. With a population of only 8.3 million on an area of 640.000 km², is has a low population density (13.3 people per square kilometer). It is estimated that only 4% of its fertile land is used. It has a rich resource base: not only oil, but also minerals and agriculture, livestock, for-ests, fishery.

But a multitude of constraints hold back their exploitation: a lack of un-ambiguous land rights, a minimal infrastructure of roads, railway, river transport, electricity, internet, a very low level of education and a low level of health. A key problem is the multitude of unresolved conflicts with Sudan of which it was part - over resource division, border demarcation, nationality, etc. The seriousness of these disagreements came to a head when South Su-dan stopped its oil production in January 2012, cutting both its own and Su-dan's main income source. This brought into the open the structural depend-encies and the fragility of the economic systems and hastened the need for economic reform.

This paper analyzes the state of macroeconomic policy formation in the new South Sudan. As the private sector is still in its infancy, the public sector plays an overriding role. Thus, the article will give particular emphasis to the quality of fiscal (revenue and expenditure) management. Three strands of discussion are relevant to this context: First, the discussion on state building, especially in a post-conflict context; second, the discussion on public finance management and its reform; and third, the discussion on the challenge of dealing with dependence on mineral and aid rents (termed as 'resource curse').

In each of these areas numerous lessons have been learnt but controver-sies remain. South Sudan has tried to adopt such lessons and its experiences can also provide interesting insights and inform the discussion.

The second section gives an overview of the current economic, social and political conditions. The following section three discusses the economic policy, the strategies, the policies, the implementation and the actors, relating all these issues to the discussion on state building. Public finance and its reform are discussed in the fourth section, while specific attention to the risks of resource curse through oil and aid inflows is given in section five. The final section six concludes with some recommendations.

2   Economic, Social and Political Conditions in South Sudan

As argued in the introduction, South Sudan is unique in several respects. It bears a number of potentials that have been largely untapped as yet. But at the same time, the barriers that need to be unlocked to realize these potentials are deep and manifold.

While oil is the resource on which the budget and the whole economy depend, the country is rich in other minerals as gold, silver, iron ore and copper. The country also has a rich agricultural potential; cassava, ground nuts, sweet potatoes, sorghum and millet, sesame, maize, rice, and beans are currently planted. Cattle and fish and also timber have a huge commercial potential.

However, the challenges abound: Health and education indicators are very low - the literacy rate is only 27% (16% among female); school enrolment rate is 44%; 30% of the children are underweight. The infant mortality rate is 102 (per 1,000 live births); the maternal mortality rate is 2,054 (per 100,000 live births); and only 17% of the children were fully immunized. As much as 51% of the population is living below the poverty line; 55% have access to improved water sources and only 20% to improved sanitation; 15% of the households own a phone/handy (59% in urban areas compared to eight percent in rural areas); 83% of the population still live in rural areas and road infrastructure is minimal - only one tarred road connects the capital city Juba to the border with Uganda (World Bank data on website, SSNBS data on website).

Another area of concern is the still very difficult business environment. The World Bank's Doing Business Index (World Bank 2012a) rates South Sudan as rank 159 out of 183 countries (where 1 is easiest and 183 the most difficult conditions). The modern private sector is still in its infancy stage and markets, with the exception of the capital Juba, are largely undeveloped.

No comprehensive analysis of the achievements of the six year Comprehensive Peace Agreement (CPA) interim period (2006 -2012) in South Sudan is available. While the promises of the CPA were at best rudimentarily implemented at the national level of the then Sudan, in the South a public administration started to get in place. Most importantly, the CPA brought a broad pacification of the South. On the background of the general experiences in post-conflict development (most of which see a return to conflict) this is a remarkable achievement. Food and basic goods were distributed, schools and health stations were built, and roads were constructed. Overall, the results of the CPA interim period were regarded as impressive by the population (Schomerus and Allen 2010).

At the same time, the achievements remained fragile and were compromised by broadening corruption and power abuse, in an environment of minimal control and accountability. Government is still weak and the dominant international partners have emphasized in the first years after the CPA humanitarian assistance, rather than capacity building and institution building.

A key challenge to maintenance of peace and development is the disarmament, demobilisation and reintegration (DDR) of the large national army (Sudan People Liberation Army - SPLA) and the numerous militias. Only very limited success has been attained in this field so far: By January 2011 less than 13% of the targeted number had entered the DDR process. Among the multiple reasons are inconsistent conceptions and aims of the then national government (all Sudan) and of the GoSS, lack of ownership of SPLA, insufficient compensation for former combatants, ineligibility of participants, and the use of 'best practice' of other post-war countries irrespective of their inapplicability (Stone 2011).

The sudden decision to cut off oil exports in January 2012 that constituted 98% of South Sudan's revenue sharpened the challenges. Even if and when the open conflicts between the two Sudans will be resolved, it will take months to return to the pre-crisis oil-production level. As a result, inflation reached a peak of 80 percent in May 2012, receding to 41 percent in November 2012.

Internationally comparable economic data on South Sudan are as yet scarce, but the national data collected and computed by the South Sudan National Bureau of Statistics (SSNBS) are expanding, on which most of the following information is based.

Economic growth has been insufficient to tackle the huge challenges, and it has actually slowed down over recent years (2009-11), from 4.3 over 4.2 to 1.9%. In 2011 GDP amounted to US\$ 19.2 billion (World Bank website). This translates into a per capita income of US\$ 1,546 (2010), being much higher than that of neighboring countries. However, this figure is misleading, as a much lower income remained in the country. The GNP is only US\$ 984 (2010), reflecting the large income outflows to oil companies and payments under wealth sharing until independence.

Oil contributes with about 80% to the GDP. Outside of the oil sector, livelihoods are concentrated in low-productivity, unpaid agriculture and pastoralists work, which accounts for around 15% of the GDP (World Bank website). According to the Census of 2008 (SSCCSE 2011), 63% of the work force are regarded as working in the agricultural sector, 16% in household production for own use, 6% in public administration, 3% in education, health and social work, only 1% each in manufacturing and construction, 7% in trade, and 3% in other services. 14% of the labor force was regarded as unemployed (this figure does not capture those who are working part time or are working in the informal sector).

Government revenues are almost completely dependent on oil income (see the following table 1).

Table 1: Revenue & Expenditure in South Sudan (2006-2012, SSP billion, current prices)

Items/Year	2006	2007	2008	2009	2010	2011 (Jan-Jun)	2012 (Jul-Apr)
Revenue	2736,1	2977,8	6789,6	4238,8	5756,8	4889,1	10182,7
Oil	2732,9	2964,5	6670,9	4121,5	5630,3	4782,1	9882,9
Non-oil revenue	3,2	13,3	118,7	118,3	126,6	107	299,8
Expenditure	3581,5	2936,5	5712,7	4234,7	5576,1	4424,1	8545,8
Revenue as % of expenditure	0,76	1	1,2	1,0	1,0	1,1	1,2
Oil revenue as % of total revenue	1,00	1,00	0,98	0,97	0,98	0,98	0,97

Source: OEA (2012: 3)

The table 1 shows a continuing and extreme dependency on oil as a source of public revenues. The share of non-oil revenues increased only marginally from 0.1% (2006) to 2.9% (2012). How urgent the task of economic diversification is for diversifying also the sources of public revenues, is drawn in perspective by the following figure 1: As far as currently known oil resources go, production has already passed its peak.

Figure 1: Historical and future expected oil revenues of South Sudan (1995-2035, billion US$)

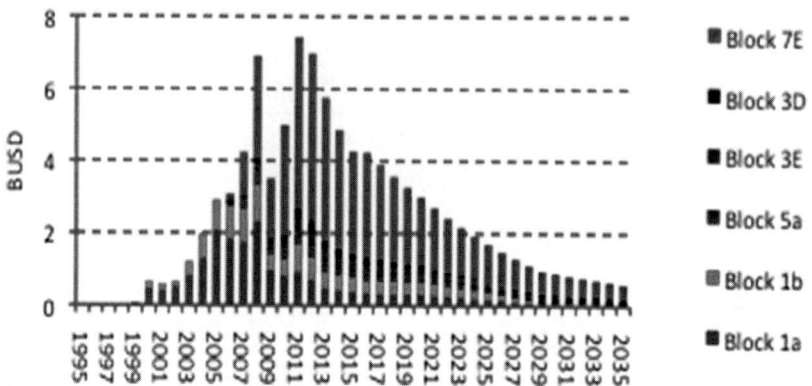

Source: GRSS (2011: 404)

The following table 2 gives an overview of the categories of spending over the past years. Almost half of the public expenditure goes to salaries, and about as much is going to operating costs, a spending pattern which leaves very little to investment. The transfers to the ten states are also very limited, which is problematic in the presence of their very limited capacities to raise their own public revenues.

Table 2: Expenditure by Category in South Sudan (2006-2012, SSP billion current prices)

Items/year	2006	2007	2008	2009	2010	2011 (Jan-Jun)	2012 (Jul-Apr)
Salaries	1185,7	1479,8	1873,4	1977,3	2205,7	1334,9	3129,2
Operating	1438,2	1058,4	2227,3	1255,3	2279,6	2145,8	1892,1
Capital	957,6	398,3	1611,9	1002	1090,9	943,4	1636,7
Transfers to states	525,5	631,6	637,6	1089,9	1219,9	773,3	1540
Expenditure	**3581,5**	**2936,5**	**5712,7**	**4234,7**	**5576,1**	**4424,1**	**8545,8**
Salaries as % of Expenditure	0,33	0,50	0,33	0,47	0,40	0,30	0,37
Operating as % of Expenditure	0,40	0,36	0,39	0,30	0,41	0,49	0,22
Capital as % of Expenditure	0,27	0,14	0,28	0,24	0,20	0,21	0,19
Transfers to the States as % of Expenditure	0,1	0,2	0,11	0,26	0,22	0,17	0,18

Source: OEA (2012: 3)

According to table 3, by far the largest amount of allocation went consistently to security (38% in latest year), followed by public administration (14%), infrastructure (12%), and rule of law (11%). Health and education only received 2% and 4-8% respectively (even with a declining trend for education). While these are alarming signs, the international donor partners have highly concentrated their activities on these sectors (but not the government!).

Table 3: Expenditure by sectors in South Sudan (2006-2012, SSP billion, current prices)

Items/year	2006	2007	2008	2009	2010	2011 (Jan-Jun)	2012 (Jul-Apr)
Accountability	258,8	71,4	656	329,7	533,3	718,6	397,1
Economic functions	45,5	52,7	0,3	94,8	162,4	98,8	133,7
Education	225,2	233,1	290,2	234,1	279,2	144	367,9
Health	136,1	67,2	114,1	97,1	139,4	94,1	174,6
Infrastructure	360,8	170,3	813,9	536,3	635,9	451,8	984,5
Natural re-sources	119,8	109,4	196,5	178,8	185,3	91,9	247,1
Public admi-nistration	185,6	234,6	512,6	345,1	844,7	2009,5	1160,3
Rule of law	351,4	257,2	515,2	529,4	665,7	421	949,4
Security	1204,8	1920	1882,1	1411,4	1514,9	1081,4	3206,7
Social Huma-nitrian	85,0	37,9	84,1	39,4	72,8	80,9	135,5
Block trans-fers	324,1	416,0	452,7	438,7	542,6	404,6	788,9
Expenditure	3297,4	2841,8	5712,7	4234,7	5576,1	5596	8545,8

Source: OEA (2012: 3)

The effectiveness of policies and the implementation of plans, budgets and programs is highly determined by the underlying quality of governance. Governance can be described as consisting of the traditions and institutions by which authority in a country is exercised. This includes the process by which governments are elected, monitored and replaced; the capacity of the government to effectively formulate and implement sound policies; and the respect of citizens and the state for the institutions that govern economic and social interactions among them (World Bank 2012b).

Comparative data on the status of governance of South Sudan are diffi-cult to get as yet. However, the World Bank's comprehensive World Govern-ance Indicators data - that process multiple sources to estimate the state of governance in six dimensions - include the new country South Sudan. The following table 4 measures the quality of governance in comparison with other countries on a scale from 0 (lowest) - 100 (highest). These aggregate indicators combine the views of a large number of enterprises, citizens and expert survey respondents in industrial and developing countries. These are based on 30 individual data sources produced by a variety of survey insti-tutes, think tanks, non-governmental organizations, international organiza-tions, and private sector firms.

Table 4: Comparative governance indicators for South Sudan and Sudan (2011; percentile rank 0-100)

	South Sudan	Sudan
voice and accountability	16,90	4,20
political stability/absence of violence	14,20	0,90
government effectiveness	0,90	7,10
regulatory quality	3,30	8,10
rule of law	2,80	8,50
control of corruption	0,90	5,70

Source: World Bank 2012b

The table 4 shows that in two dimensions (voice and accountability and political stability/absence of violence) South Sudan does markedly better than Sudan. This reflects progress. But on the four other criteria - government effectiveness, regulatory quality, rule of law, and control of corruption - the new nation is worse, and at rock bottom of all countries. And while all of the six governance dimensions are important as conditions for effective macroeconomic policy making, these latter four are directly important. One could argue that, as a new state, low ratings could be expected. However, for one point, South Sudan had already 6 years of peace, a period to build up a new administration, regulations, and laws, and for another point, it should be easier to build up a sound new system than to reform a well-established system of bad governance. In fact, all of these governance dimensions have continuously further deteriorated over the last years. In sum, these indicators disqualify heavily the laws passed and the bodies set up. This is not a basis for a sound economy.

Since 2005 a new indicator, specifically targeted at the determinants of 'failing states', is collected by an American civil society organization (Fund for Peace [2012], see table 5 below). It proposes 12 indicators: Mounting demographic pressures; Massive movement of refugees and Internally Displaced Persons (IDPs); Legacy of vengeance – seeking group grievance; Chronic and sustained human flight; Uneven economic development along group lines; Sharp and/or severe economic decline; Criminalization or delegitimization of the state; Progressive deterioration of public services; Widespread violation of human rights; Security apparatus as 'state within the state'; Rise of factionalized elites; and Intervention of other states or external actors. This comparative project points to the relative character of these characteristics by collecting the data for all states. The indicators range between zero (best) and 10 (worst).

Data for South Sudan are available for the first time for 2012. Thus, no comparison over time is possible, but only one with Sudan (see table 5 below). The table 5 shows that, expectedly, most indicators are not different from Sudan's (that has the third worst overall indicator of 177 countries). While the indicators of human flight and brain drain are notably better for the new country, state legitimacy and human rights and rule of law are only slightly so, and the indicator for public services provision is more progressively deteriorating in South Sudan relative to Sudan.

Table 5: Failed States Index (2012)

Indicator	South Sudan	Sudan
Demographic pressures	8.4	8.4
Refugees and IDPs	9.9	9.9
Uneven economic development	8.8	8.8
Group grievance	10.0	10.0
Human flight and brain drain	6.4	8.3
Poverty and economic decline	7.3	7.3
State legitimacy	9.1	9.5
Public services	9.5	8.5
Human rights and rule of law	9.2	9.4
Security apparatus	9.7	9.7
Factionalized elites	10.0	9.9
External intervention	10.0	9.5

Source: Fund for Peace (2012)

The following section 3 considers the policy, institutional and organizational base of these economic and social outcomes.

3   Context of Development Strategies and of Macroeconomic Policy Formation

The Southern Sudan region was integrated into Sudan that became independent in 1956, but this was done on pressure of the elites in the new country's capital, but not based on the opinion of the population of the South. Not surprisingly, rebellion in the South even preceded independence (1955), and continued ever since until 2005, only interrupted by a peace interval from 1972-83 (Addis Ababa Agreement). During all this time, civil administration and development remained very thin and restricted. Real state building only began after the signing of the CPA in 2005.

Following the signing of the CPA a Joint Assessment Mission (JAM) by UN and World Bank, in cooperation and with endorsement of the Government of Sudan and the South Sudanese rebel movement (Sudan People Liberation Movement - SPLM), provided a detailed assessment of recovery and development needs for the entire country (JAM 2005). Although elements of a public service existed in Sudan Government-controlled areas and starts of a rudimentary government and a public administration were made also in the SPLM controlled areas, covering most of the country (Rolandsen 2005), the JAM noted that the entire public service of South Sudan had to be built up virtually from the scratch.

Thus, the challenges of state building and post-conflict reconstruction basically coincided. In both of these fields many mistakes have been made and many lessons were learned. One key misconception in both efforts has been the serious underestimation of the tasks. A second has been the view that 'best practices' developed anywhere can easily be copied and transplanted in any context. Basically, development experts believed that building the capacity of the state to carry out its core functions - security, infrastructure development, health, education, and taxation to finance all these tasks - would be an easy endeavor.

However, as Pritchett et al. (2012) pointed out, reality has proven otherwise. 50 years after independence of many states, their capacity in these respects is still the same or even worse. This was illustrated for instance by Pritchett et al. (2012) by analyzing data on time series of quality of governance, government effectiveness and quality of public services provided. Pritchett et al. (2012) point out the dangers of over-ambition in regard of goals and standards relative to available capacity, the establishment of bodies that have the form of modern organizations but do not really execute their tasks, and the neglect of local contexts. These lessons should give a warning sign to late-comers to state building as South Sudan. Are these lessons taken on board?

During the six year peace period following the signature of the CPA in 2005, numerous governance institutions and organizations were set up and plans, laws, and concept papers were laid down. Since independence in July 2011, this process continues. While these institutions are largely following the model of a modern democracy, unsurprisingly they do not yet measure up to their standard. The country's transitional constitution of 2005 constitutes the three arms of government: legislative, executive, and judiciary. There is a wide range of powers for the president: He cannot be impeached and has the authority to fire state governors and to dissolve the parliament and the state assemblies. There is no control of powers.

The country has not less than 29 ministries (recently reduced from 37) and 21 commissions. It introduced a decentralized system of governance with the central national level, 10 states, and the local government level with 73 counties. Substantial powers are devolved to the sub-national levels (see below next section). Not all of the commissions are, however, as yet effective, nor are all the laws and policies.

A parliament with two houses - the National Legislative Assembly (NLA) and the State Council (SC) with representatives of the 10 states - has 332 and 50 resp. members. While the lower house has also members from the former Sudan parliament, and members appointed by the political parties and by the president, the members of the upper house are partly from the former Sudanese State Council and partly appointed by the president. Thus the system cannot be called 'elective democracy'. Nevertheless, in the opinion of most people, the parliament meets the aspirations of an inclusive body, covering all regions, political and ethnic groups and gender (25% of the members have to be women).

The ruling party SPLM holds 90% of the seats. While five opposition parties are in the parliament, they do neither have the resources nor the experience to formulate policies and to pose an effective and credible opposition. Moreover, these parties tend to be one man shows and/or are based on a specific ethnic group. If anything, the potential for democratization through parties is currently more within the SPLM that has various factions, including army officers, academics, activists, and modern professionals.

A major reason for the very limited control function of the parliament is the ignorance of many members about the function of a parliament and the limited competence, last not least in English language. While some are highly educated and experienced, others have little education, among them veteran civil war fighters. Whether the parliament will grow into a relevant institution will depend on the ability of the members to acquire the means and the competences that are required. However, it will be decisive for its role and the relevance that civil society will expect and demand from parliament.

The Interim Constitution provides for an independent judiciary headed by a Supreme Court. The president's Supreme Court appointments must be confirmed by a two-thirds majority in parliament (the National Legislative Assembly - NLA). The embryonic court system is under huge strain. In September 2011, the chief justice said the courts had the capacity to handle 100,000 cases a year, but in fact faced four times that number. He called for a greater use of traditional dispute-resolution systems to ease the burden of the court system (Freedom House 2012). Interference by the Executive also undermines the independence of the Judiciary.

The South Sudan Anti-Corruption Commission (SSACC) has not proven to be effective. Corruption is widespread and has not as yet been effectively addressed, as many of its beneficiaries are known to be among the top leaders and are regarded as deserved former freedom fighters that seem to be untouchable. No official has ever been prosecuted for involvement in corrupt practices since the establishment of the SSACC five years ago. In August 2011 the members of parliament initially refused to approve South Sudan's first cabinet as an independent country, demanding that the president releases the names of a list of 13 ministers suspected of being involved in corruption.

In September 2011 the SSACC released a report stating that it was investigating some 60 cases of corruption and was trying to recover more than SSP 120 million (approx. $20 million). The report to the surprise of many, including Paul Akol, a Member of Parliament/MP, made no reference to the list of the 13 top officials (Sudan Tribune 2011). Both South Sudanese and international actors are increasingly concerned about the pervasive and destructive impact of corruption, but according to many, despite statements to the contrary, 'there is little will to address it' (OECD 2011: 12). A ray of hope is the South Sudan National Audit Chamber (SSNAC), which, despite very limited means, published reports on the government financial statements for the years 2007 and 2008 (SSNAC 2012a and b) that spell out the numerous and major shortcomings (see below section 4). Although presented to the president and to the parliament, no concrete steps seem to have been taken.

Another positive and important development is the establishment of the National Bureau of Statistics (SSNBS) that continues to bring out more and more economic and social data that provide a basis for a more evidence-based policy making process. This institution thereby contributes to transparency in government and with regard of the social situation.

The Ministry of Finance and Economic Planning (MoFEP) combines the tasks of annual economic planning and longer term development planning as well as donor coordination. Its capacity has been strengthened since 2006. However, this is not the case for the remaining 28 other ministries which often have quite limited tasks and may also have overlapping functions, like those for transport and roads & bridges, or are closely related to each other (as an example, there are two ministries for education).

All in all, the large number of newly created government bodies is troublesome. First, they have to cope with the extremely limited pool of skilled staff to make them working. Second, they create a large scope for duplication, and for overlapping and conflicting functions. Most importantly, the broad number of organizations has negative implications for depth of fulfilling tasks and for effectiveness of operations. Unfortunately, they conform to the picture of 'isomorphic mimicry' of pretenders of real organizations (Pritchett 2012).

Why did this happen? What are the motivations behind? Two explanations offer themselves: First, bloated organizations are created to absorb former fighters, to create jobs, and to benefit on other elements. Second, donors press for and (part-) finance institutions they think are important and that are currently in vogue in development circles. These include for instance the SSACC. It doubles functions that should be done by others, including the Auditor General, the Ministry of Finance, and the Judiciary. Furthermore, the budget of the SSACC even surpasses that of the vital South Sudan Audit Chamber (SSAC). Similar arguments could - and should - be made for most of the Commissions, whose tasks should be executed by the ministries themselves. The effectiveness of many of these Commissions is reportedly very weak.

A great number of policy documents has been produced that is meant to give structure and guidance to policy making. The South Sudan Development Plan (SSDP) 2011-13 (GRSS 2011) sets the framework and a medium-term agenda for South Sudan on economic and fiscal policy. The very comprehensive plan (GRSS 2011, 437 pp.) presents a detailed framework of goals, objectives and performance targets, and an action plan how these are to be pursued, as well as how the resources are allocated. It also sets out indicators to monitor progress. The plan is very detailed and highly sophisticated. Overall SSDP objective is to ensure that by 2014 South Sudan is a united and peaceful new nation, building strong foundations for good governance, economic prosperity and enhanced quality of life for all. Efforts to achieve this are broken down into four core building blocks for the SSDP in the plan period:

1. Improving governance;
2. Achieving rapid rural transformation to improve livelihoods and expand employment opportunities;
3. Improving and expanding education and health services; and
4. Deepening peace building and improving security.

In addition, seven cross-cutting issues have been identified as important: preserving the environment; achieving gender equality, providing for youth employment; capacity-building; following human rights; combatting HIV/AIDS; and fighting corruption. (GRSS 2011: XX)
Its priorities include:

- expanding and strengthening the public provision of basic services;
- large scale infrastructure development (in particular roads, electricity);
- development of human and institutional capacities; and the
- establishment of a legal framework across all the levels of government

In this framework, the importance of fiscal policy and management is recognized: 'In order to achieve fiscal discipline and macroeconomic stability, GoSS will pursue sound public financial management (PFM)' (GRSS 2011: 134). The Public Financial Management Act (PFMA), the Procurement Law, the Audit Act and the Central Bank Act have been prepared for this purpose. The Government is currently rolling out a Financial Management Information System (FMIS) to states. Key institutions to implement fiscal policy are the MoFEP, the Central Bank of South Sudan (CBSS), the SSAC, the SSACC, and the SSCCSE (now SSNBS). The purpose is to bring all this into a 'comprehensive legal framework'.

Budget Sector Plans set out Government's priorities and cover key sectors across ten sectors: accountability; infrastructure; security; economic functions; natural resources; social and humanitarian issues; education; public administration; health; and rule of law. The National Budget Plan is Government's key budget strategy document. It links Government's overall policies and plans, as set out in the Budget Sector Plans, to the annual budget. To do this it highlights main macroeconomic policies, recent macroeconomic performance and future plans, available public resources, and public expenditure priorities (OEA 2012: 16-17).

The country's aid strategy from 2006 and the renewed one in 2011 (see below section 5) is to make sure that foreign aid is in line with Government's priorities and helps to build capacity.

A growth strategy for the years 2010-2012 has also been formulated in 2010 (GoSS 2010). The strategy emphasizes the role of government in promoting growth - through creating an enabling environment and an open economy, and through direct support to the private sector (whose most important actors are smallholder farmers and pastoralists), rather than direct public involvement in economic activities. The strategy then identifies the sources of growth and its constraints. It identifies insecurity, poor infrastructure, and multiple taxation as the binding constraints to growth in South Sudan - i. e. those constraints that must be addressed first in order to raise the rate of growth. Lastly, the strategy sets out the roles of GRSS sectors and agencies. As the strategy calls for strictly evidence-based policy making, it also emphasizes the need to strengthen this evidence base by further data collection and rigorous research.

These documents meet a relatively high standard. They are, however, not in line with the underlying very limited capacity to implement. They do not only lack complete consistency with each other, they do also not consistently lead to policy making. Both government and development partners experience problems in prioritizing and in sequencing the work (OECD 2011: 13). The lack of consistency is exemplified by the contrast between the very comprehensive approach of the development plan that touches all sectors and many activities, and the Growth Strategy that emphasizes prioritizing as well as sequencing according to binding constraints (as new and different immediate constraints will come up once the present ones are eased).

The limitations of the role of these comprehensive planning documents for actual policy making were thrown into light with the decision taken early in 2012 to abruptly stop oil production in the continuing dispute with Sudan on the transfer fee for the oil transport to Port Sudan. While it is understandable as a reaction to the illegitimate transfer of oil funds by Sudan's government, the decision was apparently not taken on the basis of a systematic evaluation of options with their costs and benefits, but as a unanimous cabinet decision charged with emotion and as a symbol of newly found independence (Reuters 2012). Obviously the well-articulated development plans and budget plans have become obsolete as a result.

Framing the decision to stop oil production as being without alternative (as done for example in the budget speech GRSS 2012), instead of doing a costing of the various options, contrasts with the growth strategy's aim of strictly evidence-based policy making. The aim of seeking alternative pipeline routes is understandable, and may possibly be an option for the medium term, cannot help in the short term.

Freedom of expression is guaranteed by the Interim Constitution. However, a long-awaited media law that would ensure the rights and obligations of journalists has not yet been passed by parliament, which leaves the journalists in a limbo. In fact, many in government tend to see independent press as a threat and the security agency has more than once arrested or even beat up journalists and has confiscated newspapers. At the same time, there has been an explosion of private media which provide enlightenment. Currently 37 FM frequency radio stations, more than a half dozen newspapers, and several online new sites are counted (Freedom House 2012: www.freedomhouse.org). In addition, there is a publicly owned national television channel and a private satellite channel.

There is an emergent civil society, primarily active in Juba, but it is also seen by many in government more as a threat than as a vital ingredient for a thriving society. Troubling is the recent abduction and beating of the prominent chairman of the SSCSA/South Sudan Civil Society Alliance (Freedom House: http://www.freedomhouse.org/article/south-sudan-celebrates-one-year-independence-brutal-attack-prominent-civil-society-activist). All in all, Freedom House rates South Sudan as a 'not free' country - the same ranking as Sudan's - while the press is rated as 'partly free'.

Poor performance by the GRSS in passing key legislation, acting against corruption, enforcing merit-based public service recruitment, or dealing with procurement transgressions suggests a culture of impunity (OECD 2011: 15). The result of all this is that macroeconomic policies will not be adequately discussed by the wider public in terms of objectives, instruments, implementation and outcomes. Such a discussion would be valuable and necessary in order to find out more adequate macroeconomic policy alternatives for the country.

4   Public Finance Reform

An effective state is a state that is able to mobilize resources and to spend it on infrastructure, services and public goods that both enhance well-being of its citizens and their human capital. With its management of public finance it ensures that macro-economic balance is maintained: Its policy is neither too accommodative to generate high inflation and to crowd out private investment, nor is it too restrictive to discourage private investment. Arguably, fiscal issues are thus 'at the heart of the state's role in the development process' (Addison and Roe 2004). Policy failures in taxation, public expenditure or management of fiscal deficit and public debt can easily undermine growth and poverty reduction.

The importance of establishing a fiscal policy in Southern Sudan was identified as key both in the JAM of 2005 (JAM 2005) and in the Development Plan of 2011 (GRSS 2011). No public policy can be implemented without public resources. Donors supported this process strongly. Based on the immense task of rebuilding the institutions, and considering the length of the preceding conflict and the very low level of development, a chance was seen to make a clean sweep and to establish a modern public sector and a fiscal policy structure by using 'best practices' of fiscal management, including instruments such as a Medium-Term Expenditure Framework (MTEF), the establishment of an Autonomous Revenue Agency (ARA) and an Integrated Financial Management Information System (IFMIS). The JAM (2005) recommended that core fiduciary services such as auditing, accounting and procurement be contracted out to international firms.

These instruments are part of a new approach to public management (NPM) that has been strongly pushed by IMF and World Bank and implemented in a number of African countries. These are inspired by successful reforms in countries such as New Zealand and basically are guided by the introduction of private sector management principles to public management (Fozzard and Foster 2004):

- privatization of public enterprises,
- separation of policy and implementation functions by creating executive agencies and decentralizing responsibility for service delivery,
- giving public managers greater autonomy in the use of resources and in staffing by liberating them from bureaucratic controls,
- aligning incentives for agencies and personnel with policy goals by using personal performance contracts and performance related pay,
- mechanisms to ensure feedback from and accountability to the public by creating opportunities for exit (by access to alternative private and public providers) and voice (through e. g. client surveys and participation of representatives on management boards), and

- competitive pressures through compulsory tendering, internal markets and benchmarking of performance between service delivery units

All of these principles involve major, sophisticated, wide-ranging, and costly, reforms. While they promise major gains, they also incur substantial risks. These approaches and practices have been developed in industrial countries and are advocated on a major scale in developing countries, also for South Sudan.

MTEFs are increasingly common within Eastern and Southern Africa (Fjeldstad et al. 2004). By encompassing all expenditures they provide a linking framework and facilitate the management of policies and budget realities to reduce expenditure pressure throughout the budget cycle. The result is supposed to be a generally better control of expenditure and a better value for money within a hard budget constraint (World Bank 1998). The process is said to be a 'complex task and a radical shift in perspective and the way business is done' (World Bank 1998).

An IFMIS is a common computerized financial system used in government offices. It often includes government ministries, departments and agencies and may be extended to regional and local governments. It has a single database in which the financial transactions are recorded, a uniform coding structure for the analysis of the transactions, and the possibility of entering each transaction only once. It usually comprises the core modules of budgeting, cash and debt management and accounting, and in some cases ancillary components such as payroll and procurement.

The traditional way of organizing central government revenue collection is to let it be handled by units within the Ministry of Finance. However, over the past decade several countries in the region and beyond have implemented comprehensive reforms of their tax administrations by introducing semi-autonomous revenue authorities. The choice of a revenue authority model aims partly to limit direct political interference by the Ministry of Finance, and partly to free the revenue administration from the constraints of the civil service system.

As argued above, these modern approaches are sophisticated and have high demands on finance and manpower. They have been developed in industrial countries over a longer term and typically in a piecemeal and learning by doing manner. These modern approaches and computer packages are now available to developing countries and offer them, at least theoretically, a chance to 'leapfrog' decades of costly learning and slow change. However, they also imply serious risks. They may be overly complex, not sustainable, and they create dependence on imported skills (Wynne 2005, Parry 2004). They may also undermine local ownership that is vital for sustainable development and for effective learning.

Their success has therefore, not surprisingly, been quite mixed in the context of developing countries. Many countries have implemented some of these concepts, but overall successful public expenditure management reform cannot be dissociated from more fundamental institutional reforms within government. Such reforms serving the need for transparent and clean financial management are especially pertinent in post-conflict as in mineral-resource based economies such as South Sudan. These two contexts are discussed in the following paragraphs.

Public expenditure management, revenue mobilization and establishing the overall (macroeconomic) fiscal framework are all crucial issues for post-conflict reconstruction in a country that tries to rebuild itself. But there is no mechanical relationship between economics and conflict and between economic policy and peace: Complex non-economic factors as ideologies and belief systems also play a role, as do the effectiveness of institutions in resolving conflict by non-violent means.

General principles for 'post-conflict' recovery include (Addison et al. 2004):

1. Reduction of absolute poverty
2. Reduction of (horizontal) inequality
3. Rebuilding the rules of the game and people's respect for them (the social contract)

Whatever form the new rules take, they have a fiscal dimension: people expect a new distribution of services and of infrastructure – and these must be financed. Fiscal issues during conflict and reconstruction include (Addison et al. 2004):

- Rebuilding the rules of the game and people's respect for them (the social contract) are necessary for peace.
- Building a functioning democracy that represents the interests of the majority is crucial to the effectiveness of any reform that aims to achieve a broad-based recovery from war.
- Most of the necessary improvements will be more difficult to achieve if the quality of the debate and the understanding on fiscal policy issues is not first improved. This, in turn, requires more rigorous research to inform the process.

At the same time, fiscal reforms may not be among the first measures advisable after the end of a civil war (Collier 2003). Building effective revenue and budgetary institutions requires a large measure of social stability. Fiscal reform will also have more positive effects when complemented by conflict-reducing measures.

In any case, economic policies should be distinctive in post-conflict situations - policies at the start of peace are normally much worse than in other equally poor countries. The likely cocktail of interventions that might increase growth combines policy reform, aid, and improved access to global markets. It is important to note that growth is more sensitive to policy during the first decade of post-conflict situations than in normal situations.

Attempting reform across a broad front is not sensible in a post-conflict situation. Rather, a focus on 2 or 3 policies that are politically as easy as possible and yield rapid pay-offs is advisable. In general terms, social policy is relatively more important, while macroeconomic policy is relatively less important in a post-civil war context. Specifically, policies for social inclusion are vital. Although education and health investment have only long-term impacts, their signal effects are important. It is important to prioritize addressing the grievances over resources that played a role in the war. In South Sudan these grievances concern land ownership, oil revenues, and the lack of investment in certain areas (Collier 2003).

In terms of economic development, civil war is 'development in reverse' (Collier 2003). This challenge is particularly serious in South Sudan, as, prior to 2006 the country has only seen peace once over a longer period (1972-1983). In addition to the specific reasons of a civil conflict, once a country is in a civil war, mechanisms develop to sustain this conflict: while conflict weakens the economy and leaves a legacy of atrocities, it also creates leaders and organizations that have invested in skills and equipment that are only useful for violence. It also destroys much of what has been there before the war. While the overwhelming population suffers, these leaders often do well, and have thus little incentive for peace. The difficult task of economic development is to break this mechanism by creating employment, and providing security, health and education.

History shows that the risk for post-conflict countries to fall back into conflict is very high. To reduce this risk, policy reform, aid for development, and improved access to global markets are important. As mentioned above, because of the low level of administrative competence, it is not sensible to attempt reform across a broad front. Nevertheless, practice tends to result in exactly this, due to the combination of a very weak capacity to manage, coordinate and lead policy processes by government and the diverse interests of international cooperation partners that limit the scope for donor coordination, despite all the rhetoric. South Sudan is a textbook example.

Social policy is relatively more important in a post-conflict situation than macroeconomic policy (Collier 2003: 155). This applies especially to education and health. While the effects of education will not be felt on a large scale immediately, its signal effect – showing the good intentions of the government – is vital. The same is with health sector reconstruction. Even more importantly, the returns to early rehabilitation of key infrastructure destroyed during war and conflict is likely to be extremely high. The provision of information about the ongoing process of development is needed in order to counter both rumors about corruption and the misuse of public funds and also the build-up of unrealistic expectations of quick progress by the population.

What is the experience of public finance reform in Africa? A recent analysis (Andrews 2010) of 31 Public Finance Management (PFM) reform efforts has three key findings:

1. Budgets are made better than they are executed (budget preparation processes are comparatively stronger than budget execution and oversight processes) - a fact that seriously questions the success of PFM reforms;

2. Practice in budgets execution lags behind the creation of processes and laws (laws and processes may be in place but seldom affect actual behavior); and

3. Actor concentration pays off (processes are stronger when narrower, concentrated sets of actors are involved in implementation):

Countries were – according to these studies - significantly different. However, they have alarmingly similar reform packages in place. 'Best practice' has been applied in a largely non-contextual manner. This creates new problems in administrations.

Critiques point out that instruments such as MTEFs 'act as a huge distraction to good basic budgeting, with questionable results and much wasted resources' (Wynne 2010). Instead of the risky approach of major reforms and fundamental change an organic and incremental change is advised. Tried and tested reforms should be applied and the use of local experts rather than of international consultants should be preferred, because only they really understand their systems. Critics also point to stringent conditions being necessary for the successful application of MTEFs, but these conditions are often absent - all the more in post-conflict countries: they need to be diagnostic rather than formulaic, to be based on clear, affordable and consistent national and sectoral policies (OPM 2010, Wynne 2010).

How is the experience in South Sudan? A first-hand experience in building up and assisting planning and budgeting systems in Southern Sudan is reported by Davies and Smith (2010). The World Bank has done a PFM assessment, covering the Interim-CPA period (GoSS 2011). As positive factors the report points out:

1. Upstream PFM functions: These functions have improved considerably since 2005. The budget is prepared with due regard to government policy: The budget classification indicates the purpose of spending, the budget documents are comprehensive and of high quality, and these are publicly available (nevertheless, they have a low scoring). 'Budget at a glance' overviews are prepared for public information. A robust policy-oriented annual budget preparation process provides a necessary platform on which a medium term per-

spective to budgeting is introduced - this has nevertheless a low scoring as it is in an early stage. Well-targeted technical assistance is said to have played a strong role. Rising skills capacity at the Mo-FEP is said to enable a decreasing reliance on foreign technical assistance. However, there are no indications for this in the underlying analysis. The entire report does not focus at all on means and progress of capacity building.

2. Strengthening tax administration: a solid base has been established for this task to work adequately in future years (therefore this function also gets a low rating). It is not clear why then this element is counted as a positive factor.

3. Establishment of an integrated PFM system: is also in an early stage.

4. Establishment of an electronic payroll system: there is an increasing accountability for salary payments.

5. Strengthening internal and external audit systems: this function is at an early stage - i.e. still to be seen in the future: The SSNAC is being strengthened; legislative oversight is still more an expectation when regarding the situation presently, as is effective GoSS-donor interaction.

As remaining challenges are identified:

1. Aggregate and spending agency expenditure outturns tend to be significantly different from the approved budgets. This was possible because of higher revenues than those budgeted for - nevertheless some spending agencies had lower expenditures than budgeted.

2. Constitutional and legal controls regarding changes in relation to the approved budget appear not to be fully adhered to.

3. In-year predictability in regard of availability of funds is low.

4. Build-up of payment arrears – this often occurs because the MoFEP felt obliged to make payments as contracts had been signed and procured goods and services were received, although these positions were not yet included in the budget - most obvious grain and dura for food reserves in 2007 were contracted and procured outside the approved budget.

5. Public procurement systems tend to lack transparency: despite of regulations emphasizing the use of competitive procurement methods in practice single source procurement is the norm.

6. Some internal control systems appear less than robust - control procedures either are not in place or are not complied with.

7. The PFM law is still not in place, even though the bill was drafted in 2007. The old and very comprehensive Financial and Accounting Procedures Ordinance (of 1995) is now only partly used.

Generally speaking, downstream PFM areas as budget execution, budget accounting and some internal budgetary control systems are still weak, resulting in budgets that are not credible (i.e. not realistic nor implemented as intended). The overriding issues are capacity constraints: improvements in systems can only take place at the pace that capacity and capability constraints permit.

The JAM (2005) recommendation to contract out core fiduciary services as audit, accounting and procurement to international firms was implemented. However, GoSS' experience in contracting out has been varied. While government had supported the process of contracting out key services, it had very limited capacity to design and manage the contracts: even with World Bank administered contracts, government had limited capacity to ensure that the contract design and performance met its own needs. Lengthy World Bank procurement procedures and limited government capacity to follow them led to significant delays. Costs were not only lost service delivery, but also diminished incentives for government to build its own capacity and structures. Capacity development was generally inadequately addressed: It was not at the center of design, and no exit strategy was formulated. This shows that inappropriate design can undermine effectiveness of contracting out. Furthermore, contracting out proved not to be cheap. As a better alternative contracting in temporary capacity from the diaspora has been recommended (Davies 2009).

The overall situation and progress in procurement has been evaluated in the recent South Sudan Procurement Assessment Report (World Bank 2011). The legal framework for public procurement is the Interim Public Procurement and Disposal Regulation (IPPDR), approved by the Council of Ministers in 2006. However, it has not been passed by Parliament, which creates some doubts on its legality. Further, it has some legal shortcomings. More importantly, a high amount of public entities fails to use the IPPDR - some even do not know about it. The Procurement Policy Unit (PPU) of the MoFEP has limited capacity to exercise its statutory role to guide and supervise the process. There is a clear lack of unambiguous legislative and regulatory framework establishing and assigning normative/regulatory functions and defining clear procedures. Monitoring and information tools are also lacking, as are resources and an adequate level of independence and authority to exercise these functions. There are major weaknesses in all steps of the procurement process. There is no established practice for quality control, and cases of mismanagement are frequent. Although capability in processing procurement has been increasing since 2005, it still does not meet the required level. At the state level, a number of targeted states have established procurement units. However, these are not operational and staff has little if any experience.

On a broader note, the report (World Bank 2011) states that the private sector is still dominated by traders with a short term profit orientation and a lacking business and management expertise. The legal framework is not satisfactory and legislation that has been passed is far from being implemented. Infrastructure is poor and complex and unclear import regulation and customs systems result in high and non-transparent transport costs and long transport duration.

Budgetary control is another weak point as yet. The limitations of the SSAC and the NLA have been discussed above. An important first step to systematize the budget process is fixing a budget cycle. This has been done in South Sudan (see the following table 6).

Table 6: South Sudan Budget Cycle

Date	Action
15th Nov.	Council approval of the MTEF in preliminary National Budget Plan
After 15th Nov.	Launch of planning process with training for BSWGs (Budget Sector Working Groups)
Jan.	Submission of draft 3 year Budget Sector Plans (BSP)
Feb.	BSP and preliminary National Budget Plan are presented to the Economic, Development and Finance Committee of the Parliament
15th March	Final budget ceilings are approved by the Council
31th March	Budget Call Circular issued (ceilings for each agency)
31th March	MoFEP informs the States about the estimates of transfers
April	Compilation of the draft budget Book
15th May	Submission of draft Budget Book and of National Budget Plan to Council
July	Budget Execution Circular

Source: OEA 2012: 43-45

However, it is worrying that the time window for discussions in parliament (in the resp. committee and then in the full parliament) is limited to only a maximum of 6 weeks (February - mid March). In such a short period parliament will not be able to give as comprehensive an attention to the budget as its role requires.

An important element of the NPM reform is decentralization. In difference to other elements of the NPM agenda discussed above, this seems to fit South Sudan's requirements perfectly. The centralization of power and the vast and continuing rural-urban and regional disparities can be seen as a key underlying dilemma that caused Sudan's conflicts and its recent breakup. Because of this, decentralization is a key element of South Sudan's governance set. The emphasis on decentralization addresses the country's legacy of marginalization of areas. The problem is implementation of decentralization.

According to the Transitional Constitution of South Sudan (2011) and under the Local Government Act (2009), South Sudan has a three layers system of decentralized governance - national/federal, state (10 states), and local government (83 counties). As it is the case in other countries, different levels of government (national, state, local) have different, but also concurrent, powers and tasks (i.e. tasks that are in danger of overlapping and/or are conflicting). Furthermore, the three levels are not financially independent from each other. Some local taxes are transferred upwards to federal government that, in turn, provides transfers down to states and local councils. They (the three levels of government) need to interact. However, importantly, the Local Government Act (LGA) spells out that the lowest adequate possible level of government should act (principle of subsidiarity). The division of tasks is meant to enhance provision of public goods and services at different levels of the society. The Local Government Act spells out the objectives of local government. Among them is promoting social and economic development. Appendix III of the Local Government Act lists the concrete functions which the local government has in terms of economic development (see excerpt below):

APPENDIX III: LOCAL GOVERNMENT FUNCTIONS, Part I, Finance and Economic Development

1. Preparing the economic and social plans of the Council.
2. Preparing, keeping and organizing statistical records of all the economic, development and service activities of the Council.
3. Promoting and encouraging investment, and facilitating the business of investors, in accordance with the laws in force.
4. Encouraging the self-help and charitable projects, and the business of charitable and voluntary societies.
5. Organizing markets and places of sales.
6. Spreading awareness among citizens of the approved economic and social programs.
7. Organizing the trade activities, by granting the necessary licenses for all types of trades in the Council.
8. Conducting such studies and researches which may target development of the Council and may increase its resources thereof.
9. Preparing the estimates of the revenues and expenditures for the Council annual budget.

---

10. Controlling the public funds, closing the Council accounts at specified dates and presenting the final statement of the accounts to the Council.
11. Advertising and approving tenders of the Council.
12. Assessing and re-assessing rates.
13. Monitoring weights and measures and controlling markets.
14. Caring for and organizing exhibitions in the Council.

Source: LGA/Local Government Act, 2009, p. 74

Beyond the issue of adequate revenue collection, government structures at all levels being really accountable, reliable service delivery, civil education, security, and a coordinated effort among development agencies remain currently elusive goals (Schomerus /Allen 2010). Although the development approach emphasizes the creation of strong institutions, these often lack accountability, particularly at the local level. In practice, decentralized government structures have in reality begun 'to resemble ethnic chiefdoms'. While new government structures proliferate, they are in addition to an emphasis on old governance systems, rather than replacing them or strengthening them. While new governance structures of community-based administrators are implemented half-heartedly, many aid agencies exacerbate the confusion and lack of clarity by turning to 'tribal chiefs' in their need for programming, i.e. defining channels of responsibility and funding (Schomerus/Allen 2010).

Transfers from Federal Government to the States are naturally the key source of their finance, as the collection of non-oil tax is as yet limited, as a result of the thin the tax base there. There are two sets of transfers: block grants and conditional grants. States can allocate the block grant according to their budget priorities. The block grant has been cut by nearly 39% compared to the 2011/12 austerity budget, and by just over a quarter compared to 2011. Alongside these austerity measures, there are significant reforms to the allocation of these transfers across the States. Since 2005 the block grant has been allocated equally between States, despite their different sizes and needs. A recent Report of the Inter-government Fiscal Relations Taskforce called for a more equitable formula for distributing transfers. Accordingly, 60% of the block transfer remains allocated equally to each State, but 40% is allocated on a per capita basis. The County Development Grant (CDG) will now also be allocated to each County on a per capita basis, to reflect the population the county has responsibility for delivering services to. However, poverty rates and other living standards indicators and/or the economic potential of states do not play any role in allocating block grants.

Conditional grants are provided to fund specific service delivery functions at the State and County level. They are funded from the budgets of the national line ministry responsible for that function. Conditional transfers have been affected by the austerity measures. However, conditional salary transfers have not been cut except for the Organized Forces' conditional salary transfers, which have been cut to reflect the austerity measure saying that housing allowances are reduced by 50% (MoFEP 2012: 36-38). It is not clear what the consequences of these austerity budgets will be for overall public service delivery, for socio-economic development and for infrastructure development.

5   Managing Oil Wealth and Aid Flows as a Public Finance Task

As reported above, South Sudan's revenue base is very much dependent on the oil exports. Oil exports made up 71% of its GDP in 2010 (GoSS 2011). Non-oil revenue accounted for no more than 2.4% of all public revenues in the same year.

The importance of donor funding is exemplified by the fact that for the year 2012 the donors planned to spend SSP 3.9 billion, in addition to the SSP 6.4 billion government budget expenditures - this means donor funding comes up to 37.9% of total spending. However, for the years 2007-2010, donor expenditure varied between 75% (2010) and 34% (2008) of donor commitments (MoFEP 2012: 7). Donor funds were earmarked mainly for infrastructure (21%), social and humanitarian support (18%), and health (15%; GRSS 2012).

Easily exploitable mineral resources and foreign aid are forms of rent in the terminology of economists. Rents have in common that they are available to the state at no or little cost – they create 'unearned income', at the disposal of the state and/or its agents. Such resources can play a crucial role in closing the finance gap faced by poor countries, and in particular by countries emerging from civil war. These countries face generally a huge finance need in order to rebuild infrastructure and institutions, to demobilize and reintegrate soldiers, and to invest in health and education.

Mineral resources and aid funds can directly improve the social security of the poor. They can support specifically targeted poverty reduction programs – the can fund the pro-poor provision of public services, they can help to expand the employment opportunities, they can contribute to the build-up of economic and social infrastructure, they may allow to transfer assets to the poorest to help them to improve both their skills and their income-earning abilities. In general, such rents can accelerate growth because they can support higher rates of investment and growth of the imports required to restructure the economy, to lift productivity and to sustain rising incomes.

However, at the same time, mineral resources and aid funds can trigger growth collapses, can prevent economic policy reform, and can result in increased poverty, inequality, and in declining levels of human development (the following bases on Hansohm 2009; see also Wohlmuth 2007). They may sustain repressive regimes, may feed grievances, and may lead to re-starts of civil war. This is why many call the phenomenon of high and sudden inflows of mineral rents and aid rents 'resource curses'.

Unfortunately, such negative outcomes are not only theoretical possibilities, but a likely outcome, more likely than the positive use of rents that the theory of resource-based growth also suggests, as many negative examples show. Nigeria, Iraq, Congo, and Africa's Great Lakes regions clearly illustrate 'the dramatic costs of revenue mismanagement – at the individual, regional and international levels' (Auty and Le Billon 2007: 1). Thus it is important for policy makers, non-state actors (NSA) and for international partners to fully understand the various links that lead to the resource curse, in order to design counteracting policies. Obviously, South Sudan is a case in point.

It is useful to distinguish two aspects, an economic and a political resource curse (Morrison 2007). The first one refers to the economic impacts. These can be explained in economic terms and are a matter of economic management, i.e. are resolvable technically. The political curse, however, is a matter of political economy and refers to the underlying incentives of the state and its executives. As such, they cannot be solved by technocrats, but need the involvements of non-state actors (NSA), lobbying in the interest of the disadvantaged groups, possibly supported by external actors like international NGOs. Experience has shown so far, unfortunately, only exceptional cases of success in overcoming the resource curse (Morrison 2007). The quality of governance in a country is a key determinant of the chances to overcome the resource curse.

Economically, the inflow of sizeable mineral and aid rents often leads to currency appreciations. Distortions in the economy make the traditional tradable sectors (agriculture and industry) uncompetitive and in effect such products become marginalized in the export basket, leading the economy away from its underlying comparative advantage ('Dutch disease'). High resource income is also likely to result in inflationary pressures.

These impacts are all the more serious, the higher and the more sudden they are, as developing countries, especially in Sub-Saharan Africa, have typically highly inflexible economies. The importance of mineral and aid rents depends not only on the extent of a country's dependence on commodity revenues, but also on the price and the price volatility of those commodities, the level of foreign aid, and the degree of government interventions to adjust prices (typically fixing artificially high exchange rates).

Oil and aid rents have in common that they are not safely predictable. They are subject to the risks of unexpected declines. Despite promises, donor funding is subject to yearly changes according to home policies in donor countries. Resource rents are subject to changes in prices that are internationally set and have been largely unpredictable, in particular for oil. Furthermore, they are based on declining natural resources, and so increasingly these resources have to be replaced by non-oil production and by non-oil exports. As reported above, unless new oil is found, South Sudan's peak of production has already passed its peak.

For these reasons, it is advisable to set aside considerable resource revenues in order to be able to continue planned spending in case of reduced revenue. Boom-bust cycles in public spending are very costly. While countries only grow a little more rapidly when spending booms, sudden reductions are much more costly. A counter-cyclical fiscal policy is essential to achieve a stable platform for growth. It is estimated that the fiscal buffer to smooth spending against market shocks should at least be on the order of 12 months of public earnings (Gelb 2012).

This is well recognized by GRSS: 'To achieve macroeconomic stability and long-run fiscal sustainability, it is important that a considerable proportion of our oil revenue should be put aside in savings' (GRSS 2011: 30). Most important for resource producers is the establishment of strong institutions of accountability. Unfortunately, experience has shown that to create the institutions to manage public spending properly takes time. In fact, recent years in South Sudan have shown that booms of oil revenue were used to allow high extra-budgetary spending (while even then some budgeted spending items could not be executed), rather than saving for years with lower resource prices and incomes. It is reported that wages and salaries and defense and security expenditures were higher than planned (GRSS 2012). As a result, the country was ill-prepared for the economic shock when oil production was stopped in January 2012.

One way to conceptualize longer-term fiscal sustainability for the time when reserves are exhausted is provided by the "permanent income" model. This model envisages a rate of saving of the oil revenues in order to achieve long-term sustainability of public expenditure flows. For South Sudan this would mean permanently spending half or less of the spending levels in 2010 and 2011 and building-up very large savings. It can be argued that for capital scarce economies returns may be higher on domestic investments than on those abroad. However, in post-conflict economies such as South Sudan the quality of spending is low. Poor capacity, corruption and politicization of spending result in unproductive and poorly managed spending programs. The lesson is clear that South Sudan should not scale up domestic investments before investing in the ability to manage them well (Gelb 2012). Public spending also needs to be reoriented from wages and salaries to development expenditures. Arguably rents in the hands of a government lacking accountability may be worse than having no rents at all to distribute.

Economic diversification is vital, not only to diversify revenues, to become increasingly independent from one source of revenue, to be better able to smoothen spending levels, but also to create employment. It is, however, sobering that only a few resource exporters have actually managed to develop strong alternative income sectors. This diversification also requires very good macroeconomic management to limit the booms and busts that inhibit private investment in trade sectors; as well a flexible exchange rate management is needed by devaluing the currency when needed for reaching international competitiveness. Most importantly, such a strategy requires a strong focus on public investments that bring down costs for the non-oil trade sectors and also the build-up of human capital to raise productivity. In addition, an open entry policy for new businesses is requested. This makes a good and strong relationship between government and the private sector so important. South Sudan has made a start with the establishment of the South Sudan Business Forum (SSBF).

Donor funds are the second source of rent for South Sudan. Both GoSS and donors have been conscious of the many problems of donor funding, namely the limited predictability, the lack of coordination with government and among each other - leading to overlaps, contradictions, and high administration costs (in the face of severe limitations of exactly these factors). As early as 2006 the GoSS has formulated an aid strategy (MoFEP 2006).

The strategy was based on six core principles: alignment, coordination, harmonization, predictability, mutual accountability, and institutional development. Of these principles, the coordination principle was most successfully implemented: the GoSS has established a credible, government-led approach to aid coordination that was tied to the budget planning process. The strategy was based on the following coordination structures:

1. Quarterly Donor Forum for systematic government-donor dialogue on fiscal, planning and aid coordination issues;
2. Inter-Ministerial Appraisal Committee for evaluation of projects prior to getting their signature by the MoFEP;
3. Donor participation in GoSS's Budget Sector Working Groups (BSWGs)

Coordination of aid with the budget planning process led to a rapid improvement in reporting on aid projections. However, its success remained constrained by lack of information on expenditure, a fact which limited discussions on aid effectiveness (Davies et al. 2011: 1). Alignment principle was weaker in fulfillment, as donors continued to develop projects bilaterally with NGOs. The record of the harmonization principle was extremely mixed, as the majority of aid volumes continued to be channeled bilaterally with high levels of project proliferation. The very weak government implementation capacity limited also the donors' use of government systems. Mutual accountability was hindered by limited reporting on real outcomes. Predictability was undermined by a donor practice of planning in annual cycles. On the whole, the "aid system" did not work well.

The MoFEP has introduced an Aid Information Management System (AIMS) to improve aid information and coordination. It is based upon the Aid Management Platform (AMP), which is supplied and supported by Development Gateway and which was installed in Juba in mid-2010. The AIMS was rolled out to development partners in December 2011 and is to receive data submissions from partners directly from January 2012 onwards. Roll out to government line agencies also commenced in 2012. Data input to the AIMS is the responsibility of all development partners, starting with the planning process for FY 2012/13 (due to start in January 2012).

Most aid to South Sudan is delivered bilaterally, that is coming directly from a donor agency to South Sudan. In 2010, 44% of aid expenditure was delivered bilaterally. In 2010, 25% of the funds were delivered through pooled funding mechanisms. There are five pooled funding mechanisms: Multi-Donor Trust Fund, Basic Services Fund, Capacity Building Trust Fund, Sudan Recovery Fund, and Common Humanitarian Fund. No aid was provided to South Sudan in the form of budget support, at the central or sector level.

A review maintains that strong coordination processes have established a degree of government hegemony and an improved information sharing. However, contrary to initial expectations, this did not translate into increased aid harmonization. The latter principle can realistically only be a medium-term objective, which is not just achieved through the establishment of harmonization instruments. Several other measures are required simultaneously: strengthening government implementation capacity; designing harmonization instruments that can engage NGOs to deliver services while government capacity is being built up; and designing and securing donor commitment. According to the review, 'significant onus remains on donors to improve the results-focus and predictability' (Davies et al. 2011: 5).

As a main success of South Sudan's 2006 aid strategy can be regarded the ability to quickly establish a simple set of coordination mechanisms, and enabling the government to take an early leadership over aid management. Most notable is the achievement of a pragmatic government-led approach to budget planning - including also donors and NGOs (Travis and French 2012). The Aid Strategy aims to establish a system for Aid Reporting and Evaluation which is transparent, participatory, and pays adequate attention to the evaluation of outcomes. However, there is still a wide gap from aims to practice.

Evaluations of aid in South Sudan came to the conclusion that aid was largely regarded as a technical exercise, rather than as a political process which it in fact is. 'A sophisticated and nuanced analysis of power relations, causes of vulnerability, and drivers of conflict and resilience indicators was largely missing from the design and execution of many aid programs.' Also, it was recognized that an 'over-use of 'good practice', was used, 'particularly with respect to ownership and harmonization, at the expense of field knowledge and engagement that was required (and welcomed) from 2005 onwards' (Bennett et al. 2010).

By 2009 there were increasing government concerns on behavioral problems on part of its international cooperation partners: lack of alignment (only 45% of development assistance in 2009, 51% by end of 2010 were involving government institutions in the sense of committing aid projects to government priorities), persistent lack of aid predictability, project proliferation (by 2010 24% of aid was channeled through pooled mechanisms and large scale programs). Between 2006 and 2011 no donor funds were provided through government fiduciary systems. Donors continued to prefer parallel mechanisms. Obviously, the development partners were not at all convinced of the governance mechanisms and the respective governance reforms.

There were also procedural problems: the Inter-Ministerial Appraisal Committee (IMAC) was unable to cope with the increasing project proliferation. IMAC's mandate is to review each project in excess of $1 million to ensure that it is in line with aid strategy principles. This concerns more than 400 projects. The established Quarterly GoSS Donor Forum struggled to obtain the political support required to have a meaningful discussion about priorities. Instead of a political forum it became a more technical body hampering macro level allocation.

Also a recent comprehensive review of donor involvement in South Sudan concluded that despite the formal level of coordination with the Budget Sector Working Groups (BSWGs) to support budget planning, there is no effective formal donor agreement in the country to coordinate aid intentions with government priorities. Instead, there is a wide range of informal and broad donor forums. Some of these groups focused on specific sectors with an ad hoc participation by Government. Although there are some positive examples, in overall terms the level of donor and aid coordination is weak (OECD 2011: 14). This is serious, because due to its low institutional, human and organizational capacity, the GoSS had to rely to a high degree on donor support and on high levels of technical cooperation - all of these outside of government systems. There are over 100 donor-established parallel project implementation units, again due largely to lack of capacity. The ability of both government and its cooperation partner to prioritize and to sequence has to be regarded as low (OECD 2011: 15).

Lack of improvements in budget execution and in public procurement resulted in donors avoiding to use the government systems altogether. All aid was off-budget, resulting in a lack of government ownership of development assistance. It was recognized that a revised strategy would need to be more focused on specific issues concerning fragile states and to emphasize the need to build state development capacity.

Thus, a revised aid strategy was formulated in 2011. Learning from experience, it emphasizes the special situation and the needs of a New Deal for Engagement in Fragile States, developed by the g7+, an independent and autonomous forum of fragile and conflict-affected countries to form one collective voice of which South Sudan is a member. The revised strategy sets out to be more strategic in identifying the linkages between aid delivery and institutional development and in setting out a process of transition from humanitarian to development aid.

The GRSS has begun to work with donors on designing a New Deal Compact, which outlines mutual commitment to South Sudan's development, based on these goals (GRSS 2012: 13). The Government will develop a National Aid Financing Plan, which will set out the key funding gaps for the SSDP and from this it will derive priorities for aid funding, levels of funding required and preferred ways of delivering that aid. A key input into this will be the South Sudan Development Initiative, which is costing priority programs in the SSDP (MoFEP 2012: 40).

Overall, the issues of managing mineral and aid rents are so far not yet covered adequately in the context of public finance management mechanisms.

6 Conclusions and Policy Recommendations

This contribution has looked at the success of state building and fiscal management reforms in South Sudan. The key conclusion is that the state of governance in general and macroeconomic policy making and fiscal management in particular show that organizations, laws and regulations alone do not suffice to change policy making and public management. The present institutional underpinning and the capacities are not commensurate with the sophisticated and demanding nature of the mainly externally introduced wholesale reforms. Instead, these reforms create a wide imbalance between the formation of organizations and their institutional grounding.

The results suggest that instead of wholesale reforms prioritization and sequencing of reforms would be beneficial. Most importantly, such reasoning should be based on the local context. There are limits to the use of international 'best practice', and each of these practices have been successful only in a specific local context. For most of the economic policy reforms, 'best practices' cannot be applied in a general, non-contextual manner.

A major way to improve the quality of macroeconomic policy formation and of a responsible, long term oriented and sustainable fiscal management process will be the creation of higher transparency and the more systematic involvement of the major stakeholders - the private sector, professionals, and the wider civil society. These are partly vocal, but at an infant stage and largely limited to the capital city of Juba.

Supporting this process will need a strengthening of the research function, both in government, but also outside in academic institutions and in independent think tanks. These should underpin the policy making process. Unfortunately, the importance of higher education for both building a home grown educated labor force and a domestic research capability is currently not on focus of either the GRSS or its international partners, as emphasis is mainly on primary education.

A key bottleneck of economic policy reform in South Sudan is the unresolved conflict between Sudan and South Sudan about oil, border demarcation, security, the status of Abyei, and other outstanding issues. Despite intensive pressure and involvement by external actors as the African Union (AU), IGAD and the US government, these issues have not been resolved. This shows that the stalemate between the two sides during the interim period, as explained by Elbadawi, Milante and Pischedda (2008), can be considered as a game where excessive militarization and brinkmanship is a rational response for both actors, neither of which can credibly commit to lower levels of military spending. These credibility issues could be resolved by democratization, increased transparency, reduction of information asymmetry, and efforts of increased economic cooperation. However, the situation has rather deteriorated after independence of South Sudan in July 2011 and the stop of oil production in the South in January 2012. Also the nine September 2012 agreements between the two states have not changed the picture.

References

Addison, T., Chowdhury, A. R. and Mansoob Murshed, S. (2004): The fiscal dimensions of conflict and reconstruction, in: Tony Addison and Alan Roe, 2004, Eds., Fiscal policy for development, Basingstoke: Palgrave and UNU-WIDER, pp. 260-273

Addison, T., and Roe, A. (2004): Fiscal policy for development, Basingstoke: Palgrave and UNU-WIDER

Andrews, M. (2010) How Far Have Public Financial Management Reforms Come in Africa?, Lessons from recent PEFA data and World Bank Public Financial Management Performance Reports, with an additional focus on the potential role of civil society, Harvard Kennedy School, May, RWP10-018

Auty, R. and Le Billon, P. (2007): Managing revenues from natural resources and aid, In: Brown, O., Moreno, S.P and Winkler, S. (eds.) /Trade and Security: An

Agenda for Peace and Development/, London: Earthscan, pp. 158-89

Bennett, J. S., et al. (2010): Aiding the peace. A Multi-donor Evaluation of Support to Conflict Prevention and Peace-building Activities in Southern Sudan 2005–2010, Final Report

Collier, P. (2003): Breaking the conflict trap. Civil war and development policy, World Bank and Oxford University Press

Davies, F. (2009): Contracting out core government functions and services in Southern Sudan, Discussion Paper for AfDB/PDG Conference on contracting out core government functions and services in post-conflict and fragile situations, Tunis, 8-9 June

Davies, F., and Smith, G. (2010): Planning and budgeting in Southern Sudan: starting from scratch, Lessons for planning and budgeting systems in post-conflict settings, ODI Briefing Paper, October, 4 pp.

Davies, F., Smith, G., and Williamson, T. (2011): Coordinating post-conflict aid in Southern Sudan. Background Note, ODI, September

Elbadawi, I., Milante, G., and Pischedda, C. (2008): Referendum, response and consequences for Sudan. The game between Juba and Khartoum, Washington: World Bank Policy Research Working Paper 4684, July

Fjeldstad, O.-H., Hansohm, D., Isaksen, J., Nhaimwaka, E. (2004): Budgetary processes and economic governance in Southern and Eastern Africa. Literature review, Windhoek: NEPRU Working Paper 95, September

Fozzard, A., and Foster, M. (2004): Changing approaches to public expenditure management in low-income aid-dependent countries, in: Tony Addison and Alan Roe, eds., 2004, op. cit.

GoSS/Government of Southern Sudan (GoSS; 2011): Public Finance Management Assessment. Based on the Public Expenditure Financial Accountability Framework (PEFA), Draft report, 19 June

Freedom House (2012): http://www.freedomhouse.org/country/south-sudan, accessed on 17. November 2012

Fund for Peace (2012): Failed States Index 2012, accessed from www.fundforpeace.org

Gelb, A. (2012): Managing oil rents from scarcity to abundance, Policy note, Juba, International Growth Centre, Country Office Juba, in Republic of South Sudan, as an Output from the International Growth Center/IGC workshop "From crisis to opportunity"

GoSS/Government of Southern Sudan (GoSS; 2011): 2011 budget speech, presented to the South Sudan Legislative Assembly (SSLA) by David Deng Athorbei, Minister of Finance & Economic Planning January

GRSS/Government of the Republic of South Sudan (GRSS; 2011): South Sudan Development Plan 2011-2013, Juba, in August 2011

GRSS/Government of the Republic of South Sudan (GRSS; 2012): 2012-13 budget speech, presented to the National Legislative Assembly (NLA) by Kosti Manibe Ngai, Minister of Finance & Economic Planning, June 2012

Hansohm, D. (2009): Oil and foreign aid: Chances for pro-poor development in Sudan?, in: Karl Wohlmuth et al. (Eds.), African development perspectives yearbook Vol. XIV: New growth and poverty alleviation strategies for Africa – institutional and local perspectives, Lit, pp.105-146

JAM/Joint Assessment Mission (JAM; 2005): Framework for sustained peace, development and poverty eradication, World Bank and United Nations, 18 March

MoFEP/Ministry of Finance and Economic Planning (MoFEP; 2006): Government of Southern Sudan aid strategy 2006-2010, Juba: Government of Southern Sudan

MoFEP/Ministry of Finance and Economic Planning (MoFEP; 2012): National Budget Plan for the Financial Year 2012/13, Juba

Morrison, K. M. (2007): Natural resources, aid, and democratization: a best-case scenario, in: Public Choice, 131: pp. 365-386

OEA/Office of the Economic Advisor to the President (OEA; 2012): Economic Questions and Answers. A Review of Key Economic Issues in South Sudan, Juba, 31st July

OECD/Organization and Economic Cooperation and Development (OECD; 2011): 2011 report on international engagement in fragile states. Republic of South Sudan, OECD Publishing

OPM/Oxford Policy Management (OPM; 2010): Medium Term Expenditure Frameworks – panacea or dangerous distraction?, OPM Review, Paper 2, May

Parry, M. (2004): Why Government IFMS procurements so often get it wrong, 27.9., http://www.michaelparry.com/wp-content/uploads/How-to-stop-IFMS-going-wrong.pdf

Pritchett, L., Woolcock, M., Andrews, M. (2012): Looking like a state: Techniques of persistent failure in state capability for implementation, Center for International Development at Harvard University Working Paper 239, June

Pritchett, L. (2012): South Sudan as a disruptive innovator in state building, 10 December, presentation to International Crisis Group/ICG seminar in Juba

Reuters (2012): Tricky oil puzzle as South Sudan flexes muscle over China, in: Business Daily, Nairobi, 16-17 November

Rolandsen, O. H. (2005): Guerilla government. Political changes in the Southern Sudan during the 1990s, Nordiska Afrikainstitutet

Schomerus, M. and Allen, T. (2010): Southern Sudan at odds with itself: Dynamics of conflict and predicaments of peace, London School of Economics and Political Science, Development Studies Institute, commissioned by PACT Sudan through Department for International Development/DfID, London, UK

Stone, L. (2011): Failures and opportunities. Rethinking Disarmament, Demobilization and Reconstruction/DDR in South Sudan, Small Arms Survey, Human Security Baseline Assessment, Sudan Issues Brief No. 17, May

SSCCSE/Southern Sudan Centre for Census, Statistics and Evaluation (SSCCSE; 2011): Statistical Yearbook for Southern Sudan, Juba: SSCCSE

SSNAC/South Sudan National Audit Chamber (SSNAC; 2012a): Financial Audit Report for the year ended 31st December 2007 to the President and the National Legislative Assembly, Juba

SSNAC/South Sudan National Audit Chamber (SSNAC; 2012b): Financial Audit Report for the year ended 31st December 2008 to the President and the National Legislative Assembly, Juba

SSNBS/South Sudan National Bureau of Statistics (SSNBS; 2012): South Sudan Statistical Yearbook 2011, Juba: SSNBS

Sudan Tribune (2011): South Sudan president replaces head of anti-corruption commission, 11. November

Travis, N., and French, B. (2012): South Sudan: domestic aid strategy and the New Deal for Engagement in Fragile States, ODI Budget Strengthening Initiative, Country Learning Notes, July, 6 pp.

Wohlmuth, K. (2007): Abundance of natural resources and vulnerability to crises, conflicts and disasters – an introduction, in: Karl Wohlmuth et al., African Development Perspectives Yearbook, Volume 12, Africa - Commodity Dependence, Resource Curse And Export Diversification, LIT Publishers, Münster/Hamburg/Berlin, 3-48

World Bank (1998): Public expenditure management handbook, Washington DC: World Bank

World Bank (2011): South Sudan procurement assessment report, draft, August

World Bank (2012a): Doing business Indicators, www.doingbusiness.org

World Bank (2012b): World Governance Indicators, www.govindicators.org, accessed on 16/11/12

Wynne, A. (2005): Public Financial Management Reforms in Developing Countries: Lessons of Experience from Ghana, Tanzania and Uganda, ACBF Working Paper 7, Harare

Wynne, A. (2010): What public financial management reforms actually work?, 17. September, http://publicfinanceafrica.blogspot.co.uk/2010_09_01_archive.html

Unit 2: Macroeconomic Policy Formation in West Africa

Macroeconomic Policy Formation in West Africa and the Second Monetary Zone: An Introduction

Osmund Osinachi Uzor[1] and Karl Wohlmuth[2]

1 The Issues

The West Africa region has not been able to raise growth to the level necessary to achieve the Millennium Development Goals (MDGs). The central issue in the economic development policy circles has been the role of macroeconomic policies in accelerating and sustaining growth. The macroeconomic policy framework usually consists of policy objectives, targets and instruments that guide policy implementation (IMF, 2008). The main objective of monetary policy is to provide for price stability but in the context of economic growth and employment generation. The main objective of exchange rate policy is to provide a competitive real exchange rate that allows for productive sector development. The main objective of fiscal policy is the provision of funds in a medium-term context for the regular supply of basic services and for public investment to allow for sustainable growth. Improvement in the macroeconomic policies can be achieved through an improved macroeconomic management, and for this to happen the key economic policy institutions need upgrading and a better coordination (ECA, 2009). Macroeconomic instability impacts adversely on those in lower income brackets; therefore macroeconomic stability is necessary as a complement to poverty reduction policies. For example, inflation often places a heavy burden on the poor because price jumps always erode the income of the poor and the provision of the assets for production more than of the non-poor (Ames et al., 2001). Also large budget deficits and uncompetitive exchange rates have a heavy toll on the poor as basic services are cut and unemployment follows from the decline of tradable goods production.

---

[1] Dr. O. O. Uzor, Research Associate, IWIM, University of Bremen
[2] Karl Wohlmuth, Economics Professor, University of Bremen, Faculty of Economics and Business Studies, Bremen, Germany

The concern of this Unit is macroeconomic policy formation in West Africa. The contributors focused their analyses on the economic policy formulation and management, the socio-economic impact of macroeconomic policies, and the sectoral impact of macroeconomic policies. However, regional integration as a way to harmonize macroeconomic policies in West Africa is also discussed. The feasibility of a Second Monetary Union in the region, including countries like Nigeria, Ghana and Sierra Leone, is outlined; it is asked how such a project can be advanced and if it would be possible to merge such a zone with the CFA Franc Zone to reach ultimately an ECO-WAS-wide Monetary Zone.

West Africa is a region in sub-Saharan Africa (SSA) with a complex political and cultural environment. The region is diverse in religion, ethnicity, but also in development policies and economic policies pursued. The borders and linguistic divided introduced during the colonial era provided for small markets and barriers to trade and cooperate. The region has abundant human and natural resources. Nigeria accounts for about 50 per cent of the regional population with about 68 per cent of the regional GDP (AfDB, 2011). Despite the inherent complexities, the movement of people and the intensity of intra-regional trade among the West African states are somewhat higher compared to other regions of Africa, but still the levels of economic interaction are too low because of so many barriers to interact. Some progress is however observable and has to do with the increasing role of common economic policies. This is partly a result of policies adopted and implemented by the community after the formation of the Economic Community of West African States (ECOWAS) in 1975. The aims of the ECOWAS as outlined in the ECOWAS statutes document are to promote economic co-operation and regional integration (AfDB, 2011). However, between 1975 and the early 2000s the region experienced a turbulent political period. The political instability pushed most countries in the region to the brick of economic stagnation, a situation associated with unsuccessful social policy programs (Zouhon-Bi and Nielsen, 2007).

In recent times, selected macro-economic indicators revealed a more favourable picture for the West Africa region, with the lowest real GDP growth rate of 4.00 per cent in 2000 and the highest growth rate of 13.3 per cent in 2002. In general, the real GDP growth rate in the region has remained above 5.00 per cent between 2003 and 2010 (AfDB, 2011). The average Gross National Savings (GNS) and the Gross Capital Formation (GCF) rates (expressed as a percentage of the GDP in the region) were in 2000 and in 2009 25.8 per cent and 22.2 per cent respectively. The GDP per capita persistently increased from US$351 in 2000 to US$1,027 in 2008 but fell to US$887 in 2009, reflecting the negative impact of the global financial crisis (GFC) of 2008/2009 in the region (AfDB, 2012).

The highest inflation rate in the region was 14.4 per cent in 2001 and the lowest one was 5.3 per cent in 2007. The inflation rate has gradually declined from a double digit level of 11.2 % in 2008 to a single digit level of 9.2 % in 2011. The current account balance expressed as percentage of the regional GDP explains the contribution of the external sector to the performance of the economy. Between the years 2000 and 2010 the contribution of the external sector to the regional GDP was highest in 2006, with a positive contribution of 15.7 %. The worst contribution of the external sector to regional GDP was in the year 2002 with a negative one of 8.1%[3]. The debt service as a percentage of the export in the region has declined rapidly from 28.5 per cent in 2008 to 4.3 per cent in 2010 (AfDB, 2011). However, the situation with regard of poverty is still serious. In general, about 60 per cent of the population still lives on less than one US dollar a day (AfDB, 2011, p. 3).

The oil crises and the recent global financial crisis (GFC) have provided the framework for understanding the damaging impacts of external shocks; in such periods macroeconomic instability and its contagious effects on living standards have increased. This negative impact could be largely in the form of a decline of economic activity, cost-pull inflation, increasing volatility in exchange rates and financial market assets, unsustainable budget deficits, and rising domestic and external debt levels. However, during the recent global economic crisis (GFC) Africa has managed the external shocks quite well. Prior policy reforms in Africa have contributed to a greater resilience (see Alabi et al. 2011). However, the recent GFC has endangered progress made towards achieving the MDGs especially in West Africa. Many countries in West Africa have engaged in economic reforms over the last three decades, and some fruits of these reforms are visible in terms of economic growth. However, growth has yet to become more inclusive. Despite the implementation of structural adjustment programmes and economic reform programmes, many countries in the region continue to experience a declining per capita agricultural production. The consequence is an increase of food imports and of food prices. Real food prices in some West African countries grew as much as 7 per cent per year over the 1980-1998 periods (Kargbo, 2005). Hence, economic reform is not a guarantee for macroeconomic stability and inclusive growth. A new macroeconomic policy framework is requested that

---

[3] The major imports of the West Africa region (ECOWAS) between 2000 and 2009 are coming from the following regions: USA 6.0%, Japan 2.1%, India 2.5%, EU 35.7%, China 11.7%, the other African Countries 13.9% and Rest of the World 11.3%. The major exports of the region are to the following regions: USA 28.7%, Brazil 5.2%, China 0.1%, EU 29.3%, the other African Countries 13.7% and the Rest of the World 22.2 % (ECA, 2012, pp. 19-21).

is supportive of inclusive growth, private sector development, employment, value addition, economic transformation and sustainable development.

In the 2000s, inflation averaged around 6-8% per annum in most African countries. The currency in the CFA Franc Zone countries in West Africa is tied to the Euro. As a result, the countries often experienced lower inflation than other African countries and regions (Heady and Fan, 2008). However, inflation in these countries has eroded the competitiveness in exports because of the effects on the real exchange rate. The production sectors, especially agriculture production, were hit, with consequences for employment and living standards. Other countries with no currency peg suffer from exchange rate volatility and its impact on inflation. Exchange rate stability and stable inflation are important to fight food price increases. Food price increases add to vulnerability as a result of already high levels of poverty and hunger. A substantial share of food that is consumed is imported in West African and Central African countries. The negative impact of food price increases for the consumers is however larger than the positive impact for net sellers of locally produced foods. In general, the impact of higher food prices has led to additional persons falling into poverty (Wodon et al., 2008). The implication of all this is that macroeconomic policies and production sector policies matter in preserving basic food and basic services. Exchange rates stability plays an important role in the stability of imported food prices, although many other policies are needed to increase food production and food supplies.

Designing a suitable medium-term fiscal framework that fosters a sustainable delivery of better public services and infrastructure is of great importance; at the same time maintaining a credible commitment to fiscal prudence is also part of the challenges that confronts many policymakers. Most countries in West Africa depend on external aid. Scaling up aid and the debt relief has created more fiscal space for expenditure programs for long-term growth and reduction of poverty rates. However, the positive impact of the increasing aid und debt relief depends on the fiscal discipline and the ultimate direction of the funds. As with oil revenue windfalls, a medium-term framework for expenditures is needed to avoid boom and bust events. For example, the WAEMU Commission has adopted Fiscal Rules to reconcile economic policies in the currency union with scaled-up aid (IMF, 2006).

Another challenge is that many countries in West Africa are aspiring for regional integration, but have often competing and conflicting macroeconomic policies. Because of these conflicting and overlapping policies amongst themselves there is lack of complementation and harmonisation of such policies. The consequence is that additional administrative burdens and complexities prevent macroeconomic policy harmonisation and coordination. This also leads to a wasteful duplication of policy interventions in view of constrained resources (Maruping, 2005). In general, political commitment and the will to implement coordinated and integrated programmes and/or agreed upon macroeconomic convergence criteria on a timely basis is lacking in the region. This has been partly due to a lack of broad internal consultations on the part of the member countries. In some cases, the socio-economic and political dynamics within the member states often mitigates against the implementation of regionally agreed programmes, especially where socio-economic sacrifices are concerned (Maruping, 2005).

The impact of socio-economic policy divergence and conflict within and between the member states is the persistent inconsistency or incoherence at the macroeconomic level. This has been a source of the problems for the "internalisation" of the regional integration agenda into national programmes, so that implementation fails. Inconsistencies in implementation and information have also made it impossible for policymakers to integrate policies regionally, for example by coordinating policies to target low inflation and fiscal discipline. Limited national and regional human capacities have resulted in the lack of mechanisms and resources for effective planning, coordination, implementation, monitoring and the continuous adjustment of programmes in West African regional integration programmes (Maruping, 2005). However, in recent years some progress was achieved and some speeding up of regional integration took place, but more so with regard of monetary criteria and less so in structural characteristics. The progress with WAMZ (West African Monetary Zone) and in bridging with WAEMU towards an ECOWAS currency union is an example (see on the convergence trends WAMA 2009, 2010). However, structural divergence between these member countries is still the problem.

Given the macroeconomic policy environment in Africa, Obinyeluaku and Viegi (2009) argue that a monetary union alone cannot guarantee fiscal discipline. Even when there is - at the regional level - an agency of restraint the governments faced with a weak tax revenue base can source funds by borrowing from state-owned banks[4]. The success of a monetary union in Africa depends on an effective coordination of fiscal and monetary policies. The fiscal policy coordination in the ECOWAS zone has been a major policy instrument that helped the member states to assess and to realize the benefits of fiscal and monetary harmonisation. Theoretically, this is on the premise that macroeconomic stability plays an important role in improving the living

---

[4] The analysis by Collier (1991) on the role of an "agency of restraint" recommends for a monetary union the creation of a framework to voluntarily sign on to conservative monetary and fiscal policies. The ECOWAS approach is somewhat in this direction.

standard for the people in the Western Africa sub-region. Keita (2011, p. 1)[5] questioned "whether the combination of a monetary policy set by an independent, supranational central bank and fiscal (and other) policies controlled by national governments is conducive to both price stability and economic growth". When fiscal harmonisation complements common monetary policies, the situation may be beneficial. Beyond this, common sector and social policies may be important to speed up progress in regional integration.

2   The Contributions

This Unit covers three contributions on macroeconomic policy formation in West Africa in the context of country case studies (two for Nigeria and one for Senegal) and an analysis on the feasibility of a second monetary integration zone (WAMZ/West African Monetary Zone) beside of the CFA Zone (WAEMU/West African Economic and Monetary Union). The country case studies highlight most important aspects of Nigeria's macroeconomic policy formation - the role of public expenditure management in achieving macroeconomic policy objectives, the impact of macroeconomic strategies on sectoral development, and the framework of economic policy formulation. The country case study on Senegal gives also an outline of the development strategies since 1960 and the implications for macroeconomic policy formation in the country. Emphasis is on the macroeconomic policy space of Senegal in the context of WAEMU and on the role of national and international agents/actors in shaping these policies. The feasibility as well as the prospects of a second monetary zone (WAMZ/West African Monetary Zone) is evaluated by referring to convergence criteria and their fulfilment over time. In order to understand the framework of macroeconomic policy formulation in the West African region one Francophone country and one Anglophone country provided the basis for the analysis to get insights on the most important issues. Since macroeconomic conditions and frameworks are dynamic, the papers in the unit reflect different periods before, during and after the economic reforms of the 1980s, an era associated with Structural Adjustment Programs (SAPs).

Different approaches were adopted by the authors in providing the theoretical background. For example, the macro-model theory and the development model theory were used in analysing the role of public expenditure management in achieving macroeconomic policy objectives. Two papers focus on Nigeria's macroeconomic policy formation what is important as

---

[5] Consultancy African Intelligence (CAI) online Publication Friday, 02 December 2011, 08:10

Nigeria is a SANE (South Africa, Algeria, Nigeria, Egypt) country of great economic importance. SANE countries like Nigeria impact on their sub-region through international and intra-regional trade, regional agro-industrial value chains, stock markets and capital flows, activity of African multinational corporations and direct investment, finance infrastructure and banking, but also in security arrangements for the whole region. The country case on Senegal is rich with regard of long-term development strategies and the policy space for macroeconomic policy action because of the WAEMU provisions and the limits on fiscal space because of ECOWAS treaties on taxes and the weaknesses of Senegal's taxation system. Also the new governmental reform intentions since 2012 are covered as they have important implications on macroeconomic stability and direction of public expenditures. The perspectives of the new macroeconomic policy formation framework are discussed. The theoretical and empirical analysis on the feasibility of a second monetary integration zone for West Africa (WAMZ) is based on the agreed upon convergence criteria and complements the country case studies for Nigeria. The countries in WAMZ, like Nigeria, can learn from the experiences of the countries in WAEMU, like Senegal, and so the contrasting analyses for Nigeria and Senegal matter in this very context of ways and means to improve macroeconomic policy formation.

The paper by **A. Tajudeen** and **T. W. Abraham** on **Public Expenditure Management and Macroeconomic Policy Objectives in Nigeria: An Empirical Analysis** deals with Nigeria as a case study for analysing the role of public expenditure management in the context of macroeconomic policy formation. The paper examines the impact of public expenditure management in Nigeria on three key macroeconomic policy variables: inflation; unemployment; and economic growth. First, the authors presented a well-structured theoretical analysis of public expenditure theories – the macro-model theory and the development model theory. This is followed by an analysis of the contemporary approach to public expenditure management (PEM) as used in developed and developing countries. Keynes' general theory of employment, interest and money was used to analyse the importance of macroeconomic factors with reference to developing countries. The pros and cons of deficit financing with focus on Nigeria were narrowed to its impact on inflation, investment and economic growth.

The literature review reflected the fiscal stress of the 1980s that led to a deterioration of the balance of payments position, a widening of government deficits, a drastic reduction in the external reserve position, a decline of capacity utilisation with regard of industrial production, and a collapse of the foreign exchange system. The effectiveness of public expenditure management and the causal relationship between inflation and the fiscal deficit were also reviewed. This is followed by an analysis how fiscal policy has impacted poverty alleviation, reduction of unemployment and the reduction of income disparities.

The authors further highlighted in depth the public expenditure management (PEM) approach in Nigeria. This involves the adaptation of a medium-term revenue framework (MTRF) and of a medium-term expenditure framework (MTEF). The MTRF for Nigeria involves the use of assumptions about the crude oil price and other variables, but also the setting of targets and estimating public revenue. The MTEF is about setting aggregate expenditure limits, setting the level of fiscal deficit and determining the financing of the fiscal deficit, as well as setting expenditure limits for Ministries, Departments and Agencies (MDAs). This reminds us how public expenditure management (PEM) functions in a resource-dependent economy like Nigeria. It also reveals how fiscal policy formation can lead, if PEM does not function, to spiralling inflation, to an exposure of the economy to shocks and to the consequences of the so called "Dutch Disease" in the country.

The rest of the paper is devoted to the empirical analysis and to a discussion on the empirical results. The authors employed the Autoregressive Distributed Lag (ADL) model to estimate the current period impact and the time lag it takes for public expenditure to affect selected macroeconomic objectives. The paper helps to understand the time lag and the impacts of public recurrent expenditure and public capital expenditure on economic growth. The study reveals a paradox of increasing capital expenditure, increasing economic growth and yet rising unemployment that is inconsistent with the defined expectation. Despite an increase in public expenditure that would have spurred economic growth and subsequently would have reduced unemployment, the opposite is the case in Nigeria. So much more is needed than focussing on growth and increasing public expenditures; especially important is a continuation of structural transformation. The economic growth and the public expenditures in Nigeria depend on increases in oil revenues. The increase in oil revenues is a function of the volume of crude oil produced and the price in the international market. Hence, the authors warned that a decline in the price of crude oil or a sudden cut in crude oil demand from major importers would result in macroeconomic instability in Nigeria.

The paper further reminds us of the relevance of an effective coordination of public expenditure policies and public revenue policies in the public expenditure management (PEM). The authors argue that public expenditure management (PEM) entails coordinating public expenditure and public revenue in a manner that would enhance sustainable economic growth. To reduce costs and waste of public funds, the paper reminds the policymakers about the need to understand the impact and the response lag of macroeconomic variables to public expenditure. They further argue that the diversification of the economy should be central in public expenditure policy (in public investment policy) in order to improve the performance of the non-oil sector.

The paper by **M. A. Iyoha, P. A. Adamu** and **D. E. Oriakhi** on **The Impact of Macroeconomic Policy Strategies on Sectoral Developments in Nigeria** considers the impact of macroeconomic strategies on the sectoral development in Nigeria from 1990 to 2010. A comparative approach was employed by breaking down the period of twenty years with regard of the two different governance regimes prevailing. In other words, macroeconomic policies during military dictatorship governance of 1990 to 1999 were compared with the period of democratically elected political governance of 1999 to 2010. Comparing the macroeconomic policies of the two different governance regimes means that more specific social and economic interests are at stake and have to be analysed. In this case, it is the employment and economic growth issues that made the authors to investigate how macroeconomic policies of both regimes have impacted on sectoral development in Nigeria. The paper made a detailed analysis of monetary and fiscal policies of both regimes and relates the analyses to the impact on the sectors with focus on output of agriculture, industry, manufacturing, wholesale and retail trade as well as (other) services. So the paper investigates the role of fiscal, monetary and exchange rate policies for the (still blocked) structural transformation in Nigeria.

Sector-wise, the empirical study concludes that different determinants play a role. The findings of the empirical study allow it to better structure government policy interventions. The main determinants of agriculture's share in output were first, aggregate investment and second, the exchange rate. Over the years, government has increased investment in agriculture in order to boost food security. This policy had been supported in recent years by increasing subsidization of key inputs like fertilizers and by enhancing agricultural extension services. This policy should be continued, but necessarily in the frame of PEM. Exchange rate policies play a role for agriculture development; therefore the management of oil revenues and of other foreign exchange revenues matters. Government expenditure came out as a key determinant of the share of the industrial sector in total output, and broad money supply also showed up as a main determinant of the share of industry in total output. Again, PEM is an important tool for the sector to develop dynamically. This study also suggests that, if properly conceived and implemented, monetary policy can be a driver of industrial output growth in Nigeria.

The share of manufacturing in output has been falling in Nigeria mainly due to gross inadequacy of infrastructure, particularly electricity. PEM is important to address these issues. The econometric results show that the main determinants of the share of manufacturing sector in total output are broad money supply and aggregate investment. This means that monetary policy and investment policy (for private and public investment) matter. A continuous monetary policy framework and PEM are key sources of stability for the sector. Government spending and the exchange rate showed up in the empirical analysis as the key determinants of the share of services in total output. Government spending is critical in various services sub-sectors because of the developmental role played by the government in Nigeria. The openness of the Nigerian economy explains the important role played by the exchange rate. The exchange rate changes impact on importation and exportation with regard of the various services sub-sectors. The share of wholesale and retail trade in total output turned out to be determined mainly by the aggregate level of investment in the economy. Investment policies (for private and public sectors) matter in this regard.

The authors also address the issues how the manufacturing sub-sector could be promoted. The manufacturing sector is currently characterized by low capacity utilization, the dominance of sub-standard goods that cannot compete internationally, and many other deficiencies. It is therefore imperative to introduce policies (macroeconomic and sectoral policies) that aim to change these characteristics. This will increase the growth rate of the GDP and will also generate employment. The expansion of the manufacturing sector will also benefit the agriculture sector by encouraging the growth of agro-industrial enterprises which would increase the demand for agricultural raw materials. Accelerating the development of the manufacturing sector is a well-known strategy for increasing value added in production, creating employment and reducing poverty. Also technology development and innovation depend on the development of the manufacturing sector.

Given the proven effectiveness of exchange rate policy in affecting sectoral output shares in agriculture, industry, and services, the exchange rate policy is a principal tool that the government can use to bring about structural transformation in the Nigerian economy. This instrument has to be complemented by a fiscal policy which is effective in bringing about changes in the share of agriculture. Fiscal policy should be targeted in order to achieve the desired results. In the agricultural sector public expenditure and investment should be directed towards providing improved seedlings, increasing fertilizer use and expanding irrigation. Fiscal policy can also be used to enhance the availability of infrastructural facilities which will not only benefit agriculture but will also boost manufacturing production. A medium-term framework for fiscal policies is therefore needed. Monetary policy can be used to further increase the share of manufacturing and industry in output. Monetary policy can be used to increase credit to small and medium scale enterprises as a means of expanding manufacturing production. Although such policies are already practiced in Nigeria, the authors argue for a more pro-active and better coordinated macroeconomic policy framework.

The starting point of the paper by **P. Njiforti** with the title **Analysis of the Prospects for a Second Monetary Zone for West Africa** is the conceptual background of the West African Monetary Zone (WAMZ). The idea was conceived as a mechanism to strengthen and to accelerate the integration process in the Economic Community of the West African States (ECOWAS). According to the author, besides serving as a facilitating instrument for regional integration, the success story of the European Monetary Union with the establishment of the Euro currency played an important role in motivating the regional Heads of State in the quest of forming a Second Monetary Zone for West Africa (WAMZ) beside of the CFA Francs Zone (WAEMU). The theoretical assumptions of the paper are centred on the traditional Optimum Currency Area (OCA) theory of criteria for macroeconomic convergence and the Customs Union (CU) theory that focuses on regional integration by removing barriers to trade. The literature review highlights the pros and cons of macroeconomic convergence with coordination of economic policies as a mechanism to harmonise macroeconomic policies. The cons hinge on the contagion effect of macroeconomic instability, especially in a region with a high macroeconomic volatility rate[6]. The literature review reflected on the relevance of the criteria for an OCA – the openness to trade in the region, the size and structure of the economies, the degree of commodity diversification, the possibility of asymmetric shocks affecting countries in the region, the existence of forms of fiscal federalism in the region to absorb shocks, and the degree of labour mobility as determining factors in a monetary integration process. Another part of the paper focuses on the primary and secondary criteria adopted by the WAMZ countries for the monetary union to be established and to make it work. The member countries are required to comply with these criteria more and more. Careful monitoring of progress with regard of reaching these criteria is a task of common agencies and institutes. The paper also looks at the advantages of attainment of a second economic and monetary union in West Africa in terms of cost reduction and trade facilitation. However, the very low level of formal intra-trade in West Africa (although there is a lot of unrecorded informal cross-border trade) and the

---

[6] High aggregate instability is a result of large external shocks, volatile macroeconomic policies, microeconomic rigidities, and weak institutions. Volatility entails a direct welfare cost for risk-averse individuals, as well as an indirect one through its adverse effect on income growth and development (Loayza, et al., 2007).

absence of other criteria for OCA leads to doubts about the prospects of feasible macroeconomic convergence in the region. Infrastructural deficiencies, small market sizes, political and economic instability, but also ethnic, religious and cultural divide (still also between Anglophone and Francophone countries) contribute to low productivity and impede structural transformation.

To determine whether the proposed member countries will meet the convergence criteria, co-integration analysis was adopted and selected macroeconomic convergence criteria variables for the period 1985 to 2009 were used. The presence of co-integration among the macroeconomic variables would suggest that there could be a convergence tendency. This is a necessary but however not a sufficient condition for the success of a second monetary zone. The paper argues that a sufficient condition for a monetary union rests on the nature of social capital embedded in the system. In this context, political will, commitment and trust are the basic elements that support interactions. The existence of these elements tends to diffuse fear of dominance within the groups of countries, to support policy credibility and to reduce nationalistic tendencies. The existence of sufficient social capital will help the member states to find solutions to the challenges related to asymmetric shocks. For example, the establishment of a stabilisation and cooperation fund, as a buffer to temporary shocks, is an issue. The paper concludes by recognising the influence of the recent public debt and euro crisis in Europe and its impact on the political will among the member states to go ahead with the monetary union project. In addition, poor trade integration, low labour mobility, lack of coordination of fiscal policies and a poor financial sector harmonization policy have raised concerns on the formation of WAMZ by the year 2015. Also the economic and political dominance of Nigeria in the proposed monetary union is a problem and so the country has a great responsibility to go ahead with own economic reforms in the interest of WAMZ. In order to bridge WAMZ and WAEMU so as to create an ECOWAS Monetary Union and a Common Currency, the successful establishment of WAMZ is a first step. Reforms in WAEMU will be another important step.

The challenges in the formation and coordination of macroeconomic policies in Senegal are the main focus of the paper by **Diene Mbaye** with the title **Macroeconomic Policy Formation in Senegal: Challenges in Formation and Coordination**. As Senegal is a member of WAEMU, the experiences of a small country in the first monetary union of West Africa can be discussed. The argument in the paper is that policy inefficacy impacts on growth and development so that economic reforms and sustainable macroeconomic policies by a committed government are required to improve economic performance. In this context, the author investigated the policy outcome of different policy regimes in Senegalese development phases. The focus here is on the effectiveness of policy interventions. The analysis looks into the weaknesses embedded in a central planning system in achieving policy objectives. The author also highlights the coordination problems in a decentralised planning system. The analysis further reveals why a participatory planning system that involves important interest groups and civil society organizations as well as diverse opinions and strategies at national and local levels is of great relevance for Senegal. In this context, the impact of policy formulation in different regimes on improving macroeconomic policy formation, raising the level of human capital, enhancing the food security and reducing the economic and social inequalities between regions is the subject of the analysis. The issue of rural development as a means of reducing poverty was linked to enabling macroeconomic and sector policies and to policies that favour infrastructure development in Senegal. The author reminds us that external factors like changes of prices of peanuts and other crops at the world market are not the only factor that determines the rural households' purchasing power in Senegal; well-conceived economic strategies and macroeconomic policies as well as efforts in human development and provision of infrastructure contribute to an increase in rural productivity and of rural incomes.

New economic policy visions became a central theme in the African policy circles since the year 2000. In this context, the paper looks into the new economic policy vision of Senegal which seeks to embrace the regional and global development policy initiatives. According to the author, Senegal became more committed towards sustainable macroeconomic policy formation and more involved in the regional integration process. Senegal also has adopted the declaration of the Millennium Development Goals (MDGs) and works towards its realisation. Poverty Reduction Strategy Papers (PRSPs) were developed and updated. Fiscal policy harmonization in line with WAEMU and ECOWAS objectives was adopted. However, it is argued that the fiscal space was reduced by such measures so that the country has now to implement reforms of the taxation system. To link poverty reduction and growth strategies, the Poverty Reduction Strategy Papers (PRSPs) were accompanied by an Accelerated Growth Strategy (AGS). The technical support by the donors provided the necessary framework for learning, but Senegal still aims at ownership in economic policy formation. Transparency in public budget management provided the required condition for donor participation and funding, but transparency is now seen as an important precondition for sustainable growth. Recently, a new economic and social development strategy called National Strategy for Economic and Social Development (NSESD) was established in November 2012. Arguably, this is similar to Nigeria's National Economic Empowerment Development Strategy

(NEEDS) document of 2005. This suggests that economic integration processes entail not only policy harmonization but also policy learning. A detailed analysis of the economic development issues, especially in the areas of growth, productivity and wealth creation, was presented in the policy document. On the social dimension, the NSESD document focuses on human capital, social protection and sustainable development; governance, institutions, peace and security are presented as the means of stabilizing the political and economic system in Senegal. This new document should pave the way for further economic reforms towards regional integration, globalization and human development. Macroeconomic policy formation should be facilitated by a new social contract.

The paper further investigated the macroeconomic performance in Senegal by analysing in detail the impact of tax reforms since 2000. It is obvious that deeper reforms are needed in order to follow sustainable fiscal policies. Sustainable fiscal policies will allow it to realise macroeconomic stability, growth and poverty reduction. Most important, sustainable fiscal policies will overcome the severe problem of the limited fiscal space. The assessment of the economic reform programs was done by linking the analysis of macroeconomic policies with designs of appropriate policies on poverty reduction. In this context, the paper investigated how the rate of inflation, the economic growth and the public budget have impacted on poverty reduction in Senegal, and what the next steps towards further economic reforms will be.

Furthermore, presents the basic framework on how macroeconomic policies are being conducted by the governments of Senegal. The monetary policies are within the domain of WAEMU's monetary policy and of the Central Bank of West African States (CBWAS) as the central policy making institution. The traditional instruments such as changes in interest rates and the refinancing of finance institutions are used by the CBWAS. The monetary policy tools, credit by CBWAS to the governments of WAEMU members and the nature of the fiscal policies are the central focus in the analysis. The improved real effective exchange rate in 2012 placed Senegal on a better competitive position relative to other partner countries. The improved real effective exchange was as result of the reduction of the inflation rate and of the nominal effective exchange rate. The author also highlighted the two different levels of formation and coordination of economic policies in Senegal. The first is at the national level where the government is better positioned to coordinate various policies and programs in the country. The second is at the supra-national level where the country has transferred some of its prerogative functions in economic policy formulation to multilateral organisations such as ECOWAS and WAEMU. As the policy space is shrinking at the national level, more action is needed at the supranational level to support the domestic economy.

3   The Strategies

This Unit highlighted the efforts, outcomes and challenges in macroeconomic policy formation in West African countries. The two case studies for Nigeria are complemented by a case study on Senegal. These studies reveal the impact of frequent economic policy changes on growth, macroeconomic stability and the socio-economic environment in the region. Dysfunctional interest groups and the absence of a developmental state are the major factors that induce instability in the regional political environment. Too often, visions and plans are not translated into action plans. Consequently, efforts in achieving long run policy targets are imperilled. Another paper discusses the establishment of a second monetary zone for West Africa. Under the present political and economic environment in the region and the challenges the region faces in economic integration processes, the paper questions the feasibility of the second monetary union in West Africa. In general, the lessons derived from the contributions are also the main challenges which the policymakers in West Africa face in their efforts to develop sound macroeconomic policies towards higher and inclusive economic growth. These lessons are:

Effective Macroeconomic Policy Formation depends on an Inclusive Development Policy and on steps towards a Developmental State:

Effective macroeconomic policy formation depends on long-term development policies which are based on visions and development plans. The country cases of Nigeria and Senegal show that both countries developed over time long-term visions and medium-term development plans in order to guide economic policies and macroeconomic policy formation. There is evidence that on the basis of development projections, visions and plans the main economic policy instruments (sector and regional policies, trade and investment policies, human development and infrastructure policies, social protection and welfare policies) and the macroeconomic policy instruments (monetary policies, exchange rate policies, and fiscal policies) can be used more effectively and better targeted. For the case of Nigeria it is shown that productive sector development can be enhanced by a certain mix of macroeconomic policy instruments. While agricultural sector development depends on a specific mix of exchange rate and fiscal policies, manufacturing sector policies as well demand enabling monetary policies so that development and innovation of the sub-sector can be financed. The particular mix of policies depends on the initial situation of the sector, on the business cycle, but also on the long-run objectives set for the sectors. For the development of services sectors exchange rate policies and fiscal policies matter. The oil exporter

Nigeria has a special obligation to plan public revenue and public expenditure in the medium to long-term. Otherwise Dutch Disease and Resource Curse effects will follow and impede the development of productive sectors. Any attempt to develop non-oil exports depends on a medium to long-term fiscal planning approach. In the long-term and medium-term priorities can be better set towards the incentives for developing non-extractive sectors. An inclusive development policy[7] is needed what means that macroeconomic policy is addressing also issues such as poverty reduction, providing for minimal social safety nets and creating employment via giving incentives for productive sectors by developing crafts, agriculture and the production of basic manufactures goods.

Macroeconomic policy formation is different in a developmental state. A developmental state is described as "a set of institutions, tools, capacities and capabilities committed to national development with a capacity to implement its articulated economic and social strategies" (UNCTAD 2011, p. 87). For Senegal a "catalytic developmental state" (see UNCTAD 2011, pp. 87-90) is of relevance - as a state giving guidance for the restructuring of the economy towards dynamic comparative and competitive advantages by promoting long-term investments and the creation of new productive capacities (UNCTAD 2011, p. 87). The development and structuring of markets has a role in this. Fiscal policy is a major tool to support this process in Senegal. For Nigeria, also institutional aspects play a role as the state is not free from capture by particular (oil revenue-based) interests. A developmental state in this sense requires some autonomy of the government machinery from specific interest groups which are capturing the executive and legislative branch of a country. Such autonomy implies that the government can act impartially towards social, economic and ethnic groups in order to allocate funds for long-term development and productive investment and for restructuring the economy so that genuine structural transformation can take place. Natural resources windfall revenues complicate the transition to a developmental state considerably. It is not so in Nigeria that all regions, all states, all ethnic groups and all social groups in rural and in urban areas benefit from government action and macroeconomic policies. A constitutional rule on the use of oil revenues for future generations and for key projects is one element of such a strategy. A new fiscal federalism working with effective instruments for reducing horizontal inequalities between regions, religious and ethnic groups is a second element of such a strategy. Both elements will help to solve conflicts in the society. In Nigeria and in Senegal a transition to devel-

---

[7] The term is used in the sense of Acemoglu 2012 when distinguishing extractive and inclusive institutions.

opmental states is feasible and will improve macroeconomic policy formation.

Reinforcement of Stakeholders' Involvement in the Macro-economic Policy Formation Processes is Imperative:

It is important to evaluate the prospects of reinforcing the Stakeholders' participation in the macroeconomic policy formation and implementation in West Africa. Since opportunities for rent-seeking are widespread and as there exist capacity gaps all over the region, an effective involvement of domestic experts, domestic research institutions and think tanks, and of local civil society groups (acting independently or in cooperation with government) will help in the formulation and implementation of macroeconomic policy. For example, civil society organisations can act as intermediaries between citizens and governments at all levels. They can assess the needs of people in urban and rural areas and can inform government for a better informed public expenditure management (PEM). In making key choices, especially about spending priorities as they affect geographical areas, economic sectors and social groups, the advice of such experts is needed. Government can assign tasks to the civil society groups to conduct detailed and analytic budgetary work. Such a bottom-up strategy to plan the budget will also enhance opportunities for local growth and development. They can also be involved with assignments to oversee whether those funds allocated to specific projects in sector development and poverty reduction programmes reach the intended beneficiaries. Targeted expenditures can best be spent by involving local civil society groups and independent experts. In democratic governance, feedbacks about the quality of services supplied by the government play an important role in the learning process.

Hence, information collected and administered by civil society groups and/or independent expert groups (and professional organizations) hired by the government is needed in the assessment of policy performance. The involvement of external economic and financial partners together with the social partners such as the NGOs, the trade unions and the employers' federations can help to improve transparency and budget credibility. The case of Senegal shows that new actors can improve macroeconomic policy formulation and execution. In federal states, like in Nigeria, such an involvement of independent organizations and experts is needed also at the level of states. Macroeconomic policy formation has to be based also on bottom-up assessment processes and evaluation procedures. Today, there is only a top-down macroeconomic policy formation process at work.

Strengthening the Democratic Process is needed for Effective Macroeconomic Policy Formation:

In Nigeria the overall economic growth was higher during the period of democratic governance as the annual rate of economic growth averaged 6.3 per cent between 2000 and 2010. This is in contrast to an average rate of growth of 0.2 per cent between 1990 and 1999 during the period of military dictatorship. However, growth in the democratic period was not inclusive enough so that participation at all levels is needed to reach out to the poor and the disadvantaged groups. Democratic participation at all levels is requested to improve macroeconomic policy formation. Democratic participation refers to such issues as voice and accountability, political stability and absence of violence, fair and transparent elections, government effectiveness, regulatory quality, control of corruption, rule of law, etc. Improvements in all these areas are needed for establishing a sound macroeconomic policy framework. Only so inclusive participation is possible. In Senegal, relative stability in the political environment has supported learning processes in management and implementation of macroeconomic policies. However, in areas such as government effectiveness and regulatory quality, large improvements are needed.

One can learn from Nigeria and Senegal that under democratic governance economic performance has been driven by economic policy reforms. To make such progress sustainable, governance has to be improved in all the mentioned areas. Wealth creation and poverty reduction are the basic development principles on the government agenda. Strengthening democratic processes is imperative and should be pursued with effective fiscal decentralization for grassroots development. Macroeconomic policy outcomes can be improved by inclusive participation in two forms. The first is through checks and balances, especially checks on the power of politicians, also at state and local levels. Civil society organizations and local citizen groups can balance the power relations in the country. The concept of checks and balances demands also that a separation of powers between executive and legislative organs helps in preventing the abuse of power by politicians. The second is through greater accountability of the politicians irrespective of religious and ethnic diversity in the society. Macroeconomic instability and ineffectiveness impose high costs on the economy and on the citizens. Strengthening the rule of law and the judicial system are also imperative for inclusive and democratic governance to work smoothly.

Public Expenditure Programming and Allocation towards Productive Investment is a Key Issue for Macroeconomic Policy Formation:

From the case study for Nigeria lessons can be derived on the importance of allocating public expenditures in a medium-term framework between sectors and between public recurrent expenditure and public capital expenditure as such decisions impact on economic growth but also on macroeconomic stability. A medium-term framework for revenues and expenditures also allows it to avoid policy failures. Such policy failures were severe in Nigeria where the windfall revenues from oil were not used for productive investment in infrastructure, agriculture and rural development, manufacturing and SMEs, services sub-sectors, strategic sectors like education and health and towards the development of non-oil sectors. Oil revenues were rather used to finance a massive expansion of the civil service. An Oil Revenue Stabilization and Equity Fund (ORSEF) was installed too late to save for future generations, to care for times of lower oil revenues, to finance strategic projects and to allocate funds to the poor people by some form of cash payments. In times of a decline of oil revenues the government had to resort to borrowing. Debt and other serious consequences (Dutch Disease and Resource Curse effects) led subsequently to macroeconomic instability and declining international competitiveness. The impact of the crude oil price volatility on the economy - due to the changing factors influencing price movements in the international market for oil - was great, requesting macroeconomic policy-making to adjust by specific tools of central bank policy, exchange rate policy and as well fiscal policy.

As development of new alternative energy sources have taken centre stage in global energy policy, volatility in oil markets will persist so that long-term adjustments are also necessary. Hence, objectives such as diversification of exports and investments in the productive sectors (agriculture, manufacturing, infrastructure services) should be central in public expenditure policy. Also the case of Senegal reveals that the state has the task to care for productive investment by a medium-term fiscal framework and by a proper balance of recurrent and capital expenditures. Channelling budget funds into productive sectors would not only promote economic growth but would also create employment and reduce poverty. The major message is that optimal public expenditure management should focus on altering the fiscal policy direction towards a medium term framework.

Meeting the Challenges of the Globalisation Trend will Strengthen Macroeconomic Policy Formation:

Globalization processes impact on macroeconomic policy formation. Trade globalization, finance globalization, global migration, technology globalization and global value chains affect macroeconomic policies of all countries. Although Africa is in some areas of globalization (finance and technology) less advanced and so less affected, economic policy and macroeconomic policy formation has to reflect these globalization trends. One response is that African countries increasingly harmonise their macroeconomic policies via regional economic and monetary cooperation so as to absorb shocks better in the region. However, also at national level responses to globalization trends have to be seen as a long term strategic measure. The recent global financial crisis is a lesson to policymakers to create policy space with regard of all policy instruments and especially fiscal space for unexpected shocks. Policy space allows it to fine-tune policy action in times of crisis. African countries with more fiscal space could manage far better the global financial crisis of 2008/2009 (Alabi et al. 2011). Macroeconomic shocks in a given country or a region (like the European Union) can have a large impact on the economies of other countries or regions. International economic integration proceeds rapidly such that global trade, migration and cross-border capital flows have risen substantially. The increasing trade and financial linkages across countries imply increasing interdependence. Hence, measures aimed at taking the advantages of global interdependences by improving the market conditions can strengthen the macroeconomic policy formation in African countries (like Nigeria and Senegal) and as well in regions and unions (WAMZ and WAEMU and ECOWAS as examples).

Macroeconomic Policies in SANE countries like Nigeria impact on Macroeconomic Policy Formation in the Whole Sub-region:

Macroeconomic policies of Nigeria have an important guiding role for the WAMZ and ECOWAS countries. SANE (South Africa, Algeria, Nigeria, Egypt) countries have economic and political power and affect the economy and politics of their respective sub-regions. Any progress in macroeconomic policy formation of Nigeria will have positive spill-over effects on other WAMZ and ECOWAS countries. If Nigeria's central bank policy is further strengthened - with more autonomy and independence, capacity to supervise and guide, and greater effectiveness - this will influence the central banks of the other WAMZ members and also of WAEMU. For WAMZ, this process will lead to a convergence of these institutions and ultimately will allow the transition to a joint central bank system. If Nigeria pursues a strict fiscal planning approach for the medium-term - associated with accountability and transparency - this also will spill over to the other members so that harmonisation of fiscal policies is facilitated. If Nigeria diversifies its economy successfully towards non-oil sectors this will create space for deeper regional trade integration and this process also will reduce the danger of asymmetric shocks/divergent business cycles in the WAMZ area (and in ECOWAS area too). If Nigeria starts with macroeconomic policy coordination for WAMZ by presenting its fiscal plans and its monetary policy and exchange ratite policy targets early to the other members, this will help the other members to react and to adjust. If Nigeria further reforms its financial sector and its banking systems this will definitely impact on the financial and banking systems in the other member countries.

There is evidence that political business cycles during in election years play a role in affecting the attainment of convergence criteria. Especially the larger economies in WAMZ (Nigeria and Ghana) seem to suffer from such cycles. Therefore, action is needed to minimise these dangers (Tarawalie et al. 2011). Because of fiscal dominance persisting in these countries (associated with an accommodative monetary policy), the risk of such cycles is great. For Ghana inflation and fiscal deficits as primary convergence criteria show such an influence of political business cycles. The salary mass criterion as a secondary convergence criterion may also be affected in the election year. In Nigeria as well fiscal deficits show a worsening trend in election years. But also money supply growth is higher in election years so that the inflation criterion may be affected as well. Nigeria's primary convergence criteria (inflation rate, fiscal deficit, central bank financing of the fiscal deficit, and gross external reserves) seem to be affected seriously by the political cycles, but not so much the secondary ones. However, secondary criteria such as salary mass and public investment financed from domestic sources may also be affected to some extent. Checking carefully fiscal developments in election years is therefore important for these two countries, but as well so for other WAMZ and ECOWAS countries so as to sustain integration efforts. Infrastructural programmes and other expenditure programmes should not be executed in an ad hoc way of decision-making in election times. National development plans and timetables for action and execution are important as guideposts for such expenditure programmes so that ad hoc decisions are avoided in election years. WAEMU is much more homogenous than WAMZ as only Cote d'Ivoire is economically larger than other members. So far monetary cooperation is effective in harmonization of banking legislation and payments systems, but in the future monetary cooperation should also include issues such as fiscal dominance and expenditure policies in election years.

Monetary Integration can support Macroeconomic Policy Formation if Structural Convergence is aimed at:

Since national monetary policy is no longer an economic policy tool in the monetary union framework, the challenge is how to deal with asymmetric shocks/divergent business cycles. A risk and cost sharing strategy for the member countries with high macroeconomic volatility requires political will and commitment. Nigeria as an oil exporter suffers from high volatility of public revenues and foreign exchange so that macroeconomic volatility is high. Other countries may have sources of revenue which are more stable (like tourism and remittances). If Nigeria - as a large economy and as one being driven by oil demand and price changes - enters a monetary union this can affect the common policies of the union (especially the policies of the central bank) to the detriment of the smaller and non-oil economies. If Nigeria and other countries in the union pursue vigorously a policy of supporting non-oil sectors this risk is reduced more and more.

However, also the other criteria for an optimum currency union are not fulfilled in WAMZ. The first is openness with trade integration and capital mobility in the context of flexibility of prices and wages. Openness between members and flexibility of market conditions are quite limited. Second, labour mobility in the broadest sense is not given, because of physical barriers, language barriers, cultural barriers and many institutional factors acting as barriers. Third, there is no fiscal federalism in place in the sense of automatic fiscal transfers to member states which are affected negatively by regional integration measures. Fourth, members should have similar business cycles but the WAMZ members experience different cycles (because of different primary products and other products supplied to the world market). Fifth, production diversification should exist and should be extended, what is largely not the case in WAMZ countries. Sixth, "solidarity" is another prerequisite, and it can be assumed that ECOWAS members share common objectives and that this factor is prevailing. However,

WAMZ countries have made some progress with regard of some of these criteria. The Regional Stabilization and Cooperation Fund for WAMZ countries could play an important role as a buffer to temporary shocks and adverse balance of payments situations. In general, the effectiveness of the fund depends on the political will and the commitment of the members. Contributions will be different – according to the capacity of the countries to contribute. Nevertheless, the divergence of economic conditions, economic structures and national macroeconomic policies in the WAMZ and ECOWAS regions requires that urgent attention is given to convergence of economic conditions so that the criteria for an Optimum Currency Area (OCA) can be met. Low intra-union trade, absence of fiscal federalism, low degree of labour mobility, inflexibility of prices and wages, divergent business cycles, lack of diversification and other missing criteria impede the working of the monetary union to the extent that the monetary union will not be feasible. Even in advanced economies like the EU, strengthening the Euro monetary union is an on-going challenge to policymakers. For example, the Stability and Growth Pact (SGP) has been criticised for being insufficiently flexible and for limiting the ability of governments to act during economic recession and in other times a strict application is demanded and an even more rigid framework is requested. ECOWAS countries have also started with the harmonisation of fiscal policies as a step in this direction. Arguably, each member country in the ECOWAS region has its own policy priorities, but tax policy harmonisation will facilitate economic cooperation and trade integration as well as facilitating macroeconomic policy coordination. Harmonising the fiscal and monetary policies is necessary but not sufficient for an effective monetary union. Stability in the political environment and good governance play also an important role in a monetary union. Furthermore, labour market reforms and other policies to strengthen productivity are ingredients of structural convergence. By making labour markets and product markets more flexible and more open within the region will also support the monetary and economic union.

References

Acemoglu, Daron, 2012, The world our grandchildren will inherit: the rights revolution and beyond, a manuscript for: Economic Possibilities for Our Grandchildren, edited by Ignacio Palacios-Huerta, MIT Press, forthcoming, 2012, 30 pages manuscript, Web Access: http://economics.mit.edu/files/7742

AfDB/African Development Bank, 2011, Regional Integration Strategy Paper for West Africa 2011-2015, African Development Bank, Regional Departments – West (ORWA/ORWB), Regional Integration And Trade Department (ONRI), March 2011, Tunis, Web Access: http://www.afdb.org/fileadmin/uploads/afdb/Documents/Policy-Documents/RISP%20for%20West%20Africa%20-%20REV%202.pdf

AfDB/African Development Bank, 2012, African Statistical Yearbook, African Development Bank Group Temporary Relocation Agency (TRA), Tunis/African Union Commission, Addis Ababa/Economic Commission for Africa, Addis Ababa, Web Access: http://www.afdb.org/fileadmin/uploads/afdb/Documents/Publications/African%20Statistical%20Yearbook%202012.pdf

Alabi, R., J. Alemazung, H. Bass, A. Gutowski, R. Kappel, T. Knedlik, O. Uzor, and K. Wohlmuth, 2011, African Development Perspectives Yearbook 15, Theme:

Africa and the Global Financial Crisis - Impact on Economic Reform Processes, Berlin: LIT Verlag Dr. W. Hopf

Ames, B., W. Brown, S. Devarajan, A. Izquierdo, 2001, Macroeconomic Policy and Poverty Reduction, Prepared by the International Monetary Fund and the World Bank, August 2001, Washington D.C.: IMF, Web Access: http://www.imf.org/external/pubs/ft/exrp/macropol/eng/

Collier, P., 1991, Africa's External Economic Relations1960-90, African Affairs, 90, pp. 339 – 356

ECA/Economic Commission for Africa, 2009, Macroeconomic Policies, Productive Capacity and Economic Growth in Africa, A Policy Report, Addis Ababa: UN Economic Commission for Africa, December 2009, Web Access: http://elearning.africa-devnet.org/files/macroeconomic_policies_productive_capacity_and_economic_growth_in_africa_december_2009.pdf

ECA/Economic Commission for Africa, 2012, Assessing Regional Integration in Africa V: Towards an African Continental Free Trade Area, Edited by Economic Commission for Africa/Addis Ababa: African Union/Tunis: African Development Bank, Copyright: UNECA/United Nations Economic Commission for Africa, Addis Ababa, First Printing June 2012, Web Access: http://www.uneca.org/sites/default/files/publications/aria5_print_uneca_fin_20_j uly_1.pdf

Heady, D., S. Fan, 2008, Anatomy of a Crisis, The Causes and Consequences of Surging Food Prices, IFPRI Discussion Paper 00831, December 2008, Washington D.C.: International Food Policy Research Institute, Development Strategy and Governance Division, Web Access: http://www.ifpri.org/sites/default/files/pubs/pubs/dp/ifpridp00831.pdf

IMF/International Monetary Fund, 2006, Making Fiscal Space Happen: Managing Fiscal Policy in a World of Scaled-Up Aid, IMF Working Paper, WP/06/270, December 2006, Washington D.C.: International Monetary Fund, Web Access: http://www.imf.org/external/pubs/ft/wp/2006/wp06270.pdf

IMF/International Monetary Fund, 2008, Regional Economic Outlook 2008: Sub-Saharan Africa. World Economic and financial Surveys, Washington D.C., April 2008, Web Access: http://www.imf.org/external/pubs/ft/reo/2008/afr/eng/sreo0408.pdf

Kargbo, 2005, Impacts of Monetary and Macroeconomic Factors On Food Prices in West Africa, in: Agrekon, Volume 44, No. 2, 2005, pp. 205–224, Web Access: http://ageconsearch.umn.edu/bitstream/31697/1/44020205.pdf

Keita, Y. 2011, Does fiscal policy cooperation within the ECOWAS increase GDP growth rate?, Discussion paper December 2011, Consultancy Africa Intelligence (CAI), Web Access: http://www.consultancyafrica.com/index.php?option=com_content&view=articl e&id=911:does-fiscal-policy-cooperation-within-the-ecowas-increase-gdp-growth-rate&catid=87:african-finance-a-economy&Itemid=294

Loayza, N., R. Ranciere, L. Serven, L., J. Ventura, 2007, Macroeconomic Volatility and Welfare in Developing Countries: An Introduction, in: The World Bank Economic Review, Vol. 21, No. 3, pp. 343 – 357

Maruping, M., 2005, Challenges for Regional Integration in Sub-Saharan Africa: Macroeconomic Convergence and Monetary Coordination, pp. 129-159, in: Jan Joost Teunissen and Age Akkerman (Eds.), Africa in the World Economy,The National, Regional and International Challenges, FONDAD/Forum on Debt and Development, The Hague, Web Access: http://www.fondad.org/product_books/pdf_download/5/Fondad-AfricaWorld-BookComplete.pdf

Obinyeluaku, M., N. Viegi, 2009, Can Monetary Union Alone Provide an Agency of Restraint for Africa?, Paper presented at the 14th Annual Conference on Econometric Modelling in Africa, Abuja, Nigeria, July 8-10, 2009, Web Access: http://www.africametrics.org/documents/conference09/papers/Obinyeluaku_Viegi.pdf

Tarawalie, A. B., C. R. K. Ahortor, A. Adenekan, M. Conte, 2011, Political Business Cycles And Macroeconomic Convergence In The WAMZ: The Case Of Ghana And Nigeria, in: West African Journal of Monetary and Economic Integration, Vol. 11, June 2011, No. 1, pp. 58 - 94, Web Access: http://www.wami-imao.org/ecomac/english/newreports/v11_no1/v11_no1.html

UNCTAD/United Nations Conference on Trade and Development, 2011, The Least Developed Countries Report 2011, The Potential Role of South-South Cooperation for Inclusive and Sustainable Development, New York and Geneva: United Nations 2011

WAMA/West African Monetary Agency, 2009, ECOWAS Monetary Cooperation Programme, Macroeconomic Convergence Report First Half 2009, Freetown, Sierra Leone: WAMA/West African Monetary Agency, November 2009, Web Access: http://www.amao-wama.org/fr/Publications/rep/Convergence%201%20sem%202009/MACROECONOMIC%20CONVERGENCE%20REPORT%20FIRST.pdf

WAMA/West African Monetary Agency, 2010, ECOWAS Monetary Cooperation Programmed, Annual Report 2010, Freetown, Sierra Leone: WAMA/West African Monetary Agency 2010, Web Access: http://www.amao-wama.org/fr/Publications/EMCP%20Annual%20Report%202010.pdf

Wodon, Q., C. Tsimpo, P. Backiny-Yetna, G. Joseph, F. Adoho & H. Coulombe, 2008, Potential Impact of Higher Food Prices on Poverty: Summary Estimates for a Dozen West and Central African Countries, The World Bank, Human Development Network, Development Dialogue on Values and Ethics, October 2008, Policy Research Working Paper 4745, Web Access: http://elibrary.worldbank.org/docserver/download/4745.pdf?expires=1370166872&id=id&accname=guest&checksum=27814987626E6380594E7B01570D9529

Zouhon-Bi, S. G. & L. Nielsen, 2007, ECOWAS – Fiscal Revenue Implications of the Prospective Economic Partnership Agreement with the EU, Africa Region

Working Paper Series Number 103, April 2007, Washington, D.C.: The World Bank, Web Access: http://www.worldbank.org/afr/wps/wp103.pdf

Public Expenditure Management and Macroeconomic Policy Objectives in Nigeria: An Empirical Analysis

Abbas Tajudeen[1] and Terfa Williams Abraham[2]

1 Introduction

Substantial evidence exists that, in many cases, poor fiscal management has been a major factor underlying such problems as high inflation, unemployment and weak or negative economic growth in less developed economies (IMF, 2008). For a developing country like Nigeria, the role of public expenditure management to her development process cannot be overemphasized since poor public expenditure management could have serious consequences for its economy (Ekpo, 2008; Garba, 2008). After 50 years of Independence and endowed with abundant natural resources, Nigeria still experiences huge problems of unemployment, inflation and weak or volatile economic growth. As an emerging economy that seeks to be ranked among the world's 20 most powerful economies by 2020, the need for public expenditure management is one that is of great importance to Nigeria.

Amidst the need to achieve a single digit low-inflation rate, employment creation and sustainable economic growth, public expenditure as a fiscal policy instrument has been shown to have considerable impact on macroeconomic objectives. Most of the studies (e.g. Devarajan et al, 1996; Onwioduokit, 2001; Iyoha and Oriahki, 2002; NISER, 2004; Akintoye, 2008; and Ogbulu and Torbira, 2012) however have examined the impact of public expenditure management on economic growth, unemployment and inflation by using models (such as ordinary least square) that do not adequately inform macroeconomic managers on the direction and the size of fiscal deficit or

[1] Abbas Tajudeen (PhD) (tajudeenabbas@yahoo.com) is a Member of the Federal House of Representatives, National Assembly, 3 Arms Zone, Abuja (Nigeria)
[2] Terfa W. Abraham (Lorenzcurve@yahoo.com) is an Economist/Research Officer at the National Institute for Legislative Studies (NILS), National Assembly, Maitama-Abuja (Nigeria). The views expressed in this paper, however, are those of the authors and do not represent those of the NILS, its Governing Council or of the National Assembly, Nigeria.

surplus. Other studies (e.g. Sen, 1998; Berger and Everaert, 2008; and Medee and Nenbee, 2011) have also employed other methods (such as the Vector Autoregressive model) to investigate the impact of public expenditures on economic growth, unemployment and inflation. This technique, on the other hand, does not provide public expenditure managers with the current impact of public expenditure on targeted variables. Besides, there are evolving contemporary issues that have implications for public expenditure management outcomes for developing countries and all these studies mentioned above did not situate this context in their approaches. These issues include heightened insecurity in Nigeria, for instance climate change and central bank actions and policies. This paper therefore situates its findings in the context of these emerging issues and analysed their consequences for the direction and the size of public expenditure management for macroeconomic outcomes in Nigeria.

The aim of the study therefore is to examine the impact of public expenditure management in Nigeria on three key macroeconomic policy variables: inflation; unemployment; and economic growth. The focus of the paper is on the Federation of Nigeria as a whole and does consider revenue and expenditure by states and local governments. The paper is arranged into six sections. Section one presents the introduction, while section two provides the conceptualization, and the theoretical and empirical review of literature. In section three, the research methodology is presented, and the discussion of the results is presented in section four. Finally, sections five and six present the summary and policy lessons, and the conclusion and recommendation respectively.

2   Conceptual, Theoretical and Empirical Review

2.1 Public Expenditure Management as a Concept

Public expenditure management involves how and why government and its various organs manage public funds to meet national policy objectives (Burkhead and Muner, 1971). It also involves the use of fiscal policies for the purpose of achieving a set of objectives over time, given a number of constraints (Bill, 2003).

Musgrave (1971) gave three traditional roles of public expenditure management. First is the allocation function, which is made to balance the provision of private and social goods in an appropriate mix with available resources. Secondly, the stabilization function is concerned with the attainment of full employment of labor and capital at stable prices, balance of payments equilibrium and a satisfactory rate of growth in per capita income. The third role is that of income distribution which aims at bridging the gap between the rich and the poor and ensuring an egalitarian state. In this context, government uses its public expenditures to protect individuals against the adverse outcomes of economy and public policy.

According to the World Bank (2005), government spending can be used to alter the relative economic position of individuals and families. It can also be used to promote national identity, enhance the supply of infrastructure and provide social services which in turn would stimulate economic growth and enhance overall economic development. On the other hand, unsustainable public spending could fuel inflation, increase domestic instability and constrain economic growth. Thus the World Bank report cautions that careless public expenditure management can lead to prolonged recession and place a disproportionately heavy burden on the people. Porter and Diamond (2001) stated that where public expenditure is not properly managed, it could distort economic growth. This is because sustained budget deficits would lead to inflation, exchange rate devaluation and increased domestic debt that would in turn affect growth negatively.

Development plans, medium term expenditure frameworks (MTEFs) and annual budgets are major channels that are used to execute public expenditure management (World Bank, 2005). A development plan is used by the government to influence, direct and control principal economic variables over time (say 10 to 20 years) so as to achieve certain economic objectives (Diejomaoh and NISER, 2008). Nigeria's current development plan is contained in its Vision 20:2020 blue print. The document builds in the Millennium Development Goals (MDGs) and the Transformation Agenda of the Federal Government that has a time line of 2015 respectively (NPC, 2011). On the other hand, the annual budget is used by the government to translate the policies and programs of its Ministries, Departments and Agencies (MDAs) into concrete actions along the budget lines (NPC, 2009). Finally, the MTEF is a transparent planning and budget formulation process within which the Cabinet and Central Agencies (MDAs) establish credible contracts for allocating public resources according to their strategic priorities while ensuring an overall fiscal discipline (Federal Ministry of Finance, 2010). The process entails two main objectives: the first is setting fiscal targets, while the second is allocating resources to strategic priorities within these targets.

The way government expenditure is allocated has an important impact on the development process of any nation (Abdullahi, 2008; Allan, 2008). Budgetary allocation to public sectors is classified into capital expenditure and recurrent expenditure. The Central Bank of Nigeria (CBN, 2007) has defined capital expenditure as the payment for non-financial assets used in the production process for more than one year. While recurrent expenditure is payment for non-repayable transactions within 1 year.

2.2 Theories of Public Expenditure Management

Theories of Public Expenditure can be grouped into two: the macro-model theory and the development model theory. The macro-model theory is made up of two theories: Wagner's Law and Peacock-Wiseman theory. Wagner's theory was developed by a German economist named Adolph Wagner (1835 – 1917). The law states that government expenditure must increase as the Gross National Product (GNP) increases and the government expenditure must of necessity grow at a faster rate. He argued that there was a functional relationship between the growth of an economy and the growth of public expenditure, such that, as both increase, there is a tendency for public expenditure to grow at a faster rate.

The Peacock- Wiseman theory was developed by two English economists, Allan Peacock and Jack Wiseman. The theory argues that the growth of public expenditure follows a political path. The main argument is that public expenditure does not increase in a smooth and continuous manner, but in jerks or steps like fashion. In their study of public expenditure in the UK for the period 1890 – 1955, during socio-political crises such as wars, epidemics, etc, people's tax tolerance level is high and the government often takes the advantage of this to raise the level of taxes to increase revenue to combat such crisis. The public expenditure increases and makes the inadequacy of the present public revenue quite clear to everyone. The upward review of expenditure and taxes was referred to as 'displacement effect'. This "displacement" creates a public acceptance of tax levels that would otherwise not have been possible prior to the displacement. However, after the crisis, the tax situation never reverts back to the pre-crisis level just creating a new government expenditure level until the next crisis comes.

The development model theory is otherwise known as Musgrave (1989) Theory. The theory argues that at a low level of per capita income, the demand for public services tends to be generally high. This is so because at the early stages of economic development the income level is very low and government is forced to provide the basic infrastructure facilities for economic take-off. However, when per capita income starts to rise above the low level, demand for services supplied by the public sector tends to rise. At a high level of income what is typical of developed economies, the rate of public sector growth tends to fall as more basic wants are already satisfied.

Schick (1998) presented a contemporary approach to Public Expenditure Management (PEM). Though PEM is a new approach to an old problem (i.e. the problem of allocating public money through collective choice), Schick argued that PEM differs from conventional theories of public expenditure (such as Wagner's Law and the Wiseman-Peacock hypothesis) in two ways. First, in traditional theories, allocations are made through the machinery of budgeting which is devised by government to decide the amounts to be spent, the balance between revenue and expenditure, and the allocation of funds among public activities and entities. PEM supplements the conventional procedural rules with substantive policy norms. While conventional budgeting theories operate through accepted procedural norms, PEM emphasizes substantive outcomes. These outcomes pertain to (a) total revenue and expenditure, (b) the allocation of resources among sectors and programs, and (c) the efficiency with which government institutions operate. PEM recognizes that even when a government adheres to accepted budget principles, then it may fail to obtain optimal fiscal outcomes. Therefore, to achieve its preferred outcomes, a government must manage public expenditures to implement avowed policy objectives which also entail creating institutional frameworks that could enhance the probability of achieving desired targets. Second, in conventional theories, what matters is how the process of budgeting is organized. PEM, by contrast, casts a broader net that takes into account how public institutions are managed and it is premised on the notion that budgeting is not a process into itself but is part of a broader set of institutional and governing arrangements to achieve positive public expenditure outcomes.

PEM as a framework has three basic elements: Aggregate Fiscal Discipline; Allocative Efficiency; and Operational Efficiency. The arguments surrounding the Allocative Efficiency element, which suggests that there is *a link* between public expenditures and policy objectives, are of great importance to this study.

2.3 Theories of Unemployment, Inflation and Economic Growth

Keynes (1936) in his work "The general theory of employment, interest and money" has argued that unemployment depends on two fundamental factors: the wage rate and the shape of the demand function. A higher wage rate (for skills that have an elastic demand curve) would require laying-off a portion of the employed workers to increase the wage of those to be retained. While a lower wage rate (for skills with inelastic demand curve), would require raising the wage rate to attract and retain the workforce.

The level of employment on the other hand, as Keynes (1936) argued, is determined by the propensity to consume, the schedule of the marginal efficiency of capital, and the rate of interest. A higher marginal propensity to consume implies high consumption and less saving. Consumption drives demand and demand is met by production. To increase production, investors would require a rate of discount which would equate the price of the fixed capital asset with its present discounted value of expected income as well as a reduction in interest rates.

On the price level, Keynes (1936) has argued that the quantity theory of money as presented by the classical economists has focused only on micro units (individuals and firms) rather than on the economy as whole and therefore he has identified five factors that determine the relationship between changes in the quantity of money and the price-level. They include: changes in effective demand are not proportional to the changes of the quantity of money; there is a demand for increases in wages; the size of idle resources is not absorbed into the production process; there is a rise of wage-units before full employment is achieved; and there is wage rigidity. This suggests that macroeconomic factors (employment and income) are important determinants of the general price level.

On government spending and economic growth, some authors (e.g. Gupta *et al.*, 2002; and Turnovsky, 2004) have argued that while government consumption could have negative effects on economic growth, government investment is also an important determinant of economic growth. Others (e.g. Devarajan *et al.*, 1996; and Folster and Henrekson, 2001) have argued that economic growth and government spending are negatively related. A sustained government deficit however would have a permanent effect on growth and in turn would affect overall development.

Deficit financing has been a recurring event in Nigeria. Since its independence in 1960, over 90% of Nigerians budgets have been in deficit. According to Paiko (2012), deficit financing has a positive impact on inflation and negatively impacts on investment. When there is a deficit, governments find ways of financing the deficit through borrowing from commercial banks or from the non-banking public or through the issue of short-term bonds and other monetary instruments. Prolonged deficit financing, however, has an overall negative impact on the economy by crowding out private investment as it fuels inflation and increases interest rates. Paiko (2012) found that a negative relationship between budget deficits and investment in Nigeria implies that deficit financing crowds out private investment.

2.4 Empirical Literature

Iyoha and Oriahki (2002) argued that Nigeria began to experience fiscal distress in the early 1980s when government resources fell short of its expenditure commitment. The symptoms of the adverse fiscal situation in Nigeria, they argued, were manifested in the following ways: an increased external debt position since the 1980s; a deterioration of the balance of payments position; drastic falls in the external reserve position; widening of government deficits; collapse of industrial production; and collapse of the foreign exchange system. They identified reasons why fiscal distress may arise, including: (1) when there are not enough reserves from all sources of revenue and when the available sources are not properly harnessed and managed to meet public needs; and (2) poor public expenditure management, which could distort macroeconomic policy targets such as achieving sustainable economic growth, employment creation and price stability. Crude oil price and revenue volatility, poor budget discipline, and socio-political instability, as Iyoha and Oriahki (2002) have argued, also contributed to the worsening of Nigeria's fiscal position. These factors are of relevance for the present paper.

A study by NISER (2004) examined the effectiveness of public expenditure in Nigeria. The aim of the study was to establish whether public spending in Nigeria has been geared towards reducing poverty in Nigeria. The results showed that public spending in Nigeria has not been pro-poor, and that very low attention had been devoted to the education and health sectors. It recommended that public expenditure management (PEM) could be used to improve the outcome of public expenditure in Nigeria. But the study did not link public expenditure management to other macroeconomic variables which would serve as useful pass-through mechanisms for public expenditure to impact on poverty.

Onwioduokit (2001) investigated the causal relationship between inflation and the fiscal deficit in Nigeria. The structural model of inflation adopted revealed that it took about two years for the fiscal deficit to impact on inflation in Nigeria. Rapid expansion of wages (attributed to the 1974 Udoji salary increase with minimum wages more than doubled; J. O. Udoji was head of the salary review commission at that time) during the oil boom era of 1971-1977 largely has contributed to fueling inflation in the 1980s as the study by Onwioduokit (2001) has argued. This suggests that there is a close relationship between inflation and fiscal deficits in Nigeria. The study however left out other macroeconomic variables that fiscal deficits are likely to impact on.

Ukwu *et al* (2003) examined the potency of fiscal policy as a tool for poverty alleviation, reduction of unemployment and reduction of income disparities. The study used a computable general equilibrium model for its analysis. The study observed that targeting of government expenditure seems to be the most potent tool for effective poverty reduction, improving employment levels and achieving equitable income distribution. Computable general equilibrium models however simulate for the whole system and could exaggerate the impact of a shock on the whole system due to its underlying assumptions. It could also yield results on certain variables that fiscal policy makers may not be able to influence.

Akintoye (2008) argued that government financing can be channeled towards reducing unemployment in the rural areas. Though the study focused only on the informal sector, its recommendations on the role of government spending in employment creation provide a platform to test its macro relevance.

Medee and Nenbee (2011) investigated the impact of fiscal policy variables on Nigeria's economic growth from 1970-2009 using a Vector Auto Regression (VAR) and Error Correction model. The result revealed that there is a long-run equilibrium relationship between economic growth and fiscal policy variables in Nigeria. It suggested that there should be consistency in macroeconomic policies' implementation in the non-oil sectors of the economy and that there should be an appropriate macroeconomic policy mix in managing the economy. The study focused on broad fiscal policy issues including taxation. The focus of the present paper, however, is on public expenditure only.

Ogbulu and Torbira (2012) examined the relationship between indicators of budgetary operations and economic growth (GDP) in Nigeria. Using regression analysis, they found that non-oil revenue and public expenditures (economic, administrative, social and transfer expenditures) are significant determinants of the Gross Domestic Product (GDP) in Nigeria. They therefore recommended that public fund managers should ensure budgetary discipline to optimize economic growth. Though the study included non-oil revenue in its explanatory variables, it would be important to include other explanatory variables such as inflation, exchange rate and the crude oil price as they also constitute vital indicators of budgetary operations in Nigeria.

2.5 Public Expenditure Management in Nigeria: Budget Assumptions and Figures

Public expenditure management in Nigeria involves the use of a medium-term revenue framework (MTRF) and a medium term expenditure framework (MTEF) (NPC, 2011). The MTRF involves the use of assumptions about the crude oil price and targets and expectations about public revenue. The MTEF on the other hand involves the setting of aggregate expenditure limits, setting a certain level of fiscal deficit and the financing of the fiscal deficit, and setting expenditure limits for MDAs.

Nigeria's 2012 budget, for instance, was anchored on the following pillars: macroeconomic stability, structural reforms, governance and institutions, and investment in priority sectors in line with the overall transformation agenda of the administration. The revenue forecast for the budget was N3.644trn (thousand millions) while planned expenditure was put at N4.749trn: implying a deficit of N1.105trn or 2.77% of GDP. This deficit level is lower than the 2.96% deficit recorded in 2011.

The proposed total expenditure of N4.749trn in 2012 is approximately 6.0% higher than the N4.48trn expenditure approved by the National Assembly in 2011. This increase is less than the projected inflation, implying an anticipation of real reduction in spending in 2012. The recurrent expenditure of N2.470trn was increased only by 1.7% from the 2011 level while capital expenditure of N1.320trn was increased by 15.0% from the 2011 level. The key assumptions and targets of Nigeria's budget for 2011 and 2012 are presented in Table 1 below:

Table 1: Nigeria: 2011 and 2012 Budget Assumptions and Budget Figures

	Budgetary Assumptions		Budget Estimates		
Variables	**2011**	**2012**	**Variables**	**2011**	**2012**
Oil Price	USD 75	USD 70	Total Revenue (in Naira T Million)	2.836	3.644
Oil Production	2.3million barrel per day (bpd)	2.48million barrel per day (bpd)	Total Expenditure (in Naira T Million)	4.484	4.749
Real GDP Growth	7%	7.20%	Fiscal Deficit (% of GDP)	2.960	2.770
Exchange Rate	150 Nigerian Naira = 1 USD	155 Nigerian Naira = 1 USD	Recurrent Expenditure (in Naira T Million)	2.430	2.470
Inflation	10%	9.50%	Capital Expenditure (in Naira T Million)	1.146	1.320
-	-	-	(*) % of Recurrent Expenditure to Total Expenditure	54.19	52.01
-	-	-	(*) % of Capital Expenditure to Total Expenditure	25.56	27.80

Source: Federal Ministry of Finance (2010) & Authors' Presentation, (*) Authors' Computation

The percentage of recurrent expenditure to total expenditure in 2011 was 54.19 percent and was budgeted to be reduced by 2.18 percent to 52.01 percent in 2012. On the other hand, the percentage of capital expenditure to total expenditure in 2011 was increased by 2.24 percent from 25.56 percent in 2011 to 27.80 percent in 2012. The increase in capital expenditure was aimed at providing additional funding for critical infrastructure as contained in the nation's transformation agenda, while the reduction in recurrent expenditure was also critical to achieving a 0.5 percent reduction in inflation by 2012. By the second quarter of 2012 however, Nigeria's actual inflation was 12.9 percent. This suggests poor coordination between fiscal and monetary policies towards inflation targeting.

The oil price benchmark in 2011 was $75pb while oil production was put at 2.3 million barrels per day. The oil price for 2012 was however reviewed downwards to USD 70pb following the experience from the 2007-2010 global financial crisis while production was put at 2.48 million bpd. The actual average crude oil price in 2011 however was about USD 110 per barrel while the average price for the first quarter of 2012 was about USD 115.98 (CBN, 2012). The actual crude oil production in the years 2011 and 2012 was 2.19 million bpd and 2.12 million bpd respectively. The excess of USD 35 and USD 45.98 multiplied by the actual barrels produced per day constitutes revenue in the excess of the benchmark price and are to be set aside in the Excess Crude Account (ECA) that also constitutes Nigeria's Sovereign Wealth Fund (SWF). The Federal Ministry of Finance (FMF) draws from the ECA/SWF in times of falling global crude oil prices to mitigate adverse fiscal shocks, to reduce pro-cyclicality and to delink public expenditure from crude oil price volatility. However, problems arise if the ECA is depleted by governments or if the benchmark price is unrealistic.

In terms of economic growth, it is projected that real GDP will be 7.2% by end of 2012, which would be marginally higher than the value of 2011 of 7.0%. The exchange rate projection of N155/$ is also higher than the MTFF assumption of N153/$ but is consistent with the mid-point band of the central bank. When the inflation rate rises, the Central Bank of Nigeria raises the monetary policy rate (MPR) above the inflation rate. This increases the interest rate which leads to increased savings and checks inflation. However, rising inflation and interest rates discourage private investment, devalue the Naira exchange rate and affect government policy outcomes.

Tables 2 and 3 below present the structure of revenues and expenditures for 2011 and 2012 from the MTRF and MTEF 2011-2013 framework.

Table 2: Structure of Revenue in the MTRF Framework for 2011 and 2012

Fiscal Items	2011 Projection	2012 Projection
Gross Federally Collectible Revenue	**7,202.34**	**7,826.43**
FGN BUDGET REVENUE (INFLOWS)	**2,470.26**	**2,700.54**
Unspent balance from previous FY	120.00	100.00
FGN BUDGET Share of Federation Account (48.5%)	1,972.62	2,231.07
FGN BUDGET Share of VAT (14%)	84.03	92.44
FGN Independent Revenue	250.00	267.50
Carryover from Supplementary II of 2009	0.00	0.00
DMO Bond Issuance for PHCN Arrears of Monetization (Supplementary I)	0.00	0.00
Other Revenue (Supplementary I)	0.00	0.00
Special Bond Issuance for INEC (Supplementary II)	0.00	0.00
Estimated FGN's Balances of Special Accounts end Dec.	13.61	9.53
Oil Revenue:		
Crude Oil Sales	2,938.08	3,138.01
Royalties	494.29	582.27
Oil & Gas Petroleum Profits Tax	1,230.25	1,355.40
Gas Sales	352.62	367.73
Rent, Gas Flared Penalty and Miscellaneous Oil Revenue	6.63	6.25
Total Oil & Gas Revenue	**5,021.88**	**5,449.65**
Non-Oil Revenue		
Customs	*450.00*	*450.00*
Corporate Tax	*632.80*	*738.29*
Value-Added Tax	*625.24*	*687.76*
FGN Independent Revenue	*250.00*	*267.50*
Total Non-Oil	**1,958.04**	**2,143.56**

Source: Federal Ministry of Finance (2010).

Nigeria's revenue has two major components: oil revenue and non-oil revenue. The unspent balance from the previous year is also brought forward as unspent balance. The federal government share of the federation account, the share of value added tax (VAT) and the federal government independent revenue constitute the major components of Nigeria's budget revenue (inflows). The major component of oil revenue is from crude oil sales, accounting for about 60% of the oil revenue sales. Oil and gas profit tax revenues are also significant next to gas sales. The structure of expenditure is presented in Table 3.

Table 3: Structure of Expenditure in the MTEF Framework 2011 and 2012

Fiscal Items	2011 Pro-jection	2012 Projection
FGN BUDGET REVENUE (INFLOWS)	**2,470.26**	**2,700.54**
Less		
Statutory Transfers	**179.78**	**188.76**
Debt Service Recurrent	**517.07**	**566.83**
MDA Spending	**3,933.10**	**4,257.67**
Of Which:		
Non-Debt Recurrent	**2,849.66**	**3,085.22**
Personnel Costs (MDAs)	1,634.06	1,797.47
Overheads	450.00	495.00
Pensions and Public Service Reform	294.37	323.65
Multi-Year Tariff Order	40.00	30.00
Other Service Wide Votes	431.22	439.11
Sub-Total	**2,849.66**	**3,085.22**
Percentage Change in Non-Debt Recurrent Spending	*6.77%*	*8.27%*
Capital Spending	**1,083.44**	**1,172.45**
Sub-Total	**1,083.44**	**1,172.45**
Percentage Change in Capital Spending	*-38.60%*	*8.22%*
Aggregate Expenditure	**4,629.95**	**5,013.26**
Percentage Change in Aggregate Expenditure	*-10.27%*	*8.28%*

Source: Federal Ministry of Finance (2010)

Aggregate expenditure is structured into five components: statutory transfers; debt service recurrent; Ministries, Departments and Agencies (MDA) spending; non-debt recurrent expenditure; and capital expenditure. Statutory transfers, debt service recurrent, MDA spending and non-debt recurrent spending constitutes total recurrent expenditure. Recurrent expenditure constitutes 61.55% in 2011 and 61.54% in 2012 while capital expenditure constitutes 38.45% and 38.46%.

3 Research Methodology

The literature section 2 discussed Nigeria's expenditure and revenue management framework from 2011 to 2012 as contained in the nation's 2011-2013 Medium Term Expenditure Framework & Fiscal Strategy Paper (FSP). The time series analysis for this paper was conducted using data from 1970 – 2008 to provide empirical evidence on the relationship between public expenditure and macroeconomic policy before the financial crisis. The data on public expenditure (recurrent and capital), inflation, unemployment and economic growth (as proxied by GDP) were collected from the Central Bank of Nigeria (CBN)'s Statistical Bulletin and from the National Bureau of Statistics (NBS)[3]. The Augmented Dickey-Fuller test was then used to test for unit root in the series. Data that were stationary in their level form was desirable. Those that were not stationary were transformed by differencing the series. The Granger causality test was used to establish the direction of causality between two variables. The Autoregressive Distributed Lag (ADL) Model was employed to estimate the models. This framework was chosen because of its ability to measure the current impact and the time lag it takes for public expenditure to impact on the selected macroeconomic objectives.

The models which are linking public expenditure management variables to macroeconomic policy variables were adapted from NISER (2004), Medee and Nenbee (2011) and Ogbulu & Torbira (2012) and were modified as presented below:

(1) $GDP_t = \alpha_0 + \alpha_1 GDP_{t-i} + \alpha_2 CE_t + \alpha_3 CE_{t-i} + \alpha_4 RE_t + \alpha_5 RE_{t-i} + \alpha_6 D_{pEM} + U_t$

(2) $UN_t = \beta_0 + \beta_1 UN_{t-i} + \beta_2 CE_t + \beta_3 CE_{t-i} + \beta_4 RE_t + \beta_5 RE_{t-i} + \beta_6 D_{PEM} + U_t$

(3) $INF_t = \lambda_0 + \lambda_1 M2_t + \lambda_3 CIC_t + \lambda_4 D_{PEM} + U_t$

(4) $\Delta GDP_t = a_0 + a_1 \Delta PE_t + a_2 \Delta TR_t + a_3 \Delta CO_t + a_4 \Delta ER_t + a_5 INF_t + a_6 \Delta Agric_t + a_7 \Delta MRR_t + U_t$

The *a priori* expectations for the coefficients in equations (1) to (4) are:

For equation (1), it is expected that
$\alpha_1 > 0$, $\alpha_2 > 0$, $\alpha_3 > 0$, $\alpha_4 < 0$, $\alpha_5 < 0$, $\alpha_6 > 0$;
For equation (2), it is expected that
$\beta_1 < 0$, $\beta_2 < 0$, $\beta_3 < 0$, $\beta_4 < 0$, $\beta_5 > 0$, $\beta_6 < 0$;
For equation (3), it is expected that

---

[3] Available at www.cenbank.org and www.nigerianstat.gov.ng respectively

$\lambda_1 > 0, \lambda_2 > 0, \lambda_3 > 0, \lambda_4 < 0$

For equation (4), it is expected that

$a_1 < 0, a_2 > 0, a_3 < 0, a_4 < 0, a_5 < 0, a_6 > 0, a_7 < 0$.

Equations (1) and (2) are autoregressive models while equations (3) and (4) are ordinary least square regression models. Public expenditure management involves the interplay of other variables, hence equation (4) provides a framework for analyzing the impact of public expenditure management (among other variables) on the performance on the economy.

In the equations, GDP = Gross Domestic product; CE = Capital Expenditure; RE = Recurrent Expenditure; UN = Unemployment rate; INF = Inflation rate; PE = total public expenditure; TR = totally collected revenue; ER = exchange rate; Agric = agricultural sector performance; CIC = currency in circulation; M2 = broad money supply; and MRR = minimum rediscounting rate or monetary policy rate. D_{PEM} = dummy variable used to capture public expenditure management taking the values of 0 for periods with surplus budget and 1 periods with deficit budget; α, β, λ are the coefficients relating the independent variables to the dependent variable, while U_t is the error term representing other variables but not included in the model. By proxy, U_t is 1 minus the estimated adjusted R-square in the result. The equations are estimated using the Eviews econometric software. The next section discusses the estimated results.

4   Results and Discussion

To achieve the objectives of the study, secondary data were collected for the variables identified in section three above. Before the equations were estimated, however, it is statistically required that the variables are stationary. Thus, they were tested for stationarity using the Augmented Dickey Fuller (ADF) unit root test. Only inflation was found to be stationary at levels, i.e. integrated of order zero $I(0)$, while the other variables were stationary after taking first difference, i.e. integrated of order one $I(I)$. The other variables were thus differenced by one to ensure stationarity before the equations were estimated. The stationarity results are presented in Table 4.0.

Table 4.0: Stationarity Test: Augmented Dickey Fuller (ADF) Test

ADF Stat	Variables	Critical Values		
Level $I(0)$		1%	5%	10%
-2.385	Unemployment	-3.611	-2.939	-2.608
-3.709	Inflation#	-3.611	-2.939	-2.608
-0.028	Gross Domestic Product	-3.611	-2.939	-2.608
-0.472	Recurrent Expenditure	-3.611	-2.939	-2.608
-1.524	Capital Expenditure	-3.611	-2.939	-2.608
-1.557	MRR	-3.611	-2.939	-2.608
-0.058	Exchange rate	-3.611	-2.939	-2.608
-2.082	Crude oil	-3.611	-2.939	-2.608
0.852	Agric. Performance	-3.611	-2.939	-2.608
-0.505	Public expenditure	-3.611	-2.939	-2.608
-0.590	Total revenue	-3.611	-2.939	-2.608
1st diff. $I(I)$		1%	5%	10%
-7.906	Unemployment	-3.611	-2.939	-2.608
-5.157	Gross Domestic Product	-3.611	-2.939	-2.608
-8.967	Recurrent Expenditure	-3.611	-2.939	-2.608
-7.322	Capital Expenditure	-3.611	-2.939	-2.608
-7.281	MRR	-3.611	-2.939	-2.608
-4.891	Exchange rate	-3.611	-2.939	-2.608
-5.761	Crude oil	-3.611	-2.939	-2.608
-4.463	Agric. Performance	-3.611	-2.939	-2.608
-7.206	Public expenditure	-3.611	-2.939	-2.608
-6.603	Total revenue	-3.611	-2.939	-2.608

Key: # stationary at levels; diff. means difference, **Source**: Authors' Computation using Eviews Software

ADF statistics are compared in absolute terms (i.e. by neglecting their negative signs). In the upper part of Table 4.0, the figures at 1% critical value are greater than the figures under the ADF statistics at levels I(0); except for inflation. This shows that only inflation was stationary at levels. In the lower part of Table 4.0 however, the variables had been differenced by one to ensure stationary. The ADF statistics values at 1st difference became higher than the 1% critical value. The next section discusses the results from the estimated equations.

4.1 Model Estimation

4.1.1   Estimated Equation (1)

Table 4.1: Estimated Eviews Result for Equation (1)

Dependent Variable: GDP				
Method: Least Squares				
Sample(adjusted): 1974 2008				
Included observations: 38 after adjusting endpoints				
Variable	Coefficient	Std. Error	t-Statistic	Prob.
C	2346053.	812877.3	2.886109	0.0073
RE	4.586947	1.276898	3.592259	0.0012
RE(-3)	10.31990	1.790747	5.762902	0.0000
CE(-2)	12.99709	1.718455	7.563246	0.0000
BDD(-3)	-2315014.	817206.3	-2.832839	0.0083
BSD(-3)	-2426869.	773610.3	-3.137069	0.0039
R-squared	0.775498	Mean dependent var		680890.9
Adjusted R-squared	0.736790	S.D. dependent var		1268528.
S.E. of regression	650805.3	Akaike info criterion		29.76461
Log likelihood	-514.8807	F-statistic		20.03492
Durbin-Watson stat	1.527149	Prob(F-statistic)		0.000000

Key: var = variable, **Source**: Authors' Computation using Eviews Software

The results in table 4.1 show that recurrent expenditure at present value and after a lag period of 3 years continues to influence current growth of the economy, while capital expenditure exacts a significant and positive impact on the current growth of the economy after 2 years. Though the dummy variable used to capture budget deficit and budget surplus were significant, they were found to negatively impact on the growth of the economy. The adjusted R-square of the model is 73.67%. This indicates that public expenditure influences the growth of the Nigerian economy by 73.67%. This reveals that public expenditure plays a significant role in the Nigerian economy and also suggests that private sector investment in the country revolves around government expenditure. This could crowd out private investment (those whose investments are not plugged in on government expenditure) in the long run as the central bank would raise the minimum rediscounting rate (which would hike the cost of loanable funds) in order to curb inflation. The Durbin Watson statistic had a value of 1.52 (approximately 2), indicating that the model has no first order autocorrelation problem while the computed F-statistics value (i.e. 20.03 with a probability value of 0.000) is also significant. These statistics indicates that the model has good fit.

4.1.2 Estimated Equation (2)

Table 4.2 (a): Eviews Result for Equation (2)

Dependent Variable: UN				
Method: Least Squares				
Sample(adjusted): 1975 2008				
Included observations: 34 after adjusting endpoints				
Variable	Coefficient	Std. Error	t-Statistic	Prob.
C	-2.290506	0.970930	-2.359085	0.0281
RE	7.26E-07	1.73E-06	0.419124	0.6794
RE(-1)	1.29E-06	6.90E-06	0.186414	0.8539
RE(-2)	-1.82E-06	7.70E-06	-0.236432	0.8154
RE(-3)	4.00E-06	7.19E-06	0.556355	0.5838
RE(-4)	-2.79E-06	7.37E-06	-0.378158	0.7091
CE	-3.89E-06	5.84E-06	-0.666086	0.5126
CE(-1)	-5.62E-07	6.04E-06	-0.092987	0.9268
CE(-2)	5.65E-06	5.93E-06	0.952499	0.3517
CE(-3)	-7.46E-06	5.27E-06	-1.415105	0.1717
CE(-4)	-1.40E-06	3.68E-06	-0.379576	0.7081
BDD	2.395990	0.966510	2.479011	0.0217
BSD	1.529245	0.916586	1.668414	0.1101
R-squared	0.627244	Mean dependent var		-0.029412
Adjusted R-squared	0.414241	S.D. dependent var		1.004469
S.E. of regression	0.768769	Akaike info criterion		2.594815
Sum squared resid	12.41112	Schwarz criterion		3.178424
Log likelihood	-31.11186	F-statistic		2.944764
Durbin-Watson stat	1.603389	Prob(F-statistic)		0.014668

Source: Authors' Computation using Eviews Software

The result for equation 2 is presented in Table 4.2(a). It shows that the budget deficit (BDD) has a positive and significant relationship with unemployment, indicating that an unsustainable budget deficit leads to a rise in unemployment. Sustainable budget deficits would however lead to a decrease in unemployment. Other coefficients however were not significant, suggesting that public expenditure management alone is insufficient in addressing unemployment in Nigeria. Real sector variables were then added to budget deficit and regressed against unemployment. The result is provided in Table 4.2(b).

Table 4.2(b): Estimated Equation (2) with other variables included

Dependent Variable: UN				
Method: Least Squares				
Sample(adjusted): 1985 2008				
Included observations: 24 after adjusting endpoints				
Variable	Coefficient	Std. Error	t-Statistic	Prob.
C	-1.479323	1.801468	-0.821176	0.4328
GDP	4.42E-07	2.16E-07	2.049439	0.0707
GDP(-1)	-3.13E-07	2.36E-07	-1.325742	0.2176
GDP(-2)	-1.69E-07	2.68E-07	-0.630306	0.5442
GDP(-3)	3.30E-07	3.01E-07	1.099234	0.3002
MU	-0.013397	0.061008	-0.219593	0.8311
MU(-1)	0.043353	0.064933	0.667662	0.5211
MU(-2)	-0.029130	0.064804	-0.449503	0.6637
MU(-3)	-0.003133	0.062732	-0.049947	0.9613
AGRIC	-6.58E-06	1.24E-05	-0.531896	0.6077
AGRIC(-1)	-2.50E-05	1.27E-05	-1.966040	0.0809
AGRIC(-2)	-1.82E-05	1.59E-05	-1.143008	0.2825
AGRIC(-3)	-1.08E-05	1.12E-05	-0.958274	0.3630
BDD	1.026260	1.446393	0.709531	0.4960
R-squared	0.704722	Mean dependent var		-0.079167
Adjusted R-squared	0.245401	S.D. dependent var		1.127224
S.E. of regression	0.979193	Akaike info criterion		3.064995
Sum squared resid	8.629369	Schwarz criterion		3.801278
Log likelihood	-21.77994	F-statistic		1.534270
Durbin-Watson stat	2.345447	Prob(F-statistic)		0.262439

Source: Authors' Computation using Eviews Software

The results show that economic growth does not create jobs in Nigeria as the current value of growth was significant and had a positive relationship with unemployment. The negative relationships which the first and second lagged values of growth have on unemployment, however, suggest that achieving sustainable growth is critical for providing jobs.

For agriculture, there is a negative relationship between its first lagged value and unemployment. This suggests that agriculture reduces seasonal unemployment as people get employed during farm and harvest time. Though at other lag lengths agriculture had a negative relationship with unemployment, the coefficients were not significant. This indicates the weak ability of the agricultural sector to provide stable employment opportunities and to enhance pro-poor growth in Nigeria. Government programs/projects that are aimed at addressing the challenges faced by the agricultural sector would therefore be very useful as the sector is Nigeria's dominant non-oil sector and engages over 60 percent of its rural population. How to make the sector provide sustainable economic opportunities to unemployed persons (especially women) should therefore be the focus directing government spending/intervention funds.

There is a link between the agricultural and manufacturing sectors. The agricultural sector employs over 60 percent of the rural population in Nigeria. Once agricultural productivity is low, people would be thrown out of jobs and there would be no farm output to serve as input for agro-allied manufacturing firms hence, hampering job creation by the manufacturing sector as well. Though the coefficients in the estimated equation for manufacturing capacity utilization (MU) were not significant, the negative relationship seen between MU (manufacturing utilization) and UN (unemployment) suggests that the increase in manufacturing capacity utilization would lead to a reduction in unemployment. Thus, public spending should be directed towards enhancing agriculture-led manufacturing sector development in Nigeria by addressing infrastructural gaps to allow for private investment initiatives to thrive.

4.1.3   Estimated Equation (3)

The results in table 4.3 revealed that currency in circulation (CIC) (i.e. cash outside the banking system) has a positive relationship with inflation while the broad money supply (i.e. demand deposits) has a negative relationship with inflation. This implies that the narrow money supply (for which CIC is a component) contributes to inflation in Nigeria, while the broad money supply reduces inflation. This implies that monetary authorities in Nigeria could focus on moving the economy towards a cashless society to enhance its inflation reduction targets while the country should caution policies that introduces larger currency notes as it would encourage the holding of large amounts of money outside of the banking system.

The dummy variables used as proxy for public expenditure management were also significant and had a negative relationship with inflation. This implies that altering public expenditure (using a surplus budget in inflationary times and a budget deficit in deflationary times) would be useful to bring inflation to a low single digit value.

Table 4.3: Eviews Result for Equation (3)

Dependent Variable: INF				
Method: Least Squares				
Sample(adjusted): 1971 2008				
Included observations: 32 after adjusting endpoints				
Variable	Coefficient	Std. Error	t-Statistic	Prob.
C	44.22623	16.25233	2.721224	0.0112
M2	-4.84E-06	2.41E-06	-2.010595	0.0545
CIC	2.83E-05	1.26E-05	2.238684	0.0336
BDD	-48.38364	15.31481	-3.159272	0.0039
BSD	-41.11689	14.16869	-2.901954	0.0073
R-squared	0.375321	Mean dependent var		-0.293750
Adjusted R-squared	0.282776	S.D. dependent var		16.13149
S.E. of regression	13.66162	Akaike info criterion		8.209658
Sum squared resid	5039.274	Schwarz criterion		8.438680
Log likelihood	-126.3545	F-statistic		4.055546
Durbin-Watson stat	2.231473	Prob(F-statistic)		0.010576

Source: Authors' Computation using Eviews Software

4.1.4 Estimated Equation (4)

Other factors, however, act with public expenditures (recurrent and capital expenditure) to bring about an improvement in overall economic growth. These factors include: crude oil price, exchange rate, inflation, non-oil sector (proxied by agriculture), and the monetary policy rate among others. The results showing the impact of some of these variables and their impact on economic growth are provided in Table 4.4.

The results show that public expenditures, public revenues, crude oil price, exchange rate, inflation, agriculture and the minimum rediscounting rate account for 74.32 percent of GDP (see Adjusted R-square value). Though the relationship of public expenditure (PE) with GDP is not significant, the negative coefficient suggests that reducing public expenditure would increase economic growth in Nigeria. This is so because total public revenue (TR) has a positive relationship with GDP and would require to be checked by sound fiscal management.

The crude oil price has a positive relationship with economic growth. It indicates that a decline in the price of crude oil or a drop in crude oil demand from major importers without a corresponding increase in demand by other importers would transmit a negative shock to Nigeria's economy. This is so because oil revenue is a significant component of total revenue in Nigeria and it is determined by the volume produced and its price at the international market.

Table 4.4: Eviews Result for Equation (4)

Dependent Variable: D(GDP)				
Method: Least Squares				
Sample(adjusted): 1971 2008				
Included observations: 38 after adjusting endpoints				
Variable	Coefficient	Std. Error	t-Statistic	Prob.
C	-0.020159	0.022960	-0.878002	0.3865
D(PE)	-0.018051	0.067828	-0.266132	0.7918
D(TR)	0.339029	0.077793	4.358059	0.0001
D(CO)	0.089068	0.078983	1.127683	0.2678
D(ER)	-0.008091	0.060206	-0.134382	0.8939
INF	0.025819	0.022442	1.150477	0.2585
D(AGRIC)	0.550840	0.118316	4.655677	0.0001
D(MRR)	-0.051436	0.080669	-0.637613	0.5283
R-squared	0.789292	Mean dependent var		0.093569
Adjusted R-squared	0.743199	S.D. dependent var		0.079546
S.E. of regression	0.040310	Akaike info criterion		-3.407558
Sum squared resid	0.051998	Schwarz criterion		-3.069782
Log likelihood	76.15116	F-statistic		17.12411
Durbin-Watson stat	2.697806	Prob(F-statistic)		0.000000

Source: Authors' Computation using Eviews Software

Agriculture has a positive and significant impact on economic growth. This implies that agriculture could also be used to stabilize Nigeria's public revenue base, to create employment and hence, to spur economic growth. The link between the agricultural sector and the manufacturing sector would also lead to an expansion in agro-allied industries, thus creating further employment and expanding Nigeria's public revenue base.

The relationship between exchange rate and economic growth was negative while inflation and interest rate (MRR) are positively related with GDP: an indication that inflation accompanies growth in Nigeria and that exchange rate appreciation is as well critical for achieving economic growth.

5 Summary Notes and Policy Lessons

Public expenditure management in Nigeria entails coordinating public expenditure and revenue in a manner that would enhance sustainable economic growth, a process that would in turn translate into development. It was found in the study that recurrent public expenditure has an immediate impact on economic growth while capital expenditure lags by two years before its impact on the economy is felt.

Though the study found that an increase in capital expenditure could be used to achieve a reduction in current unemployment, empirical evidence however has not been consistent with this expectation as unemployment has continued to rise despite the increase in capital expenditure. For instance, Nigeria's unemployment rate in January 2008 was 11.8 percent. By January 2012 however, the figure had more than doubled to 23.9 percent. Likewise, in 2008, Nigeria's budget deficit was 1.2trillion Nigerian naira but has more than tripled by 2012 standing at 4.648trillion Nigerian naira.

Despite the growth of the Nigerian economy, it has not brought about a reduction in unemployment. The agricultural sector, however, was found to have the potency of reducing unemployment. The sector, which has been neglected over the years, now faces challenges from climate change and from a huge infrastructural deficit. These factors have adverse effects on the sector's output. Public expenditure management, therefore, could be used to boost the performance of the agricultural sector either through tax incentives, providing infrastructure or financing climate change adaptation strategies that would help in raising and optimizing output. Since agricultural output also faces challenges that affect its pricing, there will also be a need to reintroduce agricultural commodity marketing regulation to ensure that farmers get adequate prices for their products.

The Central Bank of Nigeria (CBN) alters the monetary policy rate as a way of checking inflation. However, the paper found that public expenditure can also be used to support the government's goal of achieving a single digit low inflation rate. For instance, to achieve reduction in the inflation rate from 10 percent in 2011 to 9.5 percent in 2012, the fiscal deficit as a percentage of the GDP was projected to decline from 2.96 percent to 2.77 percent. The ratio of recurrent expenditure to total expenditure also was projected to decline from 54.19 percent in 2011 to 52.01 percent in 2012, while the ratio of capital expenditure to total expenditure was projected to increase from 25.56 percent in 2011 to 27.80 percent in 2012.

The relationship between GDP and public expenditure was found to be negative. This suggests that increased public expenditure (that has been the trend of public expenditure in Nigeria) has not brought about growth in the economy as anticipated. Oil revenue, which constitutes a significant component of revenue in Nigeria, however, is driven by the volume produced and the price of crude oil in the international market. A decline in the price of crude oil or a sudden cut in crude oil demand from major importers (without a corresponding increase in demand by other importers) would therefore lead to macroeconomic instability. Setting a budget benchmark for the crude oil price and the quantity produced would therefore be useful in addressing shocks from crude oil price. For instance, Nigeria used USD 75 per barrel as the benchmark for the crude oil price in 2011 and reviewed it downward to USD 70 per barrel for the 2012 fiscal year following lessons learnt from the global economic crisis of 2007-2011. The methodology for setting this benchmark, however, should be consistent with scientific development in statistics/econometrics by obtaining forecasts that would guide in selecting the benchmark, so as to avoid not foreseeing shocks that could have been foreseen.

Agriculture could also be used to stabilize Nigeria's export revenue base, create employment and boost economic growth. For example, the exploitation of linkages between the agricultural sector and the manufacturing sector would lead to an expansion in agro-allied industries which would create further employment and expand Nigeria's revenue base.

The monetary authorities also have a role to play in supporting public expenditure management in Nigeria through exchange rate management and inflation targeting. The Central Bank of Nigeria (CBN) raises the interest rates above the inflation rate when there is a rise in inflation, as a way of checkmating inflationary trends. Therefore, ensuring coordination between fiscal and monetary policy in Nigeria would be useful in addressing inflation, stabilize the Naira exchange rate (in relation to the dollar) and keep the monetary policy rate low, in order to boost private sector investment and promote inclusive growth in Nigeria.

6 Conclusions and Recommendations

The objective of this paper was to examine the impact of public expenditure management on macroeconomic policy objectives (i.e. employment creation, economic growth, and price stability) in Nigeria. On economic growth, it was found that recurrent expenditure has an immediate impact on economic growth while capital expenditure could take up to 2 years response lag before its impact on the growth would be recorded. More so, despite theoretical views that budget surpluses or deficits could be used to fine tune the economy, they could as well have negative impacts on economic growth in the short to medium term. To enhance public expenditure management in Nigeria therefore, this paper recommends that relevant government agencies being responsible for budget preparation and economic planning should adopt systematic ways of understanding the impact and the response lag of macroeconomic variables to public expenditure so as to minimize the waste of public resources.

Taking appropriate actions that would boost the performance of the non-oil sector (especially agriculture) is also important. Agriculture was once the main stay of the Nigerian economy, but was neglected following the discovery of crude oil. With the volatility of the crude oil price due to factors in the international market and the possibility of a fall in oil production/demand due to developments in renewable energy sources, revamping the agricultural sector would be useful in driving the diversification of the Nigerian economy. In conclusion, although it is argued that channeling budget deficits into productive sectors would promote economic growth and create employment, evidence from the paper revealed that sustained budget deficits or surpluses over time negatively impact on Nigeria's economic growth. Optimal public expenditure management should therefore focus on altering the fiscal direction within a medium term framework, depending on the evolvement of the Nigerian economy as a subset of the global economy, so as to determine the optimal direction of public expenditure management in Nigeria.

References

Abdullahi, I. B. (2008), "Budgetary Allocations and Selected Sector's Contribution to Economic Development in Nigeria", *Pakistan Journal of Social Sciences,* 5 (9)

Akintoye, Rufus (2008). "Reducing Unemployment through the Informal Sector: A Case Study of Nigeria", *European Journal of Economics, Finance and Administrative Sciences Issue 11*

Allan, Whaites (2008). "States in Development: Understanding State-building", Governance and Social Development Group Policy and Research Division: A Department for International Development/DFID Working Paper

Berger, T. and Everaert, G. (2008), "Is the Impact of Labour taxes on Unemployment asymmetric", University Gent (July), Discussion Paper D/2008/7012/32

Bill, H. J. (2003) *"Guideline for Expenditure management"*. Washington D.C.: International Monetary Fund

Burkhead, J. and Muner, J. (1971), *Public Expenditure,* Chicago: Aldine Atherto Publishers

CBN/Central Bank of Nigeria (CBN), Statistical Bulletin (2007), Abuja. www.cenbank.org

CBN (2012), Crude Oil Price (US$/Barrel), Production (mbd) and Export mbd), Central Bank of Nigeria (CBN) Data available at: http://www.cenbank.org/rates/crudeoil.asp?year=2012

Devarajan, S., V. Swaroop, and H. Zou (1996). "The Composition of Public Expenditure and Economic Growth," Journal of Monetary Economics 37, 313-344.

Diejomaoh, V. and NISER (2008), "National Development Planning, Markets and Development in Nigeria". Being Annual Public Lecture of the Nigerian Economic Society (NES), Delivered at Sheraton Hotel & Towers, Abuja 18th March, 2008

Ekpo, A. H. (2008), "Budgeting: The Nigerian Experience". Paper presented at the State High Level Workshop, organized by the United Nations Development Programme (UNDP), Abuja, in selected Nigerian States, March, April and May.

FMF/Federal Ministry of Finance (2010) 'Medium-Term Expenditure Framework and Fiscal Strategy Paper', A publication of the Budget Office of the Federation (BOF), Federal Ministry of Finance (FMF), Federal Government of Nigeria (FGN)

Folster, S. and M. Henrekson (2001), "Growth effects of Government Expenditure and taxation in rich countries," *European Economic Review 45*

Garba, A. G. (2008). "Development oriented fiscal management in states: Developing fiscal responsibility and procurement laws and systems?", Draft paper prepared for the fiscal policy capacity-building initiative for Lagos State, March 27 – 28th.

Gupta, S., B. Clements, E. Baldacci, and C. Mulas-Granados (2002), "Expenditure Composition, Fiscal Adjustment, and Growth in Low-income Countries," IMF Working Paper No. 02/77

IMF (2008), Pamphlet Series Number 49: Guidelines for Fiscal Adjustment, Washington D.C.: IMF

Iyoha, M. A. and Oriakhi, D. (2002), 'Explaining African Economic Growth Performance: The case of Nigeria', A paper presented in the Department of Economics University of Benin, Nigeria (May 2002).

Keynes, J. M. (1936), *The General Theory of Employment, Interest and Money*, New York: Chicago University Press

Medee, P. N. and S. G. Nenbee (2011) 'Econometric Analysis of the Impact of Fiscal Policy Variables on Nigeria's Economic Growth (1970 - 2009)' *International Journal of Economic Development Research and Investment*, (2)1: 171-183

Musgrave, R. (1971). *The Theory of Public Finance: A Study in Public Economy*, London: McGraw Hill.

Musgrave, R. (1989), "Excess Bias and the Nature of Budget Growth". *Journal of Public Economics, Vol. 28 No. 3*

NISER (2004), "Effectiveness of Public Expenditure in Nigeria", Paper Submitted to the Federal Government of Nigeria (EC Support), Technical Assistance Office, Ministry of Finance, Abuja December 2004. Ibadan: Okley Printers Nigeria Ltd.

NPC (2009), 'Nigeria Vision 20:2020 Economic Transformation Blueprint', A Publication of the National Planning Commission (NPC) of the Federal Republic of Nigeria (FGN), October 2009

NPC (2011), 'The Transformation Agenda of the Federal Republic of Nigeria (2011-2015)', A Publication of the National Planning Commission (NPC) of the Federal Republic of Nigeria (FGN)

Ogbulu, O. M. and L. L. Torbira (2012), 'Budgetary Operations and Economic Growth: The Nigerian Perspective', *British Journal of Arts and Social Sciences* 4(2):180-194

Onwioduokit, E. A. (2001), "Fiscal Deficits and Inflation Dynamics in Nigeria: An Empirical Investigation of Causal Relationships". *CBN Economic & Financial Review,* Vol. 37 No. 2

Paiko, I. I. (2012) 'Deficit Financing and Its Implication on Private Sector Investment: The Nigerian Experience' *Arabian Journal of Business and Management Review (Oman Chapter) 1(9): 45-62*

Porter, H. and J. Diamond (2001), *Understanding and Reforming Public Expenditure Management,* Washington D.C.: International Monetary Fund

Schick, Allen (1998). "A Contemporary Approach to Public Expenditure Management", World Bank Institute: A publication in the Governance, Regulation and Finance division (May 1998), published by the World Bank/International Bank for Reconstruction and Development (IBRD)

Sen, Hugeyin (1998). "The impact of the IMF-supported stabilization programmes on inflation in developing countries, The experience of Turkey in the last decade", Atatürk University, *Journal of Economics and Administrative Sciences, Vol. 12, No. 1 and 2*

Turnovsky, S. J. (2004). "The Transitional Dynamics of Fiscal Policy: Long-Run Capital Accumulation and Growth", *Journal of Money, Credit, and Banking, Vol. 36 No 2*

Ukwu, U. I., A. W. Obi and S. Ukeje (2003), "Policy Options for Managing Macroeconomic Volatility in Nigeria", (August 2003): African Institute for Applied Economics (AIAE), Enugu – Nigeria

World Bank (2005), 'Public Expenditure Analysis', Public Sector Governance and Accountability Series (Edited by Anwar Shah), Washington D.C.: A World Bank Publication

The Impact of Macroeconomic Policy Strategies on Sectoral Developments in Nigeria

Milton A. Iyoha[1], Patricia A. Adamu[2], and Dickson E. Oriakhi[3]

1   Introduction

The macroeconomic performance of the Nigerian economy during the first decade of the 21st Century was a sharp contrast to its lacklustre performance during the last decade of the 20th Century. For example, Nigeria's average annual real GDP growth rate has been between 6 and 7 per cent since 2000 making it one of the fastest growing economies in sub-Saharan Africa. Between 1990 and 1999, the average annual growth rate was only 0.2%, but increased rapidly to 6.3% between 2000 and 2010. In the fourth quarter of 2011, Nigeria's real GDP growth rate was as high as 7.68%. Hence, Nigeria's growth was classified as the 3rd highest in the world after Mongolia and China with 14.9 per cent and 8.9 per cent growth rate respectively (CBN, 2011). The improved economic performance since 2000 arguably was a result of good macroeconomic policies and the impact of democracy on economic governance[4]. Indeed, the implementation of economic reforms in 2003 led to an increase in the average growth rate of real GDP to 7% between 2003 and

[1] Milton A. Iyoha (PhD Yale), Professor of Economics, Department of Economics & Statistics, University of Benin, Nigeria

[2] Patricia A. Adamu (PhD), Senior Programme Manager, WAIFEM, Lagos, Nigeria, Email: paadamu@yahoo.com

[3] Dickson E. Oriakhi (PhD), Department of Economics & Statistics, University of Benin, Nigeria

[4] According to an IMF Report the Nigerian economy has grown robustly even during the 2008-09 global crisis, partly due to the effective implementation of countercyclical policies. While growth has been strong, it has not been fully inclusive. Although Nigeria's growth rate over the last decade has been among the highest in sub-Saharan Africa and there is some evidence of income gains also for the rural poor, the official unemployment rate has risen in recent years, reaching 24 percent in 2011 (IMF, 2012, p. 4).

2010. However, the impact of economic growth on the labour market remains a concern to economic analysts and policymakers (see figure 1).

Figure 1: Nigeria's Unemployment Rate 2000-2010 (in %)

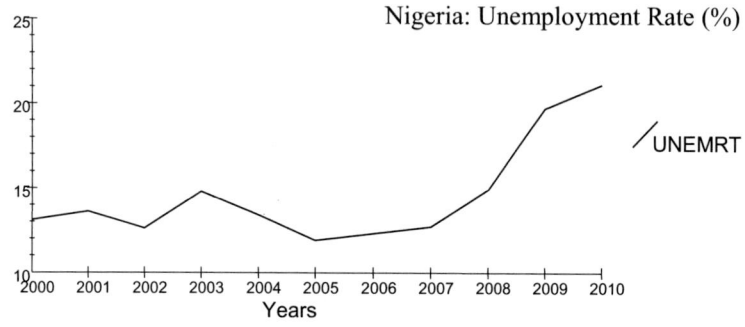

Source: NBS, 2010, 2011
Note: UNEMRT Unemployment Rate

In 2010, the national unemployment rate was 21.1 per cent while the youth (those aged between 15 and 24 years) recorded a rate as high as 35.9 per cent. The unemployment rate even worsened in 2011 - with the national unemployment rate rising to 23.9 percent and the youth unemployment rate increasing to 37.7 per cent (NBS, 2011, and also see figure 1). Furthermore, despite improved economic performance, the incidence of poverty continues to increase with the proportion of the population living below the poverty line rising to 69 percent in 2011 (NBS, various issues).

This paper investigates the impact of macroeconomic policy formulation on the sectoral performance recorded in Nigeria between 1990 and 2010. The paper questioned whether the policies and strategies were themselves backstopped by the economic reform agenda, by sound economic policies and by purposeful leadership (as argued by Iyoha 2010). The paper is structured into 7 sections. Following the introduction in section 1 is section 2 which presents the methodology. Section 3 highlights the relevant literature and the theoretical framework. Section 4 examines the macroeconomic policies and the sectoral development in Nigeria from 1990 to 2010. Section 5 provides the empirical evidence of the impact of macroeconomic policies on sectoral development in Nigeria from 1990 to 2010. Section 6 focuses on the policy implications of the empirical analysis, while section 7 concludes with lessons and recommendations.

2 The Methodology

The paper analyses the macroeconomic policy formation and economic performance in Nigeria under two alternative dispensations, namely, military and civilian between 1990 and 2010. A comparative approach is used to make an assessment of the economic performance in both regimes. First is the analysis of macroeconomic policy and sectoral development during the military regime between 1990 and 1999. This is followed by an analysis of macroeconomic policy and the development of economic sectors during the democratic regime between 2000 and 2010. To assess the impact of macroeconomic policy strategies on sectoral developments during the 1990-2010 years, both statistical and econometric techniques were used. The statistical techniques involve an analysis of the time-series of sectoral outputs using tables and graphs. The econometric analysis focuses on the estimation of sectoral output equations using the technique of cointegration and error-correction modelling.

The study estimates output share equations for 4 major sectors (agriculture, industry, wholesale and retail trade, and services) and the manufacturing sub-sector. Annual time-series data for 1990 through 2010 from the Central Bank of Nigeria (CBN) were collected and utilized. In addition to real sectoral outputs, other variables used in the econometric analysis include: real gross domestic product, real gross domestic capital formation (aggregate investment), government expenditure, broad money supply, and the exchange rate. The data were sourced mainly from the Central Bank of Nigeria (CBN) and supplemented with data from the National Bureau of Statistics (NBS) and the International Monetary Fund (IMF).

3 Review of Relevant Literature and Theoretical Framework

The overall objective of macroeconomic policy is to maximize the long-run welfare of the citizens of a country. In recent literature, the use of intermediate variables, such as price stability and balance of payments equilibrium, in economic policy is based on their importance as indicators of economic performance and wellbeing. For example, price stability is used for attaining long run objectives like greater economic efficiency and economic growth. Ideally, macroeconomic policymaking should emphasize 'real' macroeconomic objectives and the full utilization of productive capacity, in terms of employment of capital and labour as well as improved productivity (Spiegel, 2007).

Generally, three macroeconomic policy instruments have been identified in the literature. These are fiscal, monetary and exchange rate policies. Fiscal policy involves the use of government spending, taxation and borrowing to influence the pattern of economic activity and the level and growth of aggregate demand, output and employment in an economy. It is also used to stimulate the economy during recession. Usually, developing countries are persuaded to engage in tight fiscal policy in order to maintain investors' confidence. This would however result in a lower gross domestic product (GDP) (Cooper, 1992; and Taylor, 1993). Fiscal deficits are discouraged because they may crowd out private investment and may become inflationary. However, they could be growth-enhancing in the long run if channelled into productive investments. Additionally, evidence exists of complementarities between public investment and private investment through improved infrastructure that will have a crowding-in effect (Nayyar, 2000).

Monetary policy involves the use of interest rates to control the level and the rate of growth of credit and aggregate demand in the economy. Conventional monetary policy affects all sectors of the economy, while fiscal policy can be targeted at certain sectors. However, both policies should be designed and implemented according to country-specific conditions and development objectives. Monetary policy is seen to be more effective in dampening an over-heated economy than in revamping an ailing economy (Bank of Japan, 2003; Stiglitz, 2003). In recent times, some economists have shown support for the use of monetary policy rather than fiscal policy for output stabilization. This is so because it is easier for monetary authorities to react in a timely manner towards stabilizing the economy when it derails than relying on the use of changes in public expenditure and taxes which require longer political processes. However, open capital markets tend to limit the effectiveness of monetary policy.

Before the 1990s, direct controls were widely used as monetary policy instruments to manage the money supply in many countries. The direct monetary measures made the process of allocating credit to be complex and inefficient, such that the credit flow was biased towards longstanding and long existing borrowers (Reserve Bank of New Zealand, 2000). However, from the 1990s onwards, many countries switched from direct to indirect control measures. The use of indirect measures, judged from the New Zealand experience, had mixed results because higher interest rates attracted foreign buyers of New Zealand dollars, which then led to exchange rate appreciation. Thus, the burden of such adjustment is borne by the export sector. The implication is however that only one instrument (interest rate) is adjusted and so is applicable for all sectors.

In the new millennium, there has been a greater tendency to use indirect tools of monetary policy. These tools include: open market operations, changes in reserve requirements, central bank lending facilities and changes in the discount rate. Reserve requirements can be used to target specific sectors of the economy. For instance, during periods of bubbles, monetary authorities would raise reserve requirements on loans to affected sectors, such as real estate, to dampen the bubbles and to mitigate inflationary pressures, thereby stabilizing the economy. This is preferred to increasing interest rates which would discourage investment and result in unemployment. But when there is a credit constraint, changes in reserve requirements would induce increased lending to sectors experiencing credit constraints, rather than changing interest rates which will affect overall growth. However, the effectiveness of both monetary and fiscal policies in open economies is limited by the effects of capital flows.

Exchange rate management in Nigeria metamorphosed from a fixed regime in the 1960s to a floating regime in the 1970s to the mid-1980s. With the introduction of the structural adjustment programme (SAP) in 1986, a managed floating regime was introduced. In 1995 and 1999, an Autonomous Foreign Exchange Market (AFEM) and an Interbank Foreign Exchange Market (IFEM) were introduced to guarantee exchange rate stability. This was followed by the Dutch Auction System (DAS) in July 2002. The DAS was adopted in order to reduce the parallel market premium, to conserve foreign exchange reserves and to maintain a realistic exchange rate for the local currency, as well as to minimize speculative tendencies of authorized dealers (see Eme et al. 2012). In a bid to consolidate the gains of the DAS and to achieve convergence between the parallel market and the official rate, the CBN introduced the Wholesale Dutch Auction System (WDAS) in 2006 (Mordi (2006).

According to Calvo and Reinhart (2002), and Calvo (2003) many developing and emerging countries that practice a floating exchange rate regime suffer from a 'fear of floating' syndrome and hence, and so they intervene to manage the exchange rate. Therefore, the appropriate exchange rate regime that would spur growth in developing countries remains controversial (Montiel, 2003; Frankel et al. 2001; Montiel and Ostry, 1991). However, from development economic literature it is known that the level of development of a country matters in determining the type of exchange rate regime that is appropriate for economic growth (McKinnon and Schnabl 2003; Berg et al. 2002; Borensztein and Lee 2002; Lin 2001; and Mussa et al. 2000). Eme et al. (2012) concluded that exchange rate depreciation or devaluation tend to reduce output and to increase the rate of inflation. However, an effective management of the exchange rate is essential for a successful macroeconomic performance of developing countries. Often, the much desired effect of correcting an overvalued exchange rate by depreciation may not be achieved due to structural rigidities in these countries (Maku et al. 2009).

Using a simultaneous and vector auto-regression model to determine the relationship between the real exchange rate and the GDP growth in Nigeria, Eme et al. (2012) found no evidence of a strong direct relationship between changes in the exchange rate and GDP growth. Rather, they found that fiscal and monetary policies as well as the growth of oil exports have exerted great influence on economic growth in Nigeria, and therefore they concluded that the use of monetary policy and of appropriate economic reform programmes would be more effective in enhancing growth rather than exchange rate management.

4 Macroeconomic Policy and the Development of Economic Sectors 1990 to 2010

4.1 Macroeconomic Policy and Sectoral Development in Nigeria, 1990-1999

Government economic policy measures in 1990 were designed towards moderation of the inflation rate, reduction of pressure on the external sector and stabilization of the exchange rate, inducement of increased financial savings, investment and employment, and stimulation of the private sector's productive capacity. The stance of monetary policy during the period was moderately restrictive with growth in money supply declining from 14.6 per cent in 1989 to 13.0 per cent in 1990.

4.1.1 Monetary Policy Formulation in Nigeria, 1990-1999

Monetary policy refers to the use of direct and indirect monetary instruments to control the economy by maintaining a low level of inflation, a low unemployment rate, and a stable exchange rate, in order to ensure macroeconomic stability and to increase economic growth. The conduct of monetary policy in Nigeria has evolved over the years. From 1959 – 1973, the CBN has adopted the strategy of exchange rate targeting as its monetary policy framework. But from 1973 – date, a monetary targeting framework was embraced. However, from 1973 – 1993, direct measures of monetary policy were employed. These included credit ceilings, sectoral credit allocation, administrative control of interest and exchange rates, moral suasion, and movements of government accounts in and out of the deposit money banks (DMBs). From 1993 – date, indirect control measures like open market operations, liquidity and cash reserve ratios, discount window operations, have been utilized by the monetary authority for achieving its policy objectives. The official and interbank exchange rates were unified in 1999 (CBN, 2011).

    Monetary policy actions impact on the real economy through the "transmission mechanism" process. The process is complex, time consuming and difficult to manage due to time lags. Intermediate targets, otherwise known as nominal anchor for monetary policy, are employed to achieve a goal that cannot be directly measured. This nominal anchor includes a quantity-based nominal anchor and a price-based nominal anchor. The quantity-based nominal anchor targets the money stock while the price-based nominal anchor targets the exchange rate or the interest rate. Currently, the CBN uses broad money supply (M2) as the nominal anchor. The final targets of monetary policy are macroeconomic variables, normally the inflation rate. These targets are not directly affected by the central bank policy tools. The central bank chooses another set of variables called the operating targets (base money, reserves etc) which are more responsive to its policy tools. Operating and intermediate targets are used in determining the optimum level of money stock/liquidity consistent with the assumed level of expected output growth and inflation and so as to direct the monetary policy towards the achievement of its goals.

This process starts with the design of a short-term monetary programme approved by Monetary Policy Committee (MPC) using the quantity theory of money. Under the monetary targeting framework, in an indirect approach, the liquidity level that is consistent with macroeconomic objectives is determined, by using: Base Money (BM) as the operating target, M2 as the intermediate target, while inflation is the ultimate target. Conventionally, Base Money (BM) is made up of currency with the non-bank public (C) and reserves of Deposit Money Banks (DMBs). During this period, the design of the monetary policy by the Central Bank of Nigeria (CBN) was in line with fiscal year duration of one year. Monetary policy had always faced the problem of non-commitment to both intermediate and ultimate targets. The optimal long-term policy was not consistent with both the short-term objectives of government and the events that emerged over time due to time inconsistency problem (Ezema, 2009).

4.1.2   Fiscal Policy in Nigeria 1990 – 1999

In this period, the permanency of fiscal deficits characterised the pattern of fiscal policy. Some figures may present the case. In 1990, the fiscal operations of the Federal Government (FG) have resulted in an overall deficit of ₦23,357.0 million or 10.1 per cent of the GDP. The total Federal Government expenditure amounted to ₦61,149.1 million while the retained revenue was ₦37,792.1 million, hence the huge deficit could not be avoided. The total federally collected revenue was ₦66,895.4 million in 1990, and ₦66,846.5 million accrued to the Federation Account after the Federal Government's independent revenue was deducted. In the same year, Federal Government expenditure increased substantially, largely due to the growth in the debt service payments on both domestic and external debts. The expenditure, according to the CBN

(CBN 1990), amounted to ₦61,149.1 million and this amount was ₦ 20,120.8 million or 49.0 per cent higher than the total outlays in 1989. The Federal Government recurrent expenditure of ₦36,219.1 million was mainly on transfer payments, namely interest payments on domestic and external debts, pensions and gratuities. This accounted for 68.4 per cent while administration, social and community services, and economic services absorbed 18.5, 9.5 and 4.5 per cent respectively of the total outlays. Total capital expenditure which stood at ₦24,929.5 million increased over the 1989 and 1988 levels, due largely to outlays on transfer payments, administration, social and community services while outlay on economic services has declined. The share of transfer payments in capital expenditure increased from 44.2 per cent in 1989 to 65.9 per cent in 1990 while those of administration, social and community services and economic services fell from 17.4%, 12.3%, and 22.9% in 1989 to 11.7%, 8.4%, and 14% respectively of total capital expenditures in 1990 (CBN 2000)[5].

In 1994, federally collected revenue increased by 4.7 per cent to ₦ 201,910.8 million from ₦192,769.4 in 1993. Though a surplus was envisaged in the 1994 budget, the Federal Government recorded a deficit of ₦ 70,818.5 million. The banking system financed 70.7 per cent of the deficit while borrowing from the Central Bank of Nigeria (CBN) accounted for 58.3 per cent of the total deficit financing. This action resulted in the substantial growth of domestic liquidity above target and led to increased pressure on prices and the exchange rate. With decreases of 24.7 per cent and 50.8 per cent in domestic interest payments and non-debt expenditure respectively, the recurrent expenditure of the Federal Government fell by 33.5 per cent to ₦ 90,522.8 million from ₦136,177.8 million in 1993. In contrast, external interest payments rose by 74.6 per cent to ₦19,030.0 million. Total recurrent expenditure in relation to GDP fell to 10.1 per cent from 10.7 per cent in

---

[5] The *functional classification of recurrent expenditure* includes four main areas: Administration, economic sectors or services (consisting of agriculture, transport, communication, and road/construction), social and community services, and transfer payments. The personnel costs often take up the lion's share of recurrent expenditure in Nigeria.
In terms of *capital expenditure*, there are also *four principal areas in terms of functional classification*: Administration, outlays on economic services (comprising mainly manufacturing, mining/quarrying, agriculture /natural resources, transport/communication, and roads/construction), public investments on social and community services (principally education and health); and transfers.

1993. Aggregate capital expenditure increased in 1994 by 24.2 per cent to ₦ 51,091.9 million. Apart from general administration and housing, almost all other sub-headings recorded substantial increases in capital expenditure. Internal security, education and health and defence were major beneficiaries of the increase in the capital spending for 1994.

With a retained volume of revenue of ₦662,585.3 million and a total expenditure of ₦947,690.0 million in 1999, the fiscal operations of the Federal Government resulted in an overall deficit of ₦285,104.7 million or 8.4 per cent of GDP. As usual, oil revenue constituted 77.8 per cent of total gross revenue for 1999. Company income tax contributed ₦46,211.2 million to total revenue, a development largely adduced to better tax administration and an increase in voluntary tax compliance. Customs and excise duties contributed ₦87,906.9 million, what was an increase of ₦30,223.9 million or 52.4 per cent over the level of ₦57,683.0 million in 1998, a reflection of the positive impact of port reforms and reduction of tariffs on imports which attracted a large inflow of goods through Nigerian ports. Another major contributor to non-oil revenue was the Value Added Tax (VAT) with ₦47,135.8 million, representing an increase of ₦10,268.1 million or 27.9 per cent over the 1998 level.

Though the 1999 budgeted total expenditure was ₦429,931.6 million, the government expended ₦947,690.0 million, thereby recording a deficit of ₦517,758.4 million or 120.4 per cent of the expenditure. The increase was attributed to personnel cost, expenditure on transition to civil rule, and debt service payments (external and internal). At ₦449,662.4 million, aggregate recurrent expenditure increased by ₦271,554.6 million over the level of ₦ 178,097.8 million in 1998. Outlays on goods and services accounted for ₦ 321,693.3 million under recurrent expenditure in 1999. Personnel cost amounted to ₦134,888.8 million, representing 30.0 per cent of total recurrent expenditure, while overhead cost was ₦58,753.9 million, accounting for 13.1 per cent of total recurrent expenditure. Interest payments on both domestic and foreign debt amounted to ₦127,969.1 million or 28.4 per cent of recurrent expenditure. Capital expenditure in 1999 exhibited similar patterns of expenditure for economic services, transfer payments, and administration. However, outlays on social and community services were a mere ₦17,353.5 million, accounting for a paltry 3.5 per cent of total capital expenditure.

The aforementioned features highlight the endemic problems inherent in Nigeria's fiscal operations. Remarkable is persistence of high fiscal deficits, the unending story of public debt servicing, and the very weak funding of transport and communication infrastructure in the first half of the 1990s. A major dimension to the use of fiscal policy in Nigeria is the role of fiscal deficits in the growth process. Deficit financing is generally accepted by economists as an important fiscal policy instrument for moving the economy towards prosperity when the instrument is correctly utilized. Indeed, many economists have contended that deficits are not totally condemnable provided they do not exceed 3 per cent of GDP, are not chronic, and are not financed by borrowing from the banking sector, especially the Central Bank. More importantly, they should be spent on productive activities, which could generate resources to offset the deficits. When domestic resources are inadequate to place the economy on the path of sustainable economic growth and development, borrowing from both domestic and foreign sources becomes inevitable. However, classical economists are quick to point out that such borrowing, which may result in a debt crisis, has the potential of incurring high interest rates in the domestic economy and crowding out private sector investment.

In 1992, the objective of fiscal policy was the consolidation of the gains of economic restructuring and the promotion of greater efficiency, productivity and increased employment. The restoration of fiscal discipline, improvement in financial transparency and accountability, and restoration of macroeconomic stability which could stimulate the growth of the productive sectors constituted the major policy thrust of the Nigerian government in 1994. The achievement of sustainable output growth and the viability of the external sector which was predicated on the dominant role of the private sector were the concern of fiscal policy in 1997. In 1999, the framework for government intervention in the economy was established and strengthened. Hence, policy measures were directed towards the establishment of the institutional, legal and regulatory frameworks which were designed to promote reforms that could enhance growth, diversification, capacity building and utilization, expansion of the revenue base, and rehabilitation of infrastructure. The inability of Nigerian policy makers to achieve these loftily policy objectives could be ascribed to poor policy implementation and mismanagement.

4.1.3   The Impact of Macroeconomic Policy on Sectoral Development in Nigeria between 1990 and 1999

In addition to its objective of using its available macroeconomic policy tools (fiscal. monetary and exchange rate) to achieve the short-run goal of macroeconomic stability and the long-run objective of rapid economic growth, the government was keen to affect sectoral developments. In particular, it was the intention of the government to increase the relative shares of agriculture and manufacturing in GDP. Government's interest in expanding agriculture's relative share was to boost food self- sufficiency (food security) and to produce enough raw materials so as to encourage the establishment/expansion of agro-allied manufacturing industries. Since the share of manufacturing in GDP had been falling since the adoption of the Structural Adjustment Programme (SAP) in 1986, it was imperative to attempt to use macroeconomic policy tools to increase the relative share of manufacturing in GDP. Unfortunately, as a close examination of Table 1 will show, not much progress was made in achieving the intention of boosting the relative share of manufacturing in GDP although agriculture was basically able to maintain its relative share in output.

An analysis of Table 1 indicates that the industrial sector contributed most to the GDP growth during the period 1990 to 1997, followed by the agricultural and the services sectors respectively. The contribution of the manufacturing sector to the GDP growth was the least important. For instance, the contribution of the industrial sector to GDP growth increased from 41.4 per cent in 1990 to 58.7 per cent in 1993, while that of agriculture fell from 32.7 per cent to 24.2 per cent in the same period. Similarly, the contribution of the services and of the manufacturing sectors to GDP growth fell from 25.9 and 5.54 per cent in 1990 to 17.2 and 4.0 per cent in 1993 respectively. However, the contribution of the industrial sector to GDP growth witnessed a downturn from 1994, while that of agriculture and services sectors had gradual increases over the rest of the period (see Table 1 for details). However, the industry sector is dominated by oil and gas production[6]. The extent of the impact of macroeconomic policy on the sectors will be analysed in section 5.

---

[6] The principal economic sectors are: *Agriculture, Industry, Building and Construction, Wholesale and Retail Trade, and Services*. The *main sub-sectors of Agriculture* are: (i) Crop production; (ii) Livestock; (iii) Forestry; and (iv) Fishing. The *main sub-sectors of Industry* are: (i) Crude petroleum and Natural gas; (ii) Solid minerals (mainly coal mining, metal ores and quarrying); and (iii) Manufacturing (mainly Oil Refining, Cement, and Other Manufacturing). The *main sub-sectors of Services* are: (i) Transport (consisting mainly of Road transport, Rail transport and Pipelines, Water transport, and Air transport); (ii) Communication (mainly Telecommunications and Post); (iii) Utilities (mainly Electricity and Water); (iv) Hotel and Restaurant; (v) Finance and Insurance (mainly Financial Institutions and Insurance); (vi) Real Estate and Business Services (mainly Real Estate and Business Services); (vii) Producers of Government Services (mainly Public Administration, Education and Health); and (viii) Community, Social and Personal Services (mainly Private non-Profit Organizations, Other Services, and Broadcasting).

Table 1: Sectoral Contribution to GDP Growth (percent) 1990-1999

Years	Economic Sector			
	Agriculture	**Industry**	**Manufacturing**	**Services**
1990	32.7	41.4	5.54	25.9
1991	30.4	45.6	5.90	24.0
1992	23.8	58.3	4.32	17.9
1993	24.2	58.7	4.00	17.2
1994	28.6	50.2	4.94	21.2
1995	31.6	46.7	5.36	21.7
1996	30.7	49.2	4.84	20.1
1997	33.6	44.8	5.08	21.6
1998	39.8	33.4	5.24	27.6
1999	36.6	35.2	4.89	28.2

Sources: World Bank, World Development Indicators, various issues; Economist Conference 2007; **Note:** (i) Shares may not add up to 100 percent because of rounding, (ii) Manufacturing is a sub-sector of Industry

4.2   Macroeconomic Policy and Development of Economic Sectors in Nigeria, 2000-2010

4.2.1   *Monetary Policy Framework in Nigeria: Formulation and Implementation 2000-2010*

The objective of monetary policy in Nigeria is to achieve price stability and high and sustainable economic growth, by reducing the gap between actual and potential output. The institutional framework of monetary policy formulation in Nigeria is rather diversified (see Ezema 2009). The framework includes five organs, namely: the Monetary Policy Committee (MPC), the Monetary Policy Technical Committee (MPTC), the Monetary Policy Implementation Committee (MPIC), the Liquidity Assessment Group (LAG), and the Fiscal Liquidity Assessment Committee (FLAC). The MPC is at the apex of the policy hierarchy. It is mandated to formulate monetary and credit policy. The MPTC is charged with the responsibility to provide technical documents on issues of interest for the MPC meetings. The MPIC is the arm of the MPC being responsible for the monitoring and implementation of monetary policy, while the LAG is charged with the daily assessment of the liquidity situation in the economy. It also suggests policy actions to be taken. Lastly, the FLAC provides information on the operation of the Treasury to assist in the forecasting of the optimal liquidity level in the economy (Ezema, 2009).

In 2002, the CBN started a two-year medium-term monetary programme with the aim of liberating monetary policy from the problem of time inconsistency and minimizing the overreaction due to temporary shocks. In the discount window operations, the minimum rediscount rate (MRR) was introduced and used up to December 2006, while the monetary policy rate (MPR) was introduced and used from December 2006 – date; these instruments have been utilized by the monetary authority for achieving its policy objectives (Ezema, 2009). The CBN uses the base (reserve) money as its operating target, broad money supply (M2) as the intermediate target, and inflation as the ultimate target. The operating and intermediate targets are employed in determining the optimal level of the money stock, being consistent with the assumed level of expected output growth and inflation (Ezema, 2009).

To solve the problem of time inconsistency arising from time lags, the CBN adopted a medium term monetary policy framework in January, 2002. This framework enabled the Bank to set targets on a two yearly basis rather than on an annual basis, thereby minimizing the overreaction to temporary shocks. This has yielded positive results as the gap between targets and outcomes has been minimized. For instance, the M2 targets were (in per cent) 15.3 in 2002, 15 in 2004 and 27.8 in 2006; while the outcomes were 21.56, 14.02, and 30.56 in 2002, 2004, and 2006 respectively (Ezema, 2009). However, from December 2006 onwards, a new monetary policy implementation framework was introduced to reduce the interest rate volatility and to pave the way for the adoption of inflation targeting. To this end, a new monetary policy rate (MPR) was put in place to serve as an anchor for monetary policy. This new MPR replaced the minimum rediscount rate (MRR). The new MPR is advantageous since it provides a better signal of the monetary policy stance, stabilizes inter-bank rates, and moderates the deviation from M2 targets and in inflation rates. In this new framework, the operating target is the overnight interbank interest rate, while the prime lending rate is the intermediate target. The monetary transmission mechanism is basically through the term structure of interest rates (Ezema, 2009).

4.2.2   *Fiscal Policy in Nigeria between 2000 and 2010*

Fiscal policy in this period showed changes, by reducing budget deficits and by using fiscal policy instruments for stabilization, economic stimulation and for sector and social policy objectives. The retained revenue of the Federal Government in 2000 amounted to ₦597,282.1 million representing an increase of ₦305,287.3 million or 104.6 per cent over the level in 1999. The increase in retained revenue reflected the enhanced revenues which accrued to the Federation and the VAT Pool Accounts. The main components of the retained revenue included VAT (₦8,255.4 million), privatization proceeds (₦18,103.6 million) and the federal independent account (₦38,061.8) million (CBN 2000). Aggregate expenditure of the Federal Government rose by

19.0 per cent to ₦701,059.4 million, exceeding the budgeted total expenditure of ₦653,135.3 million by 7.3 per cent. The increase was attributed to higher personnel cost as a result of the upward review of salaries and allowances and the higher allocations to domestic debt service payments. Overall, the fiscal operations of the Federal Government resulted in a deficit of ₦ 103,777.3 million or 2.9 of GDP and it was financed entirely from domestic sources, that is, from the banking system. In the year 2000, there was a significant increase in the Federal Government expenditure on education and health. This was a major aspect of the budgetary reforms by the government to shift expenditure from transfers, which has constituted the bulk of expenditure in the last decade before 2000, to social and economic services in order to promote rapid economic development (CBN 2000, p. 39).

In 2005, the fiscal operations of the Federal Government recorded a modest improvement, as the fiscal deficit declined from ₦172.6 billion (or 1.5 per cent of GDP) in 2004 to ₦161.4 billion (or 1.1 per cent of GDP) in 2005. The retained revenue of the Federal Government amounted to ₦ 1,660.7 billion, representing an increase of 32.5 per cent over the level in 2004 and an excess of 11.3 per cent over the ₦1,492.0 billion estimate for 2005. There was an increase of aggregate expenditure of the Federal Government in 2005 by 27.8 per cent to ₦1,872.1 billion relative to the level in 2004 at ₦1,223.1 billion. The recurrent expenditure for 2005 accounted for 67.2 per cent of total expenditure, recording an increase of 18.5 per cent over the 2004 level. The increase in recurrent expenditure was largely attributable to personnel and overhead costs. External and domestic debt service accounted for a reasonable percentage of recurrent expenditure. In 2005, capital expenditure amounted to ₦519.5 billion and constituted 28.5 per cent of total expenditure. As a proportion of Federal Government revenue, capital expenditure was 31.3 per cent, exceeding the minimum target of 20.0 per cent under the West African Monetary Zone (WAMZ) secondary criterion (CBN 2005, p. 58).

In 2010, the balance reflected a deficit of ₦20.2 billion, or 0.1 per cent of GDP, whereas in 2009 there was a surplus of ₦515.0 billion, or 2.0 per cent of GDP. The Federal Government's retained revenue increased to ₦3,089.2 billion in 2010 from ₦2,643.0 billion in 2009. The estimated aggregate expenditure of the Federal Government increased from 2009 by 21.5 per cent to ₦4,194.6 billion in 2010. Total debt service payments amounted to ₦415.6 billion, representing 9.9 per cent of the total expenditure, or 1.4 per cent of the GDP in the same year. With ₦3,109.4 billion, recurrent expenditure accounted for 74.1 per cent of total expenditure. Capital expenditure declined by 23.3 per cent to ₦883.9 billion, or 3.0 per cent of GDP, and accounted for 21.1 per cent of the total expenditure. As a proportion of the Federal Government's revenue, capital expenditure was 28.6 per cent, exceeding the stipulated minimum target of 20.0 per cent under the West African Monetary Zone (WAMZ) secondary convergence criteria. Under capital expenditure for 2010, outlays on economic services accounted for ₦412.2 billion, or 46.6 per cent of total expenditure.

For 2010, the fiscal policy thrust was directed towards stimulating economic recovery from the negative effects of the global economic and financial crisis. With increased spending outlays, the budget was designed to transform the socio-economic fortunes of the country through the implementation of appropriate measures to counteract the problems of the global economic recession. Hence, there were targeted fiscal interventions in the priority sectors, particularly infrastructure, with the intent of providing the enabling environment for the acceleration of sustainable economic growth and development, driven by the private sector. A major component of fiscal policy in 2010 was the rationalization and prioritization of capital expenditure through the allocation of about 90.0 per cent of the Ministries, Departments and Agencies (MDAs) capital expenditure to five (5) key priority sectors, namely critical infrastructure, human capital development, land reform and food security, physical security, law and order and the Niger Delta. Others include the enhancement of power infrastructure, the establishment of a special intervention fund to provide credit facilities for commercial farming, and the creation of gainful employment and an increase in the disposable income.

In keeping with global reforms on budgetary issues, and the need to adopt rules and norms that make it appropriate for representatives (executive/legislative) and managers (public servants) to concentrate on outcomes and outputs, rather than inputs and procedures, the Federal Government commenced budgetary reforms in fiscal year 2003 (CBN, 2010). The idea was to move away gradually from the line-item budgeting to contemporary techniques of budgeting. By the year 2005, the Federal Government had instituted the fiscal strategy plan (FSP) and embraced the Medium Term Fiscal Framework (MTFF), both of which were underscored by the legal framework established by the Fiscal Responsibility Act of 2007. The FSP documents the fiscal stance of the government in the medium term and outlines the MTFF on a rolling basis. By 2008, the Federal Government had progressively embraced a budgetary system which incorporated performance-based elements as a component of the Public Financial Management (PFM) reforms. The major problem in Nigeria's fiscal policy is however the excessive concentration of expenditure on recurrent expenditure, especially on defence spending and on interest payments, so that changes require, first of all, political decisions for reallocations of funds.

The agricultural sector recorded an appreciable performance in 2005. This performance was ascribed to the federal government support for the sector through the subsidy on the supply of fertilizers and other inputs. Crude oil production increased from 2.46 m bpd or 900.4 million barrels in 2004 to 2.53 m bpd or 923.5 million barrels in 2005. The increase was attributed to the lifting of the production ceiling by OPEC on member countries, due to the increase in the demand for crude oil globally. The consumption of premium motor spirit (PMS), which makes up 72.8 per cent of the total petroleum production, has stagnated as a result of the price increases introduced by the government in the last quarter of 2004 and in August 2005.

In 2005 the government, in an attempt to improve on the provision of health services, commenced with the construction of 200 model healthcare centres across the country. And with a determination to ensure the success of the National Health Insurance Scheme (NHIS), the Federal government released the sum of N4.8 billion as its take-off grant. In the education sector, the government encouraged an enhanced participation of the private sector, and this led to the increase in the number of private primary, secondary and tertiary institutions in the country in 2005. Today, the total number of approved Universities exceeds 105.

The thrust of fiscal policy during 2005-2008 was to consolidate the gains of the years 1999-2004 and to sustain growth and development efforts. Thus, the fiscal policy template was influenced by the National Economic Empowerment and Development Strategy (NEEDS) and the Seven Point Agenda (SPA) of the government, and in particular by the Medium Term MTEF/Expenditure Framework (NPC/National Planning Commission, 2009). Hence, the economic policies that were directed at diversifying the revenue base and at rationalizing expenditure for growth were consistent with the objectives of fiscal policy for the period. Budget deficit targets were set at a maximum of 3 per cent of the gross domestic product. The Excess Crude Account (ECA) policy was initiated and implemented during the 2005-2008. By the end of 2008, over US$20,341.2 million were accumulated as savings.

4.2.3   The impact of Macroeconomic Policy Formation of Nigeria on sectoral development 2000 - 2010

Although not much progress was made in its effort to change the sectoral output shares between 1990 and 1999, the government continued with its policies to increase the relative shares of agriculture and manufacturing in GDP during the first decade of the new millennium – this was done by continued use of fiscal, monetary and exchange rate policies. However, an examination of Table 2 will show that no progress was made in increasing the relative of manufacturing in output although some success was achieved in boosting the relative share of agriculture in GDP. The success in agriculture was largely attributable to the effective use of exchange rate policy and of fiscal policy (increased use of subsidies for agricultural inputs by the government). The failure to expand the manufacturing output share can be traced to several factors, particularly the poor state of infrastructure, especially electricity, and the failure to work in this policy direction.

The contribution of the industrial sector to the GDP growth between 2000 and 2006 was higher than the contribution of other sectors. The share increased from 43.6 per cent in 2000 to 56.2 per cent in 2005. The contribution of agriculture, services and manufacturing sectors fell from 28.8, 27.6 and 4.0 to 16.9, 26.9 and 3.8 per cent respectively during the same period. The contribution of the agriculture and services sectors to GDP growth improved tremendously during 2007 – 2010 period, while that of the industrial sector declined (see Table 2 for details). However, the manufacturing sector did not benefit from these changes; the share remained around 4% only. The extent of the impact of macroeconomic policy on the sectors is studied in section 5.

Table 2: Sectoral Contribution to GDP Growth (percent) 2000-2010

Years	Economic Sectors			
	Agriculture	**Industry**	**Manufacturing**	**Services**
2000	28.8	43.6	4.0	27.6
2001	30.6	47.8	3.9	21.6
2002	31.2	43.8	4.6	25.0
2003	26.4	49.4	4.0	24.2
2004	16.6	56.9	3.7	26.5
2005	16.9	56.2	3.8	26.9
2006	17.5	54.0	3.8	28.4
2007	41.3	25.3	4.0	31.2
2008	41.3	23.1	4.1	33.3
2009	41.2	22.4	4.2	34.6
2010	40.9	20.4	4.2	36.8

Sources: World Development Indicators, various issues; Economist Conference 2007; CBN Annual Report and Statement of Accounts, 1990, 2000, 2005, 2010, 2011
Note: (i) Shares may not add up to 100 percent because of rounding, (ii) Manufacturing is a sub-sector of Industry

5   Empirical Evidence of the Impact of Macro-economic Policies on Sectoral Development in Nigeria 1990 - 2010

This section presents the statistical and econometric analysis of the impacts of macroeconomic strategies on sectoral developments in the Nigerian economy from 1990 – 2010. The available macroeconomic data show that, in many respects, the period of civilian democratic governance was more beneficial to Nigerians from an economic perspective than the years of military rule. Measuring economic growth by the percentage growth rate of real income (GDP), it can be shown that economic growth was much higher after the transition to civilian democratic government in Nigeria. Between 1990 and 1999, the growth rate of real income only averaged 0.2 per cent but it increased to 6.3 per cent between 2000 and 2010. Indeed, after adoption of economic reforms in 2003, real income grew at an even higher average annual rate of 7.0 per cent for the next eight years (that is, between 2003 and 2010). Even today, despite of the global financial and economic crisis of 2008-2009, economic growth is still buoyant, reaching a high level of 7.9 per cent in 2010 and equalling 7.68 per cent in the 4th quarter of 2011. This growth rate was said to be the third highest in the world, after Mongolia (14.9 per cent) and China (8.9 per cent (see CBN 2011, Annual Report). The growth that has taken place can be largely attributed to good macroeconomic management as high oil prices played a role for only a few years, at the start of the new millennium. During the second half of the decade, growth was driven by the non-oil sector which was galvanized by good economic policy. Note that in contrast, during the decade of military rule (1990-1999), the economy was stagnant and the growth of per capita real income was even negative. But after the transition to democratic governance, during the period between 2000 and 2010, the economy improved dramatically and the growth of real income was quite robust at 6.3 per cent per annum. This analysis of economic outcomes under military and democratic dispensations again confirms a conclusion, earlier reached by Iyoha (2010, p. 166), to the effect that Nigeria does not quite fit into the "Structural Model" of "The Logic of Authoritarian Bargains" as proposed by Desai, Olofsgard, and Yousef (2007). This arises from the fact that in Nigeria's case, little or no economic gain was present to compensate the citizens for the political rights they had relinquished to the military dictators.

It could therefore be concluded that during the 2000-2010 decade, growth of real GDP was rapid, driven by sound economic management and strategies, home-grown economic reforms, nascent institutions and high oil prices for some of the years. During the second half of the decade, growth was mainly pushed by good performances in the non-oil sector (in particular, agriculture, building and construction, and services). However, poor infrastructure, particularly deficient power supply, has been responsible for a shrinking manufacturing sector, rising unemployment and increasing incidence of poverty. Growth was however not at all inclusive, as the rising unemployment and poverty levels reveal (see also figure 1). Social indicators on health and education are very weak, and no trend of improvement is observable.

5.1 Econometric Analysis of the Impact of Macroeconomic Policies on Sectoral Developments in Nigeria 1990 – 2010

In this section, an attempt will be made to estimate sectoral output share equations for the 4 major sectors of the Nigerian economy, viz., agriculture (AGRSH), industry (INDSH), wholesale and retail trade (WRTSH), and services (SERVSH), and the manufacturing sub-sector (MANSH) in an attempt to explain the determinants of sectoral growth during the 1990-2010 periods. Figure 2 gives the development of the output shares of these four major economic sectors and of the manufacturing sub-sector for this period. It is to be recognized that the manufacturing sub-sector is even showing a continuation of the de-industrialization trend from an already very low base, so that all dynamic advantages of this sector are lost for Nigeria.

Fig. 2: Nigeria: Sectoral Output Shares, 1990-2010

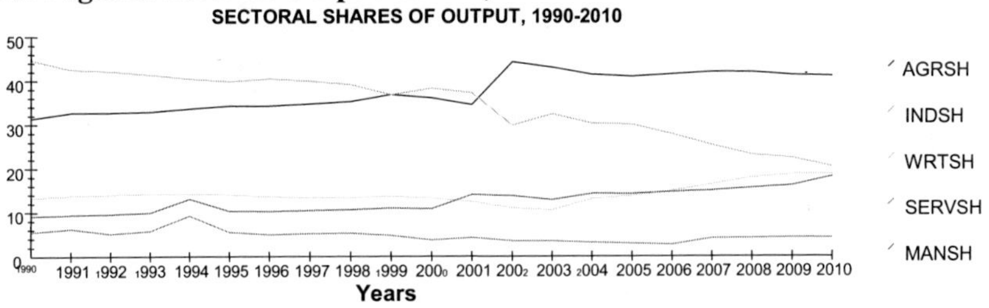

SECTORAL SHARES OF OUTPUT, 1990-2010

5.1.1 The Model Specification

In order to investigate the impact of macroeconomic policy strategies on sectoral development and growth in Nigeria, the output shares are specified to depend on key macroeconomic variables which are indicators and vehicles of macroeconomic policies and strategies. The key macroeconomic variables utilized are: aggregate investment or real gross domestic capital formation (INV), government expenditure (GOVEXP), broad money supply (M2), and the nominal exchange rate (EXRT).

Thus, the share equations are specified thus:

Agrsh = F(INV, GOVEXP, M2, EXRT) .... (1)
Indsh = G(INV, GOVEXP, M2, EXRT) .... (2)
Wrtsh = f(INV, GOVEXP, M2, EXRT,) .... (3)
Servsh = g(INV, GOVEXP, M2, EXRT) .... (4)
Mansh = h(INV, GOVEXP, M2, EXRT) .... (5)

Taking logarithms of the variables and adding stochastic error terms yields the final form of the econometric equations to be estimated as:

$\text{LAgrsh} = a_0 + a_1\text{LINV} + a_2\text{LGOVEXP} + a_3\text{LM2} + a_4\text{LEXRT} + u_1$ .... (6)
$\text{LIndsh} = b_0 + b_1\text{LINV} + b_2\text{LGOVEXP} + b_3\text{LM2} + b_4\text{LEXRT} + u_2$ .... (7)
$\text{LWrtsh} = c_0 + c_1\text{LINV} + c_2\text{LGOVEXP} + c_3\text{LM2} + c_4\text{LEXRT} + u_3$ .... (8)
$\text{LServsh} = d_0 + d_1\text{LINV} + d_2\text{LGOVEXP} + d_3\text{LM2} + d_4\text{LEXRT} + u_4$ .... (9)
$\text{LMansh} = e_0 + e_1\text{LINV} + e_2\text{LGOVEXP} + e_3\text{LM2} + e_4\text{LEXRT} + u_2$ .... (10)

Where:
L stands for logarithms
Agrsh = Percentage share of agriculture in output
Indsh = Percentage share of industry in output
Wrtsh = Percentage share of wholesale and retail trade in output
Servsh = Percentage share of services in output
Mansh = Percentage share of manufacturing sub-sector in output

This section uses annual time-series data for 1990 through 2010. The data set was sourced from the Central Bank of Nigeria (CBN).

5.1.2 Econometric estimation

Since the study uses economic time-series data, it is advisable to begin by verifying the time series properties of the variables employed. That is, it is necessary to find out if the variables are stationary or non-stationary. In sum, it is necessary to determine the order of integration of all the variables in-volved. This is best accomplished by carrying out unit root tests of the varia-bles.

Unit root tests
In order to test for the stationarity of variables used in this study, unit root testing of all the macroeconomic variables and the sectoral shares was carried out using the Augmented Dickey-Fuller (ADF) methodology. The ADF unit

root test is widely considered as the most reliable test of stationarity for economic time series variables. The unit root tests were carried out using the MICROFIT 4.0 econometric software by Pesaran and Pesaran (1997) and the following results were obtained (see table 3).

Table 3: Summary of Unit root tests using the ADF Criterion

Variable Decision	Order	ADF	Decision
LINV	1st difference	-5.41	I(1)
LGOVEXP	1st difference	-5.36	I(1)
LM2	1st difference	-3.93	I(1)
LEXRT	1st difference	-4.06	I(1)
LAGRSH	1st difference	-4.43	I(1)
LINDSH	1st difference	-3.22	I(1)
LWRTSH	2nd difference	-3.85	I(2)
LSERVSH	1st difference	-4.34	I(1)
LMANSH	1st difference	-4.03	I(1)

Note: 95% critical value for the Dickey Fuller statistics = -3.05

Note that all the macroeconomic variables, viz., aggregate investment (INV), government expenditure (GOVEXP), broad money supply (M2), and the nominal exchange rate (EXRT) are difference stationary, that is, they are I(1) variables. All the sectoral shares except the share of wholesale and retail trade in total output (WRTSH) are also difference stationary or I(1) variables. WRTSH was found to be stationary at the second difference. Given these results, the autoregressive distributed lag model and the Bounds Testing Approach (See Pesaran, Shin and Smith (2001)) can be used for the econometric estimation of the share equations provided the variables in each equation are co-integrated. Hereunder, please find the results of the tests of cointegration obtained by using the ADF technique to test for the stationarity of the residuals from the OLS regression of each share equation:

Tests for Co-integration and Error-Correction Modelling using ARDL
Note that when a given set of variables are co-integrated there exists a meaningful long-run relationship among them and the "Granger Representation Theorem" assures us that the short-run dynamics can then be aptly described by an error-correction model. The standard method of obtaining this is by using the autoregressive distributed lag (ARDL) model. However, it has also been shown that the ARDL model can still be used even when co-integration has not been established. See Iyoha (2004). Utilizing the MICROFIT 4.1 econometric software, and using the maximum R-bar squared criterion, we obtain the parsimonious error-correction representation of each share equation:

(a) AGRICULTURE Sectoral share

It can be verified from Table 4 that AGRSH is co-integrated with INV, GOVEXP, M2 and EXRT using the residuals unit root test. Note that the absolute value of the ADF test statistic (5.39) is larger than the absolute value of the 95 % critical value of the Dickey-Fuller test (5.24). Thus, there exists a long-run equilibrium relationship among the five variables.

Table 4: Co-integration Test results of DLAGRSH on DLINV, DLGOVEXP, DLM2, and DLEXRT using data for 1990 through 2010

Variable	ADF Statistics	95% ADF critical value	Remarks
Residuals	-5.392	-5.242	Stationary

Therefore, we can estimate an error-correction model using the auto-regressive distributed lag technique. The parsimonious representation of the error-correction model is reported in Table 5.

Table 5: Parsimonious Error Correction Model for the Agricultural Sector (Dependent variable is dDLAGRSH and 18 observations are used for the estimation from 1993 to 2010.)

Regressor	Coefficient	Standard Error	T-ratio[Prob]
dDLAGRSH1	.68828	.22110	3.1130[.012]
dDLINV	.46319	.13068	3.5444[.006]
dDLINV1	-.39471	.10815	-3.6496[.005]
dDLGOVEXP	-.20014	.073618	-2.7186[.024]
dDLGOVEXP1	.10305	.053840	1.9140[.088]
dDLM2	-.23219	.10715	-2.1669[.058]
dDLEXRT	.24765	.065152	3.8012[.004]
dINPT	-.081894	.054136	-1.5127[.165]
ecm(-1)	-2.7434	.40461	-6.7804[.000]
R-Squared		.94011;	
R-Bar-Squared		.83032	
S.E. of Reg.		.041286;	
F-stat. F(8,9)		11.7736[.001]	
Mean of Dep. Var.		. -.3841E-3	
S.D. of Dep. Var..		10023	
Residual Sum of Squares		.010227	
Equation Log-likelihood		41.7167	
Akaike Info. Criterion		29.7167	
Schwarz Bayesian Criterion		24.3745	
DW-statistic		1.8792	

(b) INDUSTRY Sectoral share

It can be verified from Table 6 that INDSH is co-integrated with INV, GOVEXP, M2 and EXRT using the residuals unit root test. Note that the absolute value of the ADF test statistic (5.42) is larger than the absolute value of the 95 % critical value of the Dickey-Fuller test (5.24). Thus, there exists a long-run equilibrium relationship among the five variables.

Table 6: Cointegration Test results of DLINDSH on DLINV, DLGOVEXP, DLM2, and DLEXRT using data for 1990 through 2010

Variable	ADF Statistics	95% ADF critical value	Remarks
Residuals	-5.417	-5.242	Stationary

Therefore, we can estimate an error-correction model using the auto-regressive distributed lag technique. The parsimonious representation of the error-correction model is reported in Table 7.

Table 7: Parsimonious Error Correction model for the Industrial sector (Dependent variable is dDLINDSH and 18 observations are used for the estimation from 1993 to 2010)

Regressor	Coefficient	Standard Error	T-ratio[Prob]
dDLINDSH1	.52416	.21953	2.3876[.044]
dDLINV	-.013809	.074598	-.18511[.858]
dDLGOVEXP	.23941	.076500	3.1296[.014]
dDLGOVEXP1	-.18759	.057613	-3.2560[.012]
dDLM2	-.20961	.11059	-1.8954[.095]
dDLM21	.33436	.11194	2.9870[.017]
dDLEXRT	-.10626	.050464	-2.1058[.068]
dDLEXRT1	-.062709	.048141	-1.3026[.229]
dINPT	-.061896	.049812	-1.2426[.249]
ecm(-1)	-2.3280	.41353	-5.6296[.000]

R-Squared	.96086
R-Bar-Squared	.83366
S.E. of Reg.	.042955
F-stat. F(8,9)	10.9111[.001]
Mean of Dep. Var.	-.0045089
S.D. of Dep. Var..	.10532
Residual Sum of Squares	.0073807
Equation Log-likelihood	44.6525
Akaike Info. Criterion	30.6525
Schwarz Bayesian Criterion	24.4199
DW-statistic	1.1097

(c) Wholesale and Retail trade Sectoral share
It can be verified from Table 8 that WRTSH is not co-integrated with INV, GOVEXP, M2 and EXRT as the absolute value of the test statistic (2.92) is less than the absolute value of the 95% critical value of the Dickey-Fuller statistic (5.24).

Table 8: Cointegration Test results of DLWRTSH on DLINV, DLGOVEXP, DLM2, and DLEXRT using data for 1990 through 2010

Variable	ADF Statistics	95% ADF critical value	Remarks
Residuals	-2.922	-5.242	Non-stationary

Since there is no co-integration between the variables, an error-correction model cannot be used. However, we can estimate the equation of WRTSH on the macroeconomic variables by distributed lag with OLS. These results are reported in Table 9.

Table 9: Distributed-lag model for the Whole and Retail Trade sector

Ordinary Least Squares Estimation			
Dependent variable is DLWRTSH			
18 observations used for estimation from 1993 to 2010			
Regressor	Coefficient	Standard Error	T-Ratio[Prob]
DLGOVEXP	-.098028	.080212	-1.2221[.245]
DLM2	.14683	.10886	1.3488[.202]
DLEXRT	.084910	.060828	1.3959[.188]
DLWRTSH(-1)	.72815	.23115	3.1501[.008]
DLINV(-1)	.35404	.11660	3.0365[.010]
DLM2(-1)	-.36856	.14726	-2.5029[.028]
R-Squared .53181;		R-Bar-Squared .33673	
S.E. of Reg. .061803;		F-stat. F(5,12)2.7261[.072]	
Mean of Dependent Variable .016198			
S.D. of Dependent Variable .075887			
Residual Sum of Squares .045836			
Equation Log-likelihood 28.2167			
Akaike Info. Criterion 22.2167			
Schwarz Bayesian Criterion 19.5456			
DW-stat. 2.2287;		Durbin's h-stat. -2.4796[.013]	

(d) Services Sectoral share
It can be verified from Table 10 that SERVSH is co-integrated with INV, GOVEXP, M2 and EXRT using the residuals unit root test. Note that the absolute value of the ADF test statistic (6.06) is larger than the absolute value of the 95 % critical value of the Dickey-Fuller test (5.24). Thus, there exists a long-run equilibrium relationship among the five variables.

Table 10: Cointegration Test results of DLSERVSH on DLINV, DLGOVEXP, DLM2, and DLEXRT using data for 1990 through 2010

Variable	ADF Statistics	95% ADF critical value	Remarks
Residuals	-6.0602	-5.242	Stationary

Therefore, we can estimate an error-correction model using the auto-regressive distributed lag technique. The parsimonious representation of the error-correction model is reported in Table 11.

Table 11: Parsimonious Error Correction Model for Services

Dependent variable is dDLSERVSH			
18 observations used for estimation from 1993 to 2010			
Regressor	Coefficient	Standard Error	T-Ratio[Prob]
dDLINV	-.42552	.18126	-2.3476[.043]
dDLINV1	.33719	.20584	1.6381[.136]
dDLGOVEXP	-.17056	.13380	-1.2748[.234]
dDLM2	.31434	.21652	1.4518[.181]
dDLM21	-.39783	.23238	-1.7120[.121]
dDLEXRT	.032791	.096926	.33831[.743]
dDLEXRT1	-.19990	.066207	-3.0194[.014]
dINPT	.030175	.089165	.33842[.743]
ecm(-1)	-1.3124	.22721	-5.7764[.000]
R-Squared .94786;		R-Bar-Squared .82273	
S.E. of Reg. .078778		F-stat. F(8,9) 11.3626[.001]	
Mean of Dependent Variable .0056677			
S.D. of Dependent Variable .18711			
Residual Sum of Squares .031030			
Equation Log-likelihood 31.7277			
Akaike Info. Criterion 18.7277			
Schwarz Bayesian Criterion 12.9403			
DW-statistic .88470			

(e) Manufacturing Sectoral share
It can be verified from Table 12 that MANSH is co-integrated with INV,
GOVEXP, M2 and EXRT using the residuals unit root test. Note that the
absolute value of the ADF test statistic (5.99) is larger than the absolute value
of the 95 % critical value of the Dickey-Fuller test (5.24). Thus, there exists a
long-run equilibrium relationship between the five variables.

**Table 12: Cointegration Test results of DLMANSH on DLINV,
DLGOVEXP, DLM2, and DLEXRT using data for 1990 through 2010**

Variable	ADF Statistics	95% ADF critical value	Remarks
Residuals	-5.99	-5.24	Stationary

Therefore, we can estimate an error-correction model using the autoregressive distributed lag technique. The parsimonious representation of the
error-correction model is reported in Table 13.

Table 13: Parsimonious Error Correction Model for Manufacturing

Dependent variable is dDLMANSH			
18 observations used for estimation from 1993 to 2010			
Regressor	Coefficient	Standard Error	T-Ratio[Prob]
dDLINV	-.59070	.31933	-1.8499[.094]
dDLGOVEXP	-.54810	.30821	-1.7784[.106]
dDLGOVEXP1	-.34318	.20200	-1.6988[.120]
dDLM2	1.1497	.59550	1.9307[.082]
dDLM21	-.71397	.60481	-1.1805[.265]
dDLEXRT	.15198	.18572	.81835[.432]
dINPT	-.55082	.21729	-2.5349[.030]
ecm(-1)	-1.7388	.34722	-5.0076[.001]

R-Squared .92976;		R-Bar-Squared .80099	
S.E. of Reg. .16228		F-stat. F(7,10)11.3462[.000]	
Mean of Dependent Variable .011187			
S.D. of Dependent Variable .36376			
Residual Sum of Squares .15800			
Equation Log-likelihood 17.0789			
Akaike Info. Criterion 5.0789			
Schwarz Bayesian Criterion -.26335			
DW-statistic 1.5989			

5.1.3   Interpretation of results

(a) Agricultural output share
The agricultural output share equation is very good as it has an R^2 of 0.94. Thus, the regressors in this equation explain over 94 percent of the systematic variations in the share of the agricultural sector in total output during the 21 year period, 1990 through 2010. The equation has an F statistic of 11.77 (with a p-value of 0.000). Thus, the hypothesis of a log linear relationship between the share of agriculture in output and the explanatory variables in the equation cannot be rejected at the 1 percent confidence level. The ECM (error correction mechanism) had a negative sign as expected and with a t-statistic of -6.78 has passed the significance test at the 1 percent confidence level.

The most important variables impacting on the agricultural sector during the period under study were its own lagged value, the aggregate level of investment, that is, the level of gross private domestic capital formation, and the exchange rate. These 3 variables had positive signs and were significantly different from zero at the 1 percent confidence level.

(b) Industrial output share
The industrial output share equation was very good, with an R^2 of 0.96 percent. Thus, the explanatory variables used in the equation succeeded in explaining 96 percent of the systematic variations in the share of the industrial sector in output between 1990 and 2010. The F-statistic of 10.9 (with a p-value of 0.001) easily passes the significance test at the 1 percent level. Hence, the hypothesis of a significant log-linear relationship between the share of industry in output and the regressors in this equation is validated. The ECM (error correction mechanism) had a negative sign as expected and with a t-statistic of -5.63 passed the significance test at the 1 percent confidence level.

The most important variables impacting on the share of the industrial sector in output during the 1990-2010 periods were its own lagged value (positively), government expenditure (positively), lagged broad money supply (positively), and the exchange rate (negatively). With a t-value of 3.13, government expenditure was significantly different from zero at the 1 percent confidence level. With a t-value of 2.99, lagged money supply was also significantly different from zero at the 1 percent confidence level. The coefficient of lagged share of industrial production in total output passed the significance test at the 5 percent level. Exchange rate had a negative sign but only passed the significance test at the 10 percent confidence level. The aggregate level of investment was not significant.

(c) Share of Wholesale and Retail trade in output
The equation explaining the share of wholesale and retail trade was just satis-factory, showing an R^2 of 0.53. Thus, variables used were only able to ex-plain 53 percent of the systematic variations in the output share of wholesale and retail trade during the period of 1990-2010. Nevertheless, the equation had an F-statistic of 2.72 which shows that it is significantly different from zero at the 10 percent level. Thus, the hypothesis of a significant log-linear relationship between the output share of the wholesale and retail trade sector and the regressors cannot be rejected at the 10 percent confidence level.

The macroeconomic variables having the greatest impact on the share of wholesale and retail trade in output were lagged WRTSH and lagged INV. These had positive signs and were significantly different from zero at the 1 percent confidence level. On the other hand, the lagged value of broad money supply had a negative sign but was only significant at the 5 percent confi-dence level.

(d) Share of Services in output
The equation explaining the share of services in output was very good with an R^2 of 0.95. This equation therefore explains approximately 95 percent of the systematic variations in the output share of services during the 21-year period studied. The equation had an F-value of 11.36 (with a p-value of 0.001) showing that it easily passes the significance test at the 1 percent con-fidence level. It can therefore be concluded that the hypothesis of a signifi-cant log-linear relationship between the output share of services and the re-gressors in the equation is strongly validated. The ECM (error correction mechanism) had a negative sign as expected and with a t-statistic of -5.78 passed the significance test at the 1 percent confidence level.

The most important variables impacting on the output share of services were the exchange rate (negative and significantly different from zero at the 1 percent level) and aggregate investment (negative and significant at the 5 percent level). The remaining variables were not significantly different from zero at the 1 percent, 5 percent or 10 percent confidence level.

(e) Manufacturing Share of output
The overall fit of the manufacturing output share equation is very good as it has an R^2 of 0.93. Thus, the regressors in this equation explain approximately 93 percent of the systematic variations in the share of the manufacturing sector in total output during the 21 year period, 1990 through 2010. The equation has an F statistic of 11.35 (with a p-value of 0.000). Thus, the hy-pothesis of a log linear relationship between the share of manufacturing in output and the explanatory variables in the equation cannot be rejected at the 1 percent confidence level. The ECM (error correction mechanism) had a

negative sign as expected and with a t-statistic of -5.0 passed the significance test at the 1 percent confidence level.

The most important variable impacting on the manufacturing sector during the period under study was broad money supply. This variable was positively signed and significantly different from zero at the 10 percent confidence level. Aggregate investment had a negative sign and was significant at the 10 percent confidence level. The other variables had negative signs and were not significant at either the 5 percent or 10 percent levels.

From the foregoing analysis, one may conclude that fiscal policy (through government investment spending) has had some measurable effect on agriculture while monetary policy (through variations in broad money supply) has had a substantial effect on industrial sector growth but a lesser effect on manufacturing production. Indeed, the effect of macroeconomic policy on manufacturing output has been so mild that it has not succeeded in raising the share of manufacturing in GDP as the government has been intending. Exchange rate policy seems to be the most versatile of the major macroeconomic policy tools as it has had some effect on the agricultural sector, the industrial sector, and on services.

6 Policy Implications of the Empirical Analysis

Sector-wise, different determinants play a role. The findings allow it to structure better policy interventions.

The main determinants of agriculture's share in output were aggregate investment and the exchange rate. Over the years, government has increased investment in agriculture in order to boost food security. This has been back-stopped in recent years by increasing subsidization of key inputs like fertilizers and by enhancing agricultural extension services.

As expected, government expenditure is a key determinant of the share of the industrial sector in total output. Broad money supply also showed up as a main determinant of the share of industry in total output. This suggests that if properly conceived and implemented, monetary policy can be a driver of industrial output growth in Nigeria.

However, as pointed out above, the share of manufacturing in output has been falling mainly due to gross inadequacy of infrastructure, particularly electricity. The econometric results show that the main determinants of the share of manufacturing sector in total output are broad money supply and aggregate investment.

Government spending and the exchange rate showed up as key determinants of the share of services in total output. The openness of the Nigerian economy explains the important role played by the exchange rate. A depreciation in the exchange rate favours decreased importation while an appreciating exchange rate encourages increased imports. Government spending is critical because of the developmental role played by government in a developing country such as Nigeria.

Finally, the share of wholesale and retail trade in total output turned out to be determined mainly by the aggregate level of investment in the economy.

Currently, agriculture and services are major drivers of growth in Nigeria. This is an indication that economic growth has not resulted in the desired structural changes that would make manufacturing the engine of growth, create employment, promote technological development and reduce poverty (Sanusi, 2010). In their study Obadan and Edo (2004) have noted that manufacturing has been characterized by low capacity utilization, low and declining contribution to national output, a declining and negative real growth rate, a dominance of light consumer goods manufacturing, a low value-added to production due to the high import dependence for inputs, the prevalence of unviable state-owned enterprises, the accumulation of large inventories of unsold finished products, and the dominance of sub-standard goods that cannot compete internationally. It is imperative to introduce policies to change these characteristics.

What is needed most is to raise the share of the manufacturing sector in total output in order to further increase the growth rate of GDP and more importantly to increase employment. Expansion of the manufacturing sector will also benefit agriculture by encouraging the growth of agro-industrial enterprises which would increase the demand for agricultural raw materials. Accelerating the development of the manufacturing sector is a well-known strategy for increasing value added in production, creating employment and reducing poverty. Also technology development and innovation depend on the development of the manufacturing sector.

Given the proven effectiveness of exchange rate policy in affecting sectoral output shares in agriculture, industry, and services, it seems reasonable to project it as the principal tool that the government can use to bring about structural transformation in the Nigerian economy. This should of course be complemented by a fiscal policy which is effective in bringing about changes in the share of agriculture. For best results, fiscal policy should be targeted in order to achieve desired results. For example, in the agricultural sector investment should be directed towards providing improved seedlings, increasing fertilizer use and expanding irrigation. Fiscal policy can also be used to enhance the availability of infrastructural facilities which will not only benefit agriculture but also boost manufacturing production. A medium-term framework for fiscal policies is therefore needed. Monetary policy can then be used to further increase the share of manufacturing and industry in output. In this regard, monetary policy can be used to increase credit to small and medium scale enterprises as a means of expanding manufacturing production. Although something is done in this direction, a much more concerted effort is needed.

7 Conclusions and the Way Forward

In this paper, we have undertaken a comprehensive analysis of the impact of macroeconomic strategies on sectoral developments in the Nigerian economy from 1990 through 2010. The study period spanned both years of military rule (1990-1999) and years of civilian democratic governance (1999-2010). Overall, economic growth was higher during the period of democratic governance - the annual growth rate of real GDP averaged 0.2 percent between 1999 and 1999 while the annual rate of economic growth averaged 6.3 percent between 2000 and 2010. Indeed, since the widespread implementation of economic reforms in 2003 the annual rate of economic growth has averaged a commendable 7 percent. This contrasts sharply with the economic stagnation which characterized the previous decade of military rule. Thus, from a purely economic perspective, democratic governance has greatly benefited Nigeria. This is in addition to the political gains of freedom and an environment of a more liberal society enjoyed under civilian democratic governance. It should be emphasized that the commendable economic performance under democratic governance was driven by good economic policies and strategies, far-reaching economic reforms and the installation of sound institutions. However-er, the growth process was not inclusive in Nigeria in terms of reducing un-employment and youth unemployment, alleviating poverty, and improving health and education indicators. Policies also were not conducive to manufac-turing sector development and sustained agricultural productivity increases.

The sectoral analysis undertaken showed that services (particularly tele-communications and banking) and agriculture were the big "winners" while the industrial sector and particularly the manufacturing sub-sector was the big "loser". The sectoral share of services in total output increased from 11.3 per cent during the decade of military rule to 15.6 per cent during the years of civilian democratic governance. Similarly the share of agriculture in total output rose from 33.8 per cent during the decade of military rule to 40.5 per cent during the years of democratic governance. At 39.1 per cent, the share of the industrial sector in total output was rather low by international standards during the decade of military rule. It fell even lower to 27.6 per cent after the transition to democratic governance. Thus the industrial sector was a "loser" as a result of the transition to democracy. The manufacturing sub-sector was the worst hit. By 2010, the share of manufacturing in GDP had fallen to 2.9 percent. Yet, manufacturing must be revived if growth is to be self-sustaining and if significant progress is to be made in employment creation and poverty reduction. The poor performance of the industrial sector during the entire 1990-2010 period has been attributed in large part to the deficiency of infrastructure, especially transportation and power. The share of wholesale and retail trade in total output remained stationary at approximately 14 percent during the two periods. So, this sector was neither a "winner" nor a "loser" as a result of the transition from military to democratic governance. Neither in the military governance period nor in the civilian governance period there was a sustained trend of structural transformation of the Nigerian economy. Macroeconomic policies were not effective in this regard.

The importance of good macroeconomic policies in the achievement of sustainable development in both developing and developed economies of the world is widely recognized. Good macroeconomic policies were responsible for the appreciable economic performance of the Asian countries. China is a recent example. With a GDP per capita of U$111.82 in 1970, China was ranked 114th in the world, while Nigeria had a GDP per capita of US$233.35 and ranked 88th in the world the same year. Currently, China occupies an enviable position as the second largest economy in the world and Nigeria is struggling to be rated among the 20 leading economies of the world by 2020. Thus, Nigeria needs to improve its policies and strategies to ensure that growth is inclusive, broad-based and transformational.

Overall, we may conclude that the macroeconomic policy strategies of the civilian governments as reflected in the economic reform programs such as NEEDS had a positive impact on the growth and development of agricultural and service sectors. The macroeconomic policy strategies of the civilian governments did not have a significantly positive impact on the wholesale and retail trade sector while their impact on the industrial sector, particularly the manufacturing sub-sector, was negative. It is therefore imperative for the government to improve infrastructure by building more roads and maintaining them, building more modern railways, and boosting the availability of power, especially electricity. However, also many other policy initiatives are needed to support structural transformation in Nigeria, especially also in the macroeconomic policies field. Medium-term Public Expenditure planning, social development policies and a systematic support of non-oil sectors in Nigeria are the most important policy fields. Expansion of the manufacturing sector will not only contribute to a more sustainable growth of real GDP but it will also enhance employment creation and promote poverty reduction.

References

Agu, U. and C. J. Evoh (2011): "Macroeconomic Policy for Full Employment and productive and decent Employment for all: The Case of Nigeria". *Employment Working Paper No 107, International Labour Publications, Switzerland*

AfDB/African Development Bank and AfDF/African Development Fund (2003): *Bank Group Financial Policy,* Operations Policies and Review Department

Akpobasah, M. (2004): "Development Strategy for Nigeria", A Paper Presented at a 2-day Nigeria Meeting organized by the Overseas Development Institute (ODI), London, 16-17, June.

Amadi, S. N., Ogbolo, F. and Essi, D. (2010): Fiscal Policy and Economic Growth: Evidence from Nigeria (1970 – 2006), *Journal of Economic Management Studies and Policy (JEM SAP)*, 3(1) 1-15.

Aregbeyen, O. (2007): Public Expenditures and Economic Growth, *African Journal of Economic Policy*, Ibadan University Press 1(1) 1-37.

BoJ/Bank of Japan (2003): Japan's Deflation and Policy Response, Based on a speech given by Kazuo Ueda, Member of the Policy Board, at the Meeting on Economic and Financial Matters in Nara City, Nara Prefecture. April 24, 2003

Barro, R. (1997): *"Determinants of Economic Growth: A Cross-Country Empirical Study"*. Cambridge, Mass.: MIT Press

Berg, Andrew, Eduardo Borensztein and Paolo Mauro (2002): "An Evaluation of Monetary Regime Options for Latin America". The North American Journal of Economics and Finance, 13: pp. 213-235.

Borensztein, Eduardo and Jone-Wha Lee (2002): Financial Crisis and Credit Crunch in Korea: Evidence from Firm-Level Data. Journal of Monetary Economics, 49(4): pp. 853-75

Bruno, M. and W. Easterly (1998): "Inflation Crises and Long-run Growth", *Journal of Monetary Economics*, 41/1: 3–26

Bruno, M. and W. Easterly (1996): "Inflation and Growth: In search of a stable relationship", *Federal Reserve Bank of St Louis/FRBSL*, 78/3: 139–146.

Bruno, M. (1995): *"Inflation Growth and Monetary Control: Non-Linear Lessons from Crisis and Recovery"*, Paolo Baffi Lectures on Money and Finance. Rome: Bank of Italy, Edizioni dell'Elefante.

Calvo, Guillermo (2003): Explaining Sudden Stop, Growth Collapse and Balance of Payments/BOP Crisis: The Case of Discretionary Output

Tax, The Mundell-Fleming Lecture for the Third Annual IMF Research Conference, Washington, D.C.

Calvo, Guillermo and Carmen Reinhart (2002): Fear of Floating. Quarterly Journal of Economics, 117, no. 2, May, pp. 379-408,

CBN/Central Bank of Nigeria (2010): *Monetary Policy Review*, Vol. 1, no. 1, Abuja: CBN

CBN/Central Bank of Nigeria (2011): Understanding *Monetary Policy Series. No.3, CBN Monetary Policy Framework, 2011*

CBN/Central Bank of Nigeria (2010): *Monetary Policy Review, Vol. No.1, Maiden Issue, 2010*

CBN/Central Bank of Nigeria (1990): *Annual Report and Statement of Accounts*, Abuja

CBN/Central Bank of Nigeria (2000): *Annual Report and Statement of Accounts*, Abuja

CBN/Central Bank of Nigeria (2005): *Annual Report and Statement of Accounts*, Abuja

CBN/Central Bank of Nigeria (2002): *The Changing Structure of the Nigerian Economy and Implications for Development.* Abuja: CBN

Cooper, R. (1992): *Economic Stabilization and Debt in Developing Countries.* Cambridge, Mass.: The MIT Press.

Desai, R. M., A. Olofsgard and T. M. Yousef (2007): "The Logic of Authoritarian Bargains: A Test of a Structural Model", Working Paper No. 3, Brookings Global Economy and Development Series. Washington, D.C.: Brookings Institution.

Easterly, M. and W. Easterly (1998): "Inflation Crises and Long-run Growth". *Journal of Monetary Economics, 41(1), February, Pp. 3-26.*

Ekpo, A. (1994): Public Expenditure and Economic Growth in Nigeria 1960 to 1992, Final Report, African Economic Research Consortium/AERC, Nairobi, Kenya

Economist Conference 2007 (2007): Third Business Roundtable with the Government of Nigeria. Abuja

Eme, A. D. and Olugboyega, O. A. (2012): "Exchange Rate and Macroeconomic Aggregates in Nigeria", Journal of Economics and Sustainable Development, Vol. 3, No. 2, Website: www.iiste.org, ISSN 2222-1700 (Paper) ISSN 2222-2855 (Online).

Eyo, E. O. (2008): "Macroeconomic Environment and Agricultural Sector Growth in Nigeria". *World Journal of Agricultural Sciences 4 (6): 781-786, 2008.*

Eyo, E. O. (2005): "Agricultural Development in Nigeria: Plan, Policies and Programmes". *Best Print Business Press*, Uyo - Nigeria.

Ezema, C. C. (2009): "Monetary Policy Framework in Nigeria: Formulation and Implementation Challenges". *African Institute of Applied Economics (AIAE), Enugu, Nigeria: Monthly Seminar, August, 2009.*

Fischer, S. (1996): "*Why are Central Banks Pursuing Long-Run Price Stability?*", in: Achieving Price Stability, Proceedings of a symposium sponsored by the Federal Reserve Bank of Kansas City in Jackson Hole, Wyo., August 29-31, 1996.

Frenkel, R. (2004): "Real Exchange Rate and Employment in Argentina, Brazil, Chile and Mexico". Paper prepared for the Group of 24, Washington, D.C.

Frenkel, R. and L. Taylor (2006): "Real Exchange Rate, Monetary Policy, and Employment. In: *Policy Matters: Economic and social policies to sustain equitable development,* J. A. Ocampo, Jomo K. S., and Sarbuland Khan, eds., New York, NY: United Nations.

Frankel, Jeffrey A, Eduardo Fajnzylber, Sergio L. Schmukler and Luis Servén, (2001): "Verifying Exchange Rate Regimes", in: Journal of Development Economics 66(2) pp. 351-86.

Garba, P. K. (2000): "An Analysis of the Implementation and Stability of Nigerian Agricultural Policies, 1970-1993". *AERC/African Economic Research Consortium, Research Paper 101,* Nairobi, Kenya

International Monetary Fund (IMF) (2012): Nigeria: Staff Report for the 2011 Article IV Consultation, Washington, D. C.: IMF, February 2012

Iyoha, M. A. (2010): "Leadership, policy making, and economic growth in African countries: The case of Nigeria", as Chapter 6: In: D. Brady and M. Spence (Eds.), *Leadership and Growth,* Washington, D. C.: World Bank.

Iyoha, M. A. (2004): *Applied Econometrics.* Benin City: Mindex Publishing

Iyoha, M. A. and D. E. Oriakhi (2008): "Explaining African economic growth performance: the Case of Nigeria". In: B. J. Ndulu, S. O'Connell, J. Azam, R. H. Bates, A. K. Fosu, J. W. Gunning, and D. Njinkeu (Eds.), *The Political Economy of Economic Growth in Africa, 1960–2000: Volume 2, Country Case Studies.* Cambridge, UK: Cambridge University Press.

Levine, R. and S. Zervos (1993): "What have we learned about Policy and Growth from Cross-Country Regressions, *American Economic Review*, 426-430.

Levine R. and D. Renelt (1992): "A Sensitivity Analysis of Cross-Country Growth Regressions". *American Economic Review,* 426 – 430.

Limonic, L. and S. Spiegel (2004): "Report on Nigeria Country Dialogue". *Initiative for Policy Dialogue (IPD),* Columbia University, New York, USA, May 6 – 24, 2004.

Lin, Justin Yifu (2001): "WTO Accession and Financial Reform in China", in: Cato Journal, 21(1), (Spring-Summer): pp. 13-18.

Maku, O. E. and Atanda A. A. (2009): "Does Macroeconomic Indicators Exert Shock on the Nigerian Capital Market?", online at: http://mpra.ub.uni-muenchen.de/17917/MPRA Paper No. 17917, posted 17, October 2009/03:36.

McKinnon, Ronald and G. Schnabl, (2003): "The East Asian Dollar Standard, Fear of Floating, and Original Sin, in: G. Ortiz, ed. Macroeconomic Stability, Financial Markets, and Economic Development, Bank of Mexico. - 33

Montiel, Peter J, (2003): Macroeconomics in Emerging Markets. Cambridge: Cambridge University Press.

Montiel, Peter J. and Jonathan Ostry (1991): "Macroeconomic Implication of Real Exchange Rate Targeting in Developing Countries", IMF Working Paper 91/29, Washington D. C.: IMF/International Monetary Fund

Mordi, C. N. (2006): "Challenges of Exchange Rate Volatility in Economic Management in Nigeria", Bullion, Vol. 30, No. 3, July - Sept. 2006

Mussa, M., P. Masson, A. Swoboda, E. Jadresic, P. Mauro & A. Berg (2000): "Exchange Rate Regimes in an Increasingly Integrated World Economy", IMF Occasional Paper No. 193, Washington, D.C.

NBS/National Bureau of Statistics (2010): *National Manpower Stock and Employment Generation Survey,* Abuja

NBS/National Bureau of Statistics (2011): *Annual Socio-Economic Report,* Abuja

NBS/National Bureau of Statistics (2012): *Review of the Nigerian Economy in 2011 & Economic Outlook for 2012-2015.* Abuja. May 2012

NPC/National Planning Commission Reports (2009, 2010, and 2011): *Annual Performance of the Nigerian Economy*, The Presidency, Abuja

NPC/National Planning Commission (2009): *Nigeria Vision 20:2020, Economic Transformation Blueprint*, The Presidency, Abuja.

Nayyar, D. (2000): "Macroeconomic Reforms in India: Short-term Effects and Long-run Implications, In: *Adjustment and Beyond: The reform Experience in South Asia,* Wahidudin Mahmud (ed.) London: Palgrave.

Obadan, M. I. and Edo, S. (2010): Overall Economic Direction, Strategy and Performance of the Nigerian Economy since Independence; in: *50 years of the Nigerian Project, Challenges and Prospects,* Bello-Imam, I. B. (Ed.), College Press and Publishers Limited, Ibadan.

Obadan, M. I. and Edo, S. (2004): Overall Economic Direction, Strategy and Performance, in: *Democratic Governance and Development Management in Nigeria's Fourth Republic, 1999-2003,* Bello-Imam I. B. and Obadan M. I. (Eds.), Centre for Local Government and Rural Development Studies, Ibadan.

Odusola, A. F. (1996): Military Expenditure and Economic Growth in Nigeria, in: *The Nigerian Journal of Economic and Social Studies,* 38, 1-3.

Okonjo-Iweala, N. and P. Osafo-Kwaako (2007): "Nigeria's Economic Reforms: Progress and Challenges", Working Paper #6, Brookings Global Economy and Development Series. Washington, D. C.: The Brookings Institution.

Pesaran, B. and M. H. Pesaran (2009): *Time Series Econometrics using Microfit 5.0,* Oxford

Pesaran, B. and M. H. Pesaran (1997): Working with Microfit 4.0: Interactive Econometric Analysis, Oxford University Press

Pesaran, M. H., Y. Shin and R. P. Smith (2001): Bounds Testing Approaches to the Analysis of Level Relationships", in: *Journal of Applied Econometrics,* vol. 16, pp. 289-326

RBNZ/Reserve Bank of New Zealand (2000): *Alternative Monetary Policy Instruments.* Accessed: http://www.rbnz.govt.nz/monpol/review/0096420.pdf

Robert, S. (1997): "Monetary Policy within Macroeconomic Policy: An Appraisal in the context of Reconstruction and Development". *Transformation, 32(1990)*

Spiegel, S. (2007): "Macroeconomic and Growth Policies", *United Nations Department for Economic and Social Affairs (UNDESA).*

Stiglitz, J. (2003): *The Roaring Nineties.* New York: W. W. Norton & Company.

Taylor, L. (1993): *The Rocky Road to Reform: Adjustment, Income Distribution and Growth in the Developing World.* Cambridge, Mass.: MIT Press.

Sanusi, L. S. (2010): "Growth Prospects for the Nigerian Economy". A paper presented at the Eight Convocation Lecture of Igbinedion University, Okada, 26 November 2010

Analysis of the Prospects for a Second Monetary Zone for West Africa

P. P. Njiforti P.P.[1]

1 Introduction

The conception of the West African Monetary Zone (WAMZ), also known as the second monetary zone in West Africa, reached a higher pedestal following the institutional meetings of the zone in Dakar, Senegal in December 2001. The idea of the second monetary zone was adopted by the summit of the Economic Community of West African States (ECOWAS) in Lome, Togo in December 1999 as a means of fast tracking the integration process of the community. The prospective members of the second monetary zone − including The Gambia, Ghana, Guinea, Liberia, Nigeria and Sierra Leone[2] − signed the Accra Declaration in April 2000, committing themselves to the ideals of a second monetary zone within the integration programme of ECOWAS (Ojo, 2005).

The quest for an ECOWAS common currency was further strengthened partly by the success story of the European Monetary Union (EMU). However, recent financial and economic crises within the Eurozone have raised policy questions whether the Euro model is the best option for adopting a single currency in the WAMZ (Daniel, 2011). It was the general belief that Europe's path to a monetary union could be adopted to expedite the ECOWAS common currency project. The assumption here is that it conforms to the theoretical literature on regional integration sequencing[3]. This approach requires that intending members of a monetary union must meet some defined Optimum Currency Area (OCA) criteria which focus on macroeconom-

[1] Njiforti P.P. (PH.D), Email: njifortica@yahoo.com and pivadga@gmail.com , Telephone: +2378036069211, Department of Economics Ahmadu Bello University, Zaria, Nigeria
[2] Cape Verde has an observer status.
[3] Regional integration sequencing metamorphoses from Free Trade Area (FTA) through the Customs Union (CU) and the Common Market (CM) to the Monetary Union (Balassa, 1964).

ic convergence of the intending member countries. The policy approach to the realization of WAMZ, so far, seems to draw essentially from the traditional OCA theories that business cycle synchronization and macroeconomic convergence make a currency area an optimal monetary arrangement, other things being equal (Balogun, 2008). This is so because it reduces the scope for asymmetric policy response to disturbances hitting the union-wide economy (Bayoumi and Eichengreen, 1992). However for about nine years, the proponents of WAMZ have experimented with this approach but have failed to meet the specified convergence criteria (Daniel, 2011). The inability of the member countries to implement policies towards the attainment of the ECOWAS single market objective and the WAMZ convergence criteria led to the postponement of the launching of the WAMZ monetary union to December, 1st 2009 (Obaseki, 2005). Now the year 2012 has not seen major achievements in this regard, although the project is upheld now for the year 2015.

In general, there are concerns within policy and academic circles that there is little likelihood that even three countries would be able meet these criteria given the apparent lack of policy co-ordination among members (see for instance Nnanna, 2007). These concerns over the slim prospects for macroeconomic convergence are significant given the little trade relations among WAMZ member countries, and the non-fulfilment of other OCA criteria. This paper therefore analyses the prospects for the formation of the West African Monetary Zone (WAMZ), i.e. the second monetary union in West Africa by the year 2015. The analysis is based on the macroeconomic convergence criteria and is divided into the primary and secondary convergence criteria.

The paper is divided into 7 sections, with introductory section 1 highlighting the research problems and the objectives of the study. Section 2 deals with the review of the literature on macroeconomic convergence. Section 3 highlights the rationale for the formation of a WAMZ. Section 4 provides the empirical analysis using annual time series data on the selected macroeconomic convergence criteria variables across the proposed WAMZ member countries. Section 5 presents the econometric analysis by examining time series properties of the series for both the primary and secondary criteria. Section 6 highlights the sufficient conditions for a sustainable WAMZ, while section 7 concludes the paper.

2 Review of Literature

The concept of macroeconomic convergence has gained prominence for a variety of reasons. The main reason for economic convergence, according to proponents, resides on the fact that coordination of economic policies leaves countries better off without others being worse off. However, the contagion effect of macroeconomic instability among member countries is eminent due to some common policies that bind these countries together. The recent events in the Eurozone give evidence of these contagion effects.

According to Paola (2007) economic convergence is feasible when member countries tend to reach a similar level of development and wealth. Solow's economic growth model depicts that an economy converges towards a steady state due to diminishing returns in physical capital investment. A major assumption drawn from Solow's model is that countries are identical in all aspects but differ in their initial levels of capital per capita - with poorer countries having higher marginal capital productivity than richer countries, thus giving these poorer countries room to catch up. Generally, two main strands of these theories - which member countries seek to optimize - are the Customs Union (CU) and the Optimal Currency Area (OCA) theories. The Customs Union (CU) theory basically tends to describe trade theories. Trade theories on regional integration are hinged on the assumption that 'productive efficiency' is enhanced if states undertake economic production in areas where they have relative advantage to others, thus rationalizing costs and prices (Anadi, 2005).

The Customs Union (CU) theory is premised on the assumptions of perfect competition in commodity and factor markets. The theory deals with the static welfare effects of a customs union with member countries deriving both positive and negative welfare effects. Initially conceptualized by Viner (1950), trade among member countries occurs when the output of inefficient producers is replaced after the elimination of tariffs by cheaper imports of more efficient producers within the region to the benefit of both producers and consumers. In line with Viner, Balassa (1961) noted that economic integration reduces trade barriers among countries. The central idea is that cooperation in international trade by setting zero tariffs against each other are beneficial relative to the case when countries attempt to secure short term advantages by setting optimal tariffs. Benefits can only be feasible when countries liberalize labour and capital movements across borders, coordinate fiscal and monetary policies, and coordinate resource allocation as well. Balassa (1961) noted that economic integration precedes political integration, with common markets and free movement of economic factors across national borders naturally generating a demand for further integration. These ideas have been endorsed by Mundell (1961) and Fleming (1962) who argued that factor mobility, and particularly labour mobility, within a region, is crucial to the success in the establishment of a currency area. Factor mobility will reduce the dependency on exchange rate variations for external balance, thus making the monetary union conducive for a fixed exchange rate.

Similarly, McKinnon (1963) emphasized that openness and the size of the economy as important determining features of integration while Kenen (1969) looked at the degree of commodity diversification as an important determining factor. Kendall (2000) noted that the benefits of regional integration are tantamount to increased mobility of both, labour and capital, an increase in the liquidity value of money, the reduction of exchange rate speculation within the region, and the reduced foreign exchange reserves requirement, given the fact that intraregional trade no longer would require foreign exchange. Summarily the Mundell - Fleming is enshrining in what is commonly known as the monetary policy trilemma which states that, from a menu of three potential desirable conditions, governments can achieve at most only two of three conditions: (1) domestic monetary policy is autonomous; (2) external currency stability; and (3) international capital mobility).

The traditional OCA theory is based essentially on the study of costs arising from the loss of the ability to conduct a national monetary policy – the inability to affect its exchange rates, considered to be a strong instrument for ensuring stability in the monetary field. In his work, Mundell (1961) is considered as the pioneer of the theory, and he has identified some criteria under which a monetary union will be successfully attained. According to the theory, regions or countries can be affected by different distortions (symmetric or asymmetric shocks). The essence of the theory is outlined through demand shifts from one country to another. According to Mundell (1961), because of these asymmetric shocks, both countries are confronted with adjustment problems. The first country faces a decrease in its level of employment and a deficit in its current account. The second country faces an expansion, which can result in upward pressures on its price levels and it accumulates a current account surplus.

As mentioned, for eliminating such macroeconomic disequilibria, the control of exchange rates constitutes a powerful instrument for adjustment. This means that depreciation of the currency in the first country would eliminate the current account balance problems and unemployment, on the one hand, and inflationary pressures, on the other. This is so because depreciation stimulates the demand for the goods of the domestic economy. In the absence of exchange rate flexibility, the adjustment mechanisms will be supported by variations in wages and unemployment. The nature of the criteria is diverse. Some of them emphasize adjustment mechanisms, which can substitute for exchange rate flexibility. The low degree of diversification within the monetary union can accentuate the existence of asymmetric shocks. These criteria may limit the feasibility of a monetary union and/or may determine whether or not an existing monetary union constitutes an OCA (Masson and Taylor,

1993; Dyson, ed., 1994; Aschheim and Tavlas, 1995)[4]. The above factors are very relevant to be taken into consideration for the formation of WAMZ. However, for most African countries the assumptions of the neoclassical market economy do not hold. Some countries still experience fiscal dominance externally and internally. Labour mobility is highly restricted even within the same blocks. Some of the economies are mono-cultural in nature in terms of dependence on a few natural resources which are not processed in the countries.

3 The West African Monetary Zone (WAMZ)

3.1 Towards Macroeconomic Convergence and the Rationale For the Formation of the WMAZ

The agreement of the WAMZ and the status establishing it were signed in Bamako in December 2000 by the member states, except Liberia that requested the right for more time to study them. With this critical action taken,

---

[4]   These criteria are: (i) Factors' mobility: In the case of demand shifts, labour mobility is a "natural" mechanism that will lead to a new equilibrium. This movement of labour eliminates the need for wage declines. Thereby, unemployment problems and inflationary wage pressures disappear. At the same time, current account disequilibria will also decline;

(ii) Wage flexibility: As is the case with demand shifts, total price and wage flexibility ensure a return towards initial equilibrium. If there is no labour and wage flexibility, the adjustment of the real exchange rate is necessary;

(iii) Country openness: Two opposite views are linked to the criterion of country openness. According to the first view, more openness reduces the cost of a monetary union, as it reduces the probability of the occurrence of asymmetric shocks. The second view is opposed to the first one. The costs of a monetary union increase with the degree of openness of a country. The idea behind the degree of openness is the effectiveness of the exchange rate in dealing with asymmetric shocks.

(iv) Diversification of the production structure: When an economy is well diversified in its production structure, a demand shock will have a small effect. Diversification implies a compensation of international immobility by means of inter-sector mobility (De Grauwe, 1997; De Grauwe and Vanhaverbeke, 1993).

(v) Integration and specialization dynamism: For Masson and Taylor (1993) the impact of a monetary union will depend on intra–community trade, which will condition the degree of asymmetric shocks. Asymmetric shocks refer to the differential response of member countries to economic dynamism or changes.

the monetary union mechanisms of the zone were expected to take off in January 2003. The WAMZ membership consisted of five countries viz.: The Gambia, Ghana, Guinea, Nigeria, and Sierra Leone, with Cape Verde and Liberia acting as observers. Liberia became a full member in the year 2010 while Cape Verde still maintained the observer status. The objective of the WAMZ is to establish a monetary union characterised by a common central bank and a single currency to replace the existing five (and then six) national currencies. The concept of the second monetary zone was endorsed in December 1999 by the Authority of Heads of State and Government of the Economic Community of West African States (ECOWAS) (WAMI, 2011) to facilitate the achievement of the goal of a single monetary zone in the sub - region, following a prolonged delay in its realisation due to economic and political problems. The West African Monetary Institute (WAMI) was set up to prepare member countries for the second monetary union, by implementing the WAMZ programme, consisting of a set of macroeconomic convergence criteria. The project, if successful, would lead to a common currency; the common currency of the zone would be called "The Eco" (see Ojo, 2004).

Member countries are required to comply with five convergence criteria before acceding to the monetary union. These are in the areas of fiscal deficit, inflation, interest rate and exchange rate. In furtherance of the objective of monetary integration, the Authority of Head of State and Government of ECOWAS at its 22nd summit in Lome in 1999 (Ukpong, 2002) adopted the set of macroeconomic convergence criteria including:

✓ Ratio of budget deficit (excluding grant)/GDP (Commitment basis) of less than or equal to 4 per cent by year 2002,
✓ Inflation rate of 5 per cent by 2003,
✓ Central bank financing of the budget deficit be limited to 10 per cent of previous year's tax revenue by the year 2003, and
✓ Gross foreign exchange reserves to be greater than or equal to 6 months of imports by the year 2003.

However at the Ghana/Nigeria bilateral economic meeting held in Accra between December 20 and 21 1999, it was agreed that these primary criteria be adopted subject to their implementation in two phases, beginning with the following bench marks.

✓ Single digit inflation rate by 2000,
✓ Gross foreign exchange reserves to cover at least 3 months of imports by 2000,
✓ Central bank financing of budget deficit to be limited to 10 per cent of previous year's tax revenue by the year 2000,
✓ Budget deficit/GDP ratio (to be determined later). The technical committee later proposed 5 per cent for 2000.

In addition the above primary criteria, another set of requirements in the form of secondary criteria include:

✓ Prohibition of new domestic arrears and liquidation of all existing arrears.

✓ Tax revenue/GDP ratio to be equal or more than 20 per cent.

✓ Wage bill/total tax revenue to be equal to or less than 35 per cent.

✓ Public investment/Tax revenue ratio to be equal to or more than 20 per cent.

✓ Real exchange rate stability to be maintained by each country. The exact rate will, however, be determined within the context of the ECOWAS exchange rate mechanism, and

✓ Maintenance of positive real interest rates.

The major benefits and rationale for the formation of common currency unions as argued by Madhur (2002) is that it facilitates trade and investment among the countries of the union. It promotes income growth within the region by reducing transaction costs in cross-border business, and by removing volatility in exchange rates across the union. Barro (2001) sees a currency like a language, and thus as common language facilitates effective communication among people; common currency could therefore promote trade and investment among countries. In an environment of different currencies, transaction costs, including the costs of obtaining information about prices, would be higher. This would be a disincentive to trade, commerce and investment.

The analysis and discussion so far suggest that the attainment of an economic and monetary union in West Africa is a desirable objective and hence necessary (Soyibo, 1998). The main argument in support is that the working balances in convertible currencies can be reduced because convertible currencies are used only for the settlement of net balances at the end of each transaction period (Quirk and Evans, 1995). Another major attraction of monetary integration is its trade-creating potential (in both goods and services) within and beyond the constituent states by removing some of the payments obstacles to trade (Itsede, 2002).

Despite the advantages advanced above, the experience in West African countries shows a very low level of intra-trade. For instance, intra-African trade stands at around 10 per cent compared to 60 per cent, 40 per cent, and 30 per cent of intra-regional trade that has been achieved by Europe, North America and ASEAN respectively. Even if allowance is made for Africa's unrecorded informal cross-border trade, the total level of intra-African trade is not likely to be more than 20 per cent, which is still lower than that of other major regions of the world (Mwangi et al., 2012)[5].

---

[5] For instance, Nigeria's export to the ECOWAS region, which averaged about 7 per cent of its total exports between 2001 and 2006, plummeted to 2.3 percent in 2010.

Moreover, the average freight cost in West Africa in 1997 was about 12.9 per cent of the cost of insurance and freight import values, in comparison with 4 per cent of these values for developed countries (WTO, 2004). The incredibly high volume and range of nontariff barriers that are still in force is corrosive to intraregional trade. The number of checkpoints erected by law enforcement agents along highways connecting West African countries range from seven per 100 kilometres between Lagos and Abidjan to two per 100 kilometres between Accra and Ouagadougou (WTO, 2004).

Political tension, conflict and violence also diminish the capacity for African states to engage in intra-continental trade. These factors lead to low levels of economic growth, destroy needed export infrastructure, and slow down and even reverse regional integration. Infrastructure is and has always been a major issue for Africa, especially for Sub-Saharan countries. Like conflict, infrastructural deficiencies reduce economic growth and productivity, and raise transportation costs. According to a 2010 report from regional African organizations only about 30 per cent of African roads are paved and, as a consequence, "shipping a car from Japan to Abidjan costs $1,500, while shipping that same vehicle from Addis Ababa to Abidjan would cost $5,000" (UNECA, AU and AfDB 2010, pp. 193-238).

Africa's maritime ports have their own problems; the same report estimates that the continent's port productivity is only 30 per cent of the international norm. It is likely that part of the reason for this underperformance is the unequal usage of the continent's ports; only six of its 90 total ports (three in Egypt and three in South Africa) handle 50 per cent of its trade. A related issue deals with cost; the port in Durban—Sub- Saharan Africa's busiest port—charges more to dock a ship than any other major harbour in the world and the charges are double the world's average. This same scenario is experienced in West African ports (Mwangi et al., 2012).

The vast majority of Nigeria's exports to the ECOWAS are mineral fuel and oils, which reached 97 percent and 94 percent, respectively, in 2009 and 2010. Comparatively, the share of manufacturing in Nigeria's total exports to the ECOWAS region climbed from 1 per cent in 2001 to 5.4 per cent in 2010, while the share of Nigeria's agricultural exports — which was 3 per cent in 2001— plunged to nearly nothing in 2009 and 2010 ((Mwangi et al., 2012).

4 Empirical Analysis - Convergence Performance by Criteria and Countries

4.1 Empirical Analysis - Convergence Performance by Criteria

4.1.1 Primary Convergence Criteria

a) Budget Deficit / GDP Ratio <4%
According to the WAMA Macroeconomic Convergence Report 2009[6], fiscal performance in Table 4.1 shows that the macroeconomic convergence criterion improved significantly between 2006 and 2009 compared to the situation prior to this period. Five countries, namely The Gambia, Ghana, Guinea, Liberia and Nigeria met up with this criterion, with 4 countries constantly meeting the Budget Deficit/GDP ratio criteria since 2006.

Table 4.1: Budget Deficit / GDP Ratio<4%

	2001	2002	2003	2004	2005	2006	2007	H1 2008	2008	H1 2009	2009*
Cape Verde	11.4	10.5	9.1	8.4	11.0	9.7	6.1	10.0	5.8	5.8	6.2
Gambia	-9.8	-9.1	-7.6	-10.2	-8.4	-2.7	-1.1	-2.1	-4.2	-3.3	-4.3
Ghana	13.2	8.3	7.5	8.1	6.9	12.9	14.5	11.1	19.5	11.7	18.0
Guinea	3.4	6.2	8.8	5.9	1.6	2.0	0.9	0.1	1.7	0.8	2.9
Liberia	1.9	1.0	3.7	4.4	0.9	-3.0	3.4	2.2	2.0	1.6	2.0
Nigeria	5.8	5.9	2.8	1.7	1.3	0.6	1.2	0.0	0.2	2.8	0.4
Sierra Leone	16.7	16.5	19.4	14.3	9.5	8.5	5.0	9.5	8.6	5.7	8.1
No. of countries	2	1	2	1	3	4	4	4	4	4	4

Source: WAMA[7] (2009, p. 20) and Central Banks[8], **Note**: H1= First Half; *=Projection; the areas marked are figures that met the convergence criteria

---

[6] The latest comprehensive macroeconomic convergence data report for the convergence criteria which was used in this study was published in 2009 by the West African Monetary Agency/WAMA (WAMA 2009). This analysis is therefore limited to 2009.
[7] WAMA Report/West Africa Monetary Agency Report 2009, ECOWAS Monetary Cooperation Programme, *Macroeconomic Convergence Report 2009.*
http://www.amao-wama. org/fr/Publications /convergences% 20macro%20en.pdf
[8] Annual reports from the central banks of the WAMZ countries and from the Central Bank of West African States, CBWAS/*Banque Centrale des États de l'Afrique de l'Ouest*, BCEAO); while WAMZ is servinf 6 countries plus one observer country, the

b) Inflation Rate ≤5 %

Inflationary pressures that mainly originated from the food and fuel crises was a challenge for all the countries in 2008. Some improvement was registered during the first and second half of 2009. As compared to 2008 when no country has achieved the target, two countries met the target in the first half of 2009 and three countries met the target in the second half of 2009.

Table 4.2: End of Period Inflation Rate

	2001	2002	2003	2004	2005	2006	2007	H1 2008	2008	H1 2009	2009*
Cape Verde	4.2	3.0	-2.3	-0.3	1.7	4.7	4.4	5.1	6.8	5.8	5.0
Gambia	8.1	13.0	17.6	8.0	1.8	1.4	6.0	2.2	6.8	5.4	5.0
Ghana	21.3	15.2	23.6	11.8	13.9	10.9	12.8	18.4	18.1	20.7	29.8
Guinea	5.2	6.1	12.9	27.6	29.7	39.1	12.8	24.6	13.5	1.8	7.7
Liberia	19.4	11.1	5.0	16.1	7.0	8.9	11.7	12.5	9.4	7.6	9.1
Nigeria	16.4	12.1	23.8	10.0	11.6	8.5	6.6	12.0	15.1	11.2	7.7
Sierra Leone	3.4	-1.3	11.3	14.4	13.1	7.3	13.8	16.6	13.2	7.8	10.0
No. of countries	3	3	3	2	3	3	2	1	0	2	3

Source: WAMA (2009, p.21), **Note**: H1 = First Half; *=Projection; the areas marked are figures that met the convergence criteria

c) Central Bank Financing of Budget Deficit/Previous Year's Tax Revenue ≤10%.

Performance in terms of budget deficit financing by the Central Bank remained impressive during the period. For instance, six countries complied with the criterion in the first and second half of 2009.

CBWAS/BCEAO is a central bank serving the eight West African countries which comprise the West African Economic and Monetary Union (UEMOA).

Table 4.3: Budget Deficit Financing by Central Banks

	2001	2002	2003	2004	2005	2006	2007	H1 2008	2008	H1 2009	2009*
Cape Verde	0.1	20.7	6.3	0.2	0.0	0.0	0.0	0.0	0.0	0.0	0.0
Gambia	80.7	22.0	63.1	0.0	0.0	0.0	0.0	32.8	0.0	3.2	5.4
Ghana	0.0	12.1	0.0	1.6	0.0	0.0	0.0	33.8	17.3	10.2	15.5
Guinea	-0.7	24.5	14.6	26.2	-8.8	54.0	0.0	0.0	5.8	0.6	0.0
Liberia	0.0	0.0	0.0	0.0	0.0	0.0	0.0	0.0	0.0	0.0	0.0
Nigeria	29.3	0.0	19.7	0.0	0.0	0.0	0.0	0.0	0.0	0.0	0.0
Sierra Leone	8.9	0.0	26.4	0.0	0.0	13.3	0.8	0.0	0.3	6.0	0.5
No. of countries	5	3	3	6	7	5	7	5	6	6	6

Source: WAMA (2009, p.21), Note: H1= First Half; *=Projection; the areas marked are figures that met the convergence criteria

d) Gross Foreign Exchange Reserves ≥6 Months of Imports Cover

In most of the member countries, the performance of gross foreign exchange reserves as indicated in Table 4.4 was poor throughout the period. Only Nigeria has been able to meet up with this criterion.

Table 4.4: Gross External Reserves ≥6 Months of Imports

	2001	2002	2003	2004	2005	2006	2007	H1 2008	2008	H1 2009	2009*
CAPE VERDE	1.5	2.0	1.8	2.4	3.4	3.6	4.1	3.7	4.1	3.9	4.0
GAMBIA	7.2	2.9	3.1	4.7	5.2	4.9	4.4	5.8	4.3	4.0	5.3
GHANA	1.2	2.3	4.1	3.7	4.0	3.7	3.9	5.7	2.2	4.7	2.3
GUINEA	2.8	2.3	1.6	1.2	1.1	0.8	0.4	0.5	1.1	1.2	1.8
LIBERIA	2.6	0.0	-0.2	0.2	0.1	0.1	0.7	0.1	0.7	1.0	0.7
NIGERIA	11.3	9.9	8.5	16.1	11.8	15.1	17.4	22.1	15.3	15.7	14.6
No. of	2	1	1	1	1	1	1	1	1	1	1

Source: WAMA (2009, p. 22), Note: H1= First Half; *=Projection; the areas marked are figures that met the convergence criteria

4.1.2 Secondary Convergence Criteria

a) Tax Revenue/GDP Ratio ≥20 %

Performance in terms of tax receipts remained low during the period under review. Two countries (Cape Verde and Ghana) fulfilled this criterion in June 2009, thus maintaining the same number attained in the corresponding period of 2008. This calls for a more in-depth reflection on the optimality of average tax rates in member countries. It is believed that with high tax rates in the context of an inefficient tax mobilization structure, it would be virtually impossible to maximize tax revenue. This could give rise to pervasive tax evasion and to administrative bottlenecks that would continue to make it difficult to mobilize tax revenue effectively (WAMA, 2009).

Table 4.5: Tax Revenue/GDP Ratio

	2001	2002	2003	2004	2005	2006	2007	H1 2008	2008	H1 2009	2009 *
CAPE VERDE	18.7	19.7	18.6	19.6	21.0	23.0	22.8	21.6	22.7	17.7	23.9
GAMBIA	19.2	14.1	13.8	22.4	17.2	18.8	19.4	18.2	17.6	16.8	15.9
GHANA	17.2	17.5	19.3	22.4	21.9	22.3	26.1	20.6	27.9	22.3	23.9
GUINEA	11 .4	12.0	10.5	9.5	12.2	14.8	13.5	14.4	14.7	15.3	15.5
LIBERIA	11.4	10.7	6.4	9.2	14.7	13.2	12.6	12.3	12.5	12.8	12.5
NIGERIA	19.5	14.0	15.7	14.8	17.2	14.9	11.7	18.8	16.2	11.0	13.5
SIERRA LEONE	13.4	11.4	16.7	13.7	8.1	8.5	7.8	9.8	8.6	8.9	8.3
No. of countries	0	0	0	2	2	2	2	2	2	2	2

Source: WAMA (2009, p. 23), **Note**: H1= First Half; *=Projection; the areas marked are figures that met the convergence criteria

b) Wage Bill /Tax Revenue ≤35%

The wage bill which forms a significant proportion of recurrent expenditure in WAMZ Member States is also monitored periodically to highlight its impact on fiscal performance. At the end of June 2009, two (2) countries (The Gambia and Nigeria) only met this criterion.

c) Public Investment/Tax Revenue ≥20 %

This criterion which monitors the utilization of domestic resources for the investment needs of member countries has suffered a similar fate as the tax revenue mobilization criterion. Only two countries (Guinea and Nigeria) met this criterion in first half of 2009 and one country (Nigeria) met the criterion in the second half of 2009.

Table 4.6: Wage Bill/Tax Revenue

	2001	2002	2003	2004	2005	2006	2007	H1 2008	2008	H1 2009	2009*
CAPE VERDE	50.3	46.3	63.2	47.9	47.1	46.0	41.6	42.8	38.1	46.4	42.7
GAMBIA	40.1	38.0	33.3	23.1	24.3	24.2	22.4	28.7	28.6	30.2	32.0
GHANA	52.9	57.2	49.6	46.1	44.8	55.7	51.5	45.9	53.8	58.3	49.5
GUINEA	32.0	31.0	34.3	32.5	23.2	18.4	25.9	24.8	28.0	32.4	36.7
LIBERIA	29.0	19.1	26.4	48.0	59.2	34.5	32.9	41.0	28.7	31.2	35.2
NIGERIA	26.4	47.2	32.6	33.8	17.9	19.5	31.6	32.9	31.2	34.7	24.3
SIERRA LEONE	55.0	63.9	59.7	56.0	65.5	61.6	60.9	57.6	53.3	61.3	52.6
No. of countries	3	2	4	3	4	5	5	4	5	5	2

Source: WAMA (2009, p. 24), **Note**: H1= First Half; *=Projection; the areas marked are figures that met the convergence criteria

Table 4.7: Public Investment/Tax Revenue

	2001	2002	2003	2004	2005	2006	2007	H1 2008	2008	H1 2009	2009*
CAPE VERDE	4.2	4.8	3.4	3.3	2.9	2.9	2.0	7.8	1.9	2.5	2.4
GAMBIA	6.1	7.5	11.0	14.2	4.8	3.1	6.3	8.6	16.3	14.0	10.0
GHANA	16.4	13.2	18.8	18.4	18.8	25.0	27.3	23.9	35.8	17.5	6.0
GUINEA	5.5	10.2	12.1	16.1	12.6	12.0	11.9	14.5	12.9	20.0	16.9
LIBERIA	46.1	47.3	0.0	25.6	18.3	14.9	13.8	12.5	12.5	15.1	14.7
NIGERIA	40.3	30.7	21.4	20.3	20.6	20.0	31.2	28.6	24.6	36.5	26.4
SIERRA LEONE	6.6	9.4	11.3	8.2	7.9	10.6	9.1	15.9	13.4	8.0	11.8
No. of countries	2	2	1	2	1	2	2	2	2	2	1

Source: WAMA (2009, p. 25), **Note**: H1= First Half; *=Projection; the areas marked are figures that met the convergence criteria

d)   Positive Real Interest Rates

In recent years, the real interest rates have been constantly negative in the majority of the member countries. This is also a result of high inflationary pressures experienced in the member countries. Prevalence of negative real interest rates is inimical to domestic savings mobilization and financial intermediation which underscores the importance of the observance of this criterion. As shown in Table 4.8, two countries met this criterion in the first half of 2008 and non in the second half of 2008. One country (Guinea) met this criterion in the first half of 2009 and no country met it in the second half of 2009.

Table 4.8: Real Interest Rates

	2001	2002	2003	2004	2005	2006	2007	H1 2008	2008	H1 2009	2009 *
CAPE VERDE	-1.0	0.2	5.5	3.8	1.5	-1.5	-1.2	4.6	-3.6	-2.6	-1.8
GAMBIA	0.9	-4.0	-5.1	6.8	3.2	3.6	-1.0	1.8	-1.8	-0.4	-0.5
GHANA	-6.8	-2.2	-13.9	-2.3	-7.5	-9.4	-11.3	-16.4	-15.9	-18.9	-28.0
GUINEA	2.8	1.3	-8.3	-19.2	-23.0	-20.0	1.8	-9.9	-0.5	5.2	-0.7
LIBERIA	-13.7	-5.4	-0.6	-12.7	-3.9	-6.2	-9.1	-10.5	-7.2	-3.8	-6.9
NIGERIA	4.0	-8.4	-20.6	-5.6	-10.1	-6.5	-3.0	-9.0	-12.0	-8.4	-4.9
SIERRA LEONE	1.3	8.1	-5.8	-6.6	-7.2	-1.8	-8.3	-11.1	-9.2	-4.3	-6.0
No. countries	4	3	1	2	2	1	1	2	0	1	0

Source: WAMA (2009, p. 26), **Note:** H1= First Half, *–Projection; the areas marked are figures that met the convergence criteria

e) Stability of Real Exchange Rate within ±5%
Two major exchange rate regimes exist within WAMZ: the fixed exchange rate regime for Cape Verde[9] and the flexible exchange rate regime for Liberia and the other countries of the WAMZ.
The co-existence of the two exchange rate regimes makes any evaluation based on the movements of the nominal exchange rates of little relevance, so that analyses based on real exchange rate developments are more appropriate. The real exchange rate of most economies remained stable during the first half of 2009. With a fluctuation margin of ± 5.0 %, seven (7) countries met the criterion in the second half of 2009.

f) Domestic Arrears (prohibition of accumulation of new arrears and liquidation of existing arrears)
According to the WAMA report (2009), performance under this criterion was not analysed due to the low level of responses of WAMZ countries within the period under review. In general, responses are received from the UEMOA countries, while the non-UEMOA countries hardly provide responses for this criterion. It is hoped that these countries would endeavour to provide re-

---

[9] Cape Verde - though a potential member - is still having only an observer status in the WAMZ.

sponses which would further enrich the analyses of domestic arrears accumulation in member countries.

Table 4.9: Real Exchange Rates

	2001	2002	2003	2004	2005	2006	2007	H1 2008	2008*	H1 2009	2009*
CABO VERDE	-3.9	-0.2	0.8	-3.1	5.4	3.3	3.0	-2.9	4.3	0.5	1.5
GAMBIA	-12.2	-17.5	-28.5	-1.2	6.4	-0.2	9.7	-0.6	14.4	3.0	0.3
GHANA	0.8	0.7	0.8	-1.4	0.0	7.1	1.5	-9.3	9.1	-6.9	2.8
GUINEA	-3.2	-2.3	-6.7	-5.8	-22.4	-7.0	32.6	4.9	4.9	3.2	4.6
LIBERIA	-23.2	-30.1	-7.2	-14.2	-3.1	-4.6	2.5	2.0	2.7	2.4	2.7
NIGERIA	11.1	-0.5	-5.1	2.7	15.3	7.3	-1.9	-7.2	10.8	3.0	4.6
SIERRA LEONE	10.8	-12.4	-20.0	-10.6	-11.5	6.2	1.2	1.2	7.9	0.7	0.5
No. of countries	3	4	2	4	2	3	5	5	3	6	7

Sources: WAMA (2009, p. 27), **Note**: H1= First Half; *=Projection; the areas marked are figures that met the convergence criteria

g) Convergence Criteria met by WAMZ countries
Table 4.10 provides an overview of the number of countries that complied with the convergence criteria. Most of the countries met the criteria in 2008 and 2009.

Table 4.10: Number of Countries that Met the Criteria

	2001	2002	2003	2004	2005	2006	2007	H1 2008	2008*	H1 2009	2009*
Budget Deficit	2	1	2	1	3	4	4	4	4	4	4
Inflation	3	3	3	2	3	3	2	1	0	2	3
Reserves	2	1	1	1	1	1	1	1	1	1	1
Central Bank Financing	5	3	3	6	7	5	7	5	6	6	6
Tax Revenue	0	0	0	2	2	2	2	2	2	2	2
Wage bill/ Tax revenue	3	2	4	3	4	5	5	4	5	5	2
Public Investments	2	2	1	2	1	2	2	2	2	2	1
Real Intr. Rate	4	3	1	2	2	1	1	2	0	1	0
Real Exch. Rate	3	4	2	4	2	3	5	5	3	6	7

Source: WAMA (2009); compiled from Tables 4.1 to 4.9, **Note**: H1= First Half; *=Projection

Table 4.11 gives a summary of the total number of criteria satisfied by each country. Table 4.11 indicates that none of the countries has yet been able to meet all the primary and secondary convergence criteria. As at mid-2009, the best performance with regard of the 9 targets was recorded by Nigeria. Cape Verde, Ghana and Sierra Leone as well as the other WAMZ countries achieved a lower number of targets.

Table 4.11: Total Number of Convergence Criteria Met

	2001	2002	2003	2004	2005	2006	2007	H1 2008	2008	H1 2009	2009*
CAPE VERDE	3	3	4	4	4	4	4	4	3	2	4
GAMBIA	2	0	1	4	4	6	3	5	3	4	4
GHANA	1	0	2	3	3	3	4	2	2	2	2
GUINEA	5	3	1	1	3	2	4	4	4	7	3
LIBERIA	4	4	3	2	3	4	4	3	4	4	4
NIGERIA	4	4	4	5	5	5	6	5	5	6	6
SIERRA LEONE	3	3	0	1	1	0	2	2	1	2	2

Source: WAMA (2009); compiled from Tables 4.1 to 4.9, **Note:** H1= First Half; *=Projection

4.1.3   Development of Convergence Performance between 2010 and 2012

Even though the analysis in this paper is limited to the WAMA 2009 report on macroeconomic convergence, the developments between 2009 and 2012 are of interest in this paper. A series of consultative meetings have been held to review the convergence criteria, the level of financial integration, the fiscal developments in the member countries, etc. Also important documents were published; these include the Report by the Committee of the Governors of the Central Bank of the Member States, the Report by the Technical Committee of WAMZ, etc.

For instance, the Director General of WAMI, Dr. Temitope W. Oshiko-ya, in his address on the 24th meeting of WAMI on February 10th 2011 stated that an assessment of macroeconomic convergence performance showed that at the end of June 2010 only Liberia has satisfied all the four primary convergence criteria. The Gambia, Ghana and Nigeria have satisfied three out of the four criteria. Sierra Leone has satisfied one criterion, while Guinea did not satisfy any. The two criteria on single digit inflation and on fiscal deficit, excluding grants, to GDP continued to be challenging for most Member States. Zonal performance under the secondary criteria was generally not satisfactory (WAMI, 2011).

According to the Report of the 26th meeting of the Committee of Governors of Central Banks Reporting of the WAMZ held in Freetown, Sierra Leone, on January 16th to 20th 2012, macroeconomic developments and the status of convergence in the first half of 2011 were positive (WAMZ/CG/26, 2012). Overall economic performance in the WAMZ remained robust - with real GDP expected to expand by 8.0 per cent in 2011, compared to 7.7 per cent in 2010. The strong growth in 2011 was driven by increased activities in the agricultural and industrial sectors in the member countries. Inflationary pressures in the Zone eased slightly, declining from 13.4 per cent at end-June 2010 to 11.6 per cent at end-June 2011. The Fiscal deficit to GDP ratio (excluding grants) narrowed to 2.6 per cent during the first half of 2011 compared to a deficit of 3.9 per cent to GDP in the corresponding period of 2010.

During the first half of 2011, member countries' performance with respect to the convergence criteria was encouraging as all the countries showed improvement in their compliance with the primary criteria. Ghana and Liberia achieved all the four primary criteria, while The Gambia, Guinea and Nigeria met three criteria. Sierra Leone complied with two criteria. The medium-term projections for the countries suggest a promising outlook. There was, however, no improvement in the member countries' performance on the secondary convergence scale (WAMZ/TC/32, 2012).

4.2 Empirical Analysis – Convergence Performance by Countries

4.2.1 The Gambia

a) Performance under the Primary Criteria
The fiscal deficit, which was 3.3 percent during the first half of 2009 compared to 2.1 percent in the corresponding period of 2008, was within the established benchmark. Inflationary pressures increased from 2.2 in June 2008 to 5.4 percent, thus missing the required target (table 4.12).

Apparently the central bank did not finance the budget deficit during the first half of 2009. However, there are indications that the central bank provided substantial overdraft to the Government during the course of the review period. This is not reflected in the highly aggregated central bank balance sheet and must have been subsumed under other items net (WAMA, 2009).

Gross foreign exchange reserves in terms of months of imports were 5.5 during the review period, compared to 5.8 in the first half of 2008. This could be attributable to the decline in export performance, lower worker remittances, and in tourism receipts (WAMA, 2009).

b) Performance under the Secondary Criteria

The tax revenue performance criterion (tax revenue/GDP) during the period was 16.8, which was slightly lower than that of the corresponding period of 2008 (18.2 %), and below the required benchmark. Between 2003 and 2009, Gambia's performance on the salary mass/tax revenue benchmark has been constantly below the required maximum target of 35.0 percent annually.

Table 4.12: Status of Macroeconomic Convergence in The Gambia

	Target	2003	2004	2005	2006	2007	2008		2009	
							June	Dec	June	Dec
Primary Criteria:										
i) Budget Deficit/GDP	≤4%	-5.2	-9.9	-8.4	-2.7	-1.1	-2.1	-4.2	-3.3	-4.3
ii) Inflation Rate	≤5	17.6	8.0	1.8	1.4	6.0	2.2	6.8	5.4	5.0
iii) Budget Deficit F.	≤10%	63.1	0.0	0.0	0.0	0.0	27.5	0.0	0.0	0.0
iv) Gross Foreign Exchange Reserves	≥6m	3.1	4.7	5.2	4.9	4.4	5.8	4.3	5.5	4.7
Secondary Criteria:										
i) Domestic Arrears	=0	n/a	n/a	n/a	n/a	n/a	n/a	n/a	n/a	n/a
ii) Tax Revenue/GDP	≥20%	13.8	22.4	17.2	18.8	19.4	18.2	17.7	16.8	15.9
iii) Salary Mass/Tax	≤35%	33.3	23.1	24.3	24.2	22.3	27.6	31.2	28.7	30.2
iv) Public Investment/Tax	≥20%	11.0	14.2	4.8	3.1	6.3	8.6	16.3	14.0	20.7
v) Positive Real Interest Rate	≥0	-5.1	6.8	3.2	3.6	-1.0	1.8	-1.8	-0.4	0.0
vi) Real Exchange Rate	±5%	-28.5	-1.2	6.4	-0.2	9.7	-0.6	14.4	3.0	0.3
Total No. Of Criteria Met		1	4	4	6	3	5	2	4	6

Source: WAMA (2009, p. 76)

However, the level of public investments financed from domestic resources remained low by the Community standard, at 14.0 per cent during the period, despite a significant improvement on the 8.6 per cent achieved in the first half of 2008. There was prevalence of a negative real interest rate (-0.4), which is inimical to domestic savings mobilization. With a fluctuation band of ± 5.0 per cent, the real exchange rate remained stable during the period under review at 3.0 per cent.

(c) Developments on Macroeconomic Convergence since 2009

Macroeconomic convergence performance showed that at the end of June 2010 The Gambia had satisfied three of the four primary criteria. The Payments System Development project in The Gambia has reached an advanced stage of implementation. On the WAMZ/AfDB Payments System Development Project it was reported that the implementation phase of the project had commenced in January, 2010. The project is scheduled to go-live in The Gambia with the pilot site in April 2011 (WAMZ/CG/24, 2011)

During the first half of 2011 The Gambia met three of the primary criteria. On policy harmonisation and institutional arrangements, steady progress has been made. Gambia's status of compliance with the ECOWAS Trade Liberalisation Scheme (ETLS) and the Common External Tariff (CET) was encouraging. With regard to financial integration, the College of Supervisors, in collaboration with WAMI, has issued its maiden Financial Stability Report (2011). Recognising the need to support member countries in building capacity to implement the International Financial Reporting Standards (IFRS), WAMI in collaboration with Euromoney organised a high level training on IFRS. Member countries' performance in terms of ratification of the four main legal instruments of WAMZ was mixed. The Gambia has ratified all the WAMZ statutes. However, with the adoption of the new West African Central Bank (WACB) statute in Conakry in July 2011, it is anticipated that the Statute would be presented to the Authority of Heads of State and Government for signing soon to pave the way for its ratification by the member countries. As regards contributions to the WACB capital, The Gambia has fully contributed while Ghana and Nigeria have made partial contributions. Guinea, Liberia and Sierra Leone are yet to make any contribution. With respect to the Stabilisation and Cooperation Fund (SCF), Ghana and Sierra Leone have fully contributed while partial contributions were made by The Gambia and Nigeria. Guinea and Liberia are yet to make any contribution (WAMZ/TC/32, 2012).

4.2.2 Ghana

a) Performance under the Primary Criteria
As in 2008, Ghana met in 2009 none of the primary convergence criteria and missed also the required benchmark on public investments financed from domestic sources. Thus Ghana met only one target in respect of the secondary criteria, namely the one on tax revenue relative to GDP (table 4.13). Although the restraints in regard of fiscal excesses resulted in a relative decline in the budget deficit, it was still high by about 7.7 percentage points above the required maximum benchmark of 4.0 per cent. The high inflationary pressures accelerated further. Central Bank financing of the government budget deficit was 25.7 per cent, and the level of gross foreign exchange reserves was 2.4 months of imports cover, far below the 6.0 months benchmark.

b) Performance under the Secondary Criteria

Performance under the secondary criteria was also not encouraging as the outcome on the various benchmarks showed divergences from the established benchmarks. Data on the domestic arrears were not available. Nevertheless, a review of the government's financial operations indicated conscious efforts towards liquidation of the existing arrears as the cash payments exceeded the commitments incurred during the period. Even though the country realized in 2009 the target on tax revenue relative to GDP, it marked a reduction in tax returns compared to the performance in the same period in 2008. The public sector wage burden continued to worsen owing to the decline in tax returns. At 17.8 percent of the level of public investments, this criterion was below the 20.0 percent benchmark (WAMA, 2009).

In spite of the relative improvement in the management of fiscal policy, the authorities still face a number of challenges. The prevailing constraints relate to the high public sector wage burden, increasing interest payments and the liquidation of outstanding arrears arising from commitments made in the preceding year.

The inflationary pressures observed in the first half of the year may persist during the second half of 2009. The consumer price index increased significantly by 15.9 percent in the review period, indicating a projected inflation above 21.0 percent for the year 2009. The relative improvement in fiscal operations in the first half of the year would also facilitate the deceleration of inflation process. However, the existence of certain risk factors would pose major challenges to the authorities, like the lagged effects of the fiscal accommodation undertaken in the first half of the year, the uncertainties about the short-term trends in crude oil prices, and the probability of a further depreciation of the domestic currency (WAMA 2009).

With regard to the convergence criteria, the projections for the second half of the year 2009 indicate that performance would continue to be difficult although the country would sustain the secondary criterion on tax revenue. The budget deficit and inflation would remain high on account of the emerging fiscal challenges. Despite an expected easing in the foreign exchange earning capacity, the prevailing constraints in the external sector would not permit a realization of the required benchmarks on gross foreign exchange reserves. Meeting the targets on the wage burden and public investments from domestic sources would also be difficult.

Table 4.13: Status of Macroeconomic Convergence in Ghana

	Target	2003	2004	2005	2006	2007	2008 JUNE	2008 DEC	2009 JUNE	2009 DEC
Primary Criteria:										
i) Budget Deficit/GDP	≤4%	7.7	9.5	6.9	12.6	14.5	15.8	19.5	11.7	18.0
ii) Inflation Rate	≤5%	23 .6	11.8	13.9	10.9	12.8	18.4	18.4	20.7	29.8
iii) Budget Def. Fi.	≤10%	0.0	1.6	0.0	0.0	0.0	33.8	36.0	25.7	15.5
iv) Gross External Reserves	≥6m	4.1	3.7	4.0	3.7	3.9	2.9	2.2	2.4	2.3
Secondary Criteria:										
i) Domestic arrears	=0	n/a	n/a	n/a	n/a	n/a	n/a	n/a	n/a	n/a
ii) Tax Revenue/GDP	≥20%	19.3	22.4	20.8	21.1	23.7	21.2	25.4	20.4	23.9
iii) Salary/Tax Rev.	≤35%	44.4	38.9	44.4	53.1	51.5	52.7	53.8	58.3	49.5
iv) Public Investment	≥20%	18.8	18.4	18.8	26.5	27.3	33.5	35.8	17.8	6.0
v) Real Interest Rate	≥0	-13.9	-2.3	-7.5	-6.2	-11.8	-16.4	-16.2	-18.7	-19.8
vi) Real Exchange Rate**	±5%	0.8	-1.4	0.0	7.1	1.5	4.5	9.1	5.6	7.6
Total No. Of Criteria Met		2	3	3	3	4	3	2	1	1

Source: WAMI Report 2011, p.4, and WAMA 2009, p. 86

c) Developments on Macroeconomic Convergence since 2009
As at the end of June 2010 Ghana satisfied three of the four primary criteria. During the first half of 2011 Ghana's performance with respect to the convergence criteria was encouraging as it showed a further improvement in its compliance with the primary criteria. Ghana had achieved all the four primary criteria. On policy harmonisation and institutional arrangements, also steady progress has been made. Ghana's status of compliance with the ECOWAS Trade Liberalisation Scheme (ETLS) and the Common External Tariff (CET) was encouraging. As regards contributions to the West African Central Bank (WACB) capital, Ghana has made partial contributions (WAMZ/CG/24, 2011). .

4.2.3   Guinea

a) Performance under the Primary Criteria
In respect of the first half of 2009, Guinea recorded an exceptional performance by meeting seven (7) criteria, including three primary ones. This performance is quite remarkable as, since 2000, Guinea has never gone beyond five targets. Concerning the primary criteria, the annualized budget deficit on commitment basis stood at 0.8% of GDP. This performance was due to a drastic cut in recurrent expenditure. Similarly, it was able to maintain its

indebtedness to the Central Bank at a marginal level. Inflation declined sharply compared to trends observed in recent years. The year-on-year inflation rate stood at 1.8% against 13.5% in December 2008 and 24% during same period the previous year 2007. The performance in respect of this criterion is very significant as Guinea has never achieved the ECOWAS inflation target (WAMA 2009). Gross foreign exchange reserves were far below the required minimum target of 6.0 months of imports cover (table 4.14).

b) Performance under the Secondary Criteria
With respect to the secondary criteria, the one concerning the wage bill was achieved in spite of a significant increase from 24.0 per cent to 32.4 per cent due to the recruitment of new personnel. With regard to public investments financed with internal resources, the country, for the first time, was able to achieve this target because of the financing of many infrastructure projects by the new government. Besides, the drop in inflation led to a positive real interest rate. Similarly, the relative stability of the national currency ensured the stability of the real effective exchange rate. On the other hand, compared to the minimum requirement, the tax revenue relative to GDP remained weak in spite of efforts made in recent years. Although some progress was made in this area, the absence of an official budget constitutes an obstacle to the consolidation of this performance (WAMA 2009).

Despite the positive trends recorded in the first half of 2009, the country's performance could decline at the end of the year given the assumptions contained in the macroeconomic framework of July 2009. In fact, inflation is expected to be slightly above the target. This would reflect in a slightly negative real interest rate. In addition, the wage bill would be above the 35% target. In addition, the level of internally funded public investments in relation to tax revenue would be reduced significantly.

Table 4.14: Status of Macroeconomic Convergence of Guinea

	Tar-get	2000	2001	2002	2003	2004	2005	2006	2007	2008 Jun	2008 Dec	2009 Jun	2009 Dec
Primary Crit.:													
i) Budget Def.	≤4%	5.2	3.4	6.2	8.9	5.9	1.6	2	0.9	0.1	1.7	0.8	2.5
ii) Inflation Rate	≤5%	7.2	5.2	6.1	12.9	27.6	29.7	39.1	12.8	24.6	13.5	1.8	7.7
iii) Budget Fin.	≤10%	24	-0.7	24.5	14.6	26.2	-8.8	54	0	0	0	0.6	0.0
iv) Gross External Reserves	≥6m	2.2	2.8	2.3	1.6	1.2	1.1	0.8	0.4	0.5	1.1	1.2	1.8
Secondary Criteria:													
i) Domestic A													
ii) Tax Rev.	=0	n/a	n/a	n/a	n/a	n/a	n/a	n/a	n/a	n/a	n/a	n/a	n/a
iii) Salary/Tax	≥20	10.2	11.4	12	10.5	9.5	12.2	14.8	13.5	14.4	14.7	15.3	15.5
iv) Public Inv.	≤35%	38.2	32	31	34.3	32.5	23.2	18.4	25.9	24.8	28	32.4	36.7
v) Real Interest	≥20%	7.7	5.5	10.2	12.1	16.1	12.6	12	11.9	14.5	12.9	20	16.9
vi Real Exchange	≥0	0.7	2.8	1.3	-8.3	-19.2	-23	-20	1.8	9.9	2.5	5.2	-0.7
Rate**	±5%	-22.5	-11.1	-0.7	-8.7	-23.1	-21.2	-9.9	4.8	4.9	4.9	3.2	4.2
Total No. Of Criteria Met		1	4	3	1	1	3	2	5	4	4	7	3

Source: WAMA 2009, p. 93

c) Developments on Macroeconomic Convergence since 2009

At the end of June 2010 Guinea did not satisfy any of the convergence criteria. The criteria on single digit inflation and on fiscal deficit to GDP, excluding grants, continued to be challenging for Guinea and most Member States. During the first half of 2011, Guinea's performance with respect to the convergence criteria was encouraging. There was an improvement in its compliance with the primary criteria; Guinea met three criteria. There was, however, no improvement on the secondary convergence scale.

On the policy harmonisation components of the work-programme, the Third Trade Minister's Forum, which took place at the ECOWAS Commission, Abuja, Nigeria from 20th – 21st May 2010, centred on issues relating to the proposal to establish an ECOWAS Standing Committee on Rules of Origin; the creation of a dedicated website on the ECOWAS Trade Liberalisation Scheme (ETLS) by Member States by the end of 2010 and the continuous sensitization of stakeholders on the ETLS by Ministries of Trade/Commerce and WAMI; the use of ECOWAS approved harmonized documentation for clearance of goods; actions required to speed up the introduction of the Community Customs Code (CCC) by end June 2010; the introduction of joint check points by Member States; and the introduction of a satellite tracking system to facilitate transit trade. The Forum reiterated the call to the ECOWAS Commission to develop a sanctions regime to be imposed on Member States for non-adherence to ECOWAS Protocols. There are plans to extend Trade policy development assistance to Guinea (WAMZ/CG/24, 2011).

In the Payments System Development Project Guinea and other Member States had reached an advanced stage of implementation. The Project is scheduled to go-live in The Gambia, the pilot site, in April 2011 to be followed by Sierra Leone and Guinea before the end of 2011 (WAMZ/TC/32, 2012).

4.2.4   Nigeria

a)   Performance under the Primary Criteria
Nigeria has been one of the best performing countries in recent years under the macroeconomic convergence programme. However, the country's performance deteriorated during the review period as it sustained only four targets in 2009 compared to five targets in 2008 (table 4.15). Nigeria met three out of the four primary criteria, namely those relating to budget deficit, budget deficit financing, and gross foreign exchange reserves. The country has consistently met these targets since 2003. Given the high total public revenues and the high foreign exchange reserves it is likely that Nigeria would continue to meet these targets in the foreseeable future. Even though the inflationary pressures have declined, the end-period inflation at June 2009 was still quite high at 11.2 per cent, about 6.2 percentage points above the required maximum target of 5.0 per cent (WAMA 2009).

b) Performance under the Secondary Criteria
Performance on the secondary criteria was not very encouraging as the country met the required target on only one criterion (public investment). The domestic arrears criterion could not be assessed due to inadequate data. Tax revenue declined by 6.0 percentage points to 9.0 percent of GDP. The reduction in tax revenue and the increase in personnel costs contributed to a further worsening of the salary mass ratio to tax revenue from 24.0 percent to 42.5 percent, thus missing the required maximum target of 35.0 percent. Even with the reduction in the revenue base, the level of public investments as financed from domestic sources was maintained, resulting in an increase in the ratio from 20.4 percent to 45.3 percent. Real interest rates remained negative in spite of the decline in inflationary pressures. The country also missed the target on real exchange rate stability (WAMA 2009).

Table 4.15: Status of Macroeconomic Convergence in Nigeria

	Target	2004	2005	2006	2007	2008 June	Dec.	2009 June	Dec. *
Primary Criteria:									
i) Budget Deficit/GDP	<4%	1.7	1.3	0.6	0.6	1.1	0.2	2.8	0.4
ii) Inflation Rate	<5	10.0	11.6	8.5	6.6	12.0	15.1	11.2	7.7
iii) Budget Deficit F.	<10%	0.0	0.0	0.0	0.0	0.0	0.0	0.0	0.0
iv) Gross Foreign Exchange Reserves	> 6m	16.1	13.1	15.1	17.4	22.1	15.3	15.7	14.6
Secondary Criteria:									
i) Domestic arrears	=0								
ii) Tax Revenue/GDP		n/a	n/a	n/a	n/a	n/a	n/a	n/a	n/a
iii) Salary/Tax Revenue	>20%	19.8	17.2	14.9	12.0	16.0	16.0	9.0	13.5
iv) P. Invest/Tax Receipts	>35%	33.8	17.9	19.5	30.6	24.0	24.2	42.5	24.3
v) Real Interest Rate	>20%	18.7	20.6	20.0	30.6	20.4	24.6	45.3	26.4
vi) Real Exchange Rate**	>0	-5.6	-10.1	-6.5	-3.0	-9.0	-12.0	-8.4	-4.9
	+5%	2.7	15.3	7.3	-1.9	-7.2	10.8	5.2	4.6
Total No. of Criteria Met		5	5	5	6	5	5	4	6

Source: CBN Statistical Bulletin, various issues; WAMA 2009, p. 101, **Note**: * = Projection

(c) Developments on Macroeconomic Convergence since 2009

At the end of June 2010 Nigeria satisfied three out of the four primary convergence criteria (WAMZ/CG/24, 2011). The criteria on single digit inflation and on fiscal deficit to GDP, excluding grants, continue to remain a challenge for most Member States. Zonal performance under the secondary criteria was generally not satisfactory for Nigeria in this quarter. During the first half of 2011, member countries' performance with respect to the convergence criteria was encouraging as all the countries showed improvement in their compliance with the primary criteria. Nigeria met three of the four primary criteria. There was, however, no improvement in its performance on the secondary convergence criteria. As regards contributions to the WACB capital, Nigeria has made a partial contribution (WAMZ/TC/32, 2012).

4.2.5 Sierra Leone

a) Performance under the Primary Criteria

The performance of Sierra Leone under the macroeconomic convergence programme remained poor as the country met only the secondary criterion on real exchange rate stability. The country improved its performance on certain criteria whilst others deteriorated. Thus, Sierra Leone met none of the primary convergence criteria in the first half of 2009 (table 4.16). Fiscal operations in 2009 resulted in a budget deficit (on a commitment basis, excluding grants) of 5.6 percent, indicating an improvement compared to the performance recorded in the corresponding period of 2008. The contractionary monetary policy yielded dividends as the end-period headline inflation declined further from 12.3 in 2008 percent to 7.8 percent in 2009. The Bank of Sierra Leone accommodated 12.4 percent of the government's fiscal operations in 2009, due to delays in the disbursement of budgetary support from the country's development partners in the period under review. The level of gross foreign exchange reserves, measured in number of months of imports cover, experienced a downward pressure on account of net foreign exchange outflows arising from an increasing imports bill and declining exports and remittances (WAMA 2009).

b) Performance under the Secondary Criteria
Performance on the secondary criteria was also not encouraging as the achievement on all the prescribed benchmarks was below expectation. The country's performance on domestic arrears was not assessed due to inadequate data. Tax revenue improved marginally, although the volume relative to GDP still remained relatively low, hovering below 10.0 percent. The wage burden continues to be a challenge for the fiscal authorities, with the position worsening further from 57.6 percent of tax revenue at mid-2008 to 61.3 percent in 2009. Contrary to expectation, the level of public investments financed from domestic sources represented 8.0 percent of total tax revenue in 2009, which compared unfavorably with the 15.9 percent recorded in the corresponding period of the preceding year. As usual, real interest rates, measured as the difference between the minimum savings rate and inflation, remained negative, much against the requirement for positive real interest rates. With a fluctuation band of ±5.0 percent, the real exchange rate of the domestic currency (measured by movements in real effective exchange rate) was stable (WAMA 2009).

Table 4.16: Status of Macroeconomic Convergence in Sierra Leone

	Target	2003	2004	2005	2006	2007	2008 June	2008 Dec	2009* June	2009* Dec
Primary Criteria:										
i)Budget Deficit/GDP	≤4%	9.3	8.6	9.6	8.5	5.0	8.0	7.0	5.6	8.1
ii)Inflation Rate	≤5	11.3	14.4	13.1	8.3	13.8	16.6	12.3	7.8	10.0
iii) Budget Deficit F.	≤10%	26.4	0.0	0.0	13.3	0.8	0.0	1.1	12.4	0.5
iv)Gross Foreign Exchange Reserves	≥6m	2.0	3.3	4.5	4.9	4.7	4.0	4.2	3.7	4.6
Secondary Criteria:										
i)Domestic Arrears	=0	n/a	n/a	n/a	n/a	n/a	n/a	n/a	n/a	n/a
ii)Tax Revenue/GDP	≥20%	8.3	8.3	8.2	8.5	7.8	8.3	8.7	8.9	8.3
iii) Salary/T	≤35%	56.0	65.5	61.6	61.6	60.9	57.6	56.4	61.3	52.9
iv) Public	≥20%	11.3	8.2	7.9	10.6	9.1	15.8	13.2	8.0	11.8
v) Real Int.	≥0	-7.3	-8.4	-7.6	-1.8	-8.3	-12.6	-9.2	-4.3	-9.5
vi)Real Ex	±5%	-20.0	-10.6	-11.5	6.2	1.2	8.0	7.9	3.0	0.5
Total No. Of Criteria Met			1	1	0	2	1	1	1	2

Source: WAMA 2009, p. 109, **Note**: * projection

c) Developments on Macroeconomic Convergence since 2009

Despite the slow pace of the global economic recovery, economic activity within the WAMZ region in 2010 was robust, while inflationary pressures generally eased. Regarding the macroeconomic convergence performance at the end of June 2010 Sierra Leone satisfied only one primary criterion (WAMZ/CG/24, 2011). During the first half of 2011, Sierra Leone's performance with respect to the convergence criteria was encouraging as it showed an improvement in its compliance with the primary criteria. Sierra Leone complied with two criteria (WAMZ/TC/32, 2012).

The Gambia, Guinea and Sierra Leone had reached an advanced stage of implementation of the WAMZ/AfDB Payments System Development Project, as it was reported that the implementation phase of the project had commenced in January, 2010. The project is scheduled to go-live in The Gambia, the pilot site, in April 2011 to be followed by Sierra Leone and Guinea before the end of 2011.

4.2.6 Cape Verde

a) Performance under the Primary Criteria

The overall level of performance deteriorated by meeting only two convergence criteria in the review period, compared to four in the preceding corresponding period. The state of convergence is as follows (table 4.17). The country met only one of the primary convergence criteria, the one on central bank budget deficit financing. The annual inflation rate at the end of the period was 5.8 % at mid-2009 compared to 5.1 % in June 2008. The budget deficit (excluding grants) was 5.8 % in 2009 compared to 10.0 % in the corresponding period in 2008 (WAMA 2009). Cape Verde did not meet the target on gross foreign exchange reserves (with only 3.9 months of imports cover compared to the required minimum benchmark of 6.0 months).

Table 4.17: Status of Macroeconomic Convergence in Cape Verde

	Standard	2004	2005	2006	2007	2008		2009	
						June	Dec	June	Dec
Primary criteria									
i) Budget deficit/GDP	≤4%	8.4	110	9.7	6.1	10	5.8	5.8	6.2
ii) Rate of Inflation	≤5%	-0.3	1.7	4.7	4.4	5.1	6.8	5.8	5
iii) Financing CB/FR	≤10% of FR n-1	0.2	0	0	0	0	0	0	0
iv) Gross exchange reserves	≥ 6months import	2.4	3.4	3.6	4.1	3.7	4.1	3.9	4
Secondary Criteria									
i) Domestic arrears	≥20%	na	na	na	na	na	na	na	na
ii) Fiscal Revenue/GDP	≤35% FR	19.6	21	23	22.8	21.6	22.7	17.7	23.9
iii) Wage bill/FR	≥20%	47.9	47.1	46	41.6	42.8	38.1	46.4	42.7
iv) Domestic invest-ments/ FR	≥20%	3.3	2.9	2.9	2	7.8	1.9	2.5	2.4
v) Real interest rate	>0	3.5	1.5	-1.5	-1.2	4.6	-3.6	-2.6	-1.8
vi) Real Exchange Rate	5%	-3.1	5.4	3.3	3	-2.9	4.3	0.5	1.5
Number of criteria met		4	4	4	4	4	3	2	4

Source: W AMA 2009, p. 117, **Note**: FR = Fiscal Revenue

b) Performance under the Secondary Criteria

The country met the targets on real exchange rate stability. The tax revenue ratio was 17.7 % at the end of June 2009, compared to 21.6 % in 2008. This reduction could be linked to a weakness in the tax mobilization mechanism.

There is no available data on the criterion on domestic arrears to appreciate the performance regarding this criterion. The salary mass/tax revenue ratio worsened to 46.4 per cent in the first half of 2009 compared to 42.8 % in the corresponding period in 2008. The ratio of public investments was 2.5 %, compared to 2.0 % in 2008. This extremely poor performance shows the inadequate effort being made by the government in public investments financed from domestic sources to support sustainable growth. The criterion on real interest rate was not met (WAMA 2009).

No information was available for Cape Verde for the developments from 2010 onwards – neither in the WAMZ Committee of Governors Report, 24th Meeting (WAMZ/CG/24, 2011), nor in the WAMZ Technical Committee Report, 32nd Meeting (WAMZ/TC/32, 2012).

4.2.7 Liberia

a)   Performance under the Primary Criteria
The strict macroeconomic policy measures adopted by the government enabled Liberia to sustain in 2009 all the five targets met in 2008, comprising two of the Primary criteria (budget deficit and central bank budget deficit financing) and three of the secondary criteria (tax revenue, salary mass and real exchange rate stability). So Liberia met two out of four of the primary convergence criteria (table 4.18). With the cash-based budgeting system, Liberia sustained its achievement on the budget deficit benchmark mid-2009with a surplus outturn of 1.0 percent. Albeit the country missed the target on inflation by 2.8 percentage points, there has been a significant improvement in recent months, especially since the second half of 2008, following the abatement in the global prices of food and petroleum products. As usual, the central bank did not accommodate the financial operations of the government. At 1.0 month cover of imports by foreign exchange reserves, the country has made only a marginal improvement in gross foreign exchange reserves, although it would require great efforts to build the foreign exchange stock to the minimum of 6.0 months required.

b)   Performance under the Secondary Criteria
Regarding the secondary criteria, the country did not meet any additional targets during the review period. It should be noted that performance under the domestic arrears criterion could not be assessed owing to inadequate data. With reservations that Liberia might be understating its GDP figures due to difficulties in measurement and inadequate capacity, the country has since 2007 realized the required minimum target for tax revenue of 20.0 per cent of GDP, reaching 21.4 per cent. Discussions with officials revealed that the public sector reforms and efficient auditing techniques

aimed at eliminating ghost names from the public sector payroll have been very useful as these measures contributed to a significant reduction in the wage burden in 2008 and 2009, thereby meeting this required target at 32.5 and 29.2 per cent. In spite of the reduction in inflation, real interest rates remained negative in contravention to the requirement for a positive outturn. On the basis of the real effective exchange rate fluctuation margin of five percent, the domestic currency was relatively stable during the period under review.

Table 4.18: Status of Macroeconomic Convergence in Liberia

	Target	2003	2004	2005	2006	2007	2008 June	Dec	2009 June	Dec*
Primary Criteria:										
Budget Deficit/GDP**	≤4%	3.7	4.4	0.9	-3.0	-2.4	-0.4	2.8	-1.0	-2.0
Inflation Rate	≤5	5.0	16.1	7.6	8.9	11.7	22.0	9.4	7.8	9.1
Budget Deficit Financing	≤10%	0.0	0.0	0.0	0.0	0.0	0.0	0.0	0.0	0.0
Gross External Reserves	≥6m	-0.2	0.2	0.1	0.1	0.7	0.4	0.7	1.0	0.7
Secondary Criteria:										
Domestic Arrears	=0	n/a	n/a	n/a	n/a	n/a	n/a	n/a	n/a	n/a
Tax Revenue/GDP	≥20%	6.4	9.2	14.7	13.2	21.4	22.6	22.1	21.9	20.0
Salary Mass/Tax Revenue	≤35%	26.4	48.0	59.2	34.5	41.6	30.6	32.5	29.2	35.2
P. Invest/Tax Receipts Real Interest Rate	≥20%	0.0	25.6	18.3	14.9	13.9	12.2	12.6	19.3	19.5
	≥0	-0.6	-2.7	-3.9	-6.2	-9.1	-10.5	-7.2	-3.8	-7.0
Real Exchange Rate Stability	±5%	-7.2	-14.2	-3.1	-4.6	2.5	-4.6	2.7	2.1	2.7
Total No. of Criteria Met		3	2	3	3	4	5	5	5	5

Source: WAMA 2009, p. 123, **Note**: ** (-) implies surplus; * projected figures

c)   Developments on Macroeconomic Convergence since 2009
At the end of June 2010, only Liberia satisfied all the four primary convergence criteria. The criteria on single digit inflation and fiscal deficit to GDP, excluding grants, continued to be challenging for most Member States.

On the WAMZ/AfDB Payments System Development, it was reported that the implementation phase of the project commenced in January 2010. The AfDB provided an additional grant for the extension of the project to Liberia (WAMZ/CG/24, 2011).

During the first half of 2011, member countries' performance with respect to the convergence criteria was encouraging as all the countries showed improvement in their compliance with the primary criteria. Ghana and Liberia achieved all the four primary criteria. As regards contributions to WACB capital and SCF, Liberia was yet to make a contribution (WAMZ/TC/32, 2012).

5 Econometric Convergence Analysis for WAMZ countries

5.1 Methodology

5.1.1 Nature and Sources of Data

Annual time series data on the selected macroeconomic convergence criteria variables across the proposed WAMZ member countries were collected in the period 1985 to 2009. Variables used include the ratio of Budget Deficit/GDP (BD/GDP), Inflation Rate (Inf.), Budget Deficit Financing by the Central Bank/Tax Revenue (BDF/TR), Gross Foreign Exchange Reserves (GER), Non-accumulation of Internal Arrears (IAA), Tax Revenue/GDP (TR/GDP), Wage Bill/Tax Revenue Ratio (WB/TR), Public Investment/Tax Revenue Ratio (PI/TR), Real Interest Rate (RIR), and Real Exchange Rate Stability (RER). The data were obtained from several issues/documents of the CBN/Central Bank of Nigeria Statistical Bulletin, the NBS/National Bureau of Statistics, the World Bank's African Development Indicators, the WAMI/West African Monetary Agency, the IMF and WB/World Bank Data bases.

5.1.2 Analytical Framework

To determine whether the proposed member countries will ever meet the convergence criteria, co-integration analysis has been adapted following the works of Haug et al. (2000), Karfakis and Moschos (1990) and MacDonald and Taylor (1991). This study therefore has adapted the analytical framework of Haug et al. (2000). This is so because the tendency for convergence of variables, as well as the rate at which they converge, can be revealed by the co-integration and error correction analysis. The strategy adopted therefore is to test for co-integration for each of the variables that relates to the convergence criteria for all the countries in the Zone. The presence of co-integration among the variables would imply that there is a tendency for them to converge, though this is not a sufficient condition.

According to Granger (1986), the starting point for the co-integration analysis is to investigate for the level integration of the series. The usual approach is to verify for the presence of Unit root (Granger, 1986). Therefore, all the variables were subjected to unit-root test at levels for stationarity using the Augmented Dickey-Fuller (ADF) and the Phillips Perron (PP) tests. Furthermore, the Engle and Granger (1987) two-step procedure in co-integration involves first, a preliminary analysis to find the order of integration of the data series and after that secondly, an ordinary least squares re-

gression is carried out to estimate the equations for those economic aggregates where co-integration can be found (Engle & Granger, 1987; Adam,1992).

In testing for the stationarity, the following equations are specified and
estimated;

$$\Delta Y_t = \gamma_0 + \gamma_1 Y_{t-1} + \Sigma \gamma_i \Delta Y_{t-i} + \mu_t \dots\dots\dots\dots\dots\dots\dots\dots\dots\dots \text{ Eqtn 1}$$

Where i= (1,............., m), Δ= the first-difference operator, γ = the parameters, and μ= stationary stochastic process. The number of lag length (m) is
determined based on the appropriate model criterion.

To test for the presence of unit-root with intercept and trend on the series, the above model is modified to include the trend parameter which is
stated as:

$$\Delta Y_t = \gamma_0 + \gamma t + \beta_1 Y_{t-1} + \Sigma \gamma_i \Delta Y_{t-1} + \varepsilon_{it} \, (i=1,\dots\dots, m)\dots\dots\dots\dots\dots\dots \text{ Eqtn 2}$$

Where β_1 and γ_i are constant parameters, ε_{it} is a stationary stochastic process.
The m-lagged difference terms are included so that the error terms μ_t and ε_{it} in
both equations are serially independent. Thus, if $\beta=0$, there is no presence of
unit-root but if $\beta\neq0$, it means the series contains a unit-root (Ramanathan,
1992).

5.1.3   Model Specification

This model is adopted from the work of Johansen (1995) as modified in Haug
et al. (2000); the VAR (k) model can be written in VECM (Vector Error-
Correction Model) form as:

$$\Delta X_t = \Pi X_{t-1} + \sum_{i=1}^{k-1}\Gamma_i \Delta X_{t-i} + \mu_0 + \mu_1 t + U_t \dots\dots\dots\dots\dots \text{Eqtn 1}$$

Such that; $t = 1, \dots, T,$ and where
X Denotes the vector of endogenous variables, Π and Γ_i are the p x p matrices of coefficients that can give us information about the long run relationship between the variables while μ_0 and μ_1 are p x 1 vectors of constant and
trend coefficients, respectively. The error vector U_t, which is p x 1, is assumed to be multivariate normal with mean vector zero and covariance matrix Ω, and assumed to be independent across time periods.

The VECM representation (Eqtn. 1) is convenient because the hypothesis
of co-integration can be stated in terms of the long run impact matrix Π. This
matrix can always be written as:

$$\Pi = \alpha\beta' \dots\dots\dots\dots\dots\dots\dots\dots\dots\dots\dots\dots\dots\dots\dots\dots\dots \text{ Eqtn 2}$$

Where α and β are p x r matrices of full rank. If r = 0, then Π = 0, and there
exists no linear combination of the elements of X_t that is stationary. At the
other extreme, if rank (Π) = p, X_t is a stationary process. In the intermediate

case however, when $0 < r < p$, there exist r stationary linear combinations of the elements of X_t, along with $p - r$ stochastic trends. Thus, following from equation 1, we can specify our empirical model as follows:

$$\Delta X_t = \Pi X_{t=1} + \sum_{i=1}^{k-1} \Gamma_i \Delta X_{t=i} + U_t \dots\dots\dots\dots\dots\dots\dots\dots\dots\dots\dots\dots\dots\dots\dots \text{Eqtn 3}$$

Where $X_t = (Inf_t\text{Nig}, Inf_t\text{Gha}, Inf_t\text{Gui}, Inf_t\text{Gam}, Inf_t\text{Sie})$ $Inf_t\text{Nig}$ is the inflation rate of Nigeria, $Inf_t\text{Gha}$ is the inflation rate of Ghana, $Inf_t\text{Gui}$ is the inflation rate of Guinea, $Inf_t\text{Gam}$ is the inflation rate of Gambia, and $Inf_t\text{Sie}$ is the inflation rate of Sierra Leone. Hence the model specification in **Eqtn 3** will be applied to all the convergence criteria. This follows the lead work of Johansen (1988) and Ahn and Reinsel (1990), as used by Haug et al. (2000) with little modification.

5.2 Analysis of the Econometric Results

The behaviour of the annual convergence criteria is analysed for all the member countries. The concept of co-integration may not apply to all the countries considered, if the series for the countries manifest a different level of integration. In this instance only series with the same level of integration shall be co-integrated. Consequently, the co-integration analyses have been conducted on convergence criteria of countries with the same level of inte-gration (Haug et al. 2000).

For the interpretation of the empirical results, it will claim "complete" convergence of convergence criteria among a set of p countries if it is found that $p-1$ co-integrating vectors and only a single shared common stochastic trend exist. Otherwise, if r is found to be in the interval $0 < r < p-1$, we shall say that only "partial" convergence has been achieved (Haug et al. 2000). This is the definition of convergence as used by Hafer and Kutan (1994) and by Hafer/Kutan/Zhou (1997), among others (cited in Haug et al. 2000), in the context of co-integration of variables across countries. Convergence in this context implies that criteria have been aligned enough so that the variables move towards an equilibrium in the long run and do not drift too far apart over time. The intuition of this terminology is as follows. If there exist two or more shared common stochastic trends in the convergence criteria of the WAMZ countries, then it must be the case that some countries in the group set their policies independently, at least in the long run. Hence, the circum-stances of forming and maintaining an economic and monetary union will be quite difficult. On the other hand, when finding only one shared common trend this means that a multitude of policy measures have converged to a single common long-run path, dominated perhaps by the policy preferences of some country in the union.

The co-integration analysis was not conducted for the real exchange rate and the domestic arrears because these variables were integrated of different order for the different member countries of the WAMZ.

In carrying out the co-integration tests, the appropriate lag lengths were chosen based on the Akaike and Schwarz information criteria. These are criteria which determine the appropriate lag length in the test procedure for co-integration analysis. Also the co-integration tests were conducted on each of the criteria using different lag lengths as suggested by the lag selection criteria.

Again, it has to be made clear that because of data availability only the situation up to 2009 (estimates) is covered. Only up to this year the latest available Macroeconomic Convergence Report for this study (WAMA 2009) had comparable data for the member countries of WAMZ. Co-integration tests were conducted to determine whether the series for the member countries are co-integrated. Any suspicion of co-integration is a necessary but not a sufficient condition for convergence in a potential monetary zone. Issues of sufficient conditions for monetary integration in West Africa are discussed in section 6.

The co-integration results are presented in tables 5.1 to 5.8, and the Unit Root results for primary and secondary convergence criteria are presented in Appendix A and in Appendix B.

Table 5.1: Co-integration analysis for Budget Deficit/GDP

Trace (λ trace)					
No. of CE(s)	None	At most 1	At most 2	At most 3	At most 4
Eigenvalue	0.81	0.64	0.36	0.32	0.079
λ *trace Statistic*	83.14	44.48	21.05	10.76	1.92
5% Critical Value	68.52	47.21	29.68	15.41	3.76
1% Critical Value	76.07	54.46	35.65	20.04	6.65

Maximum Eigenvalue (λ max)					
No. of CE(s)	None	At most 1	At most 2	At most 3	At most 4
Eigenvalue	0.81	0.64	0.360	0.32	0.079
λ *max Statistic*	38.66	23.43	10.29	8.85	1.92
5% Critical Value	33.46	27.07	20.97	4.07	3.76
1% Critical Value	38.77	32.24	25.52	18.63	6.65

Source: Authors' calculations

Table 5.1 shows the co-integration result for the first primary convergence criterion, the *Budget Deficit to Gross Domestic Product ratio* (i.e. BD/GDP) for Gambia, Ghana, Guinea, Nigeria and Sierra Leone. The trace statistic (λ trace) suggested 1 co-integrating equation at both 5% and 1% at significance level, and Max-eigenvalue (λ_{max}) suggested 1 co-integrating equation at both 5% and 1% significance level. The presence of at least one co-integrating vector is an indication that the Budget Deficit/GDP series for the member countries manifests a common long run stochastic trend (i.e. the tendency for long run convergence).

Table 5.2 shows the co-integration result for the *Inflation rate criterion* for the four countries Ghana, Guinea, Nigeria and Sierra Leone. The results suggest 3 co-integrating equations at both 5% and 1% significance level respectively. The presence of co-integrating vectors in the series for the WAMZ countries equally demonstrates a strong common long run stochastic trend and consequently a strong tendency for this criterion of the member countries to converge.

Table 5.2: Co-integration analysis for Inflation Rate

	Trace (λ_{trace})			
No. of CE(s)	None	At most 1	At most 2	At most 3
Eigenvalue	0.999855	0.934351	0.620010	0.013891
λ_{trace} *Statistic*	263.3732	77.80564	20.61357	0.293755
5% Critical Value	47.21	29.68	15.41	3.76
1% Critical Value	54.46	35.65	20.04	6.65
	Maximum Eigenvalue (λ_{max})			
No. of CE(s)	None	At most 1	At most 2	At most 3
Eigenvalue	0.999855	0.934351	0.620010	0.013891
λ_{max} *Statistic*	185.5676	57.19207	20.31981	0.293755
5% Critical Value	27.07	20.97	14.07	3.76
1% Critical Value	32.24	25.52	18.63	6.65

Source: Authors' Calculations

Table 5.3 shows the co-integration result for the *Budget Deficit Financing to Tax Revenue ratio* criterion (i.e. BDF/TR) for 3 countries, i.e. Gambia, Guinea and Nigeria. The trace statistic (λ_{trace}) and the Max-eigenvalue (λ_{max}) identified 2 co-integrating equations at 5% significance level and 1 co-integrating equation at 1% significance level respectively. This is equally a signal for future convergence.

Table 5.4 shows the result of the co-integration test conducted on *Gross Foreign Exchange Reserves (GER)* for the four co-integrating countries (Gambia, Guinea, Nigeria and Sierra Leone). The trace statistic (λ_{trace}) and the Max-eigenvalue (λ_{max}) identified 1 co-integrating equation at 5% and 1% significance levels respectively.

Table 5.3: Co-integration result for Budget Deficit Financing/Tax Revenue

Trace (λ_{trace})			
No. of CE(s)	None	At most 1	At most 2
Eigenvalue	0.807302	0.511931	0.061978
λ_{trace} *Statistic*	48.55824	15.62562	1.279647
5% Critical Value	29.68	15.41	3.76
1% Critical Value	35.65	20.04	6.65

Maximum Eigenvalue (λ_{max})			
No. of CE(s)	None	At most 1	At most 2
Eigenvalue 0.061978	0.807302	0.511931	
λ_{max} *Statistic* 1.279647	32.93263	14.34597	
5% Critical Value	20.97	14.07	3.76
1% Critical Value	25.52	18.63	6.65

Source: Authors' Calculations

Table 5.4: Co-integration result for Gross Foreign Exchange Reserves

Trace (λ_{trace})				
No. of CE(s)	None	At most 1	At most 2	At most 3
Eigenvalue	0.802783	0.437482	0.350160	2.49E-05
λ_{trace} *Statistic*	57.85637	22.14049	9.483198	0.000548
5% Critical Value	47.21	29.68	15.41	3.76
1% Critical Value	54.46	35.65	20.04	6.65

Maximum Eigenvalue (λ_{max})				
No. of CE(s)	None	At most 1	At most 2	At most 3
Eigenvalue	0.802783	0.437482	0.350160	2.49E-05
λ_{max} *Statistic*	35.71588	12.65729	9.482651	0.000548
5% Critical Value	27.07	20.97	14.07	3.76
1% Critical Value	32.24	25.52	18.63	6.65

Source: Authors' Calculations

Table 5.5 shows the co-integration result for the four co-integrating countries Ghana, Guinea, Nigeria and Sierra Leone on the basis of the *Tax Revenue to Gross Domestic Product (TR/GDP) ratio*. The trace statistic (λ_{trace}) and the Max-eigenvalue (λ_{max}) identified 3 co-integrating equations at 5% and 2 co-integrating equations at 1% significance level respectively. Both the λ_{trace} and the λ_{max} suggested likely future convergence by the set time target.

Table 5.5: Co-integration result for Tax Revenue/GDP

| | Trace (λ_{trace}) | | | |
No. of CE(s)	None	At most 1	At most 2	At most 3
Eigenvalue	0.905054	0.705601	0.521742	0.020825
λ_{trace} Statistic	95.39031	43.59236	16.69030	0.462997
5% Critical Value	47.21	29.68	15.41	3.76
1% Critical Value	54.46	35.65	20.04	6.65
	Maximum Eigenvalue (λ_{max})			
No. of CE(s)	None	At most 1	At most 2	At most 3
Eigenvalue	0.905054	0.705601	0.521742	0.020825
λ_{max} Statistic	51.79795	26.90206	16.22731	0.462997
5% Critical Value	27.07	20.97	14.07	3.76
1% Critical Value	32.24	25.52	18.63	6.65

Source: Authors' Calculations

Table 5.6 shows the co-integration test conducted on the ratio of *Wage Bills to Tax Revenue (WB/TR)* for the four co-integrating countries The Gambia, Ghana, Nigeria and Sierra Leone. The results indicate that there is 1 co-integrating equation for the trace statistic (λ_{trace}) at 5% significance level and no co-integrating equation at 1% critical levels, while the Max-eigenvalue (λ_{max}) shows no co-integrating equation at both 5% and 1% critical levels respectively.

Table 5.6: Co-integration result for Wage Bill/Tax Revenue

| | Trace (λ_{trace}) | | | |
No. of CE(s)	None	At most 1	At most 2	At most 3
Eigenvalue	0.613228	0.530232	0.392608	0.003883
λ_{trace} Statistic	48.57400	27.67577	11.05439	0.085594
5% Critical Value	47.21	29.68	15.41	3.76
1% Critical Value	54.46	35.65	20.04	6.65
	Maximum Eigenvalue (λ_{max})			
No. of CE(s)	None	At most 1	At most 2	At most 3
Eigenvalue	0.613228	0.530232	0.392608	0.003883
λ_{max} Statistic	20.89823	16.62138	10.96879	0.085594
5% Critical Value	27.07	20.97	14.07	3.76
1% Critical Value	32.24	25.52	18.63	6.65

Source: Authors' Calculations

Table 5.7 shows the co-integration results for the ratio of *public investment to tax revenue* for Gambia, Ghana, and Guinea. The Max-eigenvalue and the trace statistics indicated no co-integrating vectors at the 1% and 5% critical values. This means that this criterion does not show any tendency for future convergence.

Table 5.7: Co-integration result for Public Investment/Tax Revenue

No. of CE(s)	Trace (λ_{trace})		
	None	At most 1	At most 2
Eigenvalue	0.524431	0.249029	0.116051
λ_{trace} *Statistic*	26.51870	9.424116	2.837178
5% Critical Value	29.68	15.41	3.76
1% Critical Value	35.65	20.04	6.65
	Maximum Eigenvalue (λ_{max})		
No. of CE(s)	None	At most 1	At most 2
Eigenvalue	0.524431	0.249029	0.116051
λ_{max} *Statistic*	17.09458	6.586938	2.837178
5% Critical Value	20.97	14.07	3.76
1% Critical Value	25.52	18.63	6.65

Source: Authors' Calculations

Table 5.8 shows the co-integration test conducted for Gambia and Sierra Leone for the *Real Interest Rate* convergence criterion. The λ_{trace} statistic identified two co-integrating equations at 5% critical levels and no co-integrating equation at 1% critical levels. The λ_{max} value identified no co-integrating equation each at both 5% and 1% critical levels. This suggests the presence of at least one country having the stochastic trend and it is likely to converge on the basis of this criterion in the long-run.

For all the criteria analysed (Budget Deficit/GDP, Inflation Rate, Budget Deficit Financing/Tax Revenue, Gross Foreign Exchange Reserves, Tax Revenue/GDP, Wage Bill/Tax Revenue, Public Investment/Tax Revenue, and Real Interest Rate), the empirical results from all the convergence criteria considered suggest that for the West African Monetary Zone (WAMZ) countries there is a strong evidence of convergence. The results imply that there are possibilities of the WAMZ member countries for satisfying the requirements necessary for the launching of the project by 2015. However, for a more reliable long-run convergence, the WAMZ member countries will need to make some commitments for adjustments to align their policies for the single currency to be more viable.

Table 5.8: Co-integration result for Real Interest Rate

	Trace (λ trace)		
No. of CE(s)	None	At most 1	+
Eigenvalue	0.402172	20.04	
λ trace Statistic	16.20258	4.884629	
5% Critical Value	15.41	3.76	
1% Critical Value	20.04	6.65	
	Maximum Eigenvalue (λ max)		
No. of CE(s)	None	At most 1	
Eigenvalue	0.402172	0.199108	
λ max Statistic	11.31795	4.884629	
5% Critical Value	14.07	3.76	
1% Critical Value	18.63	6.65	

Source: Authors' Calculations

As part of the precondition for the take-off of the WAMZ project, at least three countries must satisfy at least three primary and three secondary criteria for at least three consecutive years; the direct implication of these results is that if the WAMZ member countries can put in more efforts towards the actualization of the project, the targets can be achieved even earlier. The results give an optimistic outlook that the WAMZ project can be realised from now on up to 2015, as it is likely to provide for the member countries in this period the frame for effective policy coordination. A clearly defined convergence period, with clear targets to be achieved by all member states, would be part of a negotiated framework to this programme.

6 Towards Sufficient Conditions for Currency Integration

As stated above, the convergence criteria (primary and secondary) are necessary but not sufficient conditions for monetary integration. There are other challenges that transcend the political, economic, institutional, and socio-cultural (including language barriers) arena, which on the surface may appear trivial, but indeed have implications for the long-term sustainability of the monetary union.

One such challenge is the political will and the commitment on the part of member states. It must be acknowledged that the six countries of the second Monetary Union, and particularly so Ghana and Nigeria, have demonstrated strong political will and great and specific commitments to proceed with the monetary integration. Indeed, such political will and commitment are unparalleled in the history of the formation of monetary unions. What is essential, therefore, is how to translate these to the larger group of the

WAMZ membership so that the planned single monetary zone for West Africa comes to fruition at the proposed date or with minimal delay. In reality, with the increased globalization and the rise in regional economic blocs, it would appear that member states of the ECOWAS sub-region are left with little choice but to act quickly on the monetary union and other economic integration objectives. Public administrators must act as leaders and catalysts to the whole integration process since anything short of that may derail the process. Thus, building up political credibility is both a challenge and a risk that monetary Union members would have to contend with (Itsede, 2003).

Related to the issues of political will and commitment is that of communication with the general public and how to deal with the uncertainties and public apprehension about relinquishing their national currencies with the introduction of a single currency. How do you encourage the public to accept the technical feasibility of the transition to a single currency? To deal with these issues, authorities in member countries will have to embark on extensive public enlightenment campaigns to get the general public buy into the whole monetary integration process. The public must be carried along as otherwise the whole integration effort will come to naught, as exemplified by the experience of the failed ECOWAS Travellers' cheque. It makes no sense to demonstrate strong political will and commitment at the highest level without the confidence of the public in the project. Central to this is also the issue of consumer protection. They must be guaranteed that there will be no added cost or special charges for the changeover to a single currency. The support of all citizens is crucial to the success of monetary union.

Another major challenge that must be tackled is that of distrust and suspicion between member states. Smaller economies/countries often fear the domination by the large ones. This fear of domination can also be seen within groups of countries from a monetary union. Such fears might be compounded by socio-cultural, historical and language difference in the case of ECOWAS countries where there exists strong potential for one group to fight to dominate the other, i.e. the Anglophone vis -à-vis the Francophone countries. For example, the distrust and suspicion between the Anglophone and Francophone countries of ECOWAS may have undermined the efforts at establishing a Free Trade Area as well as the efforts made by some member states to enhance intra-regional trade within the region through the introduction of the ECOWAS Travellers Cheque prior to the introduction of a monetary union. Thus, the authorities of the member states of the proposed Monetary Union (MU) must play the catalytic role and turn these potential barriers to an advantage rather than see them as destabilizing factors.

This experience of the ECOWAS is a good lesson for WAMZ member countries. As ECOWAS comprises the Francophone countries of the WAEMU, the WAMZ states are made up of Anglophone countries. A careful cushion is required to diffuse any ethno-linguistic supremacy that could undermine the benefit of the integration (WAMZ/CG/24, 2011).

According to the report of the 24th Meetings of the Governors of the Central Banks of WAMZ, 2011, the conceptual issues regarding federal and unitary structures of central banking, including their advantages and disadvantages, were discussed. The presentation highlighted the decision-making process in the WACB within the two structures (federal and unitary), and provided comparative analysis of the existing models of central banking (BCEAO/BEAC, ESCB, and Federal Reserve Bank). Under either structure, unitary or federal, price stability or low inflation will be the primary objective of the WACB, and the exchange rate policy will be market based. Also, for some period of time at least, the WACB system may permit credit to government, subject to clearly specified ceilings (WAMZ/CG/24, 2011).

It was indicated that under the Federal system, National Central Banks (NCBs) will continue to exist, but will give up their sovereignty over monetary policy to the WACB. The NCBs will however retain some residual powers of central banking in their countries and will be part of the central authority that governs the WACB system. The WACB Headquarters could be kept small in manpower size, with no major reorganisation required, and could benefit from technical work being shared by NCBs through reliance on working groups, committees etc. Furthermore, the challenge is the restructuring of the relationship between the Centre (the WACB) and the NCBs. There would also be the need to reach consensus on the degree to which the prospective WACB could support the general economic policy of the countries (especially economic growth objectives), while maintaining price stability as the primary objective (WAMZ/CG/24, 2011).

Under the unitary structure for the WACB, the NCBs will cease to exist and will become branches of the WACB. There will then be only one bank with central banking authority. The centralized budgetary arrangement and the need to undertake significant structural reforms (down-sizing) at the branches are the key challenges.

The Technical Committee of WAMZ has observed that the objectives and functions of the WACB should be given greater prominence than the nomenclature (federal or unitary). The main decision on the type of central bank for the WAMZ should be based on the primary objective of monetary policy.

The primary objective should endow the common central bank with the prerequisite attributes enabling it to deliver on its mandate of price stability.

The choice of the WACB structure should also take into account the most appropriate arrangement considering the pertinent issues relating to the decision-making processes in monetary policy management, the pooling of reserves, the consistency with the ECOWAS road map, and most importantly, what is appropriate for the WAMZ at this point in time. Taking cognisance of the existing realities within the Zone, it was suggested that a common central bank similar to the European Central Bank (ECB) be adopted for the WAMZ (WAMZ/TC/32, 2012).

In addition to the issue of political credibility alluded to above, the proposed single ECOWAS monetary zone has to contend with the issue of importing monetary policy credibility to the monetary union. The question is, do some member countries have well-established and credible independent monetary policies that could be imported into the MU when a single currency is eventually adopted so as to reduce the country risk premium, which is possibly associated with a depreciation risk? In this regard, therefore, the experience of the CFA franc zone (or WAEMU) in maintaining a credible monetary policy environment since its existence becomes useful and, thus, capable of giving added credibility to the larger monetary union when it eventually comes on board.

The biggest challenge posed by currency union arrangements is traditionally seen to be how to cope with the divergence of national developments from those of the currency union on average, when national monetary policy is no longer available as an economic policy tool. Basically, this concerns the issue of how to handle asymmetric shocks. Should there be particular measures for dealing with the adjustment costs associated with asymmetric shocks or not? Researches have portrayed asymmetric shocks as unambiguously undesirable on the grounds that they raise the costs of membership in a currency union. It has been suggested that monetary union members can respond to such shocks through fiscal, price and wage policies. While this may be true, it may not be so in all circumstances, thus requiring other initiatives to deal with the problem. In this context, therefore, the plan by the ECOWAS members to set up a Regional Stabilization and Cooperation Fund, as a buffer to temporary shocks and adverse balance of payments situations would certainly help. The effectiveness of such a fund, however, presumes that each member must demonstrate strong commitment to helping its neighbours.

Thus, a country like Nigeria with its very large economy and its oil resources should be able to play the "big brother" role when smaller economies within the union experience adverse shocks (Mordi, 2002). In addition to the "bail out", ensuring unimpeded regional labour mobility (and possibly mobility of other factors) could assist in cushioning shocks that affect the economies differently. This calls for labour market reforms in the converging economies to facilitate movement of people across industries and national borders where necessary to find jobs and, thus, making the labour markets more flexible. It is pertinent to note here that on paper ECOWAS has indeed facilitated mobility by the elimination of visa requirements, but in practice there is some visible resistance to labour mobility within the sub-region. This is in addition to the other administrative bottlenecks encountered by citizens of other countries seeking to establish residency in another country, as well as the existence of outright hostile responses against large-scale immigration from neighbouring countries. These attitudes need to change among the union members for the monetary union to be sustainable. Thus, harmonizing immigration laws and implementing already established protocols remains a major challenge. The ECOWAS experience is a good lesson for the WAMZ member countries to take all necessary measures to eliminate any form of barrier to mobility when eventually the MU goes operational comes 2015 (WAMA 2009).

With respect to the conduct of national fiscal policies in a Monetary Union (MU) and the credibility and sustainability of fiscal policies, the following questions must be answered. What is the role of fiscal policy in the MU? How independent can national fiscal policies really remain in the MU? Does the Monetary Union reduce or increase fiscal discipline? And what rules, if any, should be used to restrict national fiscal policies? Should there be a Stability Pact akin to the EU Stability/Fiscal Pact? How should the issue of risks of default and bailout be handled in a Monetary Union? Indeed, some of these issues are already receiving attention, as indicated by the convergence criteria, where a rule on government budget deficits has been set. The views on the relevance of a fiscal policy rule have been divergent, but there is now a growing literature on why fiscal policy rules make sense in a monetary union (see the early study by Sargent and Wallace, 1981). All the questions raised above must be addressed in a holistic manner by the converging economies for the Monetary Union to be sustainable.

Related to the role of fiscal policy is how to conduct monetary policies in a union where asymmetric shocks occur and where the same shocks are transmitted differently among member-countries. Should there be a common central bank or a coordination of the central banks of individual member countries? If a common central bank is required, what monetary policy strategy should it adopt, what should be the ultimate and final targets of monetary policy, and what instruments should it use to achieve these targets? Should there be a single objective or multiple objectives that will encompass price stability, stabilization of the business cycle, maintenance of high employment, financial stability, etc.? Should the common central bank be completely independent and accountable and should it have the necessary powers to carry out its assigned responsibilities and to build up credibility? What will be the interaction between the common central bank and the national fiscal authorities and how are conflicts to be resolved, particularly as it concerns enforcing access to monetary financing?

There is also the challenge of financial markets integration and supervision. Financial markets integration—bonds and equity markets and banking sectors—is of great importance for the smooth functioning of the MU and it can facilitate adjustment to asymmetric shocks. Financial markets integration is a worldwide phenomenon, driven by globalization and technological progress. Adoption of a single currency adds another catalytic dimension for financial markets integration in the ECOWAS monetary zone. The ECOWAS cross-border clearing and settlement infrastructure, which is essential for the smooth and efficient functioning of the securities markets, remains fragmented and rudimentary. Major steps in integrating and upgrading the infrastructure must be taken by member countries while at the same time undertaking an adjustment of the structures and operating procedures of financial markets (De Grauwe, 2000).

7 Conclusion

Meeting the macroeconomic convergence criteria, which will culminate in an economic and monetary union, especially within the time frame envisaged, poses an enormous challenge for the economies of the West African subregion. This is so because having common economic policy goals is important to the success of a monetary union; hence the important role for the convergence criteria cannot be overemphasized. The challenge is how to get the member states to implement the necessary economic policy measures that would steer them toward meeting these criteria. One crucial problem is that the economies of the countries in the intending union may be too fragile or too weak to undertake the necessary macroeconomic adjustments required for the monetary union. It is feasible that some countries may be able to meet the targets within the stipulated time frame while others might not. In other words, it may require special policy efforts on the part of failing countries to meet the convergence criteria. Under this circumstance, it may be expedient for member countries to determine how to move forward, taking into account the factors (whether internal or external) that may have constrained their ability to meet these criteria.

The recent development in the Euro zone is a good lesson for members of the WAMZ, especially with respect to the Greece's debt crisis and the debt problems of other countries such as Spain, Italy etc. The implication is that the political will among the member states of the WAMZ who have stronger economies could be reduced in terms of supporting weaker member countries. In general, poor trade integration, low labour mobility, independent and uncoordinated fiscal policies in member states and a poor financial harmonization policy are factors that could limit the successful formation of WAMZ set by 2015.

References

Adam, C. S., (1992), Recent developments in econometric methods: An application to the demand for money in Kenya, *African Economic Research Consortium (AERC)*, 15: 1–52

Afristat (2001), A Contribution to Statistical Capacity Building In Member States During The 1996- 2000 Period, A seminar on the launching of the study "*AF-RISTAT AFTER 2005*", Bamako, 7-9 May

Ahn, S. K., and G. C. Reinsel (1990), "Estimation of Partially Non-stationary

Multivariate Autoregressive Models", *Journal of the American Statistical Association*, 85, 813–823.

Anadi, Sunday (2005), "Regional Integration in Africa, the Case of ECOWAS", Thesis presented to the Faculty of Arts of the University of Zürich for the Degree of a Doctor of Philosophy.

Aschheim, Joseph and Tavlas, George S. (1995), "Monetary Economics in

Doctrinal Perspective: A Review Essay", in: Journal of Money, Credit and Banking, Blackwell Publishing, vol. 28(3), August.

Balassa, B. (1964), "The Purchasing Power Parity Doctrine: A Reappraisal", in: *Journal of Political Economy*, Vol. 72

Balassa, B. (1961), Towards a Theory of Economic Integration, in: Kyklos, February, Volume 14, Issue 1, pp. 1-17

Balogun, E. D. (2007), "Monetary Policy and Economic Performance of West African Monetary Zone Countries", *MPRA Paper* No. 4308

Balogun, E. D. (2008), "An Alternative Reconsideration of Macroeconomic Convergence Criteria for West African Monetary Zone", *MPRA Paper* No. 11367

Barro, R. (2001), "Currency Unions." Unpublished monograph, Harvard

University, Harvard, USA

Bayoumi, T. and B. Eichengreen (1992), "Shocking Aspects of European Monetary Unification", *NBER Working Paper* No. 3949.

CBL/Central Bank of Liberia, Annual Report, January 1, 2011 to December 31, 2011

CBN/Central Bank of Nigeria, (2009), Statistical Bulletin, Vol. 10, No.2, December

CBN/Central Bank of Nigeria (2010), Statistical Bulletin, Vol. 4, No.4, November

Daniel, A. (2011), "The Eurozone Currency Crisis: A Lesson for the West Africa Monetary Zone", in: Asian Journal of Business and Management Sciences, Vol. 1, No. 11 [11-25]

De Grauwe, P. (2000), "Economics of Monetary Union", Fourth Edition, New York: Oxford University Press Inc.

De Grauwe, P. (1997), The Economics of Monetary Integration, Third Edition, Oxford

De Grauwe, P. and W. Vanhaverbeke (1993), 'Is Europe an optimum currency area?: evidence from Regional data', in P. R. Masson and M. P. Taylor (eds.), Policy Issues in the Operation of Currency Unions, Cambridge University Press

Dyson, Kenneth (ed.) (1994), *The Euro at 10: Europeanization, Convergence and Power*, Oxford University Press, Oxford, Chapter 1: pp. 1-34; Chapter 7: pp.132-64; Chapter 20: pp. 378-413

ECA/United Nations Economic Commission for Africa, AUC/African Union Commission, AfDB/African Development Bank (2009), Assessing Progress in Africa toward the Millennium Development Goals, MDG Report 2009

Engle, R. F. and C. J. Granger (1987), "Co-integration and Error Correction: Representation, Estimation, and Testing", in: *Econometrica, 55, 251-276.

Fleming, J. M. (1962), "Domestic financial policies under fixed and floating exchange rates", *IMF Staff Papers* 9: 369–379, Reprinted in: Cooper, Richard N., ed. (1969), *International Finance*. New York: Penguin Books.

Granger C. W. J. (1986), Developments in the study of co-integrated economic variables, in: Oxford Bulletin of Economics and Statistics, 48, 3

Haug, A., J. MacKinnon and L. Michelis (2000), "European Monetary Union: A Co-integration Analysis", in: *The Journal of International Money and Finance*, 19, June 2000, pp. 419-432.

Hafer, R. W., and A.M. Kutan (1994), "A Long Run View of German Dominance and the Degree of Policy Convergence in the EMS", Economic Inquiry, 32, 684–695.

Hafer, R. W., Kutan, A. M., Zhou, S. (1997), Linkages in the EMS term structures: evidence from common trend and transitory components. In: Journal of International Money and Finance 16 (4), August 1997, 595–607

Itsede, C. O. (2002), "The Challenge of Monetary Union: Gains and Opportunities", CBN/Economic & Financial Review/EFR Vol. 40 - Number 4 - Paper 3

Itsede, C. O. (2003), "The Challenges of establishing the Second Monetary Zone in West Africa**, *Bullion, Publication of the CBN/Central Bank of Nigeria,* Volume 29, no. 2

IMF (2011), Data and Statistics, Access: http:// www.imf.org /external /data.htm

Johansen, S. (1995), "Likelihood-Based Inference in Co-integrated Vector Autoregressive Models", Oxford University Press, Oxford.

Johansen, S. (1988), "Statistical Analysis of Co-integration Vectors", in: *Journal of Economic Dynamics and Control, 12, 231–254.

Karfakis, S. J. and D. M. Moschos (1990), "Interest Rates Linkages within the European Monetary System: A Time Series Analysis", in: *Journal of Money, Credit and Banking, 22, 388-394.

Kendall, P. (2000), "Exchange Rate Convergence in CARICOM", Staff Papers, August 2000, Caribbean Development Bank

Kenen P. (1969), *The Theory of Optimum Currency Areas: An Eclectic View*, University of Chicago Press, 1969, Access: http://ideas .repec.org/a/ eee/inecon /v1y1971i1p127-131.html

MacDonald, R. and M. Taylor (1991), "Exchange Rates, Policy Convergence and the European Monetary System", in: *Review of Economics and Statistics, 73, 553-558.*

Masson, Paul R. and Mark P. Taylor, (1993), "Fiscal Policy within Common Currency Areas," in: Journal of Common Market Studies, Wiley Blackwell, vol. 31(1), 03, pages 29-44.

Madhur, S. (2002), "Costs and Benefits of a Common Currency for ASEAN", Asian Development Bank, *Economics and Research Department/ERD Working Paper No. 12*

Masson, Paul R. and Mark P. Taylor *(1993),* "Fiscal Policy within Common Currency Areas," in: Journal of Common Market Studies, Wiley Blackwell, vol. 31(1), pages 147-154

Mwangi S. K., Zenia A. L. and Brandon R. (2012), Accelerating Growth through Improved Intra-African Trade, Brookings Africa Growth Initiative, Brookings Institution, Washington D. C.

Mordi, C. N. O. (2002), The Challenges of Monetary Union: Risks and Pitfalls and How to Respond to them, Paper presented at CBN Executive Policy Seminar, Owerri, October 14 . 18, 2002

Mundell, R. B. (1961), "The Theory of Optimum Currency Areas", in: *American Economic Review, 51 (4), September, 1961,* pp. 657–663.

McKinnon, R (1963), "Optimum Currency Areas," American Economic Review, Vol. 53, p. 717-25

Nnanna, O. J. (2007), "ECO Currency: Is a Third Postponement Avoidable?", in: *West African Journal of Monetary and Economic Integration,* Vol. 7 No. 1 June 2007

Obaseki, P. J., (2005): "The Future of the West African Monetary Zone (WAMZ) Programme". In: *West African Journal of Monetary and Economic Integration, Vol. 5(2a):pp. 1-33.*

Ojo, M. O. (2004), "The Challenges of Introducing the Eco Currency", The Zonal Workshop for the Mass Media in the WAMZ, Conakry, Republic of Guinea, June 8, 2004

Ojo, M. O. (2005), "Towards a Common Currency in West Africa: Progress, Lessons and Prospects", in: *West African Journal of Monetary and Economic Integration, Vol. 5(2a):pp.47- 79.*

Paola, B. (2007): Theory, History and Evidence of Economic Convergence in Latin America. Access: http://ideas.repec.org/p/adv/wpaper/200713.html

Quirk, P. and O. Evans (1995), "Capital Account Convertibility: Review of Experience and Implications for IMF Policies", *IMF Occasional Paper No.131,* Washington, D. C.

Ramanathan, R. (1992), Introductory Econometrics with Application. Dryden Press (Fort Worth), Access: http://www.getcited.org/pub/102932889

Sargent, T. J. and N. Wallace (1981), "Some unpleasant Monetarist Arithmetic", Federal Reserve Bank of Minneapolis Quarterly Review, 5, 1-17.

Soyibo, A. (1998), "International Payments System: West African Common Currency", Is it Possible or Necessary?, *Paper presented at the Workshop on International Payments System within ECOWAS Countries, Accra-Ghana. March 30-31.*

Umar, A. A. (2011), Towards a Second Monetary Zone in West-Africa: A Test for Long-Run Convergence, An Unpublished M.Sc. Thesis, Department of Economics, Ahmadu Bello University, Zaria.

UNECA/United Nations Economic Commission for Africa, AU/African Union and AfDB/African Development Bank (2010), Assessing Regional Integration in Africa, Volume IV, *Enhancing Intra-African Trade,* Addis Ababa, Ethiopia

UNECA/United Nations Economic Commission for Africa (2010), Economic Report on Africa - Governing Development in Africa - the role of the state in economic transformation. Access: http://www.un.org/regionalcommissions/ERA2011.pdf

Viner, J. (1950), "The Customs Union Issues", New York: Carnegie Endowment for International Peace

WAMA/West African Monetary Agency (2010), ECOWAS Monetary Cooperation Programme, Annual Report 2010, Freetown, Sierra Leone, Access: http://www.amao-wama.org/fr/Publications/EMCP%20Annual%20Report%202010.pdf

WAMA (2009), ECOWAS Monetary Cooperation Programme, Macroeconomic Convergence Report, first half 2009, Freetown, Sierra Leone

WAMA (2007), ECOWAS Monetary Cooperation Programme, *Macroeconomic Convergence Report 2007,* Access: *.http://www.amaowama.org/fr /Publications /convergences%20macro%20en.pdf*

WAMI (2011), "Meetings of the West African Monetary Zone (WAMZ)", Abuja, Nigeria, February 7- 11

WAMI (2000), "West African Monetary Zone, The Technical Committee Report on Monetary Issues", Vol. 1, Presented to the Convergence Council, 2000

WAMI/West African Monetary Institute Website: wami-imao.org http:// www .imf.org/external/pubs/ft/weo/data/index.htm.

WAMZ/TC/32 (2012), Report of the 32nd Meeting of the Technical Committee of the WAMZ. Freetown, Sierra Leone. Jan. 16-17.

WAMZ/CG/24 (2011), Final Report on the 24th meeting of the Committee of Governors of Central Banks of the West African Monetary Zone (WAMZ), Abuja, Feb. 7-11

WAMZ/TC/30 (2011), 30th Meeting of the Technical Committee of the West African Monetary Zone, Final Report Abuja, Nigeria, February 7 - 8

WAMZ/CG/26 (2012), Report of the 26th Meeting of Governors of Central Banks of the West African Monetary Zone (WAMZ), Freetown, Sierra Leone, January 16th to 20th.

WTO/World Trade Organisation (2004), Annual Report; accessed: https://www.wto.org /english/res_e/booksp_e/anrep_e/anrep04_e.pdf

World Bank and IFC (2011), Spotlight on Africa. Access: http://africanspotlight.com/2011/11/world-bank-and-ifc-approve-us82-million-power-loan-for-cameroon/

World Bank, 2011, African Development Indicators, http:// data. worldbank.org /sites/default/files/adi_2011-web.pdf

Ukpong, G. E. (2002), Second Monetary Zone In ECOWAS: Issues, Progress And Prospects, by G. E. Ukpong, Ph.D*, Accessed: http:// www.cbn.gov.ng/OUT/PUBLICATIONS/EFR/RD/2002/ EFRVOL40-4-1.PDF

Appendix A1: Unit Root Test Results for Primary Convergence Criteria

	BD/GDP				INFR			
	LEVEL		1st DIFF		LEVEL		1st DIFF	
	ADF	PP	ADF	PP	ADF	PP	ADF	PP
GAMBIA	-3.2287	-5.4270	-5.5441		-6.4992	-2.9098		-8.4897
Order Of Integra-tion		*I(0)*	*I(1)*		*I(0)*			*I(1)*
GHANA	-1.1734	-1.7308	-2.1924	-5.7008	-3.4206	-3.5248	-4.3915	
Order Of Integra-tion			*I(1)*	*I(1)*		*I(0)*	*I(1)*	
GUINEA	-2.2228	-2.9385	-4.1802	-6.6004	-1.7488	-1.9883	-3.0567	-4.7089
Order Of Integra-tion			*I(1)*	*I(1)*			*I(1)*	*I(1)*
NIGERIA	-1.8944	-2.3317	-3.6482	-5.2627	-2.9761	-2.7245	-3.9680	-4.3055
Order Of Integra-tion			*I(1)*	*I(1)*			*I(1)*	*I(1)*
SIERRA LEONE	-3.1623	-2.9839	-5.7275	-5.3450	-2.7973	-4.0445	-3.5174	
Order Of Integra-tion			*I(1)*	*I(1)*		*I(0)*	*I(1)*	

Appendix A2: Unit Root Test Results for Primary Convergence Criteria Cont'd

	BDF/TR				GER			
	LEVEL		1st DIFF		LEVEL		1st DIFF	
	ADF	PP	ADF	PP	ADF	PP	ADF	PP
GAMBIA	-1.4492	-2.9982	-5.0340	-9.3643	-3.5963	-5.7536	-7.1501	
Order Of Integration			I(1)	I(1)	I(0)		I(1)	
GHANA	-7.4219	-4.1394			-5.4232	-4.7092		
Order Of Integration	I(0)	I(0)			I(0)	I(0)		
GUINEA	-3.4990	-7.4219	-7.2992		-2.1414	-2.2514	-3.7454	-5.4469
Order Of Integration		I(0)	I(1)				I(1)	I(1)
NIGERIA	-2.4226	-6.0211	-4.8006		-2.1596	-2.8694	-4.3602	-6.4904
Order Of Integration		I(0)	I(1)				I(1)	I(1)
SIERRA LEONE	-4.2112	-5.7585			-2.0818	-2.1312	-3.8492	-6.1447
Order Of Integration	I(0)	I(0)					I(1)	I(1)

Source: E-views 4.0. Notes: For all the series at levels, we included trend and intercept, as their line plots indicate. The critical values are based on the McKinnon criterion. The null hypothesis of the test is: a series has a unit root. I() shows the level of integration.

Appendix B1: Unit Root Test Results for Secondary Convergence Criteria

	IAA				TR/GDP			
	LEVEL		1st DIFF		LEVEL		1st DIFF	
	ADF	PP	ADF	PP	ADF	PP	ADF	PP
GAMBIA					-4.6367	-3.9659		
Order Of Integration	----	----	----	----	I(0)	I(0)		
GHANA	-5.6726	-3.0354			-2.3948	-3.1703	-3.9067	-6.7516
Order Of Integration	I(0)	I(0)					I(1)	I(1)

GUINEA	-3.0032	-4.4044	-4.1854		-2.4613	-3.9658	-3.9418	
Order Of Integration		*I(0)*	*I(1)*			*I(0)*	*I(1)*	
NIGERIA					-3.4003	-2.9989	-4.4649	-5.1359
Order Of Integration	------	----	----	----			*I(1)*	*I(1)*
SIERRA LEONE					-4.8978	-3.2830		-3.9592
Order Of Integration	------	----	----	----	*I(1)*			*I(1)*

Appendix B2: Unit Root Test Results for Secondary Convergence Criteria Cont'd

	RIR				RER			
	LEVEL		1st DIFF.		LEVEL		1st DIFF.	
	ADF	PP	ADF	PP	ADF	PP	ADF	PP
GAMBIA	-3.1908	-4.0185	-5.7354		-2.2808	-3.1524	-4.5929	-6.7524
Order Of Integration		*I(0)*	*I(1)*				*I(1)*	*I(1)*
GHANA	-4.6906	-4.6767			-4.3387	-5.6130		
Order Of Integration	*I(0)*	*I(0)*			*I(0)*	*I(0)*		
GUINEA	-2.3772	-3.7522			-6.2288	-6.3054		
Order Of Integration	*I(0)*	*I(0)*			*I(0)*	*I(0)*		
NIGERIA	-3.8548	-4.4881			-3.7764	-3.9949		
Order Of Integration	*I(0)*	*I(0)*			*I(0)*	*I(0)*		
SIERRA LEONE	-2.5285	-3.6273	-3.4020		-5.3891	-3.8839		
Order Of Integration		*I(0)*	*I(1)*		*I(0)*	*I(0)*		

Appendix B3: Unit Root Test Results for Secondary Convergence Criteria Cont'd

	WB/TR				PI/TR			
	LEVEL		1st DIFF		LEVEL		1st DIFF	
	ADF	PP	ADF	PP	ADF	PP	ADF	PP
GAMBIA	-2.6164	-3.2075	-3.7696	-5.8258	-2.4718	-1.9747	-4.6251	-4.2006
Order Of Integration			*I(1)*	*I(1)*			*I(1)*	*I(1)*
GHANA	-0.3939	-2.0458	-4.0905	-4.7016	-2.0273	-2.9770	-3.0870	-4.7405
Order Of Integration			*I(1)*	*I(1)*			*I(1)*	*I(1)*
GUINEA	-3.7092	-4.2026			-3.2764	-4.2983	-3.7133	
Order Of Integration	*I(0)*	*I(0)*					*I(0)*	*I(1)*
NIGERIA	-2.9295	-2.7410	-3.5357	-4.7797	-3.8266	-2.6739	-3.6672	
Order Of Integration			*I(1)*	*I(1)*	*I(0)*		*I(1)*	
SIERRA LEONE	-2.9512	-3.5445	-3.9501	-6.8043	-3.9802	-5.1057		
Order Of Integration			*I(1)*	*I(1)*	*I(0)*	*I(0)*		

Source: E-views 4.0. **Notes**: For all the series at levels, we included trend and intercept, as their line plots indicate. The critical values are based on McKinnon criterion. The null hypothesis of the test is: a series has a unit root. I() shows the level of integration.

Macroeconomic Policy Formation in Senegal: Challenges in Formation and Coordination

Mbaye Diene[1]

1 Introduction

Senegal has been facing many economic and social challenges which often led to ad hoc interventions of the government, although the level of political stability has been quite high. All the political regimes since 2000 have followed a liberal economic policy agenda. The country's development strategies and its economic policies can largely be explained by the economic performance of the tertiary sector as the dominant sector. As shown in Table 1a, the tertiary sector is more dynamic than the others in terms of contribution to the growth rate of GDP (Gross Domestic Product) at constant price (1999) and the value added. The contribution of the primary sector to the GDP growth is not consistent due to frequent shocks as a result of price fluctuations in the world market.

Table 1b presents the growth rates of the contributions of sectors to the GDP. These contributions are measured by multiplying the growth rate of the value added by its own ratio to GDP. It shows that the tertiary sector contributes at about 60% of the growth of GDP between 2005 and 2011. This is followed by the secondary sector which contributes about 24% to the growth of GDP. The contribution of the secondary sector comes mainly from the extraction and processing of phosphates, food processing, construction and cement industry (Direction of Forecast and Economic Studies/DFES, 2011: 4). Both, domestic and foreign investments play an important role in the development of the secondary sector. This can be explained by two factors. Firstly, Diaspora investment in the housing sector through their remittances is relevant. The estimate by the Directorate of Forecast and Economic Studies

[1] University Cheikh-Anta-Diop, CRES, Rue 10 Prolongée. BP 7988. Pyrotechnie. Dakar, Senegal; e-mail : mdiene@cres-sn.org

(DFES) revealed that the total remittances in 2011 amounted to 702.5 billion CFA francs in 2011 and 737.7 billion CFA francs in 2012 (DFES, 2012).

Table 1a: Annual growth rate of GDP (at constant prices of 1999) and growth rates of its component sectors

Years	2005	2006	2007	2008	2009	2010	2011	2012*
Value added	5.7	2.3	4.9	4.4	3.4	4.4	1.6	2.7
Primary sector	8.5	-8.9	-5.8	18.5	15.1	5.9	-12.8	2.9
Secondary sector	3.8	1.4	7.1	-1.2	1.7	4.4	6.4	0.1
Tertiary sector	5.8	5.8	6.8	3.4	1.2	4	4.1	3.9
GDP	5.6	2.5	4.9	3.7	2.4	4.3	2.1	2.9

Source: National Agency for Statistics and Demography/NASD (2011): National Accounts data. *NASD (2012): Recent economic growth data.

Table 1b: Annual growth rates (in percentage) of the sectors' contributions to the GDP

Years	2005	2006	2007	2008	2009	2010	2011	2012*
Value Added	5.0	2.0	4.3	3.8	3	3.9	1.4	5.1
Primary sector	1.2	-1.3	-0.8	2.2	2.1	0.9	-2	1.3
Secondary sector	0.8	0.3	1.4	-0.2	0.3	0.8	1.2	0.2
Tertiary sector	3.0	3.0	3.7	1.9	0.6	2.2	2.2	3.0
Taxes on products	0.6	0.5	0.6	-0.1	-0.6	0.3	0.6	0.6
GDP	5.6	2.5	4.9	3.7	2.4	4.3	2.1	2.9

Source: NASD (2011): National Accounts data. (*) Estimation from DFES (2013a)

Table 2 presents the percentage shares of the different sectors to the GDP. We see that the tertiary sector is the greatest contributor to the GDP, and its contribution mainly comes from trade, public administration, and other services (such as the financial services, and the real estate businesses: DFES 2013a: 35).

Table 2: The annual shares of the different economic sectors to the GDP (in percentage)

	2010	2011	2012	2013*
Primary sector	**15.5**	**13.6**	**14.6**	**14.9**
-Agriculture	8.4	6	7.1	7.4
-Livestock and hunting	4.2	4.4	4.2	4.2
-Fishing	1.8	2.1	2.2	2.2
Secondary sector	**20.5**	**21.6**	**21.2**	**21.5**
- Mining and quarrying	1.9	2.1	2	2.1
- Other industries	12	12.7	12.3	12.3
- Electricity, gas and	2.7	2.7	3.1	3.3
- Construction	3.9	4	3.7	3.7
Tertiary sector²	**45.6**	**45.7**	**45.5**	**45**
- Trade	15.7	15.8	15.7	15.4
- Transports, storage, etc	10.2	10.3	10.1	10.1
- Education and training	3.6	3.6	3.7	3.6
- Other services	14.7	14.6	14.6	14.5
Public administration	**18.4**	**19.1**	**18.7**	**18.7**
GDP at market price	100	100	100	100

Source: DFES (2013a): Financial and Economic Situation in 2012
(*) Estimation from the DFES

Secondly, the government investments in the infrastructure development increased since the beginning of the 2000s, especially in the energy sector which supported the recovery of the chemical industries in Senegal. However, the rising cost of production has affected the energy sector negatively. The government's efforts to liberalise the sector in 1999 and 2001 failed as a result of weak political will and the fear of job losses. The question is: how stable is a political system if it cannot pursue reforms? The fact is that the government of Senegal makes a tradeoff between sociopolitical stability and economic efficiency. The national company that provides electricity in Senegal is very largely subsidized by the government despite its weak ability to

---

[2] The tertiary sector comprises also other sectors as Posts and Telecommunications, Health and social services, Repair services, Accommodation and food services, Financial Services and Financial intermediation, Real estate activities etc.

provide good services. The government still allocates huge funds to maintain the price of electricity at socially acceptable levels for the population. The amount of subsidy to the company is 144 billion CFA francs in 2011, 99 billion CFA francs in 2012 and is expected to be 80 billion CFA francs in 2013 (DFES 2013a: 36). In addition, because of very old facilities and over-staffing, the company operates inefficiently. All the private investors who wanted to control the company felt the need to reduce the number of workers and to increase the prices of energy. The government does not accept the social consequences of such measures. This is a headlong rush towards more serious energy problems.

In the West African Economic and Monetary Union (WAEMU) countries, the economic and financial situation has improved in 2012 after a sharp economic decline in 2011 due to the post-electoral crisis in Ivory Coast and bad weather conditions that led to the decline in agricultural production in the Sahel countries. The growth rate in the Union was 5.8% in 2012 and so it is significantly higher than the growth rate of Senegal in 2012. This is partly due to the decline of the production of the country's secondary and tertiary sectors, despite an increase of the primary sector's production. In the primary sector, the production has grown by 8.9% in 2012 against a decline of 10.8% in 2011. This recovery is driven by the agricultural sub-sector, marked by abundant and well distributed rainfall distribution, by contracting publicly agricultural inputs (seeds and fertilizer), but also by the preservation of plant health (WAEMU 2012: 80). The growth rate in the secondary sector was 2.7% in 2012 against 7.2% in 2011. This decrease of the production (the value added has also decreased from 6.4% in 2011 to 0.1% in 2012, as shown in table 2a) is explained by the slowdown of the production of the sub-sectors of Construction and of Food processing (WAEMU 2012: 81).

The tertiary sector remains still important in the economy, though its light decline. The growth rate of the sector's production was 2.9% in 2012 against 4.0% in 2011. This is mainly due to the subsectors of Trade, Transport, Telecommunications and Financial services. Indeed, the sub-sector of Trade grew in 2012 by 3.7%, thanks to the increase of the imports of basic foodstuffs, reinforced by the poor crops situation of 2012, and the easing of the imports of vehicles. The sector of Transport declined in 2012 by a rate of 3%, marking a sharp slowdown due to the air transport which is affected by the decline of tourism. The sub-sector of Finance is supported by the sub-sector Insurance Services and by the short and medium term bank credits. The growth of the tertiary sector is also offset by the decline in the sub-sector Hotels and Restaurants (WAEMU 2012: 81).

In the recent decade, the major programs undertaken by the Senegalese government at the macroeconomic policy level are the Accelerated Growth Strategy (AGS) in 2005, the Poverty Reduction Strategy Paper III (PRSP) for the period from 2011 to 2015, and the Document of Economic and Social Policy (DESP) presented in 2006. The Economic Policy Support Instrument (EPSI) is also a relevant program, though it mainly concerns the public sector. The National Strategy for Economic and Social Development (NSESD), for the years 2013-2017, is replacing the DESP which was a national plan too. The NSESD is developed through a participatory process, at both central and local levels. It involves regional stakeholders, consultations with local authorities, and also with the Senegalese Army. This latter were involved because the fate of the demobilized soldiers is important for the government and the economy. Indeed, their lives are often precarious and many of them fall into poverty after leaving the army.

The NSESD document emphasizes wealth creation, strengthening governance, and the development of strategic sectors (with special focus on improving the welfare and social demand). Support measures for cross-cutting issues such as employment, gender, social protection and sustainable development were taken into account in the new strategy. The coordination process of the NSESD is based on a synergy between the economic and social policy programs such as the Accelerated Growth Strategy (AGS) and the Economic Policy Support Instrument (EPSI).

One basic impact of the macroeconomic programs as pursued is a low inflation rate that remains below 3% and is expected to be around 2.3% in 2013 (DFES, 2013a: 4) against 1.7% in 2012. This progression is due to reflect the increase in producer prices in the secondary sector (3.4% in 2013 against 2.3% in 2012) and the tertiary sector (1.8% in 2013 against 1% in 2012). The real GDP growth rate in 2011 was 4%; it is 3.5% in 2012 and is expected to be 4% in 2013. This last increase is supposed to be mainly due to the primary and secondary sectors and to the implementation of both public investments and the NSESD (DFES: 2013: 4). The tax revenues expressed as a percentage of the GDP increased from 18.8% in 2010 to 19.3% in 2011 due to an improved efficiency in the tax collection and the modernization of the management of the public finances (DFES, 2011: 5). The formulation of economic policies in Senegal has been strongly supported by the International Monetary Fund (IMF), the World Bank and other technical and financial partners such as the African Development Bank (AfDB), the United Nations Economic Commission for Africa (UNECA), and the African Capacity Building Foundation (ACBF). Nevertheless, the formation and coordination of economic policies in the country is done at national level, but supported by international partners. This means that own policies adopted in the country are decided by the government itself with the support of national stakeholders and its technical and financial partners. Nevertheless, the regional supranational organizations have recently been involved in the proposition and choice of national development programs. These are policies adopted by

Senegal as a member of the WAEMU. It is the case of the indirect tax policies as proposed by the West African Economic and Monetary Union (WAEMU) which was adopted by all the country members of the Union.

In view of the macroeconomic policy formulation as well as past and recent developmental issues in Senegal, this paper presents the framework of economic policy formulation in Senegal in a longer term perspective from 1960 to 2012. Emphasis is however placed especially on the policies from the year 2000 onwards, mainly by discussions on their political, social and economic objectives. The role of the stakeholders, such as the regional and international financial and technical partners as well as the civil society organizations, is also analysed. The paper is divided into 6 sections. Following section 1, section 2 focuses on economic policy changes since 1960s. The new vision on economic policies since the year 2000 is discussed in section 3. The conduct of macroeconomic policies is presented in section 4. The macroeconomic policy formation in Senegal is treated in the section 5, while section 6 concludes with policy recommendations.

2　The Economic Policy Changes since the 1960s

There are three different policy regimes in the Senegalese development history. First was the *centralized planning system* from 1960 to 1985 whereby central authorities enthusiastically believed in the power of planning for the development of the entire country. The second period from 1985 to 2000 was characterized by the *decentralized planning system* that involved more directly all the regions and local administrations (supported by international financial organizations). The third period from 2000 to date can be characterized as a *participatory planning system* that is nationally and locally coordinated with strategic specific options. These options are related to the creation and maintenance of pro-poor economic growth, the quality of the institutional environment, and the importance of strategic partnerships between all the stakeholders of the economic and development. The current planning system is being supported by various international technical and financial partners.

2.1　The Centralized Planning System from 1960 to 1985

The first packages of economic policies and the investment programs of the government were defined in the First Development Plan of 1961 to 1964. The objectives of the plan were to help the country to leave the colonial models of development. In fact, the economy was organized at that time in such a way that it produced the raw materials needed by France. This latter were mainly provided with agricultural products. The plan had economic and social components. The policy of import substitution was adopted within this plan. It means that the country tries to produce the goods it was used to import before, by helping domestic providers. The Second Development Plan of 1965 to 1969 was a mere reinforcement of the goals of the first development plan. The Third Development Plan (1969 - 1973) tried to improve the level of human capital and the food security in the country; the reduction of inequalities between regions was also an objective (MPI, 1962, 1965, 1969).

Between 1961 and 1973 the macro-economy of Senegal was relatively stable, with regular positive GDP rates of growth, despite the fluctuation of the prices that occurred at the end of the period, due to the oil crisis. The annual growth averaged 3% between 1960 and 1967 (Diene, 2005: 62). However, the annual growth rate of the population was 2.3% per year. The stable economic growth at that time was also a result of the positive development of peanut production in Senegal. Indeed, peanut exports accounted for nearly 80% of the domestic exports and represented a share of 12% to 15% in GDP during that period (Diene, 2005: 62). During the period between 1967 and 1974, the country's exports were vulnerable due to price fluctuations in the world. Like in most African countries, the terms of trade of Senegal began to deteriorate from 1967 onwards and Senegal's share in cash crops exports also decreased drastically in the world markets (World Bank, 2000: 22). The fall in export prices led to a downward spiral of the terms of trade (Diene, 2005: 64). The income of the rural producers consequently fell as the prices of peanuts plunged from 21.5 CFA francs to 18 CFA francs per kilogram (Ly and Sow, 1999: 7). This led to a decline in the agricultural production with an annual growth rate of only 1% and contributed to a weak overall growth in the GDP.

The Fourth Development Plan of 1973 to 1977 was designed to find a solution to the major economic and social problems, such as the public deficits, the stifling of the rural world (which created the so-called "peasant unrest."), the rural exodus, etc. The main objectives of the Fourth Development Plan were to improve the living conditions of the households and to promote the industrialization of the country. In general, the period of the Fourth Development Plan saw an increase of the export value between 1973 and 1974 by 82% (mainly due to the exports of peanuts and phosphates) and terms of trade increases from 102.5% to 105% (Diagne and Daffé: 2002: 60). Moreover, the strong growth of the prices of phosphates and peanuts (24% and 132%, respectively) helped the economy to reduce the consequences of the oil shock (AT 2012: 7). The hourly minimum wage increased from 58.19 CFA francs in 1973 to 107.05 CFA francs in 1974. The purchasing power of rural households increased as the price of peanuts increased for producers by 38% in 1975 (ILO, 2008: 43).

The Fifth Development Plan of 1977 to 1981 was designed to address the economic recession of Senegal. In 1978, the Senegalese economy entered into a deep crisis with profound impairment of the overall macroeconomic framework. The main indicators clearly show a stagnation of real output and a chronic deficit in the trade balance and in public finances (Kasse, 2008: 11). The peanut production drastically declined as export prices fell by 25% between 1978 and 1981 (Diene, 2005: 67). The growth of the imports of consumption goods contributed to the high current account deficit of 14.2% of the GDP and to the 8% decrease of budget revenues. Why and how did this happen, was it caused by lack of own production or by smuggling or by what other factors? (MEF, 2010: 66). In 1979, the price of peanuts was at a level lower than it was in the period between 1969 and 1973. This resulted in sharp decreases of rural incomes. Furthermore, the increasing public debt and the structural imbalances in the economy forced the Senegalese Government to implement a set of economic reform programs from 1980 onwards.

The Sixth Development Plan of 1981 to 1985 - under a new political regime - took different approaches and methods in terms of administration, mainly by the introduction of permanent committees for planning at the national and regional levels. As a result of the oil crisis, drought and structural imbalances, the country adopted stabilization plans and Structural Adjustment Policies (SAP) with the support from the IMF and World Bank.

2.2 The New Planning System and the Adjustment Policies

The Seventh Development Plan of 1985 to 1989 aimed at a stimulation of the production of the primary and secondary sectors as well as a reduction of the institutional barriers that may limit productivity and financial and economic recovery. A New Planning System (NPS) was introduced in 1987. An "Economic Orientation Plan" (EOP) for six years that covered economic and social development and a "Triennial Public Investment Program" (TPIP) were created in the new planning system. Budget discipline became the central policy issue in the new plan. The Eighth Development Plan of 1989 to 1995 aimed at an implementation of the New Planning System/NPS, focused on increasing the total factor productivity, adapting the national education system in line with the productive system, and controlling the urbanization process through the improvement of the rural economy (MEF, 2010: 60). The objective of the Ninth Development Plan of 1996 to 2001 was a liberalization of the economy (MEF, 2010: 62). The plans exist until now with specific programs which are managed by committees of sector-based experts or by national agencies.

The significant features of the new policy reforms were the low level of public investment and the disengagement of the State from productive and social sectors. However, the policy reforms failed to expand the economy and provided no safety net for the poorest segment of the population (Diouf,

1992:73). The economic reforms failed to promote domestic savings, while the terms of trade fell to the level of the 1970s (Fall and Sy, 2003: 8). The exports remained weak and at a ratio of only 30.5% of the GDP between 1994 and 2000 (Daffé, 2002:71). As shown in Figure 1 below, the persistent trade deficit has limited availability of foreign exchange for productive investment.

Figure 1: The trade balance as a percentage of the GDP

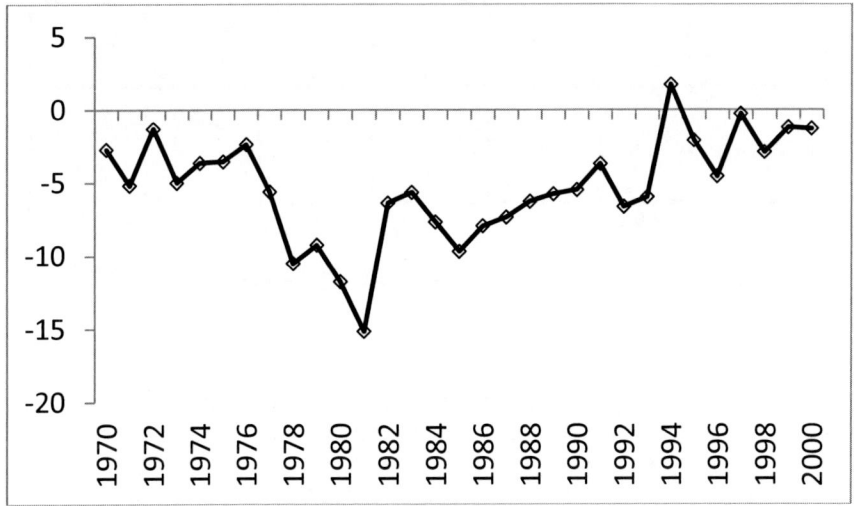

Source: NASD, 2006

The informal economy grew since the 1970s and accounted for more than 60 % of the total jobs in the country (Daffé, 2002: 77; MEF, 2012: 9). Table 3 shows the GDP growth rate and the GDP per capita between 1960 and 2000. The Table 3 reveals that the GDP increased from 1.8% between 1980 and 1984 to 5.5% between 1994 and 2000. The GDP per capita improved from -0.9% to 2.8% in the two periods respectively. Despite of low exports, the GDP growth between 1994 and 2000 was important. The explanation is that, after the devaluation of the CFA franc in 1994, the overall strategies of the government were to stimulate economic growth by bringing more resources to the sectors of non-tradable goods. The economic growth was expected to be mainly driven by the sectors of services, construction and manufacturing (AT: 2012: 24). With the devaluation, the state of the Senegalese economy was considered as successful by the authorities, with a continued reduction of fiscal deficits and current account balances and low inflation rates. But these economic reforms and austerity measures nonetheless affected negatively the living conditions of the poor people, who then engaged more intensively in the informal sector.

Table 3: Percentage growth rate of the GDP and the per capita GDP

Periods	1960 - 1969	1970 – 1979	1980 – 1984	1985 - 1993	1994 - 2000
GDP growth rate (in per cent)	2,2	3	1,8	2,2	5,5
GDP per capita growth (in per cent)	-0,5	0,3	-0,9	-0,4	2,8

Source: NASD, 2005

3 The New Vision on Economic Policies since the year 2000

3.1 The Recent Economic Strategies

The country adopted the Declaration of the Millennium Development Goals (MDGs) and became more involved in the regional integration process. It began to apply economic policies as recommended by regional integration institutions such as the West African Economic and Monetary Union (WAEMU). In this context, the harmonization of the fiscal policies proposed by the WAEMU was also adopted in Senegal. The country applied the common taxes externally and the uniform VAT tax, as the other members of the Union did. For the first time, regionally agreed common fiscal policies were adopted in Senegal. In parallel, the country developed and implemented a first Poverty Reduction Strategy Paper (PRSP I) that covered the period from 2003 to 2005, accompanied by the Accelerated Growth Strategy (AGS) since 2005. The PRSP II covers the period 2006 to 2010 and the PRSP III is from 2011 to 2015. The main feature of the government's new strategies concerning economic policies is the involvement of many private stakeholders. The international technical and financial partners (mainly the donors and the international organizations linked to the United Nations) work together with the national institutions and local partners, such as the civil society, the central government and local administrations. The donors often provide technical support and fund the training and the participation of all the actors in the formation of policies. There is a national ownership on all these economic policies but they all involve the donors as supporters. Transparency in budget management has become the key condition of the donors' participation and this is also in the interest of the Senegalese people. This explains why programs such as the PRSP III, the AGS and the Economic Policy Support Instrument (EPSI) involve many local experts from different sectors but also international experts. The EPSI is an IMF program for Senegal adopted since 2007 and running still now. It is a financing mechanism and the amount of the budget is 328 billion CFA francs in 2012. The program is designed to help the government to pursue a cautious approach to public finances and public debt in order to maintain economic stability, to increase public revenues in order to generate a greater fiscal space for financing priority expenditures, to strengthen the public financial management and governance, to promote private sector development by making structural reforms, particularly in the areas of energy and finance, and to provide for a better business environment. For example, in 2008 a major slippage in public finances was found, and it was discovered that the state had large arrears in debt settlement to the private sector. In this situation EPSI helped to tackle this situation (IMF, 2009: 6).

The second program review of EPSI, which allowed the mobilization of funds from the international community, was approved by the IMF in 2008. The EPSI is now extended over the period from 2010 to 2013. It is worth noting that the EPSI is reviewed almost every three months. The extension allows the government to complete the major infrastructure spending programs. Under the PRSP III and the AGS, structural reforms and sector-based policies were designed to bring the average growth rate of Senegal above 4% in the period between 2010 and 2015 (EPCMU, 2011). It is known that the PRSP II had failed in the reduction of poverty so that is unlikely that the country will achieve the objectives of reducing poverty by half by 2015. It is also unlikely that the goals of universal education, referred to in the MDGs and integrated into the PRSP II, access to electricity and to potable water can be realized. Access to basic infrastructure in the villages has however greatly improved (Backiny-Yetna et al., 2010: 21). The PRSP III is the framework for political, economic and social development of Senegal for the period between 2011 and 2015; arguably, it is an extension of PRSP I (2002) and PRSP II (2006) (EPCMU, 2011). PRSP III is structured around the following strategic areas:

- Wealth creation for a pro-poor growth strategy accompanied by the development of transport infrastructure and energy.
- Promotion of access to basic social services in conjunction with the MDGs to be achieved in the social sectors.
- Social protection, prevention and management of risks and disasters (drought, floods, locusts, etc.).

- Good governance, decentralized and participatory development with particular emphasis on the continued implementation of the National Program for Good Governance (NPGG) and the AGS (MI, 2002).

The PRSP III gives a central role to the current AGS for the generation of sustainable high rates of GDP growth, the creation of jobs, and the improvement of the households' living conditions. Critical assessment of the PRSP revealed that it is unlikely that the country will achieve the objectives of the MDGs by 2015. Moreover, in the sectors of health and education, some trends are still slow compared to the 2015 targets. These include the rate of infant mortality, the maternal mortality rate, and the rate of primary school achievement (UCMEP: 2012:7). However, the access to electricity and drinking water seems to be progressing in the whole country. Access to basic infrastructure in the villages has greatly improved through the PRSP (Backiny-Yetna *et al.*: 2010: 21).

The Accelerated Growth Strategy/AGS is the strategy designed to diversify and transform the economy by strengthening competitiveness. The strategy adopted in 2005 was based on two focal points. The first was the development of groups of clusters with high growth potential (growth areas) which could positively impact on the overall economy. The second was focused on the promotion of investment by continuously improving the business environment, aligning it to international standards and strengthening the efficiency of infrastructure sectors, such as transportation, energy and telecommunications. The AGS is designed to foster a dynamic process towards economic development. Operationally, it is focused on promoting private investment and growth in the areas agriculture and agro-industry, aquaculture and seafood, textiles and clothing, ICT, tourism, cultural industries and crafts. The main weakness of the AGS is its lack of evaluations, though it has become since 2012 a component of the National Strategy for Economic and Social Development (NSESD). There is no evaluation of all these efforts and the actual new political regime mainly focuses on the NSESD rather than on the policies and programs implemented by the former political regime.

3.2 The National Strategy for Economic and Social Development

The NSESD was established in November 2012 and its objectives are reflected in three economic and social policy areas. The first area comprises growth, productivity and wealth creation. The second is human capital, social protection and sustainable development, while the third is governance, institutions, peace and security.

a) Growth, productivity and wealth creation

The main objective laid down in the NSESD Document is it to target an average annual growth rate of 6.8%. To achieve this, emphasis was laid on the development of the energy sector, especially the electricity sector. In addition, the government hoped to create the conditions for economic growth by strengthening good governance and improving the efficiency of public investment. The elements of the objectives in this area are:

- Macroeconomic stability: the macroeconomic stability measures, such as control of the inflation and reduction of the volatility of interest rates, reduction of risk and uncertainty for investors, and creation of the conditions for income growth, are the central elements of the objectives. The achievement of these elements depends on the improvement of the business climate.

- Promotion of employment: To ensure full employment, the economy must generate each year nearly 150,000 jobs. Between 2013 and 2017, at least 500,000 jobs are to be created in the formal private sector and the public sector, with a gradual strengthening of the local public sector. It means that decentralized authorities are progressively involved in the process of defining the ways to create all these jobs. These objectives are supposed to be achieved by promoting public investment and self-employment of young people and by supporting the integration and reintegration of military and paramilitary personnel released from active service (MEF, 2012: 25).

- Private Sector Development: This program focuses on micro-enterprises and small businesses, rural and suburban youth, and crafts, as well as women. Regional development centres are to be involved to support export activity.

- Easy access to financial services: This has led the government to create a Guarantee Fund for Priority Investment (GFPI) and a Sovereign Fund for Strategic Investments (SFSI), and to help funding women entrepreneurs.

- Development of sectors to support the production: This is done by promoting access to energy services in terms of accelerating rural electrification, increasing the supply of renewable energy, and providing for a higher electricity production capacity. Infrastructure and transport services and telecommunication services will be promoted as an overall objective to support cross-cutting areas of production (MEF, 2012: 32).

b) Human capital, social protection and sustainable development
The main components of these policy objectives are:

- Improvement of health and nutrition, access to drinking water and sanitation, and strengthening of social protection. The strategy was designed to build health infrastructure, to strengthen the existing military medical centres, to recruit skilled health staff, and to promote generic drugs. Other major issues are measures to improve the performance of the prevention and fight against diseases such as the HIV.

- Support universal education by improving the quality of teaching and training, by building and rehabilitating schools and providing for the equipment supply to colleges, schools, institutes and universities.

- Eradication of illiteracy and promotion of national languages: there is intention to undertake the diversification of the Non-Formal Education (NFE) and to build new infrastructure for the NFEs and the codification of national languages (MEF, 2012: 40).

c) Governance, Institutions, Peace and Security
Bad governance is a hindrance to development; hence some essential rules of economic and social policies are covered in the NSESD document such as:

- Peace, democracy and security;
- Ethics and transparency in public finance management; and
- Creation of frameworks for a dialogue on public policy.

Compliance with these rules requires mutual trust among different stakeholders in macroeconomic policy formulation and implementation. The first actors that are involved in the coordination aspects of the NSESD are the local private organizations, civil society organizations and local administrations. It is a mere plan and regrettably nothing has been implemented yet. Table 4 gives the amounts needed for the realisation of the program. The government and the donors are financially involved, but still gaps remain for the funding in each year.

Different committees and councils are created to coordinate, implement and monitor the NSESD:
- A Presidential Committee for Evaluation meets once every two years and it is responsible for the evaluation of the NSESD, and it decides on the reorientation of the program, based on its major outcomes and on the international discussion of issues.
- A National Council for monitoring and guidance, chaired by the Prime Minister, is created. This Council is composed by the Government, representatives of the technical and financial partners, the civil society, the private sector, the parliament and the local administrations. It meets every six

months. Its role is to assess the progress of the implementation of the NSESD, and it gives the instructions being useful to a successful implementation of the NSESD. It makes also an annual review of the NSESD.
- A Parliamentary Monitoring Committee: This committee allows parliamentarians to monitor the implementation of the NSESD. It meets once a year. Its president is appointed by the National Assembly.

Table 4: Annual funding allocation of the NSESD (in million CFA francs)

Years	2013	2014	2015	2016	2017
Global amount need-ed	993.428	1283.669	1210.216	891.172	760.197
Amount acquired	873.428	1025.669	890.215	481.172	375.197
Given by the State	431.939	447.725	368.496	192.528	179.392
Given by the Do-nors	441.49	577.944	521.719	288.645	195.806
Gap	120	258	320	410	385

Source: MEF, 2012: 67

The Minister of Economy and Finance shall report to the meetings of these various Councils and Committees. There are two aspects in the practical level: the Coordination of the implementation of the sectoral policies defined in the program, and the Regional management of the NSESD. Thus, there are different committees:
- The Sectoral Committees for Monitoring and Evaluation: the Ministries are important channels for the implementation of the NSESD and they are ensuring the supervision of NSESD's implementation. Chaired by the Minister in charge of the sector, the Sectoral Committee is responsible for the implementation and the monitoring of the sectoral policies defined in the NSESD. Each committee meets at least once per quarter.
- The Regional Committee for Monitoring and Evaluation: it is chaired by the regional Governor while the Regional Development Agency (RDA) provides the technical secretariat. It includes all categories of actors involved in the region.
A Technical Secretariat, provided by the UCMEP, is responsible for the coordination of the overall monitoring and evaluation of the NSESD. It ensures the proper execution of the various activities of the program. All the stakeholders in economic policies are supposed to align and harmonize their actions around the NSESD's objectives that also reflect the country's commitments to achieve the MDGs. The involvement of all the stakeholders in the process of implementation is essential.

The Parliament is also involved in the NSESD, and capacity building of the parliamentarians in overseeing governmental actions is expected within the NSESD. The steering committees, both national and regional or local, mobilize all stakeholders that are state actors, local administration, civil society, the private sector, the parliament and the technical and financial partners.

4 Macroeconomic Policies and the Performance of the Economy in the period between 2000 and 2012

In 2000, poverty alleviation was among the primary policy objectives of the Senegalese government. The Poverty Reduction and Growth Facility (PRGF) program, which is supplemented by the PRSP, was initiated in 2002. The PRGF helped the government to achieve considerable macroeconomic stability. In the 2000s, the government initiated several tax reforms, especially at the sub-regional levels. Was this the problem number 1 for macroeconomic policy in Senegal? What about public expenditures, financial policies, and structural policies in Senegal? Fiscal policy, monetary policy, and exchange rate policy - some words on interactions are needed, although fiscal policy determines largely the course of development in Senegal! While section 4 covers mainly fiscal policy, section 5 will then also comment on the interrelations of fiscal and monetary policy.

4.1 The Tax reforms and other fiscal policy reforms since 2000

Over the past 12 years, three major objectives have been constantly sought in government tax policies. The first one is the preservation and consolidation of tax revenues. The second one is the rationalization and modernization of the tax system. The third one is the creation of a favorable environment for the development of investments and business promotion. These policy objectives include the adoption of indirect taxation according to the WAEMU directives in terms of a single VAT rate (18%), the rationalization of the list of VAT exemptions, the harmonization of the rates of excise duties, and the modernization of the tax system by simplifying the tax system. Other fiscal reform measures included the enhancement of the financial capacity of the local administrations by preserving the integrity of the local tax systems and the development of a new Investment Code which allows for a tax credit mechanism within the system of corporate taxation (DGID, 2012: 97).

To promote savings mobilization and the development of financial and stock markets, an incentive tax for collective investment securities, such as Unit Trusts and Open-ended Investment Trusts, was introduced. Other reforms aimed at tackling tax evasion and promoting gender equality in the taxation of men and women's incomes (MEF, 2010: 76). Diagne *et al.* (2007)

argued that the adoption of the harmonization of the tax system in Senegal has considerably reduced the protection of its economy (via a 50% reduction in customs duties) but has consolidated its domestic tax system. However, the government considered fiscal consolidation as a more important policy. It paid little attention to the possible negative effects of a higher VAT on income inequality and on the households' welfare (Diagne et al., 2007: 12). The research findings of Diene (2010) revealed that the advantages of the harmonization of the VAT and of the other indirect taxes in Senegal mainly reside on the reduction of the costs of tax collection and on the simplification of the fiscal administration procedures (Diene, 2010:23).

For purposes of macroeconomic stability and inflation control, the public finances are supposed to be more controlled within the NSESD program. Priority actions which the Government intends to use are, in the framework of the NSESD, the improvement of the performance of the tax administration and budgetary execution procedures. To this end, the implementation of the NSESD will contribute to a strengthening of fiscal revenues, resulting in an increase in tax revenues of estimated 8.9% per year. Donations are expected to increase by 4.5% per year during the period covered by the program. Current public expenditures are expected to increase by 5.1% per year during the program period while investment spending would grow at a rate of 6.3% per year over the same period (2013-2017). Regarding the management of the public debt during the implementation period of the program, the Government will continue to implement prudent debt policy by resorting primarily to concessional financing that does not compromise the viability of the total public debt. Finally, the Government undertakes not to accumulate arrears during the period under review (WAEMU, 2012: 86).

4.2 Inflation, growth, public budget and poverty

The impact of the economic reform programs can be evaluated through economic indicators such as the rate of inflation, the rate of economic growth and the situation of the public budget, but also through the impact of the macroeconomic policies on poverty. In the period of the PRGF, the average inflation rate was of 2.2% in the years 2002 - 2012. Specifically, between 2003 and 2005 the inflation stood at 1.7 %. Over the period from 2000 to 2012 the average inflation rate was 2.2% as against 6.3% in other ECOWAS countries (DFES, 2011: 5). The growth rate of the real GDP in the period 2000 - 2002 was 2.8%. Between 2003 and 2005, it passed to 6.1%. Thereafter, the average annual economic growth rate declined to 3% between 2006 and 2010. Its estimation for 2011 was 4% and its projection for 2012 was 4.2% (AfDB *et al.*, 2012: 4).

Concerning the situation of the public budget, there was a significant improvement of the taxation system and the emergence of a more efficient management of the public finances. The improvement can be traced to the policies that supported the broadening of the tax base combined with specific budget reforms, such as a gradual harmonization of the assessment of the tax expenditures (amounts to be deducted), and a modernization of the tax procedures. The tax expenditures refer to actions that have the effect of reducing or deferring taxes and charges payable by taxpayers. They can take many forms, including those of claiming non-taxable income, deductions, tax credits, tax exemptions, or tax reports. Table 5 presents the public finance components as a percentage of the GDP. The share in GDP of the tax revenues rose from 18.8% in 2010 to respectively 19.5% and 19.7% in 2011 and 2012 (AfDB *et al.*: 2012: 6).

Table 5: Public Finances (as percentage of GDP)

	2007	2008	2009	2010	2011	2012*
Total revenue and grants	22.8	21.5	21.6	22	22.5	22.6
Tax revenue	19.3	18.1	18	18.8	19.5	19.7
Total expenditure and net lending	26.5	26.3	26.8	27.2	27.8	28.9
Current expenditure	16	16.3	16.7	15.6	16.2	16.5
Primary Balance	-3.2	-4.1	-4.4	-4.2	-4	-4.9
Overall balance	-3.8	-4.8	-5.2	-5.2	-5.3	-6.3

Source: AfDB *et al.* (2012: 6). (*) Data for 2012 are projections.

Between 2000 and 2002, the public deficit was about 12% of the GDP. In the period between 2003 and 2005, the public deficit was 6% of GDP. From 2007 to 2011, the budget deficit was reduced to below 6% of the GDP. Public spending rose sharply from 2007 to 2012, with the total expenditure as a percentage of GDP increasing from 26.5% to 28.9% (see table 5). Because of the deterioration of the primary and the overall balance, the government has decided to better control and to rationalize the public expenditures. The short term measures for this are the shrink of the State. The number of ministries was reduced from 37 to 25 in 2012 and many government offices and departments have been eliminated or merged. A rationalization of the diplomatic representation abroad is also supposed to reduce the public expenditures.

The number of agencies and public entities was reduced in 2012 after a review of their usefulness and performance. The mismanagement and abuse in the public service, particularly with regard to the use of mobile phones, vehicles, fuel and electricity, public housing and rental offices, is now reduced. An improvement in the procurement of goods and services is also decided, so as a step for the reduction of other non-priority spending. The authorities have also identified non-priority spending that will be removed and have postponed non-priority investment projects, such as projects that have not yet begun, or have a limited impact on growth and poverty reduction.

Medium-term measures are taken to reduce the public expenses, such as the rationalization of subsidies and transfers to some sectors and demographic groups, so as to improve their targeting and efficiency. This includes subsidies for energy, food and water. The rationalization of education, health and other social spending is also aimed at by the government, with the support of the World Bank. Table 6 shows the evolution of the social expenditures of the government.

Table 6: Public Expenditures in social sectors (in millions of CFA francs)

Sectors	2005	2006	2007	2008	2009	2010	2011	2012
Education	245.8	254.4	310.4	321.5	384.3	459.5	447.0	190.4
Current expenditure	205.7	226.9	276.7	295.7	328.2	397.7	404.7	162.2
Capital expenditures	40.1	27.5	33.7	25.8	56.2	61.9	42.3	28.2
Health	91.9	77.3	86.3	101.6	110.6	111.6	114.7	48.0
Current expenditure	49.5	49.5	53.6	61.1	67.7	72.4	66.7	28.9
Capital expenditures	42.4	27.7	32.8	40.5	42.8	39.1	48.0	19.0
Other Social sectors	31.2	84.0	86.9	103.1	84.8	108.8	118.8	40.9
Current expenditure	15.1	24.0	36.8	33.9	36.6	35.2	46.1	13.6
Capital expenditures	16.2	60.0	50.1	69.2	48.1	73.5	72.7	27.3
Total	368.9	415.7	483.6	526.1	579.7	679.9	680.5	279.2

Source: MEF 2013

The other social sectors include the Ministries of Justice, Social Development, Environment and Rural Hydraulics and Sanitation. The social expenditures were drastically reduced since 2011, though they have seen increases from 2005 to 2011. It has to be assessed what the consequences are and will be in the future for poverty levels, unemployment levels and levels of social protection.

As one can see in table 6, there was a sharp cut of the social expenditures, from 2011 to 2012. This cut comes from the new government which

was settled in 2012. The main feature of 2012 is the advent of a new political regime that wanted to make a clean break with the past political regime concerning the public budget. This political change resulted in a budget plan with new objectives, such as:
- The objective to stop the rise of the public current expenditures,
- The objective to opt for a more investment-oriented budget.
These new objectives appeared in the Finance Act 2012 by the way of measures at controlling the staff costs and reducing the other public current expenditures, including social spending. Therefore substantial efforts to reduce the own expenditures of the public administration are undertaken by the new political regime in Senegal. These efforts do not only concern the social sectors. Indeed, there is a removing of public agencies, a streamlining of the diplomatic services, a removing of the Senate and of the Vice Presidency, among other measures taken. There was also the suspension of all mobile phone lines for government (except for defense services, security and justice). The hundred largest consumers of public administration funds for water were identified and monitored closely to make significant savings on the water bill of the central government. The reduction of social expenditures in 2012 is undertaken in this spirit of the new government. But all these cuts resulted in an increase in public capital expenditures, and more effort was undertaken of securing public funding for the implementation of new projects and programs initiated by the government.

The reduction of the social expenditures is not permanent because, in the Finance Act of 2013, priority is given to social sectors (education, health, sanitation, social protection, etc.), food security, improvement of rural incomes , energy, and employment of women and young people (DFES, 2013b: 2). In 2013, support to the social sectors is also reflected by the government's desire to create a Universal Social Protection Fund (USPF) and a Universal Health Coverage (UHC), with the intention to extend the social protection system to the workers of the informal sector. The sharp cut of the social expenditures in 2012 is therefore part of the overall government strategy to make an overall reduction of the public expenditures possible, so as to rationalize public expenditures and to reach macroeconomic stability. The cut of social expenditures is not a deliberate policy as the attitude towards social expenditures for 2013 shows.

The impact of macroeconomic policy on poverty can be explained by changes in the poverty index. Senegal remains a poor country, but the proportion of poor households has declined (see table 7). The proportion of poor individuals in the country has declined from 55.2% in 2001 to 48.3% in 2005 and to 46.7% in 2011 (MEF, 2012: 11). Poverty is measured by the Foster–Greer-Thorbecke (FGT) poverty index. What the consequences of the drastic cuts of expenditures for social sectors in 2012 are will be brought out in future research.

Table 7: The Evolution of the proportion of poor households in Senegal

Zones/Years	2001	2006	2011
Dakar	38.1	28.1	26.2
Other urban zones	45.2	41.4	41.3
Rural zones	65.2	59	57.3
Senegal	55.2	48.3	46.7

Source: MEF 2012: 10

As shown in Table 7, the proportion of poor people in Senegal stood at 46.7% in 2011. The Table 7 indicates that poverty is higher in rural areas than in urban zones. This phenomenon suggests that so far policy reforms adopted have not influenced that much poverty reduction in rural areas. The main reason is that the poor households in rural areas are mainly farmers, women and young people who survive by subsistence crops and livestock that are means being often not sufficient to cover the needs of their family. Factors such as a regularly insufficient agricultural production, a weak capacity of the economy to create permanent jobs, and a lack of public resources allocated to social services contribute to the poverty in rural zones. The most affected areas are the center, the south and the east of the country, where income is predominantly derived from agricultural work. This is due to the difficulties of the climate and to an unequal distribution of public investment. Households in rural areas have less access to migrants' remittances and rural producers and workers have more difficulty in obtaining bank loans. The regional priority actions of the NSESD should correct this situation. The drastic cut of social spending in 2012 may lead to a further deterioration of the situation if not compensated by other measures and efficiency improvements (see table 6).

Arguably, the reforms were more successful where the government initiatives were supported by the international financial and technical partners. From 1960 to the early 1980s, the government has tried to implement its own policies but failed to put the country towards a specific development trajectory or path. The involvement of the international partners (at this time, only the IMF and the World Bank were involved) in the economic policy formulation since the early 1980s helped the country to resolve the debt crisis by using structural adjustment policies. The implication is that the government obviously could not undertake a meaningful economic policy reform without the technical and financial support of its international partners. The political classes, the bureaucracy and the interest groups, whenever they are involved in the formulation of the policies or where they have the ability to influence these policies, are perverting the good intentions of plans and policies so that the financial aspects of their implementation are always becoming a problem. The power to influence the policies depends crucially on the extent of the financial capacity of the stakeholders involved. But in contrast to the external policy package of the structural adjustment programs since the early 1980s, the economic policies are developed in the period of the 2000s more by the government and by national experts coming from different economic and social sectors. For example, all the economic strategies of the PRSP III were developed by national experts but the international technical and financial partners helped in elaborating, executing and financing the PRSPs.

5   Macroeconomic Policy Formation in Senegal

The government of Senegal conducts the macroeconomic policies of the country but it has no autonomy on the monetary domain. The monetary policies in all the WAEMU countries are under the responsibility of the Central Bank of West African States (CBWAS). The traditional instruments of monetary policy used by the CBWAS are the changes in interest rates and the refinancing of the financial institutions of the economy. The country as well does not have enough space to undertake indirect taxation fiscal policies because they are directed by regional organizations, such as ECOWAS and mainly WAEMU. Harmonized international fiscal policies are applied by the countries of these organizations. In fact, the effectiveness of the instruments used for monetary policy, fiscal policies (indirect tax rates) and exchange rate policies is not completely controlled by the government because these policies depend on the common decision-making bodies for the Union. Furthermore, common polices in sectors such as agriculture (within the WAEMU) and industry (within the ECOWAS) are actually still running, despite some difficulties in their implementation and monitoring (Savadogo, 2009: 2; ECOWAS, 2010: 39).

5.1   The monetary and fiscal policies

Three issues are considered here. First, the evolution of the monetary policy tools, namely the exchange rates and interest rates, is considered. Second, the features of the monetary policy are discussed. Third, the nature of the fiscal policies is presented.

The real effective exchange rate estimated in 2012 by the CBWAS shows an improvement in the competitive position of Senegal at 1.7% compared to other partner countries. This gain in competitiveness was as a result of a combination of factors. First, it was due to an average reduction of inflation in the WAEMU countries of about 1.8%. The second was the reduction of the nominal effective exchange rate by 0.1% (CBWAS, 2012: 43). The interest rate in the first quarter of 2012 as shown by CBWAS has declined to 3.2736 % as against 3.2940% in the last quarter of 2011 (CBWAS, 2012: 28). The interest rate is the monthly average money market rate. It is the main tool which the CBWAS uses to influence the liquidity in the economy. A remarkable aspect of CBWAS's function is its support in financing the public deficit. It provided to the government an amount equal to 11.9% of the fiscal revenues in 2012 (CBWAS, 2012: 54). The official rule is that a government cannot have an amount greater than 35% of its fiscal revenues. This explains why the refinancing of the country has a high net margin valued at 219.7 billion francs in mid-2012[3]. Nevertheless, the government issues Treasury bonds and obligations to finance its deficit which are bought by the national and external economic agents such as the banks and the public.

In respect to the monetary policies in Senegal, their transmission channels rely more on the interest rates and on the monetary aggregates than on the exchange rate because the currency is pegged to the Euro. Authors Dramani, Ly and Diouf (2007) argue that there are close relationships between interest rates and real exchange rates with the aggregate real supply in Senegal on the one side, and between the real exchange rate and inflation on the other side. They show that an increase of the real interest rate will induce a transient decrease of the real output (Dramani, Ly, Diouf, 2007: 46). For example, a 10% increase of the interest rate in one year induces an increase of 4.57% of the money supply in the first year and a decrease by 4.52% in the second year. It also implies a decline in private investment by 0.4% in the first year. This affects the economic growth negatively which decreases by 0.71%, 0.35% and 0.03% in the first, second and third years respectively (Dramani, Ly, Diouf, 2007: 45).

Similarly, in the short and medium term, a depreciation of the CFA vis-à-vis to the US dollar will induce economic expansion, and high inflation based on the model estimations. In fact, the interventions of the CBWAS effectively have impacted on the real sector and on the inflation rate. The depreciation of the currency is directly linked to the fluctuations of the Euro against the US dollar because of the fixed rate between the CFA Franc and the Euro.

---

[3] This margin means that the government can borrow money up to this amount. This margin is determined by the CBWAS by deducing from the statutory limit the amount of loans granted to banks and backed by government securities.

Dramani *et al.* (2007) argued that a depreciation of the CFA franc against the dollar by 10% resulted into higher cost of imports but a restored competitiveness of the domestic products. For example, cost of imports of capital goods increase by 17% on average over the two years following the depreciation of CFA franc (Dramani, Ly and Diouf, 2007: 47). The GDP increases by 3.01% during the first year, 0.87% in the second year and 0.55% in the third year (Dramani, Ly and Diouf, 2007: 48). The research evidence of the macroeconomic model of the Senegalese economy for assessing the impact of the depreciation on inflation runs on a panel data basis from 1980 to 2000; by different authors it is shown that inflation grew by 4.73% in the first year, 3.58% in the second year, and 0.46% at the end of the third year (Dramani, Ly and Diouf, 2007: 48).

In respect to fiscal policy, the VAT rates are harmonized at 18% as a result of the reform introduced within the WAEMU countries in 2001. However, indirect taxes are still levied on imports of commodities such as sugar, oil of peanuts, etc. from other countries. In addition to customs duties, products coming from non-WAEMU countries are subject to several supplementary taxes such as the Statistical License Fee (SLF) and the Community Tax for Solidarity (CTS) at the rate of 1%. Nevertheless, the government has little policy space for conduct of fiscal policies because it uses mainly indirect taxes. It does not mean that direct taxes cannot be used, but they only concern the formal sector of the economy. That is why the government always tries to control the informal sector, aiming to make it contribute to its fiscal revenues. The recent economic statistics shows that the tax revenues increased to 1.3132 trillion CFA francs in 2011, at a rate of 9.9% compared to 2010. The indirect tax revenues grew by 10.8% in the two years, due to the VAT on oil consumption and the customs duties (DFES, 2011: 23). Direct taxes, through the income tax, grew moderately by 2.9%. In general, the ratio of taxes to GDP is estimated at 19.2% in 2011 as against to 18.8% in 2010. This slight increase reflects more an improvement of the effectiveness of revenue collection than of higher tax rates (DFES, 2011: 25). As we stated earlier, since 2011 the government, with the support of the World Bank, is trying to rationalize its expenditures, by drastically reducing the social spending and the non-efficient investments. This is considered as the best way to deal with the difficulty of increasing the tax revenues to the level of the expenditures. However, the social situation may deteriorate further. Non-efficient investments and non-priority investments can be reduced, but social spending cuts have severe limits.

5.2 The Levels of Formation and Coordination of the Economic Policies

The formation and coordination of the economic policies in Senegal are done at two different levels.

The *first* is at the national level where the government is better positioned to coordinate various policies and programs in the country. For example, in 2009 a national institution called Unit for Coordination and Monitoring of Economic Policy (UCMEP) was created. Its mission is to support the implementation and the monitoring of all national and sector-based policies. The Unit is also involved in the issues related to fund-raising for the various programs and to the control of financial resources used in the programs. The Unit is attached to the Ministry of Economy and Finance. It is made up of working groups assigned with specific functions. The groups are classified according to their functions and objectives. The following groups may be mentioned:

The Group of quantitative monitoring of policies: Its objectives are to monitor the indicators of achievement of the development programs, such as of the PRSP and/or the NSESD. This group reviews periodically the quantitative surveys undertaken by the statistical departments of the government.

The Group of qualitative monitoring of policies: This group is responsible for monitoring the changes induced by the policies. It also provides the capacity building to the regional actors and to the civil society by helping them in the implementation and monitoring of projects and programs.

The Group for the better articulation of sector-based policies: The main function of this group is to review the sector-based policies and to identify the strengths, the weaknesses and the gaps as well as providing for corrective measures.

The *second* is at the international level where the country has transferred some of its prerogative functions in economic policy formulation to regional and multilateral organisations such as ECOWAS and WAEMU. This is in the area of the international trade policies, especially the tariff issues. Senegal has adopted the common external tariff policies of ECOWAS and WAEMU. In addition, the country is actively involved in the negotiations for the effective implementation of the policies undertaken in these organizations. Like other ECOWAS member states, the country has created a National Committee of Economic Policy Coordination (NCEPC). The aim of NCEPC is to ensure the identification, formulation and monitoring of the Community Development Program (CDP). The CDP is an ECOWAS program with the objective to establish coherency between sector-based programs within the ECOWAS and its member-States development policies. CDP was launched in 2008 with its strategies focused to sectors such as common agricultural and industrial policies, interconnection of transport infrastructure, energy supply, financial and monetary integration, research and development, innovation, as well as common natural resources and environmental policies. The NCEPC is attached to the Ministry of Economy and Finance and is composed of members of the UCMEP and of the WAEMU as well as from the civil society and the private sector. The NCEPC also assists the ECOWAS in the collection, processing and analysis of economic information related to Senegal.

If the government is the first actor involved in the definition and implementation of the national development policies, there are other national actors playing a role in the formation of economic policies in Senegal, such as the Non State Actors (NSAs), comprising the private sector and the civil society. Most of these actors are grouped into committees for the dialogue on the development strategies such as for the PRSP III and the AGS. The dialogue forums are not very satisfying for the Non State Actors (NSAs) who often complain that they are not involved enough. They create their own organizations or committees, aiming to be better involved in the policy decisions, and they work together with the donors, excluding the public authorities. There are three major categories of Non-State Actors (NSAs) in Senegal: the civil society organizations, the trade unions and the employers' organizations but there is a lack of coordination and an absence of a unified structure.

The involvement the non-state actors (NSAs) in the design, implementation and monitoring of the economic policies is often presented as an objective which is announced by the public authorities and desired by the donors. Nevertheless, the recent experiences show that the supposed involvement generates more frustration than satisfaction; so new modalities have to be developed. The employers' organizations are implicated in the process of definition of economic policies, by means of the National Council of Employers. Civil society organizations and trade unions are not really involved. The political parties are involved only if they are part of a coalition with the ruling party; so the impact on policies is extremely limited.

6 Conclusions and recommendations

The government is the major actor in the definition and implementation of the national development policies. The Central Bank defines the monetary policies for the WAEMU countries and so has a great role to play in terms of monetary policies in Senegal. Besides issuance of the banknotes, coins and being a lender of last resort, it is also responsible for the centralization of the foreign exchange reserves, the management of the monetary policy, the control of the accounts of the Treasures, and the definition of the banking law being applicable to banks and financial institutions. In addition, the macroeconomic policy formation in Senegal involves other actors than the public administration and the Central Bank. The economic and financial partners work together with the social partners, such as the NGOs, the trade unions, etc. The regional and international donors are also involved in the entire process of definition and application of the economic policies. They are no longer considered as finance providers only but they are also institutional and technical partners.

It is necessary to encourage a process of innovative and continually reinforced participation in the economic policies formulation, which involves all stakeholders, including non-state actors (NSAs) from the regions and the rural areas. For this direction to emerge, it is desirable to create functional and durable mechanisms of dialogue between the government, the donors and the NSAs.

This paper therefore recommends the following specific actions:

- Effective involvement of the NSAs who have skills to participate in technical discussions. This can be done by the establishment of a national cell of the NSAs to enhance their participation in the formulation and implementation of macroeconomic policies.
- Strengthening the institutional support for the NSAs and the local authorities by the government and its partners.
- The financial partners should help to strengthen the capacity for sector work. This is to support the development of detailed proposals at national and sub-regional levels based on the analysis of the situation.
- Establishment of a national observatory to monitor the degree of partnership with stakeholders in the development of macroeconomic policies. This will help the beneficiaries to better understand the implications of macroeconomic policies.
- Strengthening the information dissemination processes on macroeconomic policies for the benefits of the economic agents.
- Effective coordination and constant monitoring and evaluation of macroeconomic policies in order to support business sector development projects.

The implementation and monitoring of the impacts of programs are the main challenges. That is why the government and its partners encourage the involvement of stakeholders at regional and local levels, to better implement the policies, as well as to better monitor their impacts.

References

AfDB, OECD, UNDP, ECA (2012), "Senegal", en: « Perspectives Economiques en Afrique: Promouvoir l'Emploi des Jeunes », Edition OCDE, Paris, France

AT/Aide Transparency (2012), Analyse de l'évolution des politiques macroéconomiques du Sénégal de 1980 a nos jours, Document No. 219413872, Dakar, Senegal

Backiny-Yetna, P., Camara, M., Ndoye D., Ndiaye P. T., Tsimpo, C. & Wodon Q. (2010): Evaluation sur base d'enquêtes des progrès accomplis dans la stratégie pour la croissance et la réduction de la pauvreté au Sénégal, CSPLP, Dakar.

CBWAS/Central Bank of West African States (2012), "Report on the Monetary Policy in WAEMU", CBWAS: Avenue Abdoulaye FADIGA, BP 3108. Dakar - Senegal

Daffé, G. (2002), La difficile réinsertion du Sénégal dans le commerce mondial, Dans: DIOP, Momar-Coumba, La société sénégalaise entre le local et le global, Paris, France: Karthala, pp.67-80

Diagne, A., & Daffé, G. (2002), Le Sénégal en quête d'une croissance Durable, CRES, Edition Karthala, Paris, France

Diagne, A., Cabral, F. J., Cisse, F., Dansokho, M. Ba, S. (2007), Trade Policies, Regional Integration, Poverty and Income Distribution in Senegal, CRES Working Papers, MPIA-PEP

Diene, M. (2005), La Fiscalité Indirecte et les Inégalités de Revenus Au Sénégal, Thèse de Doctorat d'Etat, UCAD, Faculté des Sciences Economiques et de Gestion, Dakar, Senegal

Diene, M. (2010), "Fiscal reforms and Income inequality in Senegal and Burkina Faso: a comparative study", RP 205, AERC Research paper: November 2010. Nairobia.

Diouf, M., (1992), Senegal: La crise de l'Ajustement, In: Politique Africaine, Vol. N° 45, PP. 62-85, Dakar, Senegal

DGID/Direction Generale Des Impots Et Domaines (2012), Code Général des Impôts, Loi Numéro 31 -12- 12, publiée au Journal Officiel numéro 6706 du 31 -12- 12, Dakar, Senegal

DFES (2011), Financial and Economic Situation in 2011 and perspectives in 2012, biannual publication of the DFES, NASD, Dakar, Senegal

DFES (2012), The Balance of Payment of Senegal, Publication of the DFES, NASD, Dakar, Senegal

DFES (2013a), Financial and Economic Situation in 2012 and perspectives in 2013, biannual publication of the DFES, NASD, Dakar, Senegal

DFES (2013b) Exposé général des Motifs: La Loi de Finances 2013. Publications DFES, NASD, Dakar, Senegal

Dramami, L., Ly, B., & Diouf, D. (2007), Transmission de la politique monétaire au secteur réel au Sénégal, NASD, Bureau des Synthèses et Etudes Analytiques, Dakar, Senegal

EPCMU/Economic Policy Coordination and Monitoring Unit (2011), Poverty Reduction Strategy Papers, Dakar, Senegal

ECOWAS (2010), Politique industrielle commune de l'Afrique de l'ouest, ECOWAS, Lagos, Nigeria

Fall, A. S. & Sy, O. (2003), Les économies ouest- africaines dans un contexte de mondialisation, (CRDC), Université du Québec en Outaouais, Gatineau, Québec, Canada

Floridi, M., Ngalane, M., Thiam, M. L. (2008), Cartographie des acteurs non étatiques au Sénégal, Rapport final tome 1: Analyse et diagnostic, ECO/European Consultants Organisation, Dakar, Senegal

IMF/International Monetary Fund (2009), Report on the second review of the Economic Policy Support Instrument (ESPI) For Senegal, Number 09/5, Publication Services, 700 19th Street, N. W. Washington, D.C. 20431

ILO/International Labour Organization (2008), Diagnostic national sur la situation sociale du travail et de l'emploi dans secteur de la pêche au Sénégal, By Andersen Perrine, Dakar, Senegal

Kasse, M. (2008), Politique Nationale de Dévéloppement, Université Cheikh Anta Diop de Dakar, Faculté Des Sciences Economiques et de Gestion, Dakar, Senegal

Ly, El H. & Sow, A. (1999), Diagnostic des Politiques sociales au Sénégal, Études et Travaux du Réseau RPSAOC n° l, Dakar, Senegal

MEF/Ministry of Economy and Finance (2010), Trimestrielle d'information et d'analyse du Ministère de l'économie et des finances, Echos-finances No. 8, Juin, 2010, Dakar, Senegal

MEF/Ministry of Economy and Finance (2012), National Strategy for Economic and Social Development, Republic of Senegal, Dakar, Senegal

MEF (2013), Exécution des dépenses des secteurs sociaux de 2006 à 2012, Republic of Senegal, Dakar, Senegal

MI/Ministry of Interior (2002), National Program for Good Governance, République du Sénégal, Dakar, Senegal

MPI/Ministry of Planning and Industry (1962), Premier plan quadriennal de développement pour la période de 1961-1964, Imprimerie Nationale, 174p., Dakar, Senegal

MPI/Ministry of Planning and Industry (1965), Deuxième plan quadriennal de développement économique et social, 1965-1969: Programmes régionaux, Vol. 3, Dakar, Senegal

MPI/Ministry of Planning and Industry (1969), Troisième plan quadriennal de développement économique et social, 1969-1973: IIIe plan, Imprimerie Nationale, 690 p., Dakar, Senegal

NASD/National Agency for Statistics and Demography (2005), National Accounts Data, Editions 1980-2004, Dakar, Senegal

NASD/National Agency for Statistics and Demography (2006), Senegalese Social Indicators Database (SSID), Editions 2005-2006, Dakar, Senegal

NASD/National Agency for Statistics and Demography (2011), National Accounts Data, Editions 2005-2011, Dakar, Senegal

NASD/National Agency for Statistics and Demography 2011), Situation économique et sociale du Sénégal, Edition 2010, Dakar, Senegal

NASD/National Agency for Statistics and Demography (2012), Recent Economic Evolutions Data, Edition 2012, Dakar, Senegal

Savadogo, K. (2009), La Politique agricole de l'UEMOA: Etat de mise en œuvre et defies, Burkina Faso, Colloque Régional WAEMU / IDRC on: Intégration régionale et stratégie de réduction de la pauvreté

UCMEP/Unit for Coordination and Monitoring of Economic Policy (2010), The MDGs: Progress made and Prospects, Ministry of Economy and Finance, Dakar, Senegal

WAEMU (2012), Rapport semestriel d'exécution de la surveillance multilatérale, Report of The WAEMU Commission, Ouagadougou, Burkina Faso

World Bank (2000), Can Africa claim the 21st century?, The World Bank, Washington D. C.

Unit 3: Book Reviews and Book Notes

Contents

Macroeconomic Policy Formation in Africa

International Labour Organization, Employment Sector, Employment Policy Department, *Employment Working Papers,* Geneva: ILO, since number 53, 2010. Web Access to the Series: http://www.ilo.org/ employment/Whatwedo/Publications/working-papers/ lang--en/index.htm

Various issues of the *Employment Working Papers* since the year 2010 have relevance for macroeconomic management in Africa and give examples of macroeconomic policy formation, by including employment-targeting and social protection aspects. A considerable number of African countries is covered in the form of case studies these papers. The paper Number 53 by Muhammed Muqtada of 2010 was of importance for the framing of Unit 1 of the *African Development Perspectives Yearbook* (see the article by this author in Unit 1 of the Yearbook). Especially the following discussion papers are relevant for this volume 16 of the African Development Perspectives Yearbook:

Towards more inclusive employment policy making: Process and role of stakeholders in Indonesia, Nicaragua, Moldova and Uganda

Claire Harasty, Zulfan Tadjoeddin, Mikhail Pouchkin, Gijsbert van Liemt

Employment Working Paper No. 137

Cities with Jobs: Confronting the Employment Challenge; An examination of approaches to employment in two South African case study cities

Glen Robbins, Sarah Hobbs
Employment Working Paper No. 127

Tackling the youth employment crisis: A macroeconomic perspective

Makiko Matsumoto, Martina Hengge, Iyanatul Islam
Employment Working Paper No. 124

Contribution of labour market policies and institutions to employment, equal opportunities and the formalisation of the informal economy: Morocco

Aomar Ibourk

Employment Working Paper No. 123

Regional Trade and Employment in ECOWAS

Erik von Uexkull

Employment Working Paper No. 114

Macroeconomic policy for full and productive and decent employment for all: The case of Nigeria

Ugochukwu Agu and Chijioke J. Evoh

Employment Working Paper No. 107

The impact of the financial and economic crisis on ten African economies and labour markets in 2008-2010: Findings from the ILO/World Bank policy inventory

Catherine Saget and Jean-François Yao

Employment Working Paper No. 100

Macroeconomic policy for employment creation: The case of Malawi

Sonali Deraniyagala, Ben Kaluwa

Employment Working Paper No. 93

Macroeconomic policy for "full and productive employment and decent work for all": Uganda country study

Elisa van Waeyenberge, Hannah Bargawi

Employment Working Paper No. 91

Growth, Employment Policies and Economic Linkages: Egypt

Heba Nassar

Employment Working Paper No. 85

Growth, employment and decent work in Namibia: A situation analysis

Godfrey Kanyenze, Frédéric Lapeyre

Employment Working Paper No. 81

Employment Diagnostic Analysis: Malawi

Dick Durevall, Richard Mussa

Employment Working Paper No. 73

Labour Market Policies and Institutions: a Synthesis Report. The cases of Algeria, Jordan, Morocco, Syria and Turkey

Mariangels Fortuny and Jalal Al Husseini

Employment Working Paper No. 64

Growth, Economic Policies and Employment Linkages in Mediterranean Countries: The cases of Egypt, Israel, Morocco and Turkey

Gouda Abdel-Khalek

Employment Working Paper No. 63

Rwanda forging ahead: The challenge of getting everybody on board

Per Ronnås (ILO), Karl Backéus (Sida), Elina Scheja (Sida)

Employment Working Paper No. 62

Employment, poverty and economic development in Madagascar: A macroeconomic framework

Gerald Epstein, James Heintz, Léonce Ndikumana, and Grace Chang

Employment Working Paper No. 58

Trade contraction in the global crisis: Employment and inequality effects in India and South Africa

David Kucera (ILO), Leanne Roncolato (American University) and Erik von Uexkull (ILO)

Employment Working Paper No. 54

The crisis of orthodox macroeconomic policy: The case for a renewed commitment to full employment

Muhammed Muqtada

Employment Working Paper No. 53

All these papers have in common the view that employment and social protection policies can support macroeconomic policy formation and economic policy implementation; also the view is shared that more effective macroeconomic policies and more comprehensive economic policies will help to improve the design, formation and implementation of more balanced employment creation and social protection policies. Many of these papers highlight the very important issue of pursuing non-orthodox economic and macroeconomic policies in Africa as a possibility to overcome structural barriers and binding constraints to development. As the structural transformation process – in the sense of the writings of A. Lewis – is still blocked in wide parts of Africa, issues such as factor mobility, labour mobility and employment creation have to be put at the center stage of macroeconomic policy formation.

Karl Wohlmuth, Bremen

Pedro Martins, *Unearthing productive employment: a diagnostic tool for sub-Saharan Africa,* **Working Paper 01, ODI Development Progress, London: ODI, February 2013, pages: 8.**
Web Access:
http://www.developmentprogress.org/sites/developmentprogress.org/files /resource-document/unearthing_productive_employment_- _a_diagnostic_tool_for_sub-saharan_africa.pdf

This is a useful publication as employment-targeting in macroeconomic and development policies is considered as a key issue. It is argued that productive employment creation should be the key focus of economic policy in Sub-Saharan Africa. The familiar Growth Diagnostics approach – using a decision tree for evaluations and recommendations - is brought in as a tool to study the possibilities of productive employment creation at various levels; the Growth Diagnostics approach is then translated into an Employment Diagnostics approach, by looking at quantity of growth, quality of growth, and unequal access to productive employment opportunities. As productive employment is a key driver of poverty reduction, of social cohesion, citizen empowerment and personal dignity, this bridge between growth and local livelihoods is important. The growth and employment diagnostics approach allows it to improve the frame of policy reforms considerably, with the intention to increase employment. Infrastructure policies in the broadest sense, agriculture sector policies to create incomes for the rural poor and productivity increases, structural policies to increase the role of employment-intensive sectors, and social policies so as to build economic resilience and opportunities for vulnerable groups are mentioned as binding constraints at local and sub-regional levels. Strengths and weaknesses of applied economic policies and reforms can be identified and used for improved policy frameworks. Binding constraints can be identified and lead to non-conventional policy measures which are more specific to the situation in a particular locality/municipality, sub-region, region, and in a particular country. Because of the labour market characteristics in SSA of large informal sectors, high levels of underemployment and vulnerable work conditions which have to be considered in analysis and prescription, better targeted policy measures come out from such a diagnostics exercise.

Karl Wohlmuth, Bremen

IMF, *Working Paper Series,* **Washington D.C.: IMF:**

Ebeke, Christian; Ölcer, Dilan, *Fiscal Policy over the Election Cycle in Low Income Countries,* **2013, Working Paper no. 13/153, pages: 24.**

Focusing on Low-Income Countries (LICs), the paper consisting of five chapters investigates the behaviour of fiscal variables during and after elections. The results indicate that during election years, government consumption significantly increases and leads to higher fiscal deficits. During the two years following elections, the fiscal adjustment takes the form of increased revenue mobilization in trade taxes and cuts to government investment, with no significant cuts in government consumption. Using a new dataset on national fiscal rules and IMF programs, the authors find that both the presence of fiscal rules and IMF programs help dampen the magnitude of the political budget cycle in LICs.

The paper concludes that elections not only imply a macroeconomic cost when they take place but also trigger a painful fiscal adjustment in which public investment is largely sacrificed.

Richmond, Christine et al, *Investing Volatile Oil Revenues in Capital-Scarce Economies: an application to Angola,* **2013, Working Paper no. 13/147, pages: 34.**

Natural resource revenues are an increasingly important financing source for public investment in many developing economies. Investing volatile resource revenues, however, may subject an economy to macroeconomic instability. This paper consisting of seven chapters applies to Angola regarding its fiscal framework that incorporates investment inefficiency and absorptive capacity constraints, often encountered in developing countries. The sustainable investing approach, which combines a stable fiscal regime with external savings, can convert resource wealth to development gains while maintaining economic stability. Stochastic simulations demonstrate how the framework can be used to inform allocations between capital spending and external savings when facing uncertain oil revenues. An overly aggressive investment scaling-up path could result in insufficient fiscal buffers when faced with negative oil price shocks. Consequently, investment progress can be interrupted, driving up the capital depreciation rate, undermining economic stability, and lowering the growth benefits of public investment.

Samaké, Issouf et al, *Fiscal Sustainability, Public Investment and Growth in Natural Resource-rich Low-Income Countries: the case of Cameroon,* **2013, Working Paper no. 13/144, pages: 35.**

This paper consisting of seven chapters assesses the implications of the use of oil revenue for public investment on growth and fiscal sustainability in Cameroon. The authors develop a dynamic stochastic general equilibrium model to analyze the effects of such investment on growth and on the path of key fiscal indicators, such as the non-oil primary deficit and public debt. Policy scenarios show that Cameroon's large infrastructural needs and relatively low current debt levels could justify a temporary deviation from traditional policy advice that suggests saving part of the oil revenue to smooth expenditure over time. Model simulations show that a relatively high degree of efficiency of public investment is needed for scaled-up public investment to make a significant contribution to growth, while maintaining fiscal sustainability.

all by Achim Gutowski, Bremen

IMF, *Country Reports,* **Washington D.C.: IMF:**

Islamic Republic of Mauritania: Poverty Reduction Strategy Paper, **2013, Country Report no. 13/189, pages: 126.**

In March 2011, Mauritania adopted its third Poverty Reduction Strategy Paper (PRSP) action plan, covering the medium term (2011-2015). Poverty reduction as the ultimate objective of all of the country's economic and social and institutional development policies has informed the context in which the third action plan is being implemented. This status report presents the results for the year 2011 and the outlook for the period 2012-2015.

The report consists of four parts. After the executive summary and the introduction, part III summarizes the implementations of one year of PRSP. It highlights the growth and macroeconomic framework. Priority areas are analyzed such as education and training, health and nutrition, water and sanitation, rural development, food security, urban development and economic development of the natural capital. The institutional capacity building and governance, monitoring and evaluation as well as lessons learnt from the implementation of the PRSP in 2011 are discussed. Part IV consists of an outlook for 2012-2015.

The priority actions carried out during the first year of implementation of PRSP included: (i) continuation of implementation of economic financial and policies and of reforms aiming at maintaining macroeconomic stability and improving the competitiveness of the economy; (ii) expansion of policies that anchor growth in the economic sphere of the poor by continuing rural development programs, adopting a policy aimed at bringing the country's food security situation under control, tackling the crop and pasture land shortages. Further implementing programs aimed at combating poverty and improving the living standards of the population by means of the refurbishment of shantytowns; (iii) human resources development and expansion of basic services; (iv) governance and capacity building.

Despite an unfavourable international economic climate and the effects of the drought on the livestock sector, PRSP implementation in 2011 had positive results in a context of sustained and stable growth characterized by: (i) an economic growth rate of 4 per cent, explained by results in the fisheries, public works and construction and service sector, offset in part by the significant decline in agricultural output (20 per cent year-on-year); (ii) inflation kept to 5,7 per cent (annual average) due to a reduced rate of transmission of imported inflation affecting food and petroleum products; and (iii) a lower current account deficit as the increase in prices for export products offset the higher petroleum and food bill throughout 2011.

The government wants to continue to implement the PRSP action plan during 2012-2015 with a view to consolidating achievements made during the first year of PRSP implementation, while emphasizing acceleration of growth and the redistribution of the results of growth in order to intensify efforts to combat poverty and keep the country on its path towards achieving the Millenium Development Goals. This action plan will be based on five core strategies that will work together to achieve the primary objective of sustainable and poverty-reducing growth.

Ghana: *2013Article IV Consultation*, 2013, Country Report no. 13/187, pages: 113.

Under Article IV of the IMF's Articles of Agreement, the IMF holds bilateral discussions with members, usually every year. In the context of the 2013 Article IV consultation with Ghana, the following documents have been released and are included in this publication:

A Staff Report for the 2013 Article IV consultation, prepared by a staff team of the IMF, following discussions that ended on April 12, 2013, with the officials of Ghana on economic developments and policies. Based on information available at the time of these discussions, the staff report was completed on May 29, 2013.

A Debt Sustainability Analysis has been prepared by the staffs of the IMF and the World Bank.

An enhancing Financial Sector Surveillance, Informational Annex and Public Information Notice (PIN) summarizing the views of the Executive Board as expressed during its June 12, 2013 discussion of the staff report that concluded the Article IV consultation.

The report consists of six parts named: recent developments and outlook; high potential but short-term risk; policy discussions, economic policy agenda; advancing middle-income status, fiscal policy; realigning priorities, monetary policy; and little room for easing and staff appraisal.

The following four key issues are mentioned:

(i) near term outlook: strong growth momentum, but significant stability risks. GDP growth of 8 percent in 2012 is projected to continue into 2013, with inflation back above 10 percent. Ghana's strong democratic institutions and favorable prospects for oil and gas are attracting significant foreign direct investment (FDI). Yet, a large current account deficit, thin external buffers, and rising public debt expose the economy to serious risks. Energy sector problems could curtail growth, while heavy government borrowing is raising the cost of credit to the private sector.

(ii) Economic policy agenda: advancing middle-income status. Ghana has made great strides in reducing poverty and has recently reached lower middle-income status. The economy, however, still relies heavily on agriculture and natural resources, particularly for exports, and most jobs are in the informal sector. The newly elected government has adopted an ambitious transformation agenda, centered on economic diversification, shared growth and job creation, and macroeconomic stability.

(iii) Macroeconomic policy mix: Need for realignment: with a near tripling of the cash deficit relative to 2011 to almost 12 percent of GDP, fiscal policy was highly expansionary in 2012. Monetary policy was tightened with some delay to halt rapid currency depreciation, but success in stabilizing the currency came at the cost of double digit real interest rates. The immediate policy priority is to safeguard stability by rebuilding fiscal and external buffers and reduce debt, while keeping a tight monetary policy stance. Decisive fiscal consolidation will, in due course, allow for a reduction in interest rates. Going forward, successful economic transformation will require a realignment of spending away from wages and subsidies toward investment in infrastructure, while structural fiscal reforms are needed to restore policy credibility and build institutional resilience to the political cycle.

(iv) Financial sector: containing vulnerabilities and removing structural constraints. The banking system has grown steadily in assets and profitability, but high interest rates are pricing out profitable investment projects, while raising the risk of a renewed increase in non-performing loans. The Bank of Ghana should consider requiring banks to hold higher minimum capital buffers against a future downturn, while addressing gaps and inconsistencies in the banking laws, and deepening cooperation with regional counterparts to improve the regulation and supervision of foreign banks.

Papageorgeogiou, Chris; Spatafora, Nicola, *Economic Diversification in LICs: Stylized Facts and Macroeconomic Implications*, 2013, Staff Discussion Notes no. 12/13, pages: 22.

Limited diversification is an underlying characteristic of many low-income countries (LICs). Concentration in sectors with limited scope for increases in productivity and quality may result in less broad-based and sustainable growth. Moreover, lack of diversification may increase exposure to adverse external shocks and macroeconomic instability. This staff discussion note has specific objectives. Firstly, to review and extend the evidence from the existing literature and ongoing IMF work, that points to diversification as a crucial aspect of the development process. A major focus is on cross-country and cross-regional differences in the pace of diversification. Secondly, to draw lessons from the experiences of those countries having successfully diversified their economies. Thirdly, to analyze the relationship between diversification, growth, and volatility.

It consists of eight parts: after the introduction and the question on how diversification is measured, patters of diversification are analysed. Quality upgrading and country case studies (eg Tanzania and some Asian countries) with regard to diversification are included. The topics macroeconomic stability through diversification as well as growth through diversification are stated. Final remarks conclude.

all by Achim Gutowski, Bremen

Macroeconomic Policies in Africa

WAMA (West African Monetary Agency), *ECOWAS Monetary Cooperation Programme, Annual Report 2010*, Freetown, Sierra Leone, pages: 199.
Web Access: http://www.amao-wama.org/fr/Publications/EMCP%20Annual%20Report%202010.pdf

This Report documents monetary cooperation programme of the ECOWAS countries. The West African Monetary Agency (WAMA) conducts every two years multilateral surveillance missions. These surveillance missions enable it to evaluate the macroeconomic performance of the ECOWAS countries and to make relevant recommendations to the member states for policy conduct. These surveillance mission also make it possible to interact directly with the Authorities and Executives of Central Banks, relevant Ministries and regional Institutions (the ECOWAS Commission, and the UEMOA Commission), involved in the Economic and Monetary Integration Programme. This Programme is on issues relating to the status of the Macroeconomic Convergence and Policy Harmonization programmes, such as: statistical harmonization; harmonization of banking legislations and regulations; capital and financial account liberalization; the development and interconnection of payment systems; etc. Information which is collected through the multilateral surveillance missions are used to produce the annual ECOWAS Monetary Cooperation Programme (EMCP) Report.

The Report contains an Executive Summary, a General Introduction, a Chapter 1 with a Review of the Global and the ECOWAS economic situation (with an analysis of the ECOWAS situation by issues such as real sector, public finance and public debt, monetary sector and external sector developments. In Chapter 2 is a reporting on the ECOWAS macroeconomic convergence situation (with a status analysis of policy harmonization and institutional arrangements in ECOWAS. In Chapter 3 there is a country-by-country analysis of macroeconomic convergence and the status of policy harmonization. The country-by country reporting is done for the eight UEMOA (Union Economique et Monetaire Ouest Africaine/ West African Economic and Monetary Union) countries and for the six WAMZ (West African Monetary Zone) countries plus Cape-Verde as an observer to WAMZ. General Conclusions and Recommendations follow, as well as Appendices. More information about the function of WAMA for ECOWAS can be found at the WAMA website: http://www.amao-wama.org/en/present.aspx.

In Unit 4 of this volume of the *African Development Perspectives Yearbook* is a discussion about macroeconomic convergence in WAMZ and ECOWAS countries, looking also at the perspectives of monetary integration on the basis of the first West African Monetary Zone (UEMOA) and the Second West African Monetary Zone (WAMZ).

Karl Wohlmuth, Bremen

IMF (International Monetary Fund), *West African Economic And Monetary Union (WAEMU), Staff Report on Common Policies for Member Countries,* **IMF Country Report No. 13/92, April 2013, Washington D. C.: International Monetary Fund 2013, pages: 106.**
Web Access: http://www.imf.org/external/pubs/ft/scr/2013/cr1392.pdf

The Report discusses the issues of common macroeconomic policies in the West African Economic And Monetary Union (WAEMU) countries. The region has seen new political and security challenges in 2012. Military coups have taken place in Guinea-Bissau and Mali, and the northern part of Mali was taken over by terrorist groups. However, the area-wide growth is estimated to have exceeded 5.5 percent in 2012, driven by the post-crisis recovery in Côte d'Ivoire and a rebound in agriculture. Growth is expected to remain robust in the year 2013, and inflation is expected to remain moderate.
The IMF consultation focused on the appropriate mix of macroeconomic policies, including in response to the risks to the regional outlook; improving the effectiveness of policies and the stability of the Union through better coordination, financial deepening and stability; and accelerating growth through deeper integration.

The Main Staff Report contains an Introduction, a chapter on Recent Developments, Outlook, and Risks, a chapter on Improving Effectiveness of Policies through Better Coordination, a chapter on Deepening and Strengthening the Financial Sector, a Chapter on Increasing Growth and Competitiveness through Regional Integration, and the Staff Appraisal. Important Appendixes follow the Main Report. Very important is the Supplement Staff Report on Financial Depth and Macro-Stability. Weaknesses of the financial sector are identified and proposals for reforms are made. According to the IMF a significant strengthening of the regulatory and supervisory framework is necessary to address existing and new risks. The emergence of regional banking groups requires the development of supervision on a consolidated basis and strengthening of cooperation with banking supervisors in countries where these groups operate. According to the IMF the financial crisis prevention and management framework could also be strengthened. Crisis prevention requires greater transparency, including through the regular and timely compilation and publication of financial soundness indicators for all the member countries.

Key policy recommendations were presented on four important issues: First, the policy mix between fiscal and monetary policies has to be considered. Fiscal consolidation is warranted in countries with higher deficits, in light of the projected high growth and the need to reconstitute policy buffers. The modest easing of monetary policy has been appropriate, taking into account the benign outlook for inflation. Official reserves remain adequate.

Second, fiscal policy coordination is of importance. More coordination is needed to safeguard the stability of the Union. Convergence criteria on public debt and the fiscal deficit need to be reconsidered and implementation of the framework needs to be strengthened to improve adherence and traction.

Third, Financial sector development and strengthening is requested. Further development and strengthening are desirable to boost investment and growth. Completing reforms of the interbank and government debt markets is a priority. Bank supervision and regulation and crisis prevention and resolution frameworks need to be strengthened.

Fourth, conditions for accelerating growth and for strengthening competitiveness have to be improved.

Reinvigorating the regional integration agenda would strengthen competitiveness, raise potential growth, and boost employment.

This Staff Report is based on discussions with regional institutions of the West African Economic and Monetary Union (WAEMU) and was prepared by a staff team of the International Monetary Fund in the context of the periodic regional surveillance of the WAEMU. The regional perspective of such discussions is intended to strengthen the bilateral discussions that the IMF holds with the members in the region under Article IV of the IMF's Articles of Agreement. Various documents have been released and are included in the package (Staff Report, Supplement on Financial Depth and Macro-Stability, Public Information Notice (PIN) which is summarizing the views of the Executive Board as being expressed during its March 25, 2013 discussion of the staff report; and the Executive Director's Statement). This Report complements the ECOWAS Monetary Cooperation Programme reports. As a convergence of the West African Economic and Monetary Union (WAEMU) and the West African Monetary Zone (WAMZ) are intended with a near time horizon and a clear convergence perspective by the governing ECOWAS institutions, such a reporting is increasingly important.

Karl Wohlmuth, Bremen

United Nations Economic Commission for Africa (UNECA), *Policy Briefs***, Addis Ababa: UNECA, no ISBN/ISSN, available at www.uneca.org.**

The UNECA Policy Briefs are based on various analytical work and research on social and economic development in Africa. UNECA's mandate is to promote economic and social development in member states as well as fostering regional integration in Africa.

Fast-tracking progress on the Millennium Development Goals in Africa, 2012, no. 004, pages: 4.

With two years remaining until the 2015 Millennium Development Goals (MDGs) target deadline, African countries must ensure that policies sustain and fast-track gains made thus far, especially for lagging MDGs. While performance across countries and within targets has been mixed, overall, the current pace of progress is insufficient to achieve the MDGs by 2015.

This policy brief deals with recent trends on Africa's progress on the Millennium Development Goals; areas of progress and areas requiring further attention are analyzed. Policy options to sustain and fast-track MDG progress in Africa are highlighted. Best practice examples as Algeria and Botswana are described. Recommendations are made on how Africa can reach the MDGs.

African Social Protection Schemes: Implications for achieving and sustaining the Millennium Development Goals, 2011, no. 003, pages: 4.

In the last couple of decades social development has not received the attention it deserves. More recently, social development has gained impetus as an important objective of the development agenda as embodied in the Millennium Declaration, which was a combination of previous international agreements on social development. This has further been strengthened through the global financial and economic crisis that has exposed the vulnerability of the small gains achieved in social development.

To better inform member States on the scope, efficiency and effectiveness of social protection as an anti-poverty instrument, UNECA conducted nine country-studies on *"The scope for social safety nets and social protection schemes to advance progress on the MDGs in Africa"*. The countries studied are Algeria, Ethiopia, Kenya, Malawi, Mauritius, Namibia, Nigeria, South Africa and Tunisia. The studies examined the various social protection instruments in use and explored the extent of their entrenchment in national development plans. They focus on the countries' medium-term expenditure frameworks and their financing mechanisms and analyzed the outcomes of the social protection schemes on poverty and inequality. Additionally, they propose policy options for deploying social safety nets as an additional instrument for accelerating progress in Africa towards the targets of the MDGs.

This policy brief draws on these nine country studies to identify commonalities in the development of formal social protection policies in Africa. Further, the object is to inform policymakers in articulating and implementing national social protection schemes as part of an overall strategy to protect the poor and advance progress towards the targets of the MDGs.

Achim Gutowski, Bremen

James K. Boyce; Léonce Ndikumana, *Capital Flight from Sub-Saharan Countries: updated Estimates, 1970-2010,* **2012, Amherst: University of Massachusetts, Political Economy Research Institute (PERI), Research Report, no ISSN, pages: 26.**

The performance of sub-Saharan African economies over the past decade has inspired optimism on the region's prospects for accelerating progress towards its development goals. Before the global financial and economic crisis, sub-Saharan Africa grew by an average of over five percent per annum, a major turnaround from the "lost" decades of the 1980s and 1990s. Even during the crisis, the sub-continent grew by three percent in 2009, trailing only East Asia as the second fastest growing region in the world.

However, sub-Saharan Africa faces major development challenges. It is now clear that the majority of the countries in the region will not achieve the key millennium goals.

A key constraint to sub-Saharan Africa's growth and development is the shortage of financing. Indeed, the region faces large and growing financing gaps, hindering public investment and social service delivery. At the same time, the sub-region is a source of large-scale capital flight, which escalated during the last decade even as the region experienced growth acceleration. The group of 33 countries covered in this report has lost a total of 814 USD from 1970 to 2010. This exceeds the amount of official development aid (659 billion USD) and foreign direct investment (306 billion USD) received by these countries. Oil-rich countries account for about 72% of the total capital flight from the sub-region (591 billion USD). The escalation of capital flight over the last decade coincided with the steady increase in oil prices prior to the global economic crisis.

The report provides updated estimates of capital flight for 33 sub-Saharan Countries from 1970-2010. It describes the methodology used to estimate capital flight and highlights important methodological differences with other existing studies.

Further, it presents key results on capital flight both in absolute terms and in comparison to other capital flows, especially debt, aid and foreign direct investment. It includes tables regarding capital flight in relation to the size of the different economies (as percentage of GDP and in per capita terms).

The report stresses the urgency of efforts to stem capital flight and repatriate stolen assets as a part of the broader goals of scaling-up development financing, combating corruption and improving transparency in the global financial system.

Achim Gutowski, Bremen

Society for International Development (SID), *The State of East Africa 2012, Deepening Integration, Intensifying Challenges,* **Nairobi, Kenya: Society for International Development 2012, with the support by TradeMark East Africa, Nairobi (headquarters), pages: 100. Web Access: http://www.sidint.net/docs/SoEAR2012_final.pdf**

The Report is informing about various sectors and policy issues of the five East African countries Tanzania, Kenya, Uganda, Rwanda and Burundi, the countries belonging to the East African Community (EAC). There are chapters on various aspects of EAC development. Chapter 1 is a summary chapter highlighting the key issues and options. Chapter 2 is on The People of East Africa, Chapter 3 on the Natural Resource Base, Chapter 4 on Human Development, Chapter 5 on Infrastructure, Chapter 6 on the Economic Profile, and Chapter 7 on Politics and Government. There is also a complete list of Figures, Tables and Boxes. There is also a short Data Sources and Methodology section in the Report. In order to present a holistic view of the EAC countries, the consistency of data across sources and time, the comparability of data across countries, and the focus of data-gathering on the "big picture" trends was guiding the selection of data by sources. The Report is an update from the report on The State of East Africa 2006. All these chapters present major trends of EAC countries, like the growing number of children and young people, the poverty increases, the income distribution worsening, the governance issues, the infrastructure deficits, and as well the new roles and commitments in the region and in the world because of the geostrategic importance of the EAC countries. The country differences come out quite well by so many tables, figures and boxes presented.

The Report has four main objectives: to inform by presenting facts and figures; to provide insights about what is behind the data, facts and images; to spark the imagination for interactions with groups, actors and forces that may be shaping the future; and to use the Report as a tool for engagement (businesses, civil society organizations/CSOs, and ordinary citizens should be empowered to engage with official authorities at different government levels in supporting specific advocacy initiatives). By this way the Report is conceived as a tool for changing economic policies and the way of macroeconomic policy formation, but also as a tool for changing sector policies, functional policies and regional integration policies. The purpose is then to address all the issues which are of importance for the citizens. Governance and accountability in the political process will become improved by such a process of dialogue and discourse between ordinary citizens and official authorities.

In the Overview Chapter 1 Key Highlights are presented, and also Conclusions and Recommendations concerning the Deepening Integration (in so many fields from the economy to regional security) and the Intensifying Challenges (like the high and increasing poverty levels, the food insecurity, the increasing inequality within and between the countries, but also the world's interest in the EAC region because of their natural resources abundance, the role in regional security issues, and the position of instable countries in the neighbourhood, like Somalia and the DR of Congo). All these challenges request leadership, openness and transparency, from the side of governments and from the side of the citizens. The Report therefore emphasizes strongly the options which are available for the engagement of the citizens for responding to these challenges. The last point in the Overview Chapter 1 is on the options of creating more engagement for citizens, especially by taking on responsibility as the base of constructive responses and not taking a back seat position in the process or a gambling attitude for personal profit.

According to the Report, the citizens can take charge of the process and they can influence its evolution by redefining their relationship with their governments. They can do this through the business and civil society organizations that represent their interests. They can make it a truly people-centered process with a people-centered outcome.

Karl Wohlmuth, Bremen

IMF, *Finance and Development*, magazine, Washington D.C.: IMF, online available at www.imf.org/fandd, ISSN: 0015-1947.

"Finance and Development" is a quarterly magazine of the IMF, publishing analysis of issues related to the international financial system, monetary policy, economic development, poverty reduction, and other world economic issues. The print and web editions are published quarterly in English, Arabic, Chinese, French, Russian and Spanish by the IMF.

***Women at Work*, June 13, Vol. 50, no. 2, pages: 60.**

This issue titled Women at Work is about reductions in gender disparity, potential implications for national policy making and the placing of female leaders in positions of power in India that can dramatically change public attitudes. One article is about the employment in high-return activities that is the pathway to economic empowerment for African women. It is critical for women to be active in business climate reform, not only because they themselves are strongly engaged as entrepreneurs, wage workers, and employers, but also because the obstacles and constraints they face – and their perspective – often are quite different from those of their male counterparts. African women tend to have different experiences of legal, regulatory, and administrative barriers to economic participation. At the same time, they are largely excluded from policymaking in the private sector and from dialogue between the public and private sectors. Consequently, women's presence in the private sector, as important economic actors in their own right, is not matched by their representation in private policy- and decision-making institutions. This exclusion is costly, not just to individual women and their businesses, but to the economy as a whole. Another article related to Africa deals with a growing number of countries in Sub-Saharan Africa that tap international capital markets.

Other articles include female connections on Wall Street, secrets of success of five women leaders, equal treatment within OECD-countries stating that closing the gender gap would boost economic growth in OECD-countries, China related subjects and book reviews.

Changing Africa – Rise of a middle class, **December 2011, Vol. 48, no. 4, pages: 57.**

This Africa related issue looks to its middle-class consumers to drive prosperity, deals with high unemployment rates in South Africa and discusses that poor households are benefiting from Sub-Saharan Africa´s high growth and wider global reach. Regarding the building of an African infrastructure, key political decisions are needed to build critical rail networks for a continent will suited to them. Another article deals with the ongoing drought and famine problems at the Horn of Africa which make it difficult for using global risk management to achieve food security. Increased intra-regional trade and lower tariffs pave the way for faster growth in some regions. Africa – a look into the future is about the development of the African continent fifty years ahead. Other mixed articles and a book review section conclude the magazine.

Achim Gutowski, Bremen

Lorenzo Fioramonti, *Gross Domestic Problem – the Politics behind the World's most Powerful Number*, 2013, London: Zed, ISBN: 978 1780322 728, pages: 208.

According to the author, gross domestic product (GDP) is arguably the best-known statistic in the contemporary world, and certainly amongst the most powerful. It drives government policy and sets priorities in a variety of vital social fields – from schooling to healthcare. Yet for perhaps the first time since it was invented in the 1930s, this popular icon of economic growth has come to be regarded by a wide range of people as a "problem". After all, does the quality of life really improve when economies grows 2 or 3 per cent? Can we continue to sacrifice the environment to safeguard a vision of the world based on the illusion of infinite economic growth?

In Gross Domestic Problem, the author takes apart the "content" of GDP in four chapters – what it measures, what it doesn't and why – and reveals the powerful political interests that have allowed it to dominate today's economies. In doing so, he argues just how little relevance GDP has to moral principles such as equity, social justice and redistribution. He wants to show that an alternative is possible, as evinced by the "de-growth" movement and initiatives such as transition towns.

Achim Gutowski, Bremen

Global Economic Reports

World Bank, *World Development Report 2013, Jobs*, Washington D. C.: International Bank for Reconstruction and Development/The World Bank 2012
Softcover: **ISSN: 0163-5085/ISBN: 978-0-8213-9575-2/e-ISBN: 978-0-8213-9576-9/DOI: 10.1596/978-0-8213-9575-2/*Hardcover:* ISSN: 0163-5085/ISBN: 978-0-8213-9620-9/DOI: 10.1596/978-0-8213-9620-9, pages: 422.**
Web Access:
http://siteresources.worldbank.org/EXTNWDR2013/Resources/8258024-1320950747192/8260293-1322665883147/WDR_2013_Report.pdf

The *World Development Report 2013* on *Jobs* places employment creation at the center stage of development policy. There is an Overview and an Introductory Chapter on the Jobs Challenge. In Part One there is a discussion about jobs and living standards, jobs and productivity, and jobs and social cohesion. In Part Two the quality of jobs is considered, by looking at the value of jobs, the job agendas in various sectors, and the connecting agendas of migration, considering migration of workers and of jobs. In Part Three the respective policies to create good jobs are discussed (labour policies, and moving beyond labour policies). Also to be found in the Report: Appendixes, Glossary, Bibliographical Note, List of Background Papers and Notes, Selected Indicators, and an Index. There is lot of references to African countries and to macroeconomic policies in the context of employment creation and improving the quality of jobs.

Karl Wohlmuth, Bremen

World Bank, *World Development Report 2012, Gender Equality And Development*, Washington D. C.: International Bank for Reconstruction and Development/The World Bank 2011
Softcover: **ISSN: 0163-5085/ISBN: 978-0-8213-8810-5/eISBN: 978-0-8213-8812-9/DOI: 10.1596/978-0-8213-8810-5/*Hardcover:* ISSN: 0163-5085/ISBN: 978-0-8213-8825-9/DOI: 10.1596/978-0-8213-8825-9, pages: 458.**
Web Access:
http://siteresources.worldbank.org/INTWDR2012/Resources/7778105-1299699968583/7786210-1315936222006/Complete-Report.pdf

In the *World Development Report 2012* on *Gender Equality and Development* there is an Overview Chapter and an Introductory Chapter to Guide the Reader of the Report. In Part I there is done a stock-taking on gender equality, with Chapters on the Wave of Progress and the Persistence of Gender Inequality. In Part II the driving forces of progress and the factors being responsible for the persistence of gender inequality are discussed. Chapters are on Education and Health as factors explaining gender differences, on Women's Agency, on Gender Differences in Employment, and on the Globalization's Impact on Gender Equality. Chapter summaries give the main messages in Part II. In Part III the role of and potential for public action is presented. There are chapters on Public Action for Gender Equality, on the Political Economy of Gender Reform, and on A Global Agenda for Greater Gender Equality. Also found in the Report: Bibliographical Note, List of Background Papers and Notes, Selected Indicators, Selected World Development Indicators, and an Index. There is lot of information contained on African countries and on macroeconomic as well as economic policies to facilitate more gender equality.

Karl Wohlmuth, Bremen

OECD, *Looking to 2060: Long-Term Global Growth Prospects. A Going for Growth Report*, **Asa Johansson et al, 2012, Economic Policy Paper no. 03/2012, Paris: OECD, ISSN: 2226583X, pages: 30.**

This report presents the results from a new model for projecting growth of OECD and major non-OECD economies over the next 50 years as well as imbalances that arise. A baseline scenario assuming gradual structural reform and fiscal consolidation to stabilize government-debt-to GDP ratios is compared with variant scenarios assuming deeper policy reforms. South Africa is often compared with other countries; other low-income countries are analyzed.

One main finding is that growth of the non-OECD G20 countries will continue to outpace OECD countries, but the difference will narrow substantially over coming decades. In parallel, the next 50 years will see major changes in the composition of the world economy. In the absence of ambitious policy changes, global imbalances will emerge which could undermine growth. However, ambitious fiscal consolidation efforts and deep structural reforms can both raise long-run living standards and reduce the risks of major disruptions to growth by mitigating global imbalances.

The report consists of 4 parts. After part 1 including the introduction and a vision of growth, part 2 covers growth determinants assumptions regarding the future: eg population ageing will reduce the share of the working-age population in most countries, net migration will only modestly lower old-age dependency ratios, structural reforms will be needed to sustain labour force participation, unemployment will return to pre-crisis levels, human capital will continue to improve, capital intensity is assumed to gradually stabilize, efficiency improvements will be the main driver of growth, global growth will be sustained by emerging countries, though at a declining rate, the relative size of economics will change dramatically over the next half century, GDP per capita gaps will shrink but significant cross-country differences will persist.

Chapter 3 deals with global savings and current account imbalances. Chapter 3 covers bold structural and macro policies that can enhance growth and reduce imbalances.

Achim Gutowski, Bremen

OECD, *Agricultural Policies for Poverty Reduction,* **J. Brooks (ed.), 2012, Paris: OECD, ISBN: 978-92-64-16863-3, pages: 191.**

This book is an outcome of an OECD project on agricultural policy choices in developing countries. The material forms the basis for a shorter policy synthesis, agricultural policies for poverty reduction: a synthesis which was declassified by the OECD's working party on Agricultural Policies and Markets in June 2011.

The study addresses the role of agricultural policies in raising incomes in developing countries. Chapter 1 introduces a strategic framework for strengthening rural incomes in developing countries. Examples of African countries are included since the evolution of agriculture's share on GDP in Africa, Asia and Latin America is compared and analysed. Chapter 2 stresses distributional impacts of commodity prices in developing countries. Ghana and Malawi are included in a comparison study. Chapter 3 deals with the distributional implications of agricultural policies in developing countries. Findings from the development policy evaluation model and agricultural policy simulations are mentioned with the country cases Ghana and Malawi. Chapter 4 is about the stabilization policies in developing countries after the 2007-2008 food crisis. Policy instruments and institutional arrangements are discussed. Regional trade across several southern African countries is described with the example of variability of maize production. Chapter 5 concludes with the use of input subsidies in low-income countries. Disadvantages of input subsidies and experiences as well as the design of subsidy progammes are explained.

Achim Gutowski, Bremen

OECD, *Trade for Growth and Poverty Reduction. How Aid for Trade can help,* **2011, Paris: OECD, ISBN: 978-92-64-10105-0, pages: 89.**

History has shown that trade can be a powerful engine for economic growth and, depending on its pace and pattern, reduce poverty. Trade can therefore be an important tool to help countries reach their development goals. However, particularly in the case of the least developed countries, harnessing the power of trade often remains challenging.

The Aid for Trade Initiative was launched 2005 at the Hong Kong WTO Ministerial Conference to address these constraints. The OECD, the Development Assistance Committee (DAC) and the Trade Committee (TC) have worked jointly to provide analytical input to the WTO Task Force on Aid for Trade. The focus of this joint work is on implementing the Aid for Trade Initiative in order to enable partner countries to use trade effectively to promote economic growth and achieve poverty reduction objectives in order to achieve the Millennium Development Goals (MDGs).

Chapter 1 presents the background of the report. Chapter 2 shows that achieving the four most common objectives of aid-for-trade programmes and projects has the potential to boost growth in developing countries and to reduce poverty. Chapter 3 discusses the impacts of trade reform and expansion on the poor that depends on consumption patterns as well as areas and sectors where the poor live and are economically active. Country cases as Zambia and South Africa are integrated. Chapter 4 demonstrates that most countries benefit from opening up to trade; however, some are unable to benefit from trade opportunities due to capacity constraints and the lack of adequate trade-related infrastructure as well as domestic constraints. Chapter 5 concludes.

Achim Gutowski, Bremen

OECD, *Better Policies for Development, Recommendations for Policy Coherence,* **2011, Paris: OECD, no. ISBN, pages: 76.**

The report examines the way in which wider policy tools can be used to support common development objectives, also referred to as policy coherence for development.

The report covers eighteen development policy topics, together spanning virtually and horizontally the whole of the OECD´s work. Its structure is divided into four broad categories: sustainable economic growth, economic governance, the environment and natural resource security and society. Together these reflect the OECD´s mission to help building a stronger, cleaner and fairer global economy.

The first premise is that policies ranging from trade and investment to tax and fiscal transparency, corporate governance, climate change, resource security and social policies such as labour, education and skills, migration and health have a profound impact on the prospects for achieving sustainable development objectives in a national and global context. Secondly, these policies require action by national governments and regional organisations in both developed and developing countries. However, according to the report, they also require collective action by the entire international community.

Achim Gutowski, Bremen

OECD, *Economic Policy Reforms, Going for Growth,* **2012, Paris: OECD, ISBN: 978-92-64-16825-1, pages: 218.**

Going for Growth was launched in 2005 as a new form of structural surveillance complementing the OECD´s long-standing country and sector-specific surveys. In line with the OECD´s 1960 founding convention, the aim is to help to promote sustainable economic growth and improve the well-being of OECD citizens.

This edition of Going for Growth assesses progress that countries have made on structural reforms since the start of the financial crisis, covering the period 2007-2011. The crisis has delivered new policy challenges and lessons, but is has also made the necessity of many Going for Growth priorities more apparent. The main reform patterns that emerge over the years since the start of the crisis are mentioned and analysed in chapter 1. In chapter 2, they are described in greater detail in individual country notes. Since this relates to partners such as the BRIICS-countries, South Africa is covered. Chapter 3 deals with structural policy indicators. Chapter 4 follows the question of structural reforms that can start the recovery; new evidence and lessons from 30 years of reform in OECD countries. Chapter 5 is about reducing income inequality while boosting economic growth. Policy trade-offs and complementarities between growth and income equality objectives are discussed. Chapter 6 analyses the spread of macroeconomic risks trough macroeconomic risk sharing from OECD and BRIICS countries. How do public risk-sharing mechanisms work in practice?

Achim Gutowski, Bremen

OECD, *Perspectives on Global Development 2012 – Social Cohesion in a Shifting World,* **2011, Paris: OECD, ISBN: 978-92-64-11314-5, pages: 259.**

As the OECD celebrates its 50th anniversary, it has reaffirmed its strong commitment to promote development worldwide including the design of a broader development strategy. Social cohesion is an important block in this endeavour; one that applies to emerging and developing countries, but also to OECD countries.

This report was prepared by a team of the OECD Development Centre Thematic Division and is part of a broader effort to put social issues more firmly on the global agenda. The OECD supports countries that continue to innovate, redesign and implement better policies that foster social cohesion for growth, development and a better living standard. The report examines social cohesion in fast-growing developing countries and provides policy makers with recommendations for ways to strengthen it. It looks at social cohesion through three different, but equally important points of view: social inclusion, social capital and social mobility. It is argued that social cohesion is a valuable goal itself and contributes to maintaining long-term economic growth. The report stresses the need for co-ordinated policy making in fiscal and tax design, employment, social protection, civic participation, education, gender and migration. However, all areas interact with each other in their effect on social outcomes.

The report consists of two main parts; part I is called "Opportunities and Challenges for Social Cohesion", part II is named "Building a Policy Agenda for Social Cohesion in Times of Shifting Wealth".

Chapter 1 deals with the spread of convergence in the developing world comparing trade balances in Sub-Saharan Africa, Eastern Asia and South America. Chapter 2 defines social cohesion and introduces a simple framework about shifting wealth, social cohesion and development. Chapter 3 is about structural transformation challenges such as employment, migration and agricultural challenges. Chapter 4 names trends in inequality between and within countries. Chapter 5 introduces the linkage of social cohesion and fiscal policies, the taxation in developing countries, sustainable fiscal policies and key principles of fiscal reform. This includes perceptions of corruption among local and central government officials in African countries and cases of building fiscal legitimacy in e.g. Malawi and Rwanda. Chapter 6 deals with employment and social protection policies for social cohesion including labour market institutions and wage determination. Chapter 7 provides information about new government challenges in the period of shifting wealth, women´s role in political participation and service delivery, accountability and decentralization. Chapter 8 is about policy issues, education, gender equality, food policy and the integration of immigrants and the transformation and adaptation of institutions. Finally, chapter 9 develops a fiscally sustainable social cohesion agenda, frames social cohesion policies and names the role of donors in promoting social cohesion.

Achim Gutowski, Bremen

OECD, *Development Co-operation, Report 2011, 50ᵗʰ anniversary edition,* **2011, Paris: OECD, ISBN: 978-92-64-09437-6, pages: 254.**

The year 2011 was a landmark for the OECD and its Development Assistance Committee (DAC), marking their 50ᵗʰ anniversary. This special 50ᵗʰ anniversary report features contributions from noted actors in development who have helped in their various capacities to shape thinking on important issues and needs today.

Chapter-contributions are included from the following experts: the former World Bank President James Wolfensohn, an UNDP-Administrator, African Development Bank President Donald Kaberuka, the President of the Institute for Liberty and Democracy, Japan's Administrator of Development Assistance, the Chairman of the Intergovernmental Panel on Climate Change, former DAC Chair Richard Manning and from the former Director General of the French Development Agency.

The report consists of three parts; part I is called "Fifty years of development co-operation: what have we learned?"; part II is named "Gender equality, empowerment, human rights and the environment: what's stopping progress?"; part III is entitled "New challenges, new goals: is there a future for official development assistance?" .

After the introduction including aspects of the future of development, the perspectives of development regarding co-operation past, present and future of the OECD is analysed. Chapter 1 deals with the OECD Development Assistance Committee (DAC) with its age of 50 years and the challenges of a changing world. Chapter 2 is called the real wealth of nations: lessons from the Human Development Report. Chapter 3 highlights Development and aid in Africa: what have we learned from the past 50 years? Chapter 4 is about gender and development: translating commitment into results. Chapter 5 is called the Amazon is not Avatar, stating that a series of myths and misconceptions continue to marginalise indigenous people and exclude them from integrating into the world economy. Chapter 6 deals with inclusive development facing the future. Chapter 7 includes information about climate change, equity and sustainable development: striking the balance. Chapter 8 highlights the future of international concessional flows. Chapter 9 is about the resurrection of aid. Several annexes regarding the efforts and policies of bilateral donors as well as trends in development co-operation from 1960 to 2010 are included.

Achim Gutowski, Bremen

International Labour Organization (ILO), *Global Employment Trends 2013, Recovering from a second jobs dip*, Geneva: International Labour Office 2013
Publication Classification Details: ISBN 978-92-2-126655-6 (print)/ISBN 978-92-2-126656-3 (pdf)/ISSN 2304-4365 (print)/ISSN 2304-2893 (pdf), pages: 172.
Web Access:
http://www.ilo.org/wcmsp5/groups/public/---dgreports/---dcomm/---publ/documents/publication/wcms_202326.pdf

There is an Executive Summary in the report *Global Employment Trends 2013*. In Chapter One the worsening of the Macroeconomic Challenges is discussed. In Chapter Two the Global Labour Market Trends and Prospects are presented. In Chapter Three the Regional Economic and Labour Market Developments were analysed. Chapter Four is on Structural Change for Decent Work, while Chapter Five is on Recovering from the second jobs dip. While chapters 1 - 3 give important trends, the chapters 4 and 5 reveal what could be done to improve the employment situation. Most important, structural change is benefitting labour, decent work and employment.

It is outlined that four areas of global, regional and national policy changes will help to improve the situation of labour and employment. First, policies are needed to tackle uncertainty so as to improve investment; second, a coordinated stimulus for global demand and employment creation is requested; third, addressing labour market mismatches and promoting structural change are important policy actions; fourth, increasing efforts to promote youth employment are on the policy agenda. It is not so obvious that at the global level one or more of these four policy areas are considered as priority issues. There is also doubt about policy action at the regional levels and at the national levels. Also found in the Report: Bibliography, Annexes, Tables, Boxes, Country Spotlights (also on Egypt and Morocco, and on South Africa and Mauritius), and Figures.

Many references are found in the Report on the situation in African countries and on necessary macroeconomic policy adaptations to cover labour and employment issues more actively.

Karl Wohlmuth, Bremen

International Labour Organization (ILO), *Global Employment Trends 2012, Preventing a deeper jobs crisis*, Geneva: International Labour Office 2012
Publication Classification Details: ISBN 978-92-2-124924-5 (print)/ISBN 978-92-2-124925-2 (web pdf), pages: 121.
Web Access:
http://www.ilo.org/wcmsp5/groups/public/@dgreports/@dcomm/@publ/documents/publication/wcms_171571.pdf

There is an Executive Summary in the report *Global Employment Trends 2012*. In Chapter 1 the deteriorating Macroeconomic Situation is considered. In chapter 2 the Global Labour Market Situation is outlined. In chapter 3 the Regional Economic and Labour Market Developments are presented. Chapter 4 is on Policy Options for Growth with Jobs. In this Chapter 4 macro policy options are discussed, but also specific policies to reduce youth unemployment and to recover the jobs which were lost during the crisis. Also found in the Report: Bibliography, Annexes, Tables, Boxes, Country Spotlights (also on Egypt and Morocco, and on South Africa), and Figures. It is not so obvious that any of the recommendations for global, regional and national action were taken up by policy makers. There is information in the Report on African countries and on ways to adapt macroeconomic policies towards action on labour, decent work and employment creation.

Karl Wohlmuth, Bremen

International Labour Organization/International Institute for Labour Studies, *World of Work Report 2013, Repairing the economic and social fabric*, Geneva: International Labour Office/International Institute for Labour Studies 2013
Publication Classification Details: ISBN 978-92-9-251017-6 (print)/ISBN 978-92-9-251018-3 (web pdf)/
ISSN 2049-9272 (print)/ISSN 2049-9280 (web pdf), pages: 133.
Web Access:
http://www.ilo.org/wcmsp5/groups/public/---dgreports/---dcomm/documents/publication/wcms_214476.pdf

In Chapter 1 of the *World of Work Report 2013* there is an Overview of Employment Trends and Projections. Chapter 2 contains an analysis of Income Distribution and Middle-income Groups across the world. Chapter 3 is on the role of Minimum Wages in Rebalancing the Economy, while chapter 4 is on Investment for a Job-friendly Recovery. Chapter 5 is considering how to shift to a more equitable and job-friendly economic path. Also to be found in the Report: Recent Publications, List of Figures, Tables, and Boxes by chapter. All the chapters have a short section on Main Findings. Chapter 5 synthesizes the lessons for the policymakers. It comes out in Chapter 5 that the political economy of a job-friendly and equitable approach has to be considered so as to come to successful policy action. There is evidence on African countries in the Report, and there are also suggestions on how to adapt macroeconomic policies towards improving the position of labour, decent work and employment creation.

Karl Wohlmuth, Bremen

International Labour Organization/International Institute for Labour Studies, *World of Work Report 2012, Better jobs for a better economy,* Geneva: International Labour Office/International Institute for Labour Studies 2012
Publication Classification Details: ISBN 978-92-9251-009-1 (print)/ISBN 978-92-9251-010-7 (web pdf) /ISSN 2049-9272 (print)/ISSN 2049-9280 (web), pages: 128.
Web Access:
http://www.ilo.org/wcmsp5/groups/public/@dgreports/@dcomm/@publ/ documents/publication/wcms_179453.pdf

There is in the *World of Work Report 2012* an Editorial from the Director of the International Institute for Labour Studies, Raymond Torres, on *How to move out of the austerity trap?* The Editorial reemphasizes the need for a three-pronged strategy to come out of the austerity trap; it was discussed already in the *World of Work Report 2011*. The three-pronged strategy emphasizes the strengthening of labour market institutions, the restoration of credit conditions and of a favourable business environment for small enterprises, and the promotion of employment while meeting fiscal goals. An alternative job-centred and growth-oriented strategy is requested along these lines. Nothing less than a Global Jobs Pact is considered as necessary. In Chapter 1 the Employment, Job Quality and Social Implications of the Global Crisis are analysed, followed in Chapter 2 by an analysis of Employment Protection and Industrial Relations so as to assess recent employment trends and labour market impacts. Chapter 3 is on Fiscal Consolidation and Employment Growth, while Chapter 4 is on Investing in a Sustainable Recovery. Investment policies for employment growth and providing better jobs are the major issues of the Chapter 4. Also to be found in the Report: Recent Publications, and Lists of Figures, Tables, and Boxes by chapter. All the chapters have a short section on Main Findings. There is some evidence on African

countries in the Report, and there are also suggestions on how to adapt macroeconomic policies for improving the position of labour, the employment
level, the conditions for decent work, and the quality of labour market institutions.

Karl Wohlmuth, Bremen

Regional African Economic Reports

**African Development Bank (AfDB)/Development Centre Of The Organi-
zation For Economic Co-operation And Development (OECD)/United
Nations Development Programme (UNDP)/United Nations Economic
Commission For Africa (UNECA),** *African Economic Outlook 2013,* **Special Theme: Structural Transformation and Natural Resources, Paris:
OECD Publishing, 2013, ISBN: 978-92-64-20053-1 (print), ISBN 978-92-
64-20054-8 (PDF), DOI: http:/dx.doi.org/10.1787/aeo-2013-en, pages:
357.**

This twelfth edition of the *African Economic Outlook* was also prepared by
four teams – from AfDB, OECD, UNDP, and UNECA. As a collaborative
effort it is of outstanding importance for Africa and for all those working in
and for Africa. The *African Economic Outlook* project started in 2002 with
only 22 African countries covered, and now the number of countries included
is 53, and only Somalia is left out. The twelfth edition is therefore unique in
covering all of Africa with one exception. The *African Economic Outlook
2013* is – as it was the case with the eleven prior issues – presenting the differences in conditions, policies and prospects of the African countries. The
analysis is differentiating between cases like oil exporters and oil importers;
least developed, low income and medium-income countries; countries undergoing reforms and countries without substantial reforms; countries with good
and bad governance; coastal countries and land-locked countries; and economically small and large countries. The fact that only Somalia is left out
from the *African Economic Outlook* is a signal and means that something has
moved in the positive direction in Africa; data and analysis on social, economic and political conditions are now available for 53 African countries.

The special theme of the eleventh edition is "Structural Transformation
and Natural Resources", and so a most important aspect of development
economics, how to reallocate resources within and between sectors (agriculture, manufacturing/industry, and services), was considered by the Editors.
Part One is on Africa's Performance and Prospects, covering sections on

Macroeconomic Prospects; Foreign Investment, Aid, Remittances, and Tax Revenue; Trade Policies and Regional Integration; Human Development; and Political and Economic Governance. Part Two is covering the special theme "Structural Transformation and Natural Resources". Part Three contains short Country Notes for 53 African countries with key messages for the respective country, but full length Country Surveys are available at: www.africaneconomicoutlook.org. The Country Surveys are highly informative analyses of the country's situation, covering Macroeconomic Prospects, Domestic and External Financial Flows, Trade Policies and Regional Integration in Africa, Human Development, and Economic and Political Governance. Part Four contains the Statistical Annex with many comparative data on the issues which are covered in Part One.

Concerning Part One, analysis of macroeconomic prospects reveals the fact that the recovery in Libya after the political changes added more than 2% to Africa's growth in 2012. The prospects for 2013 and 2014 are considered as favourable, with agriculture, services, and oil and minerals sectors becoming the growth engines, and the growth also being based on improved demand conditions (consumption and investment). West Africa, East Africa and Central Africa will lead in the growth rally, so that the African powerhouses (North and South Africa) have to solve their internal problems. Because of inflation pressures, the trade-off between supporting growth and controlling inflation is delicate in many African countries. Other African countries with limited fiscal space have to consolidate their fiscal balances for reasons of debt sustainability. There are two great tasks for policymakers – to stabilize macroeconomic conditions and to improve institutions and regulations so as to be able to cope with increasing volatility in the economic environment. While the external financial flows are favourable and are very important for the low-income countries (LICs), but also for the lower middle income countries (LMICs), aid dependence is still a major problem for half of African countries, especially the LICs, while the LMICs rely more on remittances, and the upper middle income countries (UMICs) more on portfolio inflows and foreign direct investment. All these sources of external flows have their problems: aid dependence of so many countries is too high, remittances depend on the situation in the countries where the migrants are working, portfolio investment is volatile, and foreign direct investment is mainly of a resource-seeking type. It may have been a chance to go deeper in this Part One on Performance and Prospects and in the Part Two with the Special Theme on ways out of all these dependencies. However, the Report does not propose in Part One ways out of these dependencies (this was the theme of various issues of the *African Development Perspectives Yearbook*). Africa's fragmentation is still seen as a major problem, despite of some progress in some regional economic communities (RECs). But the Report is right to emphasize again the many constraints for regional integration. Ambitious plans are there, but institutional arrangements and coordination mechanism are still weak. Also emphasized is in the Report the deterioration of some important indicators of human development (income inequality indicators, education and health indicators). Again, the African "development challenge" is mentioned (p. 11), to transform renewable and non-renewable natural capital into national wealth – into infrastructure, shared income, and human capital. As human development is an important enabler of structural transformation, more emphasis has to be put in this direction. Progress with regard of political and economic governance is at best to be considered as mixed, because of the erosion of progress in some countries and the lack of a stable progress in others, and so this complex is a heavy burden on the way to structural transformation and to the use of natural resources for sustainable development. Also new cycles of violence and conflict in some areas of Africa threaten a stable progress (Mali, Egypt, Tunisia, DR of Congo, etc.).

Also this Report bases the proposed macroeconomic and development strategy on a broader growth and redistribution framework. Macroeconomic policies need to be embedded into a broader framework for growth in Africa, and more so a framework of inclusive or pro-poor growth is requested. However, this is not enough as also internal and external risks and stresses have to be considered according to the analysis presented. The international and the regional environment create uncertainties for policymakers and for business. Policy space and fiscal space are therefore important issues to be able to handle such risks and stresses. The strategy framework for growth as proposed in the *African Economic Outlook 2013* has various important elements. Concerning external financial flows and tax revenue, much more effort is needed in terms of stimulating productivity-enhancing FDI, productive use of remittances and aid funds, and in terms of growth-stimulating and redistributive tax reforms. Both policy packages will be helpful so as to diversify the economy, to reduce poverty, and to create employment. However, these efforts depend also on progress in governance and human development, but also on progress in regional integration. Beside of proposed incentives to diversify the external finance flows to Africa with regard to forms, sources and partners, more effective tax policies are requested for growth stimulation, income redistribution and poverty reduction. Progress in regional integration is needed so as to reduce the impact of external shocks on African countries; various proposals are submitted in the Report, but progress in implementation is slow. New trade and integration policies as proposed in the Report will help to diversify production and trade patterns and will allow it to strengthen the relations with traditional and emerging trade partners. Concerning inclusive and pro-poor growth, the state of human development is still a problem in many parts of Africa as poverty reduction is quite slow and as there is an erosion of some gains in education and health. Despite of fast progress in human development, the aggregate level is still low. The Report from last year (*African Economic Outlook 2012*) emphasised the need to reverse capital flight from Africa to finance economic and social infrastructure. International cooperation was recommended to make possible a turnaround towards securing the US$ 700 billion which were accumulated between 1970 and 2008[1]. This is a main outcome of the Report 2012, and it the first time that an international report emphasises in an outspoken way the need to cooperate internationally so as to bring back the huge flight money to Africa for productive investment purposes. This issue is not brought up again in the *African Economic Outlook 2013* but definitely remains on the agenda. All this is part of a broader inclusive growth concept. Inclusive growth is a concept which is since years on the agenda and there is tremendous work undertaken to make the concept more operational[2], with consumption, income and inclusion coefficients being refined and combined. Every year the *African Economic Outlook* adds some new elements to this very important concept.

A comprehensive strategy and policy approach is therefore outlined also in this *African Economic Outlook 2013*, although this is done in a more implicit than explicit way – by considering inclusive growth and pro-poor growth in a broader framework; by looking at external finance flows and taxation, trade and regional integration, human development and social sector development, and rural and agricultural development; by focussing on the structural transformation and natural resources agenda, on specific human development policies for gender equality, and on economic opportunities for large and so far disadvantaged segments of the population; and by emphasizing also strongly the role of governance reforms and of quality increases of economic policy. Improving the quality of economic policy is related to political and economic governance, and these issues are covered strongly in all the *African Economic Outlook* reports. There is some optimism spread that African citizens will adopt peaceful ways to increase their participation, although the danger of repeated cycles of violence is as well mentioned. A maturing political process is observed, but this process needs stabilization. The

---

[1] Assessment of capital flight from Africa is based on various assumptions; see the resource base developed by PERI (Political Economy Research Institute), University of Massachusetts, Amherst, USA, Web Access with page on capital flight from Africa and section on Data and Methodology: http://www.peri.umass.edu/ 300/

[2] See for example M. H. Suryanarayana, What is Inclusive Growth? An Alternative Perspective, International Policy Centre for Inclusive Growth (IPC-IG), One pager no. 2015, June 2013.

indicators which are used for analysing this theme of governance and participation show however mixed perceptions, and it is clear that African countries
have achieved progress only in some areas. Corruption is still a major problem for improving the quality of economic policy and for allowing a broader
participation of the people in governance. It is a very important issue in the
context of the special theme as the structural transformation process and a
sustainable use of natural resources are endangered by corruption and mismanagement. As with issues of growth, poverty and income distribution also
in this regard the performance is mixed in Africa. This means that the African
Union (AU), the New Partnership for Africa's Development (NEPAD), and
the African Peer Review Mechanism (APRM) as well as other important
Pan-African institutions will have to work hard for speeding up structural
transformation, for better using the natural resources for sustainable development, and for aiming at a shared growth and a more balanced development
process in Africa. The regional economic communities (RECs) have a strong
role in Africa, to improve governance and participation, to speed up structural transformation, and to realise inclusive growth and pro-poor growth. The
role of the RECs goes therefore much beyond organising cross-border and
regional economic exchanges.

Of great importance in the *African Economic Outlook 2013* is the special
theme on *Structural Transformation and Natural Resources* in Africa. A
basic idea is presented in this chapter: the revenues from the natural resource
sector production can be used for structural transformation, especially for
investing into the development of the agricultural sector. If this process is
well managed, this can help to diversify the economy and to increase value
added and employment. A strategy is outlined, based on taking stock of structural transformation in Africa, building on a strong primary sector as the
basis for structural transformation, and learning from the state of the primary
sector in Africa. To this effect a four-layer policy approach is developed. It
becomes quite clear in the *first* section of Part Two that the structural transformation process has not worked for decades in Africa. Reallocation of
economic activity away from the least productive sectors and activities has
not worked for decades. Empirical assessments reveal: Structural change was
growth-reducing in the period 1990 to 1999, but it was growth-enhancing
between 2000 and 2005. Structural change was benefitting from better governance, better schools and competitive exchange rates. Despite of some
progress made in the last decade, much more effort is needed to accelerate
structural change with growth-enhancing effects. Although interesting, the
empirical evidence is limited to few countries. The Report discusses then in
the *second section* of Part Two the role of the primary sector as the basis for
structural transformation. The primary sector can drive structural transformation via linkages and diversification into adjacent activities, via employ-

ment and demand potentials, via government revenue from extractive sectors, and via attracting foreign investment with capital and knowhow. As a diversified primary sector is a good base for a diversified manufacturing sector, a better environment for the primary sector will also help to extend the manufacturing production base. Regrettably, the environment was not created in many African countries to achieve just this process of widening and deepening the production base. If the right environment is not there, only natural resources with high rents (oil and gas, diamonds, rare metals) may be exploited profitably. However, these high rent resources offer the least possibilities for structural transformation. Then, in the *third section* of Part Two of the *African Economic Outlook 2013* the role of the primary sector in Africa over the past and in the present is analysed, mainly in the form of a literature survey. Emphasized is again the poor performance of the agricultural sector and the fact that the minerals sector remained far below of its potentials. Some recent (positive) changes are mentioned since the occurrence of the commodity price boom in 2007/08, but it is more an increasing global and Asian interest in the African commodities than an increasing interest in better management of the sector what can be observed. There is also a positive note on the export of processed products relative to raw materials exports. However, it is not made clear to what extent the level of processing has increased and to what extent African lead firms are able to manage these exports. It is also coming out that the agricultural transformation is not progressing despite of the commodity price boom and the global demand for raw materials and food. More interest in exploration in the minerals sector is observed and is credited with job creation, but too often these jobs are highly vulnerable. Some of this activity is to be expected in institutionally weak states and in fragile states, like the DR of Congo. These issues are not covered in the Report. Again the "window of opportunities" is emphasized, but not many examples are cited to substantiate the view that these opportunities are really exploited so as to transform successfully the economic structures. It is argued that Africa is getting better at avoiding the "resource curse", but the examples given may not be so relevant as the future will show if the new management intentions of a government will really work (such as the new and widely praised natural resource sector legislation in Ghana). In the *fourth section* of Part Two a four-layer policy approach is presented. First, the general framework conditions have to be established for structural transformation, such as education, infrastructure, and access to regional markets. Second, specific conditions have to be met for natural resource sectors to thrive, such as proper rules for exploration of minerals, ownership rights and specific skills. Third, the revenues from natural resources have to be optimised and spent wisely for structural transformation, by optimising taxes, managing the volatility of revenues, and managing the impact on the environment. Fourth, structural transformation has to be addressed directly, by increasing agricultural productivity and by enabling economic linkages between the natural resource sector and the economy as a whole. The graphical presentation of these four layers (on page 144) shows how important the fundamentals (layer 1) are, such as public services, regulations and transparency, government capacity and commitment, and access to finance and markets. Also the layers 2 and 3 are presented as very important cornerstones of the pyramid so as to create the specific environment for the natural resource sector (layer 2) and to establish an effective management system for the natural resource sector (layer 3). If all this works (layers 1 - 3), structural transformation can be supported "on the top of the pyramid" via increasing agricultural productivity, via establishing linkages and via building capabilities. Although this is an interesting presentation, reality is different from this ideal model of good governance in natural resource-rich countries in Africa. Country case studies would have shown much better how and if such a four layer approach really works. The examples presented for practical action, especially so for layer 4, do not show if and how the minerals sector will push agricultural development and manufacturing. Some positive effects may be there, some interconnections may work, some incentives may be provided and may work, but what is the overall impact of all this? Too many issues remain open and only country case studies would have shown how feasible such a policy approach really is. Regrettably, the Part Three with country notes does not show which countries could be seen as models for the applicability of this four-layer approach. The Part Two of the *African Economic Outlook 2012* on *Promoting Youth Employment* was so relevant because country experts from nearly all African countries reported on their country experiences; but this seems not to have worked in the *African Economic Outlook 2013* project. The Report 2013 does not present enough country evidence on *Structural Transformation and Natural Resources* to allow for the dissemination of best practice interventions.

The twelfth edition again makes it very clear that the *African Economic Outlook* project has become a forum for monitoring the growth process in Africa and for identifying best practice so that sustainable policy reforms can be proposed and implemented all over Africa. Although this new edition for 2013 did not meet all the expectations it is a valuable contribution to the development of Africa literature. The twelfth edition also investigates into the role of the deeper factors for generating higher growth, structural transformation and more sustainable development in Africa, a trend which was seen over the last ten years, supported by factors such as economic policy reforms, improving governance, aspiring for more effective relations with donors, using new technologies more broadly, and enabled by the emergence of a new class of politicians and entrepreneurs. With its online platform –

www.africaneconomicoutlook.org – the *African Economic Outlook* project is able to reach more and more decision makers in Africa and elsewhere.

It is necessary to see the wealth of information which was accumulated over the last twelve years in the *African Economic Outlook* project, and it is also helpful to look at the methodology used in modelling the African economic prospects. All the other volumes of the *African Economic Outlook* were as well reviewed in various issues of the *African Development Perspectives Yearbook*, and also the *African Economic Outlook* methodology for modelling economic perspectives for Africa was considered in these reviews.

In the *African Economic Outlook 2012* the focus was on *Promoting Youth Employment*, and in the *African Economic Outlook 2011* the special theme was *Emerging Partners of Africa*, while in the *African Economic Outlook 2010* the special focus was on *Public Resource Mobilisation and Aid to Africa*. Specific topics were covered also in the other Reports: the major theme in the *African Economic Outlook 2009* was *Innovation and ICT in Africa;* and *Technical and Vocational Skills Development* was the special theme in the *African Economic Outlook 2007/2008*, while *Drinking Water and Sanitation* was the special theme in the *African Economic Outlook 2006/2007*. In the *African Economic Outlook 2005/2006* the crucial issues of *Transport Infrastructure Development* in Africa were discussed, while in the *African Economic Outlook 2004/2005* the key issue introduced was the *Financing of Small and Medium-sized Enterprises*. In the *African Economic Outlook 2003/2004* a discussion of another important key policy issue for Africa was presented – *Energy Sector Policies*, and the interaction of energy and poverty issues was analysed as well in the Report. The first two *African Economic Outlook* reports for *2001/2002* and *2002/2003* did not contain specific themes, but were already discussing some structural issues of African countries.

A gradual improvement and strengthening of the *African Economic Outlook* project can be observed. With all these special themes which were discussed in the various volumes, a wealth of information about important policy issues was presented. Looking at all these policy reviews and recommendations and best practice analyses, policymakers in Africa and working for Africa can take from it useful suggestions. The gradual enlargement of the number of countries which are considered with Country Notes and Country Surveys in Part Three of the *African Economic Outlook* is also an important improvement to the overall project. This means that the special theme is related to more and more country surveys and that work on it is drawing on more and more country experiences; this allows it to compare the country position with regard of a specific policy issue. As an example, the *African Economic Outlook 2012* contains country-by-country information about the role of public interventions with regard of youth employment schemes, and country officers for 53 countries have reported on this issue. As observed above, the *African Economic Outlook 2013* was not so successful in this regard. The Statistical Annex which is presented in Part Four of the Report allows it to further deepen the view on the country case by looking at the comparative data. The Methodology for all these tables is carefully explained. The Statistical Annex is valuable as it is including a selection of very important economic, social, and political data for African countries. The extension to various political, economic and doing business governance indicators is helpful; the comparisons with economic and social data for the country are revealing.

An explicit aim for the *African Economic Outlook* is the analysis of the trends and of the short-term evolution of selected African countries for the next two years by using a unique analytical model design for all the country case studies. The common framework includes a forecasting exercise for the current and the following two years by using a simple macroeconomic model, while the results from the modelling are related to analyses of the social and political situation in Africa. Mainly policymakers, donor agencies, academic experts, and business people are benefitting from these analyses. A problem with the *African Economic Outlook* is the fact that the background to the modelling work is not explained more deeply. Reference was made to a standard macroeconomic model called Africalook (see the short description of the prediction models in the *African Economic Outlook* 2001/2002, p. 19). It is argued that the specific structural peculiarities of the countries are also considered in this framework. The African Development Bank (AfDB) has now some lead role in this exercise, and seems to have further developed the model. The modelling for the *OECD Economic Outlook* is used to forecast world demand as well as the prices of the non-traditional imports and exports being of relevance for the particular African countries that are included in the form of case studies, while predictions of the (traditional) raw materials prices come from World Bank sources.

A much greater problem is it that there are two important competing reports coming from Africa, the *African Development Report* from the African Development Bank (AfDB) and the *Economic Report on Africa* from the UN Economic Commission for Africa (UNECA) and the African Union (AU)[3].

---

[3] See the *Economic Report on Africa 2013* on *Making the Most of Africa's Commodities: Industrializing for Growth, Jobs and Economic Transformation*, by the Economic Commission for Africa and the African Union, Addis Ababa 2013, while the *African Development Report 2013* was not released yet; the *African Development Report 2012* is on *Towards Green Growth in Africa,* by the African Development Bank Group, Tunis 2012. Also the UNCTAD Report *Economic Development In Africa, Report 2012:*

Therefore it is not yet clear to what extent the joint project *African Economic Outlook* of the OECD, the AfDB, the UNDP and the UNECA really can contribute to a better understanding of Africa's development, and what the comparative advantage of the three reports on Africa really is, as also the other two reports present analyses, forecasts, special themes, regional economic profiles, and country case studies. Both, the *African Development Report* of the AfDB and the *Economic Report on Africa* of the UNECA and the AU are very rich in analyses, in forecasts, in policy recommendations, and in informative special themes, regional economic profiles, and in country cases. It may be that a "new division of labour" emerges over time between the editing institutions with regard to the three reports. However, the publicity around the *African Economic Outlook* is huge and so the other two reports are regrettably overshadowed (although their content is rich). It could be that a "new division of labour" which is based on comparative advantages of the involved institutions is envisaged for the longer-run; it could be that the *African Economic Outlook* focuses more and more on country reports and on specific policy themes of relevance for donors, the *African Development Report* more and more on key policy reforms for Africa and on major development financing issues from the side of the African Development Bank, and the *Economic Report on Africa* more and more on sector problems and regional integration issues (although some of these issues are covered in specific programmes of UNECA, AfDB and AU on strengthening regional economic communities).

But, compared with earlier reports of the *African Economic Outlook*, the messages from the more recent ones are much clearer and stronger – the focus on international assistance strategies for Africa is stronger, structural impediments and solutions to Africa's development problems are highlighted more deeply, more and more country reviews are included (covering all African countries with the exception of Somalia), the comparability of country cases is strengthened, and the relevance of the presented data and of the forecasts has improved. The specific policy field that is covered – in this *African Economic Outlook* report the role of *structural transformation and natural resources* in Africa – is always important and the analysis is mostly to the point, and so the information presented is useful for further analyses and for projections. The researchers on country notes and surveys give valuable information for the specific theme and provide recommendations on country policies for the donors. It may however be quite important to work further on

---

Structural Transformation And Sustainable Development In Africa, New York and Geneva: United Nations 2012 is related to the theme of Structural Transformation.

a clear division of labour between these three reports, in order to strengthen them as instruments for policy assessment, policy formation and policy reform at the international, regional and national levels.

The *African Economic Outlook* can play a great role if the new trends in global development cooperation with Africa are reflected even more in the context of the annual focus theme of the *African Economic Outlook*, and as well in the frame of the recommendations for policies of the specific African country cases that are considered and reviewed. The *African Economic Outlook* is highlighting the development cooperation issues in general and also with regard to specific structural, policy, and infrastructure development issues. So the country cases highlight now more than in the past the role of national priorities and policies and the development assistance implications of macroeconomic policies and sector development policies. The issues of aid dependency and the debt (and debt relief) problems of the countries are also reflected, as well as the objectives, means and strategies for improving aid assistance to these countries. This is where the basic competences of the OECD policy departments, of the OECD/DAC forums, and of the OECD Development Centre really lie, and this vast knowledge should be utilised properly. It should also be made quite clear that the *African Economic Outlook* is a joint OECD-Africa project with considerable and fast increasing African inputs and additional inputs provided from UN organisations, like the UNDP. This is not so clear and obvious from the image and the logo of the presented volumes of the *African Economic Outlook*. The inputs coming from Africa – towards making possible and relevant these informative volumes – are becoming greater, and this can be made better visible in the format and the layout of the Reports. So it would be better to show that these are really joint OECD/Africa reports and not just OECD reports on Africa which were assisted by some African institutions.

Karl Wohlmuth, Bremen

African Development Bank (AfDB)/Development Centre Of The Organization For Economic Co-operation And Development (OECD)/United Nations Development Programme (UNDP)/United Nations Economic Commission For Africa (UNECA), *African Economic Outlook 2012*, **Special Theme: Promoting Youth Employment, Paris: OECD Publishing, 2012, ISBN: 978-92-64-17609-6 (print), ISBN 978-92-64-17611-9 (PDF), pages: 291.**

This eleventh edition of the *African Economic Outlook* was prepared by four teams – from AfDB, OECD, UNDP, and UNECA. As a collaborative effort it is of outstanding importance for Africa and for all those working in and for Africa. The *African Economic Outlook* project started in 2002 with only 22 African countries covered, and now the number of countries included is 53, and only Somalia is left out. The eleventh edition is therefore unique in covering all of Africa with one exception. The *African Economic Outlook 2012* is – as it was the case with the ten prior issues – presenting the differences in conditions, policies and prospects of the African countries. The analysis is differentiating between cases like oil exporters and oil importers; least developed, low income and medium-income countries; countries undergoing reforms and countries without substantial reforms; countries with good and bad governance; coastal countries and land-locked countries; and economically small and large countries. The fact that only Somalia is left out from the *African Economic Outlook* is a signal and means that something has moved in the positive direction in Africa; data on social, economic and political conditions are now available for 53 African countries.

The special theme of the eleventh edition is "Promoting Youth Employment", and so the most important aspect of benefiting from the "demographic dividend" in Africa of a very young population was considered. While Part One is on Africa's Performance and Prospects, Part Two is covering the special theme. Part Three contains short Country Notes for 53 African countries, but full length country surveys are available at: www.africaneconomicoutlook.org. The country surveys are highly informative analyses of the country's situation, covering Macroeconomic Prospects, Domestic and External Financial Flows, Trade Policies and Regional Integration in Africa, Human Development, and Economic and Political Governance. Part Four contains the Statistical Annex with many comparative data on the issues covered in Part One.

Concerning Part One, analysis of macroeconomic prospects reveals the need to consider the potentially negative impact of the European debt crisis on Africa. While the growth prospects for 2012 are favourable, considerable risks are there. Increasing fuel and food prices presented a policy dilemma for African countries – between fighting inflation and preserving growth amidst global risks. Public finance is also seen as a problem, in some oil-importing countries with fiscal deficits and in some resource-rich countries when medium-term fiscal planning is not working properly and when these countries are not preparing for falling resource prices by investing into sovereign wealth funds. A further deepening of the crisis in Europe could have severe impacts on trade, foreign direct investment, official development assistance, and also on the banking systems in Africa. Further risks for macroeconomic prospects arise according to the *African Economic Outlook 2012* from the situation in North Africa, the relations between Sudan and South Sudan, and because of drought and floods as affecting agricultural production and food security. Most important, high unemployment rates and very high rates of youth unemployment show the need for new policy orientation – demand-side and supply-side measures are requested to tackle this problem. These issues are discussed in detail in Part Two, but not so much in Part One, although the "demographic growth dividend" of a young population in Africa is mentioned as a chance. However, the report does not propose in Part One specific forms of employment-targeting in macroeconomic policies (as it is the theme of Unit 1 of this issue of the *African Development Perspectives Yearbook*).

Also this Report bases the proposed macroeconomic strategy on a broader growth and redistribution framework. Macroeconomic policies need to be embedded into a framework for growth in Africa, and more so a framework of inclusive or pro-poor growth. However, this is not enough as also risks have to be considered according to the analysis presented. Risk management is important as global and domestic risks interact in African countries and create uncertainties for policymakers and for business. The strategy framework for growth as proposed in the *African Economic Outlook 2012* has various important elements. Concerning external financial flows and tax receipts, much more effort is needed in terms of stimulating productivity-enhancing FDI, productive use of remittances and aid funds, and in terms of growth-stimulating and redistributive tax reforms. Both policy packages will be helpful so as to diversify the economy, to reduce poverty, and to create employment. Beside of proposed incentives to diversify the external finance flows to Africa with regard to forms, sources and partners, more effective tax policies are requested for growth stimulation, income redistribution and poverty reduction. Progress in regional integration is needed so as to reduce the impact of external shocks on African countries; various proposals are submitted. New trade and integration policies as proposed in the Report will help to diversify production and trade patterns and will allow it to strengthen the relations with traditional and emerging trade partners. Concerning inclusive and pro-poor growth, the state of human development is still a problem in many parts of Africa as poverty reduction is quite slow. Despite of fast progress in human development, the aggregate level is still low. The report emphasises the need to reverse capital flight from Africa to finance economic and social infrastructure. International cooperation is recommended to make possible a turnaround towards securing the US$ 700 billion which were accumulated between 1970 and 2008[4]. This is a main outcome of the Report,

---

[4] Assessment of capital flight from Africa is based on various assumptions; see the resource base developed by PERI (Political Economy Research Institute), University of Massachusetts, Amherst, USA, Web Access with page on

and it the first time that an international report emphasises the need to cooperate internationally so as to bring back the flight money to Africa for investment purposes. All this is part of a broader inclusive growth. Inclusive growth is a concept which is since years on the agenda and there is work undertaken to make the concept more operational[5], with consumption, income and inclusion coefficients combined.

A new strategy and policy approach is therefore outlined in the volume of the *African Economic Outlook* for 2012, although this is done more implicit than explicit – considering inclusive growth and pro-poor growth in a broader framework, by looking at external finance and taxation, trade and regional integration, human development, social sector development, rural and agricultural development, specific human development policies for gender equality, economic opportunities for large and so far disadvantaged segments of the population, governance reforms and quality increases of economic policy. Improving the quality of economic policy is related to political and economic governance, and these issues are covered strongly in the Report. There is some optimism spread that African citizens will adopt peaceful ways to increase their participation. A maturing political process is observed. The indicators which are used for analysing this theme of governance and participation show however mixed perceptions, and it is clear that African countries have achieved progress only in some areas. Corruption is emerging as the greatest problem for improving the quality of economic policy and for allowing a broader participation of the people in governance. As with growth, poverty and income distribution as it was discussed in the Report also in this regard the performance is mixed in Africa. This means that the African Union (AU), the New Partnership for Africa's Development (NEPAD) and the African Peer Review Mechanism (APRM) as well as other important Pan-African institutions will have to work hard for a more balanced development process in Africa. The regional economic communities (RECs) have a strong role to improve governance and participation and to realise inclusive growth and pro-poor growth all over Africa. The role of the RECs goes therefore much beyond organising cross-border and regional economic exchanges.

Of great importance in the *African Economic Outlook 2012* is the special theme on *Promoting Youth Employment* in Africa. This issue is discussed in great detail in Part Two, Chapter 6. It becomes quite clear in the *first section*

---

capital flight from Africa and section on Data and Methodology: http://www.peri.umass.edu/ 300/

[5] See for example M. H. Suryanarayana, *What is Inclusive Growth? An Alternative Perspective*, International Policy Centre for Inclusive Growth (IPC-IG), One pager No. 2015, June 2013.

of Part Two why the *African Economic Outlook* deals with the issue. As Africa has the youngest population in the world and as its youth is getting better educated, the problems of high youth unemployment and of very high poverty of the youth is not any longer acceptable, especially with regard of the lost development potential. More than 70 % of the youth in Africa live on less than US$ 2 per day. The potential of the youth for productive development has to be used as a valuable input to the structural transformation process. Also the definitions and measurement procedures are outlined in the section one of Part Two; these are useful methodological contributions as too many different definitions and measurement procedures prevail in the literature. The Report discusses then in *section two* of Part Two the role of the youth in the African labour markets by showing the differences between the poor and the better-off African countries. The problem of bad jobs (unproductive and low paid) in the poor countries and of too few jobs in middle income African countries is highlighted. Five distinct types of labour markets are shown (depending on GDP per capita, level of wage employment, level of vulnerable employment, and NEET (Not in Employment, Education and Training). There is a "quality of jobs" problem in low income countries and a "quantity of jobs" problem in the middle income countries. The category "Not in Employment, Education, and Training" (NEET) is of great importance for policymakers, and many initiatives are proposed. Then, in *section three* of Part Two of the *African Economic Outlook 2012* the employment outlook for the African youth is discussed. Insufficient public and private formal sector hiring is identified as a major problem, and so a new and more effective policy approach for informal sector employment creation is requested. Nothing is really new with this position and the concrete proposals, but so far practically nothing was done in Africa to use the informal sector as a dynamic absorber of the growing labour force side by side with initiatives for the private formal sector. The messages are clear since decades, but no strengthening of the informal sectors could be observed in Africa. Specific support programmes and an improvement of the environment for promoting entrepreneurial qualities for the young labour force are again recommended in order to make the informal sectors more dynamic and labour-absorbing. In the *fourth section* of Part Two the obstacles and the needs of young people in African labour markets are discussed. There is a severe labour demand problem as there is not enough demand in sectors which are able to pay better wages and to provide adequate working conditions. So, structural transformation of the economy is still an important issue as too few jobs are offered with higher productivity and better wages. There are some supply-side hurdles on behalf of the young labour force, but these problems are not as important as the demand factors according to the Report. Adaptation to the needs of the informal sector and the rural sector is important as long as these sectors are so important for employment and survival. Some strategies are recommended in this direction, such as education and vocational training, entrepreneurship promotion and some forms of public works programmes. Despite of this outcome of analysis on major constraints, the *section five* on government action to promote youth employment reveals that demand-side action from the side of governments in Africa is not so important relative to supply-side interventions. The quality of interventions is also not high. So there is a problem of policy orientation and also one of quality with regard of public labour market interventions. There are only few success stories to be reported by country officers and the editorial staff. It is obvious that public interventions only will work successfully if all relevant constraints are considered (demand side, supply-side, and matching demand and supply side) and not only some supply-side constraints. Most of the programmes are not addressing all these constraints, and too often only one constraint is covered (such as lack of specific skills). In *section six* some policy conclusions are presented. The Part Two of the African Economic Outlook 2012 is so relevant because country experts from nearly all Africa countries report on their experiences; this allows dissemination of best practice interventions.

The eleventh edition again makes it clear that the *African Economic Outlook* project has become a forum for monitoring the growth process in Africa and for identifying best practice so that sustainable policy reforms can be proposed and implemented all over Africa. The eleventh edition also outlines the role of the deeper factors for generating higher growth and more sustainable development in Africa which was seen over the last ten years, such as economic policy reforms, improving governance, aspiring for more effective relations with donors, using new technologies more broadly, and the emergence of a new class of politicians and entrepreneurs. With its online platform – www.africaneconomicoutlook.org – the *African Economic Outlook* project is able to reach more and more decision makers in Africa and elsewhere.

It is necessary to see the wealth of information accumulated over the last eleven years in the *African Economic Outlook* project, and it is also helpful to look at the methodology used in modelling the African economic prospects. All the other volumes of the *African Economic Outlook* were as well reviewed in various issues of the *African Development Perspectives Yearbook*, and also the *African Economic Outlook* methodology for modelling economic perspectives for Africa was considered in these reviews.

In the *African Economic Outlook 2011* the focus was on *Emerging Partners of Africa*, while in the *African Economic Outlook 2010* the special focus was on *Public Resource Mobilisation and Aid to Africa*. Specific topics were covered also in the other Reports: the major theme in the *African Economic*

Outlook 2009 was *Innovation and ICT in Africa;* and *Technical and Vocational Skills Development* was the special theme in the *African Economic Outlook 2007/2008,* while *Drinking Water and Sanitation* was the special theme in the *African Economic Outlook 2006/2007.* In the *African Economic Outlook 2005/2006* the crucial issues of *Transport Infrastructure Development* in Africa were discussed, while in the *African Economic Outlook 2004/2005* the key issue introduced was the *Financing of Small and Medium-sized Enterprises.* In the *African Economic Outlook 2003/2004* a discussion of another important key policy issue for Africa was presented – *Energy Sector Policies,* and the interaction of energy and poverty issues was analysed as well in the Report. The first two *African Economic Outlook* reports for *2001/2002* and *2002/2003* did not contain specific themes, but were already discussing some structural issues of African countries.

A gradual improvement and strengthening of the *African Economic Outlook* project can be observed. With all these special themes which were discussed in the various volumes, a wealth of information about important policy issues was presented. Looking at all these policy reviews and recommendations and best practice analyses, policymakers in Africa and working for Africa can take useful suggestions. The gradual enlargement of the number of countries which are considered with Country Notes and Country Surveys in Part Three of the *African Economic Outlook* is also an important improvement to the overall project. This means that the special theme is related to more and more country surveys and that work on it is drawing on more and more country experiences; this allows it to compare the country position with regard of a specific policy issue. As an example, the *African Economic Outlook 2012* contains country-by-country information about the role of public interventions with regard of youth employment schemes, and country officers for 53 countries have reported on this issue. The Statistical Annex in Part Four allows it to further deepen the view on the country case by looking at comparative data. The Methodology for all these tables is carefully explained. The Statistical Annex is valuable as it is including a selection of very important economic, social, and political data for African countries. The extension to various governance indicators is helpful; the comparisons with economic and social data for the country are revealing.

An explicit aim for the *African Economic Outlook* is the analysis of the trends and of the short-term evolution of selected African countries for the next two years by using a unique analytical model design for all the country case studies. The common framework includes a forecasting exercise for the current and the following two years by using a simple macroeconomic model, while the results from modelling are related to analyses of the social and political situation in Africa. Mainly policymakers, donor agencies, academic experts, and business people are benefitting from these analyses. A problem with the *African Economic Outlook* is the fact that the background to the modelling work is not explained more deeply. Reference was made to a standard macroeconomic model called Africalook (see the short description of the prediction models in the *African Economic Outlook* 2001/2002, p. 19). It is argued that the specific structural peculiarities of the countries are also considered in this framework. The African Development Bank (AfDB) has now some lead role in this exercise, and seems to have further developed the model. The modelling for the *OECD Economic Outlook* is used to forecast world demand as well as the prices of the non-traditional imports and exports being of relevance for the particular African countries that are included in the form of case studies, while predictions of the (traditional) raw materials prices come from World Bank sources.

A much greater problem is it that there are two important competing reports coming from Africa, the *African Development Report* from the African Development Bank (AfDB) and the *Economic Report on Africa* from the UN Economic Commission for Africa (UNECA) and the African Union (AU)[6]. Therefore it is not yet clear to what extent the joint project *African Economic Outlook* of the OECD, the AfDB, the UNDP and the UNECA really can contribute to a better understanding of Africa's development, and what the comparative advantage of the three reports on Africa really is, as also the other two reports present analyses, forecasts, special themes, regional economic profiles, and country case studies. Both, the *African Development Report* of the AfDB and the *Economic Report on Africa* of the UNECA and the AU are very rich in analyses, in forecasts, in policy recommendations, and in informative special themes, regional economic profiles and country cases. It may be that a "new division of labour" emerges over time between the editing institutions with regard to the three reports. However, the publicity around the *African Economic Outlook* is huge and so the other two reports are regrettably overshadowed (although their content is rich). It could be that a "new division of labour" which is based on comparative advantages is envisaged for the longer-run; it could be that the *African Economic Outlook* focuses more and more on country reports and on specific policy themes of relevance for donors, the *African Development Report* more and more on key policy reforms for Africa and on major development financing issues from the side of the African Development Bank, and the *Economic Report on*

---

[6] See the *Economic Report on Africa 2012* on *Unleashing Africa's Potential as a Pole of Global Growth,* by the Economic Commission for Africa and the African Union, Addis Ababa 2012, and the *African Development Report 2012* on *Towards Green Growth in Africa,* by African Development Bank Group, Tunis 2012.

Africa more and more on sector problems and regional integration issues (although some of these issues are covered in specific programmes of UNECA, AfDB and AU on strengthening regional economic communities).

But, compared with earlier reports of the *African Economic Outlook*, the messages from the more recent ones are much clearer and stronger – the focus on international assistance strategies for Africa is stronger, structural impediments and solutions to Africa's development problems are highlighted more deeply, more and more country reviews are included (covering all African countries with the exception of Somalia), the comparability of country cases is strengthened, and the relevance of the presented data and of the forecasts has improved. The specific policy field that is covered – in this *African Economic Outlook* report the role of *promoting youth employment* in Africa – is always important and the analysis is to the point, and so the information presented is useful for further analyses and for projections. The researchers on country notes and surveys give valuable information for the specific theme and provide recommendations for donors. It may however be quite important to work further on a clear division of labour between these three reports, in order to strengthen them as instruments for policy assessment and reform at the international, regional and national levels.

The *African Economic Outlook* can play a great role if the new trends in global development cooperation with Africa are reflected even more in the context of the annual focus theme of the *African Economic Outlook*, and as well in the frame of the recommendations for policies of the specific African country cases that are considered and reviewed. The *African Economic Outlook* is highlighting the development cooperation issues in general and also with regard to specific structural, policy, and infrastructure development issues. So the country cases highlight now more than in the past the role of national priorities and policies and the development assistance implications of macroeconomic policies and sector development policies. The issues of aid dependency and the debt (and debt relief) problems of the countries are also reflected, as well as the objectives, means and strategies for improving aid assistance to these countries. This is where the basic competences of the OECD policy departments, of the OECD/DAC forums, and of the OECD Development Centre really lie, and this vast knowledge should be utilised properly. It should also be made quite clear that the *African Economic Outlook* is a joint OECD-Africa project with considerable and fast increasing African inputs and additional inputs provided from UN organisations, like the UNDP. This is not so clear and obvious from the image and the logo of the presented volumes of the *African Economic Outlook*. The inputs coming from Africa – towards making possible and relevant these informative volumes – are becoming greater, and this can be made better visible in the format and the layout of the Reports. So it would be better to show that these are really joint OECD/Africa reports and not just OECD reports on Africa which were assisted by some African institutions.

Karl Wohlmuth, Bremen

African Development Bank (AfDB)/ Development Centre Of The Organization For Economic Co-operation And Development (OECD)/United Nations Development Programme (UNDP)/United Nations Economic Commission For Africa (UNECA), *African Economic Outlook 2011*, **Special Theme: Africa and its Emerging Partners, Paris: OECD Publishing, 2011, ISBN: 978-92-64-11175-2 – No. 581172011, pages: 303.**

This tenth edition of the *African Economic Outlook* was prepared by four teams – from AfDB, OECD, UNDP, and UNECA. As a collaborative effort it is of outstanding importance for Africa and for all those working in and for Africa. The *African Economic Outlook* project started in 2002 with only 22 African countries covered, and now the number of countries included is 51. The tenth edition therefore celebrates the success of a project which started in a period of African growth pessimism. Although the growth pessimism has now given place to growth optimism (although quite often unqualified), the *African Economic Outlook 2011* as well as the prior issues is not following this course but presents the differences in conditions, policies and prospects of the African countries. The analysis is differentiating between cases like oil exporters and oil importers; least developed, low income and medium-income countries; countries undergoing reforms and countries without substantial reforms; coastal countries and land-locked countries; and economically small and large countries.

The special theme of the tenth edition is "Africa and its Emerging Partners", and so the new-style partnerships of Africa with emerging economies, especially BRIC (Brazil, Russia, India, and China), South Korea and Turkey, are highlighted. While Part One is on Africa's Performance and Prospects, Part Two is covering the special theme. In Part Three short Country Notes for 51 African countries are presented, but full length country surveys are available at: www.africaneconomicoutlook.org. The country surveys are highly informative analyses of the country's situation, covering macroeconomic developments, structural transformation trends and governance issues, and as well containing a lot of data and indicators. Part Four contains the Statistical Annex with many comparative data on the issues covered in Part One.

Concerning Part One, analysis of macroeconomic policies reveals the need to consider core inflation and inflation expectations as main threats to stabilization, but there is also the problem of a rather high vulnerability of fiscal deficits due to political (election) cycles. Both phenomena highlight the issues of good governance. In the context of pre-election expenditures in African countries and with regard of untargeted subsidies for food and fuel fiscal deficits can easily get unmanageable. Also the sensitiveness of African countries to current account imbalances remains rather high, because of commodity price fluctuations and demand fluctuations. Most important, high unemployment rates and very high rates of youth unemployment show the need for new policy orientation – demand-side and supply-side measures are requested to tackle this problem. However, the report does not propose specific forms of employment-targeting in macroeconomic policies (as it is the theme of Unit 1 of this issue of the *African Development Perspectives Yearbook*).

Macroeconomic policies need to be embedded into a framework for growth in Africa, and more so of inclusive or pro-poor growth. However, this is not enough as also risks have to be considered according to the analysis presented. Risk management is important as global and domestic risks interact in Africa countries and create uncertainties for policymakers and for business. Concerning inclusive and pro-poor growth, the state of human development is still a problem in Africa as poverty reduction is quite slow. This is a main outcome of the Report. Growth rates are not high enough, growth originates in sectors and areas where the poor do not work and live, and growth is not reducing poverty enough because of high and even increasing inequality. Still, an inclusive growth concept is on the agenda[7], with consumption, income and inclusion coefficients combined. Bringing jobs to the areas where the poor are living and searching for rewarding work is crucial.

A new policy approach is outlined in the volume, although more implicit than explicit – considering inclusive growth and pro-poor growth, social sector development, rural and agricultural development, specific human development policies for gender equality, economic opportunities for large segments of the population, and quality increases of economic policy. Improving the quality of economic policy is related to political and economic governance, and these issues are covered strongly in the Report. The indicators which are used for analysing this theme show mixed perceptions, and it is clear that African countries have achieved progress only in some areas. Corruption is emerging as the greatest problem for improving the quality of economic policy. As with growth, poverty and income distribution as it was discussed above also in this regard the performance is mixed in Africa. This

---

[7] See for example M. H. Suryanarayana, What is Inclusive Growth? An Alternative Perspective, International Policy Centre for Inclusive Growth (IPC-IG), One pager No. 2015, June 2013.

means that the African Union (AU), the New Partnership for Africa's Development (NEPAD) and the African Peer Review Mechanism (APRM) as well as other important Pan-African institutions will have to work hard for a more balanced development process in Africa.

Although the Emerging Partner Countries are important for Africa, in terms of new options and opportunities, the *African Economic Outlook 2011* shows that all these new forms of cooperation are of advantage to African countries only if a home-grown strategy is in place so that the cooperation with the new partners does not lead to new forms of indebtedness, to the stagnation of the structural transformation process by exporting raw materials to new regions, and to the absorption of products and technologies from the emerging countries with a low potential for development. Therefore, agriculture, industry and technology policies need to be developed so as to frame the cooperation strategy properly. Also Sovereign Wealth Funds (SWFs) can be instruments to increase the policy space, as otherwise oil-exporters and other natural resource-rich countries may stick too long on the path of primary raw materials exports. It is necessary for Africa to enhance systematically the bargaining position with regard of traditional partners (USA, EU, and Japan, etc.) and emerging partners (BRIC, Turkey, South Korea, etc.). The Report outlines that the cooperation activities of the emerging partners seem to be complementary to those of the traditional partners. Negotiation strategies of African countries matter with regard of traditional and emerging partners. So far this aspect was neglected in Africa. While traditional partners are more concerned to support social sectors and governance reforms, emerging partners are more interested in infrastructure projects. However, this "division of labour" between partners must not last forever. Policy space can be increased by exploiting the comparative advantages of both groups of partners.

The tenth edition again makes it clear that the *African Economic Outlook* project has become a forum for monitoring the growth process in Africa and for identifying best practice so that sustainable policy reforms can be proposed and implemented all over Africa. The tenth edition also outlines the deeper factors for higher growth and more sustainable development in Africa over the last ten years, such as economic policy reforms, improving governance, more effective relations with donors, using new technologies more broadly, and the emergence of a new class of politicians and entrepreneurs. With its online platform – www.africaneconomicoutlook.org – the *African Economic Outlook* project is able to reach more and more decision makers in Africa and elsewhere.

It is necessary to see the wealth of information accumulated over the last ten years in the project, and it is also helpful to look at the methodology used in modelling the African economic prospects.

In the *African Economic Outlook 2010* the special focus was on *Public Resource Mobilisation and Aid to Africa*. Covered are in this section important definitions and concepts, analyses of the state of Public Resource Mobilisation, challenges for African policy makers, and Policy Options. The African Economic Outlook 2010 shows that African countries with sustained fiscal policy reforms in the past could use successfully countercyclical fiscal policy measures to combat the consequences of the global financial crisis of 2008/09. Obviously for this reason the editors of the volume presented a special survey on the role of public resource mobilisation. Public resource mobilisation can reduce the high dependence on external funds, and so also the negative impacts of global crises can be constrained. Africa had been affected during the global financial crisis by the decline of exports, foreign capital and of remittances, and it is therefore important to see how public resource mobilisation can make the country more resilient in times of crises, but also more stable in pre- and post-crises periods.

This volume of the *African Economic Outlook* for 2010 and also the other volumes of the *African Economic Outlook* were all reviewed in various issues of the *African Development Perspectives Yearbook*, and also the *African Economic Outlook* methodology for modelling economic perspectives for Africa was considered in these reviews.

Specific topics were covered also in the other Reports: the major theme in the *African Economic Outlook 2009* was *Innovation and ICT in Africa; Technical and Vocational Skills Development* was the special theme in the *African Economic Outlook 2007/2008; Drinking Water and Sanitation* was the special theme in the *African Economic Outlook 2006/2007*. In the *African Economic Outlook 2005/2006* the crucial issues of *Transport Infrastructure Development* in Africa were discussed. In the *African Economic Outlook 2004/2005* the key issue introduced was the *Financing of Small and Medium-sized Enterprises*. In the *African Economic Outlook 2003/2004* a discussion of another important key policy issue for Africa was presented – *Energy Sector Policies*, and the interaction of energy and poverty issues was analysed. The first two *African Economic Outlook* reports for *2001/2002* and *2002/2003* did not contain specific themes, but were already discussing some structural issues of African countries. A gradual improvement and strengthening of the project can be observed. With all these special themes which were discussed in the various volumes, a wealth of information about important policy issues was presented. The gradual enlargement of the number of countries which are considered with Notes and Surveys in the *African Economic Outlook* is also an important improvement to the overall Yearbook project. This means that the special theme is related to more and more country surveys; this allows it to compare the country position with regard of a specific policy issue. As an example, the *African Economic Outlook 2011* contains country-by-country information about the role of emerging partners. The Statistical Annex in Part Four allows it to further deepen the view on the country case by comparative data. The Methodology for all these tables is carefully explained. The Statistical Annex is valuable as it is including a selection of very important economic, social, and political data for African countries. The extension to various governance indicators is helpful; the comparisons with economic and social data for the country are revealing.

An explicit aim for the *African Economic Outlook* is the analysis of the trends and of the short-term evolution of selected African countries by using a unique analytical model design for all country case studies. The common framework includes a forecasting exercise for the current and the following two years by using a simple macroeconomic model, while the results are related to analyses of the social and political situation in Africa. Mainly policymakers, donor agencies, academic experts, and business people are benefitting from these analyses. A problem with the *African Economic Outlook* is the fact that the background to the modelling work is not explained more deeply. Reference was made to a standard macroeconomic model called Africalook (see the short description of the prediction models in the African Economic Outlook 2001/2002, p. 19). It is argued that the specific structural peculiarities of the countries are also considered in this framework. The African Development Bank (AfDB) has now some lead role in this exercise, and seems to have further developed the model. The modelling for the OECD Economic Outlook is used to forecast world demand as well as the prices of the non-traditional imports and exports being of relevance for the particular African countries that are included in the form of case studies, while predictions of the (traditional) raw materials prices come from World Bank sources.

A much greater problem is it that there are two important competing reports coming from Africa, the *African Development Report* from the African Development Bank (AfDB) and the *Economic Report on Africa* from the UN Economic Commission for Africa (UNECA) and the African Union (AU). Therefore it is not yet clear to what extent the joint project *African Economic Outlook* of the OECD, the AfDB, the UNDP and the UNECA really can contribute to a better understanding of Africa's development, and what the comparative advantage of the three reports on Africa really is, as also the other reports present analyses, forecasts, special themes, regional economic profiles, and country case studies. Both, the *African Development Report* of the AfDB and the *Economic Report on Africa* of the UNECA and the AU are very rich in analyses, in forecasts, in policy recommendations, and in informative special themes, regional economic profiles and country cases. It may be that a new division of labour emerges over time with regard to the three reports. However, the publicity around the *African Economic Outlook* is huge and so the other two reports are overshadowed (although their content is rich). It could be that a new division of labour which is based on comparative advantages is envisaged; it could be that the *African Economic Outlook* focuses on country reports and on specific policy themes of relevance for donors, the *African Development Report* on key policy reforms for Africa and major development financing issues from the side of the African Development Bank, and the *Economic Report on Africa* on sector problems and regional integration issues (although some of these issues are covered in specific programmes on strengthening regional economic communities).

But, compared with earlier reports of the *African Economic Outlook*, the messages from the more recent ones are much clearer and stronger – the focus on international assistance strategies for Africa is stronger, structural impediments and solutions to Africa's development problems are highlighted more deeply, more and more country reviews are included, the comparability of country cases is strengthened, and the relevance of the presented data and of the forecasts has improved. The specific policy field that is covered – in this Report the role of emerging partners for Africa – is always important and the analysis is to the point, and so the information presented is useful for further analyses and for projections. The researchers on country notes and surveys give information for the specific theme and provide recommendations for donors. It may however be quite important to work further on a clear division of labour between these three reports, in order to strengthen them as instruments for policy assessment and reform at the international, regional and national levels.

The *African Economic Outlook* can play a great role if the new trends in global development cooperation with Africa are reflected even more in the context of the annual focus theme of the *African Economic Outlook*, and as well in the frame of the recommendations for policies of the specific African country cases that are considered and reviewed. The *African Economic Outlook* is highlighting the development cooperation issues in general and also with regard to specific structural, policy, and infrastructure development issues. So the country cases highlight now more than in the past the role of national priorities and policies and the development assistance implications of macroeconomic policies and sector development policies. The issues of aid dependency and the debt problems of the countries are also reflected, as well as the objectives, means and strategies for improving aid assistance to these countries. This is where the basic competences of the OECD policy departments, of the OECD/DAC forums, and of the OECD Development Centre really lie, and this vast knowledge should be utilised properly. It should also be made quite clear that the *African Economic Outlook* is a joint OECD-Africa project with considerable and fast increasing African inputs and additional inputs from UN organisations, like the UNDP. This is not so clear and obvious from the image and the logo of the presented volumes of the *African Economic Outlook*. The inputs coming from Africa – towards making possible and relevant these informative volumes – are becoming greater, and this can be made better visible in the format and the layout of the Reports. So it would be better to show that these are really joint OECD/Africa reports and not just OECD reports on Africa which were assisted by some African institutions.

Karl Wohlmuth, Bremen

African Development Bank Group, *Bank Group Policy on Program-Based Operations,* **Operational Resources and Policies Department, February 2012, Tunis: African Development Bank Group, no ISBN/ISSN, pages: 22+8 annexes.**

Africa has severely been affected by the international financial crises. The African Development Bank Group has responded by offering among other means to mitigate the impact of the current economic framework an instrument called program-based operations. The policy is perceived as an appropriate instrument to provide financial resources and to a minor degree technical assistance. It is intended to promote economic growth, social stability, eradication of poverty and ecological balances on the continent.

The strategy implies mainly a strong ownership of the recipient countries, a logical framework which defines targets and action and a risk management. The Bank will pursue a close harmonization with other donors and embeds its operations into the national policies. The guidelines are flexible to be designed to the needs of fragile and crisis states on the one hand and imply for all parties being involved a long-term approach which prevents short-term interventions.

The paper is produced as a manual for policy makers in the bank as well as in African states and in the donors' community. The concept should be positively assessed because the procedures being recommended stress the need of internal adjustments in African countries as well as a flexible response to changes in the international financial markets. The conditions to be met by the recipient countries define a strong institutional economic and financial decision-making and implementation capacity. The envisaged policy option is elaborated to the specific conditions in the African continent.

Karl Wolfgang Menck, Hamburg

African Development Bank Group, *Development Effectiveness Review 2012, Thematic review: Promoting Regional Integration,* **Tunis: African Development Bank Group, no ISBN/ISSN, pages: 47.**

African states have for a long time defined regional cooperation as a means of development policy and economic growth, and there are some examples which indicate the political commitment of states in West Africa and in Eastern Africa. Special concern to establish and to enhance regional cooperation has been negotiated in the Cotonou Agreement and its preceding trade, development and political treaties. However, these efforts did not provide results which were expected by the international donor community and by the participating governments.

The thematic review focusing indicates the commitment of the bank referring to regional cooperation. The program includes setting up infrastructure connections and development corridors, the strengthening of regional industrial policy and the development of new regional development strategies. The conclusions are elaborated in the report which outlines the state of art of regional trade flows, energy transmission and distribution, water facilitation and sanitation, agriculture and food production and human capital development. An assessment of the regional policies defines as critical inputs national administrative, institutional and financial capacities being inappropriate to meet the challenges of regional cooperation. Furthermore a sufficient knowledge management in the participating states is needed. Further principles for future actions are deducted from the Paris Declaration: ownership, alignment, harmonization, managing the results and accountability. The paper stresses the necessity to substitute national policies in African states by a different policy approach which focusses regional policies. The report defines technical assistance as a complementary part of financial commitments within the regional policy strategies as NEPAD.

The Bank's paper is helpful as a comprehensive survey of the regional cooperation in Africa and a well-founded deduction of policy needs. In the context of former publications on regional cooperation in Africa, the report adds to the state of art of thinking and invites policy makers to hamper their efforts in extending regional cooperation in Africa.

Karl Wolfgang Menck, Hamburg

International Monetary Fund (IMF), *Regional Economic Outlook Sub-Saharan Africa, Sustaining Growth amid Global Uncertainty,* **April 2012, World Economic and Financial Surveys, Washington D. C.: IMF 2012 Publication Classification Details: ISBN-13: 978-1-61635-249-3, pages: 137.**
Web Access:
http://www.imf.org/external/pubs/ft/reo/2012/afr/eng/sreo0412.pdf

The Report contains four chapters. In chapter 1 there is a view on the global economy as affecting Africa in the years 2012 and 2013. The global economic opportunities are mentioned. Also the downside risks revealed by the projections are mentioned. It comes out that still the African growth process is robust despite of huge differences by regions and countries. In chapter 2 the impact of Global Financial Stress on Sub-Saharan African Banking Systems are discussed. Despite of considerable resilience shown by African banking systems during and after the global crises, the rapid spread of pan-African banking groups across countries in Africa (and probably also globally) means that the speed of internationalization is outpacing the supervisory capacity of the nation-states in Africa. A lot has to be done to improve the banking supervisory capacity by nation-states, the Regional Economic Communities (RECs) and even Africa-wide. In chapter 3 the problems of the Africa region's natural resource exporters are analysed. Although natural resources are important for close to half of the 45 countries in sub-Saharan Africa, the share of resource exports that accrues to national budgets varies widely across countries, thereby creating a lot of economic management problems. Because of high rents, oil exporters are the most successful resource exporters in terms of revenue extraction. However, the problem is volatility as a factor impeding economic management. The countries with considerable fiscal revenues from natural resources experience a much higher volatility in exports, revenue, and also in non-resource GDP growth than other African countries. Economic management could prevent negative effects from this volatility. But, fiscal policy is still pro-cyclical and many policy actions have to be undertaken to overcome this trend (such as medium-term fiscal planning, permanent income expenditure policy, and sovereign wealth funds for macroeconomic stabilization and inter-generational equity by providing funds for future generations. There are also a Statistical Appendix and References in the Report. Also the Publications of the IMF African Department are listed for the years 2009-2011. The Report is informative and complements the various other important reports on Africa which are as well reviewed in this volume of the *African Development Perspectives Yearbook.*

Karl Wohlmuth, Bremen

International Monetary Fund (IMF), *Regional Economic Outlook Sub-Saharan Africa, Building Momentum in a Multi-Speed World,* **May 2013, World Economic and Financial Surveys, Washington D. C.: IMF 2013 Publication Classification Details: ISBN-13: 978-1-48436-515-1, pages: 117.**
Web Access:
http://www.imf.org/external/pubs/ft/reo/2013/afr/eng/sreo0513.pdf

This Report contains 4 chapters. In Chapter 1 the projections for the global economy and for Sub-Saharan Africa (SSA) until 2013-14 are presented. External and internal risk factors are discussed. The downside risks are substantial, coming from inside and outside sources; outside factors, like the Eurozone crisis and growth reductions in emerging economies, and inside factors, like climatic developments and internal conflict in Africa, may be relevant. Policy space is considered as important for SSA, and countries are advised to build up policy buffers so as to handle adverse shocks. Fiscal space can be widened if opportunities are there as resulting from the global and the regional African situation. In Chapter 2 the ways and means to strengthen the fiscal policy space are discussed. While public debt is not a problem in most SSA countries as limiting fiscal space, it may be difficult to finance larger deficits in the case of an economic downturn. The constraint is the small domestic financial market, so that this issue of underdeveloped financial markets has to be addressed by adequate long-term policy measures. However, most countries in SSA can increase the fiscal space by expenditure rationalization and revenue mobilization programmes. Aid can also play a role in capacity-building for undertaking such reforms. In Chapter 3 the issuing of international sovereign bonds is discussed. The advantages and risks of issuing such bonds are discussed while considering also the broader fiscal policy considerations. Medium-term debt management strategies should be the base for examining such financing options. It comes out that not all sectors and projects can be financed by such bonds when looking at the medium-term finance and debt plan. In Chapter 4 reforms with regard of energy subsidies are discussed. As these subsidies are commanding a huge share of the budget expenditures in so many African countries (not only in low-income countries but as well so in middle-income countries) and as they are not well targeted (favouring to a large extent the well-off population) reforms are urgently needed so as to create fiscal space for public investment and key social expenditures. Political economy of reform considerations are needed in order to introduce and implement successfully these reforms. Successes depend on a gradual phasing-in of such reforms, on well-targeted mitigating measures for the poor, and on a reform of the state-owned enterprises in the energy sector. In most cases of failure with regard of such reforms, one or even all the three elements of successful action were not built in. So, this Report is tackling all the issues of increasing policy space and fiscal space. The issue of successful and well-targeted reforms of energy subsidies is a good example what should be done to increase the fiscal space and how it could be implemented. As Africa has gained a lot from such a fiscal space during and after the global financial crisis of 2008-09, it is wise to move in this direction with balanced reforms.

There are also a Statistical Appendix and References in the Report. Also the Publications of the IMF African Department are listed for the years 2009-2013. The Report is informative, readable and complements the various other important reports on Africa which are as well reviewed in this volume of the *African Development Perspectives Yearbook*.

Karl Wohlmuth, Bremen

IMF (International Monetary Fund), *Regional Economic Outlook UPDATE,* **May 2013, Middle East and Central Asia Department, Washington D. C.: International Monetary Fund 2013, pages: 15, Middle East and Central Asia Department, pages: 15. Web Access: http://www.imf.org/external/pubs/ft/reo/2013/mcd/eng/mreo0513.htm**

The Regional Economic Outlook (REO) Update 2013 gives evidence also on the countries in Northern Africa, although countries in the Middle East, Afghanistan, and Pakistan, and countries in Caucasus and in Central Asia are part of the whole Report. It is mentioned in the Update of REO 2013 that two years after the "Arab Spring" commenced, many countries of the Middle East and North Africa (MENAP/abbreviation for Middle East, North Africa, Afghanistan and Pakistan) region are still undergoing complex political, social, and economic transitions. It is also argued that economic performance was mixed in 2012. Although – according to the Report – most of the region's oil-exporting countries grew at healthy rates, economic growth remained sluggish in the countries being oil importers. In 2013, these differences are expected to narrow down because of a scaling-back of hydrocarbon production among oil exporters and a mild economic recovery among oil importers. However, there are considerable differences between countries. Many countries face the immediate challenge of re-establishing or maintaining macroeconomic stability amid political uncertainty and social unrest. The example of Egypt shows that political instability is even accelerating and that the economic consequences are severe. Beyond of this state of affairs, the region must not lose sight of the medium-term challenge of diversifying its economies, creating jobs, and generating more inclusive growth.

The report is containing informative tables with many comparative data considering MENAP oil-exporting countries (in Africa: Algeria, Libya) and MENAP oil-importing countries (in Africa: Djibouti, Egypt, Mauritania, Morocco, Sudan, Tunisia). Most of the MENAP countries in Africa are oil-importers and these countries are affected not only by high political instability but also by major economic and social imbalances. The Report is providing relevant comparative data and valuable information on two groups of countries (oil-exporters and oil-importers).

Karl Wohlmuth, Bremen

IMF (International Monetary Fund), *Regional Economic Outlook Middle East and Central Asia*, **November 2012, World Economic and Financial Surveys, Middle East and Central Asia Department, Washington D. C.: International Monetary Fund, November 2012, pages: 131, International Monetary Fund, Middle East and Central Asia Department, Publication Classification Details: ISBN: 978-1-47551-081-2 Web Access: http://www.imf.org/external/pubs/ft/reo/2012/mcd/eng/pdf/mreo1112.pdf**

This Report is of importance for assessing the situation in MENAP (Middle East, North Africa, Afghanistan and Pakistan). Regrettably North Africa is bundled together with so many Asian countries, while the Regional Economic Outlook by the IMF on Sub-Saharan Africa covers only this group of countries, but not the Northern African countries. The Regional Economic Outlook Report on Middle East and Central Asia covers the MENAP (Middle East, North Africa, Afghanistan and Pakistan) countries and also the CCA (Caucasus and Central Asia) countries. To have a complete picture on Africa, the IMF's Regional Economic Outlook on Sub-Saharan Africa and the IMF's Regional Economic Outlook Middle East and central Asia have to be studied.

The REO 2012 on Middle East and Central Asia is documenting the developments in the MENAP Oil Exporters and in the MENAP Oil Importers in separate chapters. This is a useful distinction as the two groups of countries have quite different economic problems. The discussion about the MENAP Oil Exporters is supplemented by informative Annexes, like an Annex on The Natural Gas Market so as to look at the perspectives, and an Annex on Inward Spillovers to MENA Countries from a GDP Shock in G3 Countries (China, USA, and the Euro Area). The discussion about MENAP Oil Importers is supplemented by an Annex on MENAP and CCA Countries as Highly Vulnerable to Food Price Hikes.

The Report is warning the MENAP oil exporters on severe risks from large drops of oil prices; such price changes would affect the fiscal balance severely. So for the MENAP oil exporters the advice is to look carefully at the potential fiscal problems and also at inflation trends. The Report argues also for strong reforms towards more inclusive growth. For the MENAP oil importers a rather pessimistic outlook is presented, as reserve buffers are diminished, expenditures for food and fuel subsidies are rising, and fiscal positions are deteriorating. There is also a mixed record on financial sector performance. Because of high and increasing downside risks, a careful macroeconomic management is needed, but there is also urgent need for structural reforms to enhance inclusive growth.

There are also sections such as a Statistical Appendix, References and a List of IMF Publications on the Middle East and Central Asia for 2011 – 2012 in the Report.

The Report covers seven African countries (Morocco, Tunisia, Mauritania, Algeria, Libya, Egypt, and Sudan). African oil exporters are Algeria and Libya, and the other five African countries are classified as oil importers (Sudan as well, because in July 9, 2011 South Sudan became independent and this country owns he major share of the oil reserves of the former unified Sudan).

In the section MENAP Highlights crucial messages for the oil exporters and for the oil importers are mentioned. For the oil exporters, the major issue is fiscal planning as a large drop of oil prices will reduce sharply the fiscal buffers to withstand oil price volatility. Medium-term fiscal planning on the basis of a Permanent Income and Expenditure Approach (PIEA) and an Oil Fund for Stabilization and Intergenerational Equity (OFSIE) is important in order to manage savings, consumption and investment wisely in the oil exporting countries. For oil importers, the high public debt level at more than 70 per cent of the GDP is seen as a major problem, so that the overall fiscal vulnerabilities are high. Fiscal breakeven prices in the oil exporting countries and high public debt ratios in the oil importing countries are critical variables in macroeconomic management.

Karl Wohlmuth, Bremen

Trade Law Centre (Tralac), *Monetary Union: the Experience of the Euro and the Lessons to be learned for the African (SADC) Monetary Union,* **Colin McCarthy, March 2012, Tralac working paper no. S12WP02/2012, Stellenbosch: Tralac, no. ISBN/ISSN, pages: 32.**

The working paper deals with the declared intention of the African Union (AU) and other regional integration arrangements such as the Southern African Development Community (SADC) to evolve into a monetary union in the final stages of linear regional integration. In the latter regard the Eurozone was widely considered to be a role model of monetary integration and an exercise that could and should be replicated in Africa.

The sceptical views expressed in the paper were not based on inherent weaknesses of the euro as regional currency. The euro was accepted to be a stellar phenomenon in European integration. The argument was that conditions in Southern Africa and Africa as a continent did not meet the requisite conditions for successful monetary integration such as macroeconomic convergence, which was a fundamental building block of the Eurozone, and furthermore, that in regions of disparate economies exposed to diverse external shocks a loss of policy space in exchange and interest rate determination would be inappropriate.

Recent developments in the Eurozone, however, have revealed that the euro construct has fundamental weaknesses which strengthen the argument that monetary union is a step in the process of regional integration that calls for extreme caution. Hence, this paper extends the argument in support of caution in deciding on monetary union by emphasizing certain conditions that the euro crisis has revealed as crucial for monetary union to work. The role model, which started out with acclaim, has in its operation exposed certain structural weaknesses in design. These weaknesses and the conditions for successful union that they imply add more stumbling blocks in the way of achieving monetary union in an African setting.

After the introduction in section 1, section 2 briefly defines monetary union within the context of the linear model of regional integration, which places it in a particular sequence of deeper integration. In section 3, attention is given to two monetary integration arrangements in Africa – the Common Monetary Area (CMA) in Southern Africa and the CFA (Communauté Financière Africaine) franc of francophone Africa – that have their roots in colonial history. It is argued that these two arrangements cannot be offered as evidence that monetary union can work in Africa. Section 4 deals with the benefits and costs and the conditions of success of an optimized currency area. Sections 5 and 6 discuss the recent Euro experiences and the lessons that can be learned for African policy makers. A conclusion is presented in section 6 stating that it is unlikely that African countries will meet the above mentioned conditions.

Achim Gutowski, Bremen

Society For International Development (SID), *The State of East Africa 2012: Deepening Integration, Intensifying Challenges,* **2012, Nairobi: SID, ISBN: 978-9966029 102, pages: 100.**

The Society for International Development (SID) is an international nongovernmental network of individuals and organizations founded in 1957 to promote social justice and foster democratic participation. Through locally driven international programmes and activities, SID strengthens collective empowerment and facilitates dialogue and knowledge-sharing worldwide. In addressing issues from a multi-disciplinary perspective the Society emphasises systemic and long-term approaches with a central focus on institutional and social transformation. SID has 39 chapters and 3,000 members in 50 countries. Its secretariat is located in Rome, Italy and it operates a Regional Office for Eastern Africa based in Nairobi, Kenya.

The report 2012 seeks to answer the following main questions: firstly, what are the facts about different social, economic, political, cultural and technological transitions currently taking place in East Africa? The report responses by compiling, packaging and presenting a wide range of facts and figures on the East African countries Tanzania, Kenya, Uganda, Rwanda and Burundi. The objective is to present a wide range of information that is easily accessible to the region's decision-makers and its ordinary citizens. Secondly, what hidden trends and narratives can be extrapolated from the data? The data essentially summarize important social, economic and political challenges as well as opportunities that the region faces. The report uses national-level data to provide insight and analysis on what implications they have for regional integration. Thirdly, the report seeks to inform and encourage a collective process of critical and creative thinking about the different ways in which emerging trends might shape the future of the East African region. While the report presents national statistics, it tries as much as possible to paint a regional picture by aggregating national data, analysing regional trends and comparing countries with each other to reveal the range of experiences and outcomes across East Africa.

Fourthly, the debate about the purpose, pace and outcomes of East Africa's regional integration is intensifying. This report contributes to that debate by providing some evidence, analysis and a common fact base on which to base the discourse.

The report encompasses seven main chapters with specific overarching themes. Within each chapter, it analyses specific trends that have occurred in the region over the past six to seven years. After an introduction and key insights in chapter 1, chapter 2 deals with the people in East Africa; namely population profiles, population density, urbanization and migration topics. Chapter 3 is about the natural resource base such as land use, food and agriculture and water resources and fisheries. Chapter 4 covers human development and poverty; healthcare, maternal and child health; life expectancy rates; and educational topics. Chapter 5 is about infrastructure in East Africa: the road network, non-tariff barriers, railways, pipelines, airports, ports and energy sources and use. Chapter 6 for the economic profile includes topics such as size, structure and performance of the economy, trends in foreign financing, volume and direction of trade, public finance profiles as well as labour and employment. Finally, chapter 7 called politics and government covers the political and institutional structures, corruption and political freedom, military and conflicts and internally displaced people in East Africa.

Achim Gutowski, Bremen

Friedrich-Ebert-Foundation; Centre for Conflict Resolution (CCR), *The African Union at Ten. Aspirations and Reality,* **2012, policy brief no. 13, Cape Town: CCR, no ISBN/ISSN, pages: 7.**

The Centre for Conflict Resolution (CCR), Cape Town, South Africa's latest policy brief is based on a colloquium jointly hosted by the CCR and the Friedrich-Ebert-Foundation (FES-Stiftung), Berlin/Germany from 30 to 31 August 2012 in Berlin.

The colloquium analysed the African Union's (AU) achievements and challenges and crafted concrete recommendations to strengthen its effectiveness. The meeting considered the history of the AU and reviewed the ten years since the implementation of its peace and security architecture. It compared the regional integration efforts of the AU and the European Union (EU), assessed its strategies to achieve socio-economic development and reviewed the AU's global role.

Ten key policy recommendations emerged from the Berlin Colloquium that were summarized in the policy brief.

Achim Gutowski, Bremen

Arab Spring Economies in North Africa

UNDP (United Nations Development Programme), *Arab Development Challenges Report 2011, Towards The Developmental State In The Arab Region,* Cairo: United Nations Development Programme, Regional Centre for Arab States, Cairo: 2011, pages: 172, Location of Office: 1191 Corniche El Nil, World Trade Centre, Boulac, Cairo, Egypt; for more information: http://arabstates.undp.org/
Copyright 2011, UNDP
Web Access: http://204.200.211.31/Update_Feb_2012/ADCR_En_%208-2-2012.pdf

This *Arab Development Challenges Report 2011* was produced by a Task Force to respond timely to the "Arab Spring" events in African Arab states and in Near East Arab states. The Task Force was led by the United Nations Development Programme's Regional Center in Cairo (RCC). The core team was composed of experts and staff from RCC's Poverty and Governance Practices Department. The report is the result of a fruitful collaboration between the UNDP, ILO, FAO, OXFAM and other leading regional and international experts. The main intention was it to influence the public debate in the Arab countries on governance reforms and to inform interested circles in donor countries. The Report follows the first one which was published jointly with the League of Arab States (LAS) and was endorsed by the Arab Economic and Social Development Summit in 2009.

There are Overview and Scope and Methodology sections. The Part One is on Arab Development Challenges containing sections on Human Development and Human Poverty; Money Metric Poverty and Expenditure Inequality; Growth and Structural Transformation; Employment, Social Protection and Fiscal Policy; and Water Security, Food Security and Climate Change. Part Two is on Understanding and Responding to Aspirations For Dignity, with sections on Facets of Exclusion Across the Region; Governance Deficits Perpetuating Exclusion; Towards Accountable States with Inclusive Participation; Supporting Sectoral and Local Level Initiatives; Regional Integration; and What Can be Done Now?. In Part Three on Promises and Challenges of the Arab Spring some summary views are presented and some projections are given. The Report also contains a Bibliography and References section and an Annex Tables section. All this gives the impression that the Report is well-researched.

The Report is definitely of great relevance to understand the causes of the uprisings in Tunisia and in Egypt, and elsewhere, and there is a lot of material presented to substantiate the hypotheses why the uprisings have occurred at a particular point in time). The lack of job creation in a period of economic growth and the extent of youth unemployment in Arab countries play a great role in such explanations, as well as misleading poverty and income distribution measurement in the region which may have led to an underestimation of the extent of exclusion from participation in governance. There is also some action-oriented agenda in the Report to show what can be done in the short-term, the medium-term and the long-term to address the issues, although this part is less strong than the analytic parts. New data are generated for the Report with new methodologies to measure progress in human development, human poverty and income inequality in the Arab countries. This is valuable as it adds to the explanation of the "Arab Spring" events. African countries are grouped in the Report in the Maghreb Countries group (Algeria, Libya, Morocco, and Tunisia), the Mashreq Countries group (Egypt), and the LDC/Least Developed Countries group (Comoros, Djibouti, Mauritania, Somalia, and Sudan), so that in total ten African countries are covered as Arab states in the Report. Two years after the "Arab Spring" events the politics of improving inclusion in Arab states so as to overcome exclusion from participation in society and economy seems to be the main problem; recent events show the difficulties of organizing a broader economic, social and political participation in these countries.

The Report gives a lot of comparative information which is important for further researches, and for best practice work in policy reforms. Because of the importance of the Report, the editors of the *African Development Perspectives Yearbook* have invited members of the Task Force to contribute to Volume 16 with an essay on Understanding the Causes of the Arab Spring so as to complement the essays on the "Arab Spring" countries Egypt and Tunisia (see Unit 2 in this Volume).

Karl Wohlmuth, Bremen

African Development Bank Group, *Unlocking North Africa's Potential through Regional Integration, Challenges and Opportunities,* **Edited by Emanuele Santi/Saoussen Ben Romdhane and William Shaw, Tunis-Belvedere 2012, pages: 186.**
Publication Classification Details: ISBN 978-9973-071-89-7
Web Access:
http://www.afdb.org/fileadmin/uploads/afdb/Documents/Project-and-Operations/Unlocking%20North%20Africa%20RI%20ENG%20FINAL.pdf

The report *Unlocking North Africa's Potential through Regional Integration, Challenges and Opportunities* is to some extent a shocking one. The degree of regional integration among North African countries is the lowest in the world as intra-regional trade accounts for less than 4% of total trade; and also other facets of regional integration in North Africa are very much underdeveloped. The Report is a stock-taking exercise for six countries (Tunisia, Morocco, Algeria, Egypt, Libya, and Mauritania) and for six areas of importance for regional integration (energy sector; climate change and the environment; financial sector; transport infrastructure and trade facilitation; human development; and information and communication technologies). The economic opportunities of a deeper integration with regard of these six areas are presented in great detail. Many economic problems can be solved: growth and structural transformation can be accelerated; employment creation, income redistribution, and poverty reduction can be speeded up; infrastructure can be built up region-wide; conflict prevention and peaceful coexistence will be grounded on development progress. All this can be the outcome of new and effective regional integration policies.

However, there are so many constraints. The countries are members of different regional integration groupings; the countries are locked-in by various and divergent cooperation agreements with the economies of the European Union. Also, these countries have unsolved political problems which divide the North African region politically, such as the West Sahara problem between Morocco and Algeria. But, there is no escape to follow a new route towards regional integration in order to solve the major problems in the region, like youth unemployment and human poverty.

The Report is of great relevance for policymakers in these countries and also for policymakers in European partner countries as it is shown quite drastically that the path of the past decades cannot be continued in North Africa. The "Arab Spring" countries need a deep regional integration in order to attack just the causes of the uprisings (lack of employment prospects, lack of larger markets, lack of migration possibilities, lack of cooperation in infrastructure and public services provision, lack of common regional integration strategies, etc.). The Report is a wake-up call for policymakers in North African countries.

Karl Wohlmuth, Bremen

AfDB (African Development Bank)/OECD Development Centre (Development Centre of the Organization for Economic Co-operation and Development)/UNDP (United Nations Development Programme)/UNECA (United Nations Economic Commission for Africa), *African Economic Outlook 2012, Regional Edition – North African Countries (Algeria, Egypt, Libya, Mauritania, Morocco, and Tunisia),* **Paris: OECD 2012, pages: 88. Web Access: http://www.africaneconomicoutlook.org/fileadmin/uploads/aeo/PDF/Regi onal_Edition/AEO%20North%20Africa%20Outlook%20EN.pdf**

The *African Economic Outlook 2012, Regional Edition North African Countries* contains an Overview section and sections with the Country Surveys for these six countries. While the *African Economic Outlook* for all of Africa (see the reviews in this Unit) contains only short Country Notes, this *Regional Edition North African Countries* has full Country Surveys along the entries accessible in the online edition at: www.africaneconomicoutlook.org/en.

There is an Overview section, a section Recent Developments & Prospects, a section on Macroeconomic Policy, a section on Economic & Political Governance, a section on Social Context & Human Development, and a section on the Thematic Analysis: Promoting Youth Employment. This Regional Edition is helpful and useful for policymakers, for the research community and for donor institutions. Together with the reports from the Arab regional institutions and the UN regional offices (League of Arab States, Regional Centres of UNDP, ILO, etc.) and from the (North African) Regional Economic Communities, this edition presents evidence on further reform necessities and gives information about short-term economic prospects of these six countries. Three Regional Economic Communities (RECs) matter for these six states: the Arab Maghreb Union (AMU) with all the countries except Egypt, the Common Market for the Eastern and Southern Africa (COMESA) with Egypt, and the Community of Sahel-Saharan states (CEN-SAD) with all countries except Algeria. The RECs may become in the future important drivers of North African economic progress. So far the RECs with North African countries as members have worked far below their potential for these countries.

Karl Wohlmuth, Bremen

Samir Amin, *The People's Spring, The Future of the Arab Revolution,* **2012, Oxford: Pambazuka Press, ISBN-10: 085749 1156, pages: vi-204.**

The 2011 outburst of uprisings by the Arab peoples caught the world's attention. But can the "Arab Spring" live up to the hopes invested in it? The author's analysis shows that although this "spring" coincides with the "autumn" of capitalism, the current Arab uprisings are primarily anti-imperialist and not anti-capitalist movements. To take control of shaping their future, people in Arab countries need to avoid a retreat into Islamization to unify in a positive and genuinely new alternative for secular democracy, and struggle alongside other people against both capitalism and imperialism.

Chapter 1 is called An Arab springtime?, chapter 2 deals with the Middle East as a turntable of the ancient world system, chapter 3 is named The decline: the Mameluke state, the miscarriage of Nahda and political Islam. Chapter 4 is about a leap forward: the Bandung era and Arab popular nationalisms. Chapter 5 handles the drift of the national popular project toward's "recompradorising". The last chapter concludes.

According to the author, if workers in the imperial centers increase the resulting alliance this could lead to a transition towards socialism. Alternatively capitalism's decline could pull humanity into widespread barbarity. There are powerful forces pulling in this direction: the US/NATO project for military control of the planet, the decline of democracy in the imperialist countries and the rejection of democracy by religious fundamentalists in countries of the South. The 2011 uprisings offer a glimpse of an alternative future. But the challenge is huge, not only for the Arab and Islamic world but also for all the radical left, in the South and the North. The events currently taking place become comprehensible, enabling people to face up to their challenges, only understanding them in the long run.

Achim Gutowski, Bremen

Post-Conflict Countries in Africa

Benjamin Leo/Vijaya Ramachandran/Ross Thuotte, *Supporting Private Business Growth in African Fragile States, A Guiding Framework for the World Bank Group in South Sudan and Other Nations,* **Center for Global Development/CGD, Washington D. C.: Center for Global Development/CGD 2012, pages: 112**
Publication Classification Details: ISBN 978-1-933286-68-6
Web Access:
http://www.cgdev.org/files/1426061_file_Leo_Ramachandran_Thuotte_f ragile_states_FINAL.pdf

This is a useful study as private sector development is considered as of crucial importance for fragile states. Conflict prevention and conflict management are viewed as being largely associated with greater economy activity. When employment increases via more private sector development there is a great chance to preserve peace and to avoid new rounds of violent conflict. The reason is simple. The public sector cannot take over the tasks of employment creation and of securing livelihoods in such countries – because of institutional weaknesses and severe resource constraints. The state can only initiate some public works programmes and create an enabling environment for private sector activity. This is so even in countries like South Sudan which are rich in oil reserves and have high oil revenues (if oil then regularly flows to the export market, what is not the case in South Sudan since January 2012). In such countries the public sector is using large shares of public expenditures for security (defense, police, militias, intelligence, etc.) and for administration (wages and salaries), but not so much for infrastructure and other preconditions of private sector development (PSD). Especially the agriculture and manufacturing sectors are weak and are not promoted strongly by the governments of such fragile countries.

The study starts with an Executive Summary and an Overview Chapter 1. Chapter 2 is on Private sector development in fragile states, Chapter 3 is on Constraints to business growth in African fragile states, Chapter 4 is on Government priorities in fragile states, Chapter 5 is on the theme What works – proven PSD successes in fragile states, and chapter 6 is on the Country case study – South Sudan. In chapter 7 the Conclusions are presented. There are also useful Appendixes on specific issues and further case studies (as on Zimbabwe and Somaliland). The main methodological approach is firstly, to look at the binding constraints to PSD as seen by the firms, then secondly, to investigate into the government priorities towards PSD support, and thirdly, to analyze which of the donor projects and programmes have worked and why (out of the various bilateral and multilateral projects and programmes). If there is a correspondence of the three levels, then the PSD strategy will work in fragile states. For South Sudan, there is not such a correspondence. The problem in South Sudan is that the binding constraints like electricity supply and finance are not reflected in government priorities (as only the urban firms get some infrastructure support and have some access to finance). The study uses a minimal list of 14 fragile countries, based on IDA Resource Allocation Index (IRAI) scores between 2005 and 2009.

Although the study is quite general in the analysis and interpretation of outcomes, the Report is valuable and should guide further work by donors in such countries.

Karl Wohlmuth, Bremen

European Communities, Robert Schuman Centre for Advanced Studies, European University Institute, San Domenico di Fiesole, *European Report on Development 2009, Overcoming Fragility in Africa, Forging A New European Approach*, Brussels: European Communities 2009, pages: 164 Web Access: http://ec.europa.eu/europeaid/what/development-policies/research-development/documents/erd_report_2009_en.pdf

This Report is part of the European Union's activities to develop new concepts for development aid towards post-conflict and fragile countries. The list of fragile countries is much longer than in other studies – 29 countries of Sub-Saharan Africa (SSA) were included, and these countries were selected on the basis of various indicators of fragility (indicators on policy reform, on state weakness, and on foreign policy issues). The Report analyses the costs and characteristics of fragility, the capacity of fragile states to cope with negative shocks (such as the global financial crisis of 2008/09), and the EU policies towards such countries. Major issue is how to build up resilience in such countries so as to be able to act in times of crisis and to react timely to internal and external shocks (whatever the sources of such events may be). In order to improve aid policies, a deep knowledge of the characteristics of such countries is needed. Although there are common structural characteristics of such countries, there is also a great heterogeneity to be observed among such countries. For this reason the Report had been structured in this way.

The new EU approach towards fragile countries should be constructed on the basis of this knowledge gained. The many weaknesses of EU development policy (lack of policy coherence, lack of coordination, lack of long term perspective, lack of resource transfer stability, etc.) are mentioned, and a long-term approach is recommended. It is obvious that with so many fragile countries (more than half of the countries in SSA being fragile!), a new approach is inevitable to achieve something with the considerable aid volumes. Regrettably, not much has been learned since 2009 from these insights as still the EU development policy is fragmented, uncoordinated, incoherent, short-term, and not building up resilience in the many fragile countries in SSA. Four key priority issues are mentioned but it does not seem that any improvements with regard of EU policy are discernible (such as more long-term oriented policies, doing better on enhancing human and social capital, supporting more strongly regional governance and regional integration processes, and promoting really in an integrated way security and development in the Sub-Saharan Africa region). In the meantime, new SSA countries have to be added to the list of fragile countries (Mali, South Sudan), and regrettably the European Union (EU) has not played a great role in conflict prevention and in crisis management.

The Report contains an Overview and a Section One with four chapters on the analysis of fragility in SSA. In Section Two there are three chapters on building resilience and reducing vulnerability, with lessons from the global financial crisis of 2008/09 and with implications for state-building in fragile countries. In Section Three there are two chapters on the future EU policies fragile countries in SSA and the Conclusions. There are also References and an Annex in the Report. Although the current Report is useful as well as the whole series of Annual Reports (see Web Access: http://www.erd-report.eu/erd/index.html), the observed discrepancy between the recommendations and the actually practiced EU development policy is quite shocking.

Karl Wohlmuth, Bremen

World Bank, World Development Report 2011, Conflict, Security, and Development, Washington, D. C.: The International Bank for Reconstruction and Development/The World Bank, 2011, pages: 416
Publication Classification Details:
Softcover: ISBN: 978-0-8213-8439-8/ISSN: 0163-5085/eISBN: 978-0-8213-8440-4/DOI: 10.1596/978-0-8213-8439-8
Hardcover: ISBN: 978-0-8213-8500-5/ISSN: 0163-5085/DOI: 10.1596/978-0-8213-8500-5
Web Access:
http://siteresources.worldbank.org/INTWDRS/Resources/WDR2011_Full_Text.pdf

This major Report on the issues of *Conflict, Security, and Development* is reporting on new dimensions for national and regional development policies and for development assistance in order to create the basis for a peaceful and prospering world. As around 1.5 billion people are living in countries which are affected by repeated cycles of political and criminal violence, it is urgent to devise strategies so as to break these cycles. Such strategies encompass many elements at various levels and are based on strengthened national institutions and governance mechanisms and on improved regional and international environments that support peace and development. As civil wars often are recurring, as criminal violence undermines gains made by successful peace processes, and as weak and illegitimate institutions are unable to provide citizens with security, justice and jobs, the risk is great that even countries which have on the surface some stability are threatened to turn to violence. These fragile countries cannot reach the Millennium Development Goals (MDGs) and have poverty rates which are more than 20 per cent higher than in countries without such wide-spread prevalence of violence. Many of these countries are in Sub-Saharan Africa (SSA). The impacts of violence in one country are even more severe as they spread to other areas – via criminal networks, refugee flows, drug trafficking, epidemic diseases, and price shocks because of interrupted supplies. All these effects and impacts are analysed in this Report in great detail, and the analysis is supported with so many examples and case studies.

Civil wars and violence have to do with weak government, unemployment, human rights abuses, and other causal factors. In order to break such cycles of violence at national level it is required that the underlying problems are solved which lead to forms of violence and civil war. This is a strong message in the report. Confidence-building will only work if institutional transformation is successful and if this goes hand in hand with sharing economic prospects for all groups and people. Strategies are therefore requested that consider the context for successful reforms. Beside of national action new international strategies are requested. Adapting international assistance is needed by investing in prevention of conflicts and crisis management – through confidence-building, by providing citizen security, justice and jobs, and by reforming internal agency procedures to manage risks (by redesigning of budgets and of staffing systems, by using new risk management tools with longer-term mediation support, and by negotiating more flexible peacekeeping arrangements). Acting regionally and globally in international assistance programmes is an urgent requirement – by focussing more on cross-border development programming, by implementing new standards on land resource purchases and the management of natural resource revenues, and by initiating dialogue forums on international norms for governance, transparency, accountability and leadership.

There is a long Overview Section describing in great detail the findings of the three major parts. Part One is on the Challenge of Repeated Cycles of Violence (with two chapters). Repeated violence and vulnerability to violence are the issues in Part One. Part Two is on Lessons for National and International Responses (with five chapters). Restoring confidence and building resilience are main issues as well as transforming institutions to deliver security, justice and jobs; other issues are the ways and means of providing international support to transforming institutions and to build resilience, and international action to mitigate external stresses. In Part Three there are two chapters giving Practical Options and Recommendations. Practical country directions and new directions for international support are presented. Also there are in the Report a Bibliographical Note, the References, Selected Indicators and selected World Development Indicators, as well as an Index.

The Report is a huge work and contains a lot of valuable and practical suggestions for breaking the cycle of violence. However, the reviewer of the Report cannot see enough progress towards implementing the main lessons in international aid projects and programmes. Such projects and programmes should consider the causes of the repeated cycles of violence and should adapt the assistance strategies accordingly. The aid strategies towards Sudan and South Sudan are cases in point. Development assistance should focus much more on integrated border development programmes for the areas around the new international border, but just this is not done by bilateral and multilateral donors. The assistance focus remains as usual quite national and so it is divisive by separating further the two countries (see Unit 3 of this volume).

Development aid should be in many cases a cross-border project, a cross-sectors project, a cross-issues project, a coordinated project of various donors (bilateral, multilateral, and NGOs), etc. All this is not happening, although there is in the meantime an increasing number of such cross-border projects and programmes. But they are regrettably not there where they could help to prevent conflict and war.

The weakness of the Report has to do with the political mandate of the World Bank (and of other donor agencies). The talk is about stresses, conflict and violence, and about civil war and security and development. There is not much reference to the power of large countries and firms, to the economic interest to exploit resources in other countries, to the politico-economic interventions to gain access to markets, natural resources and land, and there is not much discussion about market distortions, market power and market failures. As so many resource conflicts have to do with oil and gas, a treatment of such contracts would be useful. There are many practical examples and useful proposals, but a global and deep picture of the causes of repeated cycles of violence is not presented. External "stresses" are mentioned in the context of trafficking, resource conflicts, and conflicts over water and land. Also cross-border conflicts are mentioned and considered as "stresses". The wording is inappropriate as it draws attention away from the major driving forces which are shaping the societies and which are producing and perpetuating conflict.

Karl Wohlmuth, Bremen

Development Finance and Development Aid

UNCTAD/United Nations Conference On Trade And Development, Economic Development In Africa, Report 2013 *Intra-African Trade: Unlocking Private Sector Dynamism*, Geneva: United Nations 2013, pages: 158
Publication Classification Details: UNCTAD/ALDC/AFRICA/2013, UNITED NATIONS PUBLICATION, Sales Number E.13.II.D.2/ ISBN 978-92-1-112866-6/eISBN 978-92-1-056143-3/ISSN 1990–5114
Web Access:
http://unctad.org/en/PublicationsLibrary/aldcafrica2013_en.pdf

This Report investigates into the intra-African trade and makes proposals for a new developmental regionalism. It is asked how private business can benefit from this new developmental regionalism.

Karl Wohlmuth, Bremen

UNCTAD/United Nations Conference On Trade And Development, Economic Development In Africa, Report 2012 *Structural Transformation And Sustainable Development In Africa*, Geneva: United Nations 2012, pages: 160
Publication Classification Details: UNCTAD/ALDC/AFRICA/2012, UNITED NATIONS PUBLICATION, Sales No. E.12.II.D.10/ ISBN 978-92-1-055595-1/ISSN 1990–5114
Web Access:
http://unctad.org/en/PublicationsLibrary/aldcafrica2012_embargo_en.pdf

This Report investigates into the context of environmental sustainability, growth and structural transformation. Issues of resource use and productivity in Africa are discussed. A Strategic Framework for sustainable structural transformation is presented. Policies for sustainable structural transformation are elaborated. A final chapter summarizes the main findings.

Karl Wohlmuth, Bremen

UNDP/United Nations Development Programme, Africa Human Development Report 2012: *Towards a Food Secure Future*, New York: UNDP, Regional Bureau for Africa (RBA), 2012, pages: 190
Publication Classification Details: ISBN: 978-92-1-126342-8/eISBN: 978-92-1-055606-4/Sales No.: E.12.III.B.7
Web Access:
http://www.undp.org/content/dam/undp/library/corporate/HDR/Africa %20HDR/UNDP-Africa%20HDR-2012-EN.pdf

This Report presents a strategy for moving in Africa towards a food secure future. The strategy is built around four pillars: first, increasing agricultural productivity in a sustainable way; second, initiating effective nutrition policies so as to allow for a proper use and absorption of calories and nutrients; third, providing for access to food by increasing food availability and purchasing power through measures towards more stability of food systems; and fourth, empowerment of the rural poor, especially of the women, by harnessing the power of information, innovation and markets towards these people.

A Summary of the Report (22 pages) is also available under: http://www.undp.org/content/dam/undp/library/corporate/HDR/Africa%20H DR/UNDP-Africa%20HDR-2012-Summary-EN.pdf

Karl Wohlmuth, Bremen

UNECA; African Union, *Economic Report on Africa, Making the Most of Africa's Commodities, Industrializing for Growth, Jobs and Economic Transformation*, 2013, Addis Ababa: UNECA, ISBN-13: 978-92-1-125119-7, pages: 260, available at www.uneca.org.

Africa's recent economic performance has not generated enough economic diversification, job growth or social development to create wealth and lift millions of Africans out of poverty. A key challenge, therefore, is how Africa can pursue more effective policies to accelerate and sustain high growth and make that growth more inclusive and equitable. African countries must use this global interest in order to achieve broader structural transformation based on the needs and priorities of Africans.

This topic is important because commodity-based industrialization can provide an engine of growth for the continent, reducing its marginalization in the global economy and enhancing its resilience to shocks. According to the report, African countries have a real opportunity, individually and collectively, to promote economic transformation and to address poverty, inequality and youth unemployment. They can capitalize on their resource endowments and high international commodity prices as well as changes in how global production processes are organized.

The 2013-report argues that the deindustrialization of many African economies over the last three decades, resulting in their increasing marginalization in the global economy, was mainly the result of inadequate policies. It offers a policy framework for these countries to trigger resource-based industrialization. Key among the components of this framework is the need to design and implement effective development plans and industrial strategies to address constraints and tap opportunities for African countries to engage in value addition and commodity-based industrialization. For industrial policies to be effective there is a need for policy space. Many African countries saw notable improvements in policy space especially before the recent global financial crises thanks to prudent macroeconomic management. Successful industrial policy would assist African countries strengthen and sustain their policy space through higher and sustainable growth rates and tax revenue.

The report also underscores the need for African countries to develop appropriate local content policies, boost infrastructure, human skills and technological capabilities, and foster regional integration and intra-African trade. In this regard, the implementation of the Continental Free Trade Area (CFTA) and the regional and continental priorities of the Accelerated Industrial Development of Africa's (AIDA) Action Plan, for example, will be crucial.

This report is based on nine studies of African countries, which have helped to generate evidence-based policy recommendations. The studies show that African countries are adding value to their commodities and developing local backward and forward linkages to the soft, hard and energy commodity sectors. But the depth of linkages varies among countries and value addition remains generally limited, mainly because of country- or industry-specific constraints that require strategic and systematic industrial policies.

The report consists of six chapters as follows: Chapter 1: Economic and Social Developments in Africa and Medium-term Prospects; Chapter 2: Trade, Financing and Employment imperatives for Africa's Transformation; Chapter 3: State of Value Addition and Industrial Policy in Africa; Chapter 4: Making the Most of Linkages in Soft (Food) Commodities; Chapter 5: Making the Most of Linkages in Industrial Commodities and finally Chapter 6: Making the Most of Policy Linkages in Commodities.

Against this backdrop, the report examines key constraints and opportunities for African countries to make the most of their commodities by adding value through linkage development. It then addresses how African countries can design and implement industrial and other development policies to promote value addition and economic transformation, and to reduce their dependence on producing and exporting unprocessed commodities.

The analysis uses desk research and country specific background policy information, primary firm-level data and information from questionnaires and interviews to underpin evidence-based policy recommendations. The primary data were collected and country case studies prepared for nine African countries in the five sub-regions – Algeria, Cameroon, Egypt, Ethiopia, Ghana, Kenya, Nigeria, South Africa and Zambia.

As in previous years, the report begins by examining recent trends in Africa's economic and social development as well as selected issues, namely trade and financing for economic transformation and the question of how to translate growth into decent job creation, before focusing on "Making the most of Africa's commodities: Industrializing for growth, jobs and economic transformation" – a very brief synopsis of which is distilled into the following paragraphs.

The findings and recommendations of this report strongly complement those of previous years that emphasized the need for African countries to pursue effective policy actions to address the factors constraining economic transformation. For example, the 2012 report pursued the theme that, to address the failures of state-and market-led development experiences and to unleash Africa's potential as a pole of global growth, the continent required developmental states that design and implement innovative and bold long-term actions.

The 2013-report underscores the point that commodity based industrialization in Africa should not – and cannot – be the only way for African countries to industrialize. Not all African countries are rich in natural resources and, in the long-term, even resource-rich countries have to venture into innovative non-resource-based activities to sustain their industries when resources are exhausted.

Achim Gutowski, Bremen

UNECA; African Union, *Economic Report on Africa, Unleashing Africa's Potential as a Pole for Global Growth*, **2012, Addis Ababa: UNECA, ISBN-13: 978-92-1-125118-0, pages: xiii+186, available at www.uneca.org.**

The dynamism of African economies has captured the imagination of the world. Having been written off as "the hopeless continent" for decades, Africa is now being courted by powerful economic actors with a keen interest in its natural resources and untapped market.

While the new narrative of "a rising Africa" is warmly welcomed, it must be made clear at the outset that the continent's new fortunes are not the outcome of good luck; they are the result of years of hard work and better macroeconomic management. Indeed, the economic revival of the continent is attributed to improved economic and political governance, reduction in armed conflicts, increasing foreign capital inflows (especially direct investment) and improvements in the business climate – as well as rising commodity prices.

A positive portrayal of Africa in international circles is encouraging, but the *Economic Report on Africa 2012* presents a more cautious and nuanced analysis of the continent's growth trajectory. The report situates the story of a rising Africa in a broader context, by pointing out the challenges and opportunities that lie ahead as governments push forward a series of policies to achieve structural transformation in an environment of global uncertainty. The report identifies the key binding constraints for unleashing Africa's productive capacity and proposes a series of bold measures that governments must implement to position the continent as the next pole of global growth and rebalancing.

Finally, the *Economic Report on Africa 2012* argues that sustaining the growth momentum and taking Africa's development potential much further depends on strong political leadership with the capacity to mobilize the population around a common national development vision. This must be complemented by an effective institutional framework that delineates the roles and responsibilities of the three drivers of transformational change – the State, the private sector and civil society – for realizing the common vision and for ensuring mutual accountability.

Thus the theme – and title – of the *Economic Report on Africa 2012* is *Unleashing Africa's Potential as a Pole of Global Growth* and consists of five chapters. Chapter 1 presents a review of the developments in the world economy and implications for Africa. This includes aspects of world commodity prices, trade, foreign direct investment, aid and policy recommendations. Chapter 2 offers an overview of economic, social and human developments and conditions in Africa in 2011 and prospects for 2012. Trends in international and intra-African trade are highlighted. The remaining three chapters focus on how to harness the continent's productive capacity by taking bold measures to ease the binding constraints that still stifle Africa's potential. Chapter 3 – the focus of the growth pole analysis – looks at Africa's growth in the last half century, particularly the drivers of growth in different development strategies. Through the optic of the global growth pole, it proposes several imperatives that Africa must fulfill, including sustained high growth, as well as economic transformation (mainly of infrastructure, human resources and local entrepreneurship). It also discusses options for capitalizing on the opportunities, and for managing the risks, of the emerging multi-polar world and the gradual shift in the resource balance from the developed world to Asia and other developing regions. In more detail, chapter 4 presents how to unleash Africa's productive potential. Emphasizing that Africa's marginal position in the global economy can be reversed with the right type of political leadership committed to mobilizing all sectors of society around a common national development vision and strategy, the chapter suggests the need for two other elements: a capable and pragmatic bureaucracy and a social compact in which the State, the private sector and civil society are mutually accountable for implementing that vision. The chapter then propos-es options for improving political and economic governance, for relaxing constraints from deficits in human capital, infrastructure and local entrepre-neurship, for unlocking Africa's agricultural potential, for stepping up re-gional integration initiatives and for harnessing new partnerships, particularly with the emerging economies of the global South. Chapter 5 reviews the various resource-mobilizing channels open to Africa given the pressing need to transform itself structurally. It outlines innovative proposals on mecha-nisms for mobilizing, using and distributing resources for setting a founda-tion of shared growth and inclusive development. It begins by reviewing past experience as well as new opportunities and challenges facing policymakers in mobilizing and using external resource flows – official and private – for socio-economic structural transformation. The chapter then looks at new financial instruments for mobilizing private savings from international and domestic investors, as well as issues in mobilizing domestic public resources. Finally, conclusions and policy recommendations are stated.

Achim Gutowski, Bremen

UNECA; African Union, *Economic Report on Africa, Governing Devel-opment in Africa – the Role of the State in Economic Transformation*, 2011, Addis Ababa: UNECA, ISBN: 978-92-1-125116-6, pages: xiii+147, available at www.uneca.org.

Sustainable economic growth and social development constitute the primary goals of economic policy in Africa. It is expected that solid advances towards these goals will not only result in rising living standards across the continent but will also lead to full employment of resources as well as reduced income inequality and poverty.

Through the prism of changing development strategies, the Report reviews Africa's economic growth and social development experience since the 1960s to establish the strengths and weaknesses of these strategies. It also examines the experiences of other developing regions where countries have achieved significant economic transformation and social development, and pays particular attention to the role of the state.

The report consists of six parts. Part one is about the developments in the world economy and implications for Africa. Part two deals with economic and social conditions in Africa in 2010 and prospects for 2011. Part three suggests ideas regarding selected current and emerging development issues in Africa in 2010. Part four covers the role of the state in economic transformation in Africa. Part five is about Africa's need for a developmental state including its opportunities and challenges. The final part six analyses the governing development in Africa and its needs and responses.

Economic activity rebounded across Africa in 2010. However, the pace of recovery was uneven among groups of countries and sub-regions. Oil-exporting countries generally expanded more strongly than oil-importing countries. West Africa and East Africa were the two best performing sub-regions in 2010.

Africa's inflation trended downward in 2010, reflecting the increased supply of agricultural products, the strength of some currencies, excess capacity and competitive pressures. A few countries bucked the trend for specific reasons, including increased domestic demand (Republic of Congo, Libyan Arab Jamahiriya and Nigeria), robust public spending (Algeria) and a depreciating domestic currency (Mozambique, Sierra Leone and Sudan).

Africa's fiscal deficit deteriorated marginally in 2010, from 5.7 per cent of GDP in 2009 to 5.8 per cent. Similarly, its aggregate current account balance worsened. In both cases, divergences across broad groups of countries reflected differences in economic structure and policy stance. In particular, most countries that witnessed improvements in their current account balances were oil exporters. Continued fiscal loosening, combined with an accommodative monetary policy, largely accounted for the deterioration of fiscal balances.

The prospects for improved economic performance in Africa during 2011 are quite favourable. Average growth rates in both oil-exporting and oil-importing countries are projected to be higher in 2011 than in 2010. West Africa and East Africa are set to be the fastest-growing sub-regions once more in 2011, followed by North Africa, Central Africa and Southern Africa. Although the projected growth rates for 2011 are markedly higher than those attained in 2009 and 2010 for most sub-regions, they are generally lower than pre-crisis rates. They also seem to be below the rates needed to significantly reduce the continent's unemployment and poverty.

The outlook for economic performance in 2011 is subject to several risks and uncertainties. Africa's growth performance will, as usual, be affected by the pace and duration of growth in its major trading and development partners through the continent's exports and tourism receipts, as well as inflows of remittances, foreign direct investment and official development assistance. Other key factors include ongoing, as well as possible, political disturbances associated with elections as well as adverse weather conditions.

The state in Africa has a crucial role to play in facing various current and emerging development challenges. Diversification of production and exports is an important element of transformation. Yet state leadership and vision are required for designing and pursuing policies to move Africa from its heavy dependence on primary commodity exports. Generating domestic sources of development finance calls for strong and effective states endowed with the legitimacy to raise the necessary revenue as well as the capacity for efficient delivery of public services. Attracting international development finance, too, requires states with such attributes.

Despite the diversity of country experiences on the continent, Africa's growth performance between the early 1960s and early 1970s was similar to that of other developing regions. After the oil price shock of 1973, however, its growth faltered and generally declined, until 2000–2007 when growth improved again. During 1960–2007, 16 African countries achieved average annual real per capita growth rates above 2 per cent, 26 countries recorded less than 2 per cent growth, and 11 countries contracted. None of these African countries enjoyed economic growth that was associated with very low volatility (a coefficient of variation of less than one).

Africa's growth experience was not associated with full structural transformation. Incomplete transformation in some countries may be traced to the influence of abundant resource endowments and ineffective policies. Distorted economic transformation may have resulted from the failure of the modern industrial sector to absorb rural surplus labour and other resources.

The role of the African state in achieving rapid and sustained economic growth and social development combined with deep structural transformation should be based on a developmental state. This approach should be operationalized through disciplined planning, where social and economic policies are interwoven in a complementary and mutually reinforcing manner. In avoiding the pitfalls of state intervention, such as capture of parts of the state apparatus by elites, a developmental state in Africa must be able to administer such key elements as an autonomous and competent bureaucracy with responsibility for development planning and implementation and a developmentalist coalition among committed political leadership, bureaucracy, private sector and civil society.

According to the report, African developmental states should also implement measures such as relating state assistance to performance targets (and withdrawing assistance if necessary); empowering regulatory agencies to set and enforce product standards; and establishing and enforcing competition law.

Achim Gutowski, Bremen

The Brookings Institution, Africa Growth Initiative, *Foresight Africa, Top Priorities For The Continent In 2013*, Africa Growth Initiative at Brookings, Washington D. C.: The Brookings Institution, January 2013, pages: 34
Web Access:
http://www.brookings.edu/~/media/research/files/reports/2013/01/foresig ht%20africa/foresight%20africa_2013.pdf

It is the mission of the Africa Growth Initiative to deliver research from an African perspective – by collaborating with research partners in the area so as to raise the African voice in global policy debates. Such output should inform sound policy, so as to create sustained economic growth and development for the people of Africa.

Major issues in the Report are: Creating jobs for the youth; closing the energy poverty gap; reviewing the role of China-Africa relations, looking at Kenya's future role in Africa, continuing action on removing the causes of insecurity; narrowing the education deficit, impacting on the lack of infrastructure; and engaging the Diaspora.

Since 2010 the Brookings Institution is doing this activity under the umbrella of the Africa Growth Initiative (AGI) by presenting the top priorities for the coming year. As the list for the year 2013 covers most of the known development deficits, the list is not really a list of priorities but a list of known development constraints.

Karl Wohlmuth, Bremen

International Policy Centre for Inclusive Growth (IPC-IG), series, Brasilia DF: IPC-IG/UNDP, no ISSN, www.ipc-undp.org, pages: 1:

The International Policy Centre for Inclusive Growth (IPC-IG) is jointly supported by the Poverty Practice, Bureau for Development Policy, UNDP and the Government of Brazil.

What is Inclusive Growth? An Alternative Perspective, June 2013, one pager no. 205.

Ever since the UNDP started advocating for "inclusive growth", developing countries have set this as an objective for their long-term strategies. However, there is no universally accepted definition of the concept or how to measure it, which are important considerations for policy formulation as well as evaluation.

This note (i) provides a critical perspective on diverse conceptualizations and therefore, policy advocacy to realize the outcomes specified; further (ii) it proposes a concept and measure to address such issues.

As regards the outcome of the evaluation, the contemporary approach emphasizes a reduction in deprivation measures such as incidence of poverty and extent of inequality. The following questions are examined: how valid are such diverse characteristics from a methodological perspective? How sustainable would the advocated policy measures be for realizing the proposed inclusive growth outcomes from an economic perspective?

The Future of Global Poverty, June 2013, one pager no. 204.

This paper adds to the debate by introducing a long-term model of poverty, inequality and growth. It has three conclusions. Taking the scenario of optimistic economic growth, the number of people living below 2 USD/day could fall from around 2 billion people today to 600 million by 2030 – if every country returned to "best ever" inequality. However, if recent trends in inequality continue, it could rise so that (based on the survey means analysis) there could be an extra 400 million poor people at 2 USD/day in 2030 than today.

In sum, the authors argue that, despite all uncertainties in the modeling, there is evidently benefit in using the available data to attempt to estimate global poverty in the future. As long as one´s approach recognizes these uncertainties and the wide range of possible estimates that might be derived from the various different ways of allowing for them.

Inequality in Post-Independence Namibia: the Unfinished Agenda, December 2012, one pager no. 186.

The economic, political and social transition of Namibia over the past two decades has been remarkable. Hit by a guerilla war and after a century of colonial rule, the country is now widely regarded as one of the more stable and well-governed democracies on the African continent. Moreover, it is classified as "upper middle income", with a per capita gross domestic product almost three times the average for sub-Saharan Africa. Nevertheless, because of extreme levels of inequality, average GDP remains a particularly deceptive measure of welfare in Namibia.

The authors working for the Human Sciences Research Council document a significant decrease in the poverty headcount – from 49 to 38 per cent – and small but insignificant decreases in the country's extremely high levels of inequality. Using decomposition analysis the authors find that poverty reduction in Namibia is largely driven by growth of mean incomes rather than redistribution. The authors highlight some important changes in inequality between different social groups especially as educational attainment has replaced ethnicity as the main determinant of between-group inequality.

Analytical Framework for Evaluating the Productive Impact of Cash Transfer Programmes on Household Behaviour, **December 2012, one pager no. 185.**

This paper by two authors working for the Food and Agriculture Organization of the United Nations (FAO) states that cash transfer programs have become an important tool of social protection and poverty reduction strategies in low- and middle-income countries. However, most of their impact evaluations pay little attention to economic and productive activities. The "From Protection to Production" project aims to study the impact of cash transfer programs on household economic decision-making and the local economy.

This research project is implemented jointly by the FAO and UNICEF and builds on ongoing or planned impact evaluations in seven sub-Saharan African countries: Ethiopia, Ghana, Kenya, Lesotho, Malawi, Zambia and Zimbabwe.

The paper discusses several impact evaluation methods to identify the impact of the cash transfer programs on beneficiaries. The objective is to test the hypothesis that households who receive regular cash transfer may overcome the obstacles that limit their access to credit or cash. This, in turn, can bring about changes in household behaviour, increase income-generating investments, influence beneficiaries' role in social networks, increase access to markets and inject resources into local economies. If this is corroborated then one can conclude that besides serving its primary object of smoothing consumption, cash transfers can also be regarded as a means of promoting farm-level production gains.

Qualitative Research and Analyses of the Economic Impacts of Cash Transfer Programmes in Sub-Saharan Africa, **December 2012, one pager no. 184.**

A "From Protection to Production" project aims to identify the productive impacts of cash transfer programmes on household economic decision-making and the local economy. It takes advantage of ongoing impact evaluations of cash transfer programmes in seven sub-Saharan African countries to analyze the impact of these programmes on broader household economic activities. This includes labour supply and risk-sharing mechanisms and networks as well as the local economy. The project is led by the Food and Agriculture Organization of the United Nations (FAO) and uses a mixed-methods approach, combining econometric analysis of impact evaluation data, simulation modeling of the village economy and qualitative methods.

A qualitative research guide provides an overview and guidance on four thematic areas of research: household economy, local economy, social networks and economic impacts and operational issues – training, fieldwork preparation and research process to be implemented in each case study country. The guide also introduces participatory tools used to collect and analyze information and includes guidance for conducting key informant interviews and facilitating focus group discussions.

all by Achim Gutowski, Bremen

World Institute for Development Economies Research (WIDER); The United Nations University (UNU), Helsinki: UNU/WIDER, Working Paper Series:

Entrepreneurship and Violent Conflicts in developing Countries, **2013, Brück, T.; Naudé, W.; Verwimp, P., Working Paper no. 28, ISSN: 1798-7237, ISBN: 978-92-9230-605-2, pages: 17.**

There is a paucity of studies on dealing with violent conflict impacts at the micro-level on firms or entrepreneurs in developing countries. The authors of this paper review two recent special journal issues on violent conflict and entrepreneurship: these are the special issue of the Journal of small Business and Entrepreneurship (2011) and the Journal of Conflict Resolution (2013).

The authors assess how the two journal paper addresses the gap. It points out that violent conflict has diverse impacts on entrepreneurs, firms, investments and production processes particularly in developing countries, where violent conflicts impose a disastrous cost in terms of development.

The paper is divided into five sections; the first is the introductory part. The second section entails the concept of violent conflict and entrepreneurship. While the third section comprises of brief review of relevant literature, successfully pointing out that there is a dearth of empirical studies of micro-level studies and understanding of the micro-level impact of violent conflict on entrepreneurial behavior is actually required. Section four examines seven points' insights on the recent special issues on entrepreneurship and conflict. These involve varieties of factors that can impact positively and could also have detrimental effect on entrepreneurship in a violent conflict zone. The fifth section concludes by evaluating some policy implications in the new studies contained in these special journal issues.

The authors finally suggest a task for further research with a resolute qualitative and quantitative research combined approach.

The Role of Training in Fostering Cluster-Based Micro and Small Enterprises Development, **2012, Sonobe, T.; Otsuka, K., Working Paper no. 99, ISSN: 1798-7237, ISBN: 978-9230-565-9, pages: 26.**

The paper examines the role of training in fostering cluster-based micro and small enterprises development in developing countries. The authors argue based on some case studies conducted in Asia and Sub-Saharan Africa that management training programmes are veritable tools to small entrepreneurship success. The paper explores questions based on why firms in developing countries are less able to innovate and manage in comparison to their counterparts in developed countries, and how their entrepreneurship can further be nurtured.

The working paper consists of four sections. Section 1 provides an introduction. Section 2 describes how cluster-based MSEs in various industries developed in different countries in Asia and Africa. Section 3 discusses the possible reasons that hinder skills improvement and what governments and foreign aid can do to support training. Section 4 concludes by inciting that much remains to be studied on design of management training programmes and for its overall strategy of dissemination and adoption.

all by Rabi Sidi Ali, Bremen

German Development Institute (GDI), Discussion Paper Series, Bonn: GDI, ISSN 1860-0441:

Mario Negre, *Towards renewal or oblivion? Prospects for post–2020 co-operation between the European Union and the Africa, Caribbean and Pacific Group*, 2013, Discussion Paper 9/2013, pages: 67.

This paper is part of a joint research project conducted by the German Development Institute/Deutsches Institut für Entwicklungspolitik (DIE) and the European Centre for Development Policy Management (ECDPM) about the future of the partnership of the European Union (EU) and the African, Caribbean and Pacific (ACP) Group.

Following the adoption of the Rome Treaty, the European Union developed a formal and privileged cooperation framework for its relationship with countries in Africa, the Caribbean and Pacific (ACP). Since 2000 cooperation between the EU and the ACP is governed through the Cotonou Partnership Agreement (CPA), which encompasses three complementary dimensions: political dialogue, economic and trade cooperation, and development cooperation. The changing global context, along with institutional, political and socioeconomic developments in the EU and the ACP, raise questions about whether this approach to cooperation has sufficiently delivered on its objectives, and which evolutions – or revolutions – may be necessary for these regions' future cooperation.

This paper seeks to complement existing evidence with the findings of a detailed review of the literature and the perceptions of past, present and future ACP–EU cooperation gathered from a wide range of stakeholders in ten ACP countries. It consists of five chapters and includes case studies of the following African countries: Botswana, Cameroon, Ethiopia, Ghana, Tanzania, Zambia and Nigeria.

Florence Dafe, *The Politics of Central Banking and Implications for Regulatory Reform in Sub-Saharan Africa: the Cases of Kenya, Nigeria and Uganda*, 2012, Discussion Paper 2/2012, pages: 52.

This discussion paper is part of a wider study on the political economy of financial reforms within the research project "Making Finance Work for Africa" commissioned by the Deutsche Gesellschaft für Internationale Zusammenarbeit (GIZ).

As regulators, central banks can firstly play a stabilizing role, using prudential regulation to ensure financial system stability. Secondly, they can play a transformative role, using regulation to promote financial system development and so encourage financial deepening and inclusion. While there are strong arguments for central banks seeking to strike a balance between their stabilizing and transformative roles in financial regulation, African central banks have had difficulties in this respect.

This paper consisting of six chapters presents case studies from Nigeria, Uganda and Kenya that show how central banks have historically tended to emphasize one role rather than the other. Reforms that seek to improve the balance between the stabilizing and transformative roles of central banks in financial regulation are difficult because interest groups with the power to shape central bank behavior tend to prefer the regulatory status quo and may try to capture regulatory reform processes (chapter four). As facilitators of financial reform processes in many African countries, donors should systematically address the challenges posed by regulatory capture. This is also necessary with a view to maximize the effectiveness of their support for regulatory reforms.

Marino, Roberto; Ulrich Volz, A Critical Review of the IMF's Tools for Crisis Prevention, Discussion Paper 4/2012, pages: 50.

Against the backdrop of the International Monetary Fund's (IMF) increasing focus on crisis prevention measures and the G20's discussion of "global safety nets", this paper analyses the IMF's tools for crisis prevention in six chapters. It focuses on particular on the emphasis on the recently developed Flexible Credit Line (FCL) and Precautionary Credit Line (PCL), (chapter 4).

The paper reviews why it took the IMF so long to develop crisis prevention facilities that would find subscribers and scrutinizes initial experiences with the FCL and PCL. Moreover, it discusses the systemic implications of problems associated with such crisis prevention facilities and examines why only a few countries are using these facilities thus far (chapter 5).

Based on this analysis, it offers policy recommendations for the development of the IMF's crisis prevention facilities (chapter 6).

Grävingholt, Jörn; Sebastian Ziaja; Merle Kreibaum, *State Fragility: Towards a Multi- Dimensional Empirical Typology*, Discussion Paper 03/ 2012, pages: 50.

The purpose of this paper is to demonstrate that, empirically, state fragility – conceptualized as a multi-dimensional phenomenon along the categories of authority, capacity and legitimacy – comes in several distinct configurations, yet that the number of such configurations is rather limited.

The authors suggest that this finding has useful, previously unexplored implications for policy design vis-à-vis fragile states. They do not intend to call into question the necessity of country-specific analysis. A better grasp of "typical" forms of fragility, however, should help development agencies to better prepare for the types of situations they are most likely to be confronted with. The final section of the paper explores some of the practical implications that can be derived from the classification.

all by Achim Gutowski, Bremen

Danish Institute for International Studies (DIIS), Copenhagen: DIIS, ISBN: 978-87-7605-573-8:

Regional Security Institutions in East Africa, **2013, Katja Jacobsen; Johannes Nordby, DISS Report 14/2013, pages: 56.**

For the past decade, peace and security in East Africa have gained increasing focus internationally. The region has experienced armed conflicts, civil wars, rebellion, drought and famine. Yet, at the same time, there is an emerging ambition among a number of African states to handle security issues on the continent independently.

Such ambitions have fostered a variety of military capacity building programmes supported by external donors. The report explores in six chapters how up until now Denmark has sought to contribute to strengthening political and military security in East Africa. This has mainly been done through capacity building projects anchored in different regional security institutions. The report illuminates some of the risks that such capacity building projects might confront.

Furthermore the report points out some of the challenges that exist in the cooperation between the Ministry of Foreign Affairs of Denmark and the Danish Ministry of Defence. Finally, the report discusses lessons learned and presents some considerations for future capacity building programmes.

Immediate versus Sustainable Poverty Reduction? Supporting Agro-Industries in Africa, **2012, Lindsay Whitfield, DISS Policy Brief, no ISBN/ ISSN, pages: 4.**

To help smallholders out of poverty, an integrated industry-wide approach is necessary. Focusing on smallholders alone will not do the job. However, the dominant poverty reduction approach of many official aid agencies focuses on livelihoods, marginal income increases and food security.

When operating in productive sectors, donors mainly want to support production by small-scale farmers or informal sector producers. But many of these initiatives are not sustainable, because they fail to see small-scale producers as embedded within an industry and forget to ask what economic transformation is necessary to make that industry grow as a whole and to integrate the small-scale farmers or informal sector producers.

The paper includes two practical examples: the case of smallholders and pineapple exports in Ghana and the case of palm oil industry in Ghana.

all by Achim Gutowski, Bremen

Richard Jolly et al/Oxfam International, *Be outraged – there are Alternatives,* **2012, Sussex: University of Sussex, no ISBN/ISSN, pages: 72.**

An international group of economists and social scientists argue in this book that austerity is bad economics, bad arithmetic and ignores the lessons of history. They are outraged at the narrow range of austerity policies which are bringing so many people around the world to their knees, especially in Europe. Supported by the Oxfam organization, the book argues that austerity measures and cutbacks are reducing growth and worsening poverty and that there are alternatives – for Britain, Europe and all countries that currently imagine that government cutbacks are the only way out of debt.

Achim Gutowski, Bremen

Contents Volume 16
African Development Perspectives Yearbook, 2012/2013
MACROECONOMIC POLICY FORMATION IN AFRICA - GENERAL ISSUES

Call for Papers

Volume 18 of the African Development Perspectives Yearbook with the title „Africa's Progress in Regional and Global Economic Integration"

Invited are contributions for Volume 18 of the African Development Perspectives Yearbook with the title *"Africa's Progress in Regional and Global Integration"*. The contributions should be evidence-based and policy-oriented. High academic standards are requested and will be checked by referees. Non-technical papers with deep analysis and which are readable as well for practitioners in development cooperation also have a high priority. The methodological framework of analysis should be outlined in the Abstract submitted to the Editors.

Upon acceptance of the paper, the *contributors* will receive Editorial Guidelines and a Template. Accepted papers will be grouped into Thematic Units, and the respective Unit Editors will contact the contributors quite regularly.

Guest Editors for various Thematic Units are also invited to apply. Editors of Thematic Units are also becoming automatically Volume Editors. Guest Editors are responsible for a Thematic Unit with 3 – 5 contributions and an Introduction. For specific themes see the Main Issues proposed by the Editors for Volume 18 as presented below.

See the *context* of the Africa Research Programme of IWIM (Institute for World Economics and International Management):

http://www.iwim.uni-bremen.de/africa/africanyearbook.htm

The Editors also invite publishers and institutes to send books and issues of periodicals as well as discussion papers being of relevance to the theme for use in the *Book Reviews/Book Notes Section of the African Development Perspectives Yearbook* (Book Review Editor: Professor Dr. Achim Gutowski, Email: Prof. Dr. Achim Gutowski agutowski@uni-bremen.de)

Main Issues proposed by the Editors for Volume 18 (only some examples for possible themes are mentioned below):

Strategies of Successful African Exporters: by Large and Small Firms, by Domestic and Foreign-owned Firms, and by African-led and Foreign-led Value Chains

- *Conditions and Criteria for Success of African Exporting Firms on Regional and Global Markets*
- *Firms from SANE (South Africa, Algeria, Nigeria, Egypt) countries as Investors in Africa and Globally*
- *Strategies of African Leaders of Global Value Chains (Cases like Breweries, Oil and Gas, Mining Products, Fruits and Vegetables, Wine, etc.)*
- *Learning to Compete (Infrastructure, Innovation and Comprehensive Policies as Ingredients needed for African firms to be able to compete globally)*
- *Strengthening African Value Chains for Export Activity and Successes on Regional Markets*

National Economic Policy in Africa and International Competitiveness of African Firms

- *National Trade, Investment and Regional Integration Policies (Country Case Studies)*
- *Lessons from WTO negotiations for African membership applicants(Country Case Studies)*
- *Redirection of Trade and Investment Policies (and of Africa's trade administration capacity)*
- *Successful Exporters of Manufactured Goods (Country Case Studies)*
- *National and Local Policies for Export Success (Role of Decentralization and Local Growth Diagnostics)*
- *African countries and their cooperation with regional and international economic organizations (contribution of regional and international economic organizations to Africa's global and regional integration process)*

Regional Integration and Regional Value Chains: Impacts on the Competitiveness of African Firms

- *Regional Economic Communities as Engines of Growth in Africa (Cases of RECs and Cooperation of RECs towards a Tripartite Free Trade Agreement)*
- *Sub-Regional Cooperation between African Countries (Success Cases of Border Development Programmes with Focus on Tourism, Infrastructure Provision, and Production)*
- *South-South Cooperation (New Cooperation Frameworks between BRICS countries and African countries, and between BRICS and Regional Economic Communities)*
- *EU - Africa relations (future of EPAs, EBA, Cotonou Preferences, etc.) and experiences of African firms*
- *Future of USA - Africa trade and investment relations and experiences of African firms*
- *Progress of Regional Economic Communities in Africa (by Scoreboard Approach)*

Structural Transformation in Africa, Private Sector Development and the Dynamics of the Foreign Trade Sector

- *Exports and Economic Growth in Africa (by countries and regions)*
- *Exports, Employment and Livelihood in Africa (household, sector and country case studies)*
- *Structural Transformation in Africa: The Role of Exports and of Foreign Investment (Country Cases)*
- *From Mining to Beneficiation and from Raw Materials Production to Processing and Manufacturing (Cases by Countries)*
- *Sector-specific Cases of African Export Successes: Agriculture and Agro-industries, Crafts and Manufacturing Sectors, Service Sectors*
- *Africa Responding to Globalization Pressures (in trade, technology, finance, labour migration, and value chain integration)*

To the Contributors: Please send an Abstract and a short CV not later than March 15, 2014 to both Editors (see below). The Editors will respond within 4 weeks to your proposal. If you have already contributed to a former volume of the Yearbook, please send only an Abstract.

Contact the Editors:

Professor Tobias Knedlik, Managing Editor:

Fulda University of Applied Sciences
Marquardstrasse 35
D-36039 Fulda
Germany

Phone: +49-(0)661-9640-268
Fax: +49-(0)661-9640-252
Email-Address: Tobias.Knedlik@w.hs-fulda.de

Professor Karl Wohlmuth, Scientific Coordinator and Volume Editor:

University of Bremen
Department of Economics and Business Studies
P.O. Box 330 440
28334 Bremen, Germany

Phone: +49 421 218-66517
Fax: +49 421 218-4550
Email-Address: wohlmuth@uni-bremen.de